Japanese Culture

Japanese Culture

FOURTH EDITION

Updated and Expanded

Paul Varley

UNIVERSITY OF HAWAI'I PRESS *Honolulu*

10   09   08   07   11   10   9   8

Library of Congress Cataloging-in-Publication Data
Varley, H. Paul
    Japanese culture / Paul Varley.—4th ed.
        p.   cm.
    Includes bibliographical references and index.
    ISBN-13: 978-0-8248-2292-7 (cloth) — ISBN-13: 978-0-8248-2152-4 (paper : alk. paper)
    ISBN-10: 0-8248-2292-7 (cloth) — ISBN-10: 0-8248-2152-1 (paper : alk. paper)
    1. Japan—Civilization.   I. Title.
DS821.V36   2000
952—dc21   99-057345

Printed by The Maple-Vail Book Manufacturing Group

To Donald Keene

Contents

Preface

MORE THAN A QUARTER of a century has passed since the publication of *Japanese Culture*. With each edition, it has expanded in size. Thus, whereas the first edition ended with World War II, the second edition included a postwar chapter (which remains the book's longest chapter). When the University of Hawai'i Press published the third edition in 1984, it reset the entire text and allowed me to add material throughout. Once again, in this fourth edition, the text has been reset and I have been able to add extensive new material on subjects such as samurai values, Zen Buddhism, the tea ceremony *(chanoyu)*, Confucianism in the Tokugawa period, the story of the forty-seven *rōnin*, Mito scholarship in the early nineteenth century, and mass culture and the comics in the present age.

As stated in the preface to the first edition, *Japanese Culture* is intended as a survey, for the general reader, of Japanese culture, including religion, thought, the visual arts, literature, the theatre, the cinema, and those special arts, such as the tea ceremony and landscape gardening, that have been uniquely cherished in Japan. I have in particular sought to relate cultural developments to political, social, and institutional trends without burdening the text with an excess of the names, dates, and other details of those trends.

I would like to take this opportunity to thank my editor at the University of Hawai'i Press, Patricia Crosby, who encouraged me to undertake the revision and expansion of *Japanese Culture* for this fourth edition and who has supported and assisted me in various projects for the press over the years.

Honolulu   P.V.
February 1999

Major Periods and Cultural Epochs of Japanese History

Jōmon period	*ca.* 10,000–300 B.C.
Yayoi period	*ca.* 300 B.C.–A.D. 300
Tomb period	*ca.* 300–552
Age of Reform	552–710
Asuka epoch (552–645)	
Hakuhō epoch (645–710)	
Nara period	710–784
Tempyō epoch (mid-eighth century)	
Heian period	794–1185
Jōgan epoch (mid- to late ninth century)	
Fujiwara epoch (tenth century to late eleventh century)	
Kamakura period	1185–1333
Kemmu Restoration	1333–1336
Muromachi (Ashikaga) period	1336–1573
Kitayama epoch (late fourteenth and early fifteenth centuries)	
Higashiyama epoch (second half of the fifteenth century)	
Age of Unification	1568–1600
Azuchi-Momoyama epoch (1568–1600 or 1615)	
Namban epoch (late sixteenth and early seventeenth centuries)	
Tokugawa (Edo) period	1600–1867
Genroku epoch (*ca.* 1675–1725)	
Bunka-Bunsei epoch (late eighteenth and early nineteenth centuries)	
Meiji period	1868–1912
Taishō period	1912–1926
Shōwa period	1926–1989
Heisei period	1989–

Chinese Dynasties since the Time of Unification under the Han

Han dynasty	206 B.C.–A.D. 220
Period of the six dynasties	220–589
Sui dynasty	589–618
T'ang dynasty	618–907
Period of the five dynasties	907–960
Sung dynasty	960–1279
Southern Sung dynasty (1127–1279)	
Yüan (Mongol) dynasty	1279–1368
Ming dynasty	1368–1644
Ch'ing (Manchu) dynasty	1644–1911

Author's Notes

Japanese names: The order is family name followed by given name. Thus, Tokugawa Ieyasu is Ieyasu of the Tokugawa family. Until about the early thirteenth century, it was also common to use the possessive *no* ("of") in names—for example, Fujiwara no Michinaga was Michinaga "of" the Fujiwara family.

Year-periods: Adopting the Chinese practice, the Japanese of premodern times designated "year-periods" or "calendrical eras" that lasted, as they saw fit, from a few months to several decades. Important events, such as the Taika Reform of 645 and the Ōnin War of 1467–77, came to be known by the year-periods in which they occurred or began. A number of cultural or art epochs, including the Tempyō epoch of the eighth century and the Genroku epoch of the late seventeenth and early eighteenth centuries, also were identified by the year-periods with which they roughly coincided. Beginning with the Meiji Restoration of 1868, the year-periods have been made coterminous with the reigns of emperors.

Use of macrons: The macron is used in the transcribing of Japanese to show when the vowels *o* and *u* should be prolonged in pronunciation. In keeping with a common practice, I have omitted the macrons from such well-known place names as Tokyo, Kyoto, and Honshu, and from historical terms like "daimyo" and "shogun," which appear in most modern English-language dictionaries and which I have used without italicization.

1

The Emergence of Japanese Civilization

MUCH MYSTERY—and controversy—surrounds the origins of the Japanese people. Before the end of World War II, it was generally believed that human occupancy of Japan dated to only about 4000 B.C. and that the inhabitants of that earliest period were Neolithic or New Stone Age people. Then, in 1949, new archaeological finds dramatically revealed that humans had lived in Japan from a much earlier time and that there had been a Paleolithic or Old Stone Age before the New Stone Age. Today, a conservative estimate of the date of the beginning of the Old Stone Age is between 30,000 and 50,000 B.C. Some archaeologists, however, assert that the age commenced as far back as about 600,000 B.C.[1]

During the glacial age (about 1,000,000–10,000 B.C.), when much of the water of the earth's Northern Hemisphere was drawn into polar ice packs, Japan was connected in the west (Kyushu) and north (northern Honshu and Hokkaido) to the Asian continent, and the present Japan Sea was a lake. Very likely Japan's first inhabitants crossed over from the continent by foot. In any case, better scientific dating of archaeological materials developed since the end of World War II, including radiocarbon dating, has established that the Old Stone Age, whenever it may have begun, ended with the glacial age about 10,000 B.C. and was succeeded by the New Stone Age.

Since the first discovery of Old Stone Age civilization, some five thousand Old Stone Age sites have been uncovered all over Japan. These sites typically yield roughly shaped stone tools and an assortment of human bone fragments. Because no full skeletons have yet been found, it has been difficult for archaeologists to make judgments about the racial character of the Old Stone Age Japanese. The rudimentary level of their lives is perhaps best attested by the fact that, so far as we know, they did not advance culturally to the point of making pottery. And it is for this reason that archaeologists have labeled them, rather unpoetically, the "non-pottery" people.

The beginning of the New Stone Age is now dated to about 10,000 B.C., when there was a great warming in the Northern Hemisphere, much of the polar ice mass melted, and Japan evolved into an archipelago. In the preceding Old Stone Age, people had shaped stones into tools by chipping or flaking or had even used stones as tools just as they found them. The main index marking the transition to the New Stone Age was the appearance, from about 10,000 B.C., of stone tools of much higher quality, including skillfully shaped and polished axes, knives, arrowheads, and fish hooks.

Another major advance of the New Stone Age was the production of pottery; and indeed, archeologists now date the beginning of pottery making in Japan to the commencement of the age itself, or roughly 10,000 B.C. This means that, on the basis of what we know about the origins of pottery making in other countries, the Japanese (or the occupants of Japan during the New Stone Age) produced the world's first pottery. It is possible that future finds on the Asian continent—for example, in China or Korea—will reveal pottery that antedates Japan's and that even served as models for the New Stone Age potters of Japan. But, for the present, the Japanese stand as the first to have made pottery not only in East Asia but in the world.

Japan's New Stone Age pottery was earthenware shaped by hand in a process known as coiling, whereby clay is formed into a rope and a vessel is created by circling the rope around and around from the bottom up and then smoothing out the surface to disguise the "coiling." The earliest type of pottery made in this manner was a simple, bullet-shaped cooking vessel that was apparently inserted into sand or soft earth. Later pieces were much more elaborate and had deeply impressed and intricate surface patterns, widely flared rims, and thick handlelike appendages (fig. 1). Because the most common pattern on New Stone Age pottery was achieved by impressing cord or rope into the soft clay, archaeologists have designated the New Stone Age itself, which lasted until about 400–300 B.C., the Jōmon or, literally, "rope pattern" age.

The Jōmon Japanese were primarily hunters, gatherers, and fishers. They tended to move about with the seasons, although later in the age they established at least semipermanent settlements. Many Jōmon settlements were near the coast, where their inhabitants had easy access to food from the sea, especially shellfish, which they consumed voraciously. Jōmon remains were first discovered in modern times by an American, E. S. Morse, who in 1877 uncovered "kitchen middens" (the garbage mounds or refuse heaps of primitive people) at Ōmori south of Tokyo. Because these middens were composed largely of discarded shells, archaeologists called them "shell mounds" *(kaizuka)*. These mounds are of great value for several reasons. In addition to providing information about the diet of the Jōmon people (for example, there are many bones of small animals as well as shells in the mounds) they also contain tools, pottery, and other objects of Jōmon life.

Jōmon people lived first in caves and later in shallow pits covered with

Fig. 1 Jōmon pottery *(courtesy of the Brooklyn Museum)*

thatching. These pit dwellings *(tateana)* were uniformly small—a typical *tateana* was about two feet deep and fifteen feet in diameter—and could accommodate at most four or five people (that is, a nuclear family). Jōmon graves were also small; indeed they were merely holes into which bodies, in flexed or fetal position, were inserted. Along with the pit dwellings, these unpretentious graves provide proof that New Stone Age society in Japan was essentially classless.

Among the most striking objects from the Jōmon age are earthenware figurines, known as *dogū*, that in their distorted representations of half-human, half-beastlike beings seem to be the creation of minds absorbed with superstition and primitive magic (fig. 2). A number of *dogū* depict female creatures with prominent breasts and pregnant stomachs, physical features that suggest these figurines were used in some sort of fertility rites. Still other *dogū*, whose limbs appear to have been deliberately broken off, were quite likely employed by medicine men for the purpose of curing ailments of the arms and legs.

The Jōmon period came to an end about 400–300 B.C. as the result of

Fig. 2   Dogū figurine (The Metropolitan Museum, Gift of
Mr. and Mrs. Jerome Koizim, 1978)

major new cultural influences from the continent. By far the most important of these was wet-rice (paddy field) agriculture, a type of farming
that flourishes in central and south China (the colder climate of north
China is not hospitable to it) and that may have been transmitted almost
simultaneously at this time to both southern Korea and western Japan.[2]
Three hundred B.C. is historically close to the date (221 B.C.) when the
great civilization of north China, centered on the Yellow River, was unified for the first time by the Ch'in dynasty. It seems possible that im-
pulses from the Ch'in unification, which had been under way for many
years, spread outward to both Korea and Japan and, in the case of the
latter, brought the Yayoi period (ca. 300 B.C.–A.D. 300), so named because of the site in modern Tokyo—Yayoi—where the remains of this
phase of Japanese civilization were first discovered.

    Before World War II, it was generally believed that the Yayoi period
was begun by a migration of people from the Asian continent via Korea,
and that the new "Yayoi people," moving first eastward (to the Kantō
region of Honshu) and then northward, gradually displaced the Jōmon

people and became the Japanese of historic times. More recently, however, scholars have come to believe that the shift from Jōmon to Yayoi was essentially cultural: that is, the Jōmon people became the Yayoi people under influences from China.[3] (See the beginning of Chapter 3 for more remarks about the possible relationship between the Jōmon and Yayoi peoples.)

With the introduction of agriculture, the Japanese moved into the alluvial lowlands, formed permanent farming communities, and became differentiated into social classes. Rice, from this time on, became overwhelmingly the main staple of the economy. It also exerted a profound influence on society, since, in the form of paddy field production, it required a great and unremitting input of physical labor. The units of the agricultural world—the farming family and village—became tightly organized groups, providing a bedrock stability to Japanese life at the basic level that has persisted into modern times.

The use of metals, both bronze and iron, was also introduced to Japan in the early Yayoi period. Bronze was employed primarily for ornamental and iron for practical purposes. But probably the most important use to which metal was put, as we shall see, was the making of weapons, which brought a sharp increase in warfare and the consolidation of control over ever larger territorial units in late Yayoi times.

The transition from Jōmon to Yayoi brought important changes in pottery making (fig. 3). The serene and elegant appearance of the new Yayoi pottery suggests that the civilizing influences that brought new technology to Japan in this age also advanced the mentality of its people. The untamed spirit reflected in the shape and ornamentation of some Jōmon pottery and in the *dogū* figurines was either lost or suppressed by the craftsmen of Yayoi. But perhaps the most striking difference between the two kinds of pottery is that in Jōmon the stress is on decoration, and in Yayoi it is on form. Many Yayoi pieces have no decoration at all, whereas others have bands of thinly incised geometric designs that contrast sharply in their simplicity with the typically florid patterning of Jōmon pottery.

Pottery making in Japan, whose real origins lie in the Yayoi period, is of great importance in cultural history not only because of its inherent artistic worth but also because it is based on some of the most enduring values in the Japanese aesthetic tradition. Most peoples, as they progress technologically in the making of pottery from plain, unglazed clay pieces to fine porcelains, tend to leave their earlier works in the past. The Japanese are unusual in having retained through the ages a love for primitive ceramics even as they have made progressively finer pottery, mainly under the influence of China. The most impressive example of this love for the primitive in pottery is to be found in the culture of tea, which evolved during the medieval age.

Fig. 3   Yayoi pottery *(courtesy of the Brooklyn Museum)*

In aesthetic terms, the cherishing of primitive pottery rests on the value of naturalness, or the preference for things in their original, unaltered states. For the artist or craftsman, naturalness means staying close to his materials. Thus the maker of primitive pottery does not seek to disguise the clay he uses; and the products of his work are admired not only for their natural texture but also for the imperfections that inevitably appear in "primitively" produced things. Another example of the aesthetic taste of the Japanese for naturalness is to be found in the architecture of Shinto shrines, the wood of which is often left unpainted. In this case, practicality is clearly sacrificed to aesthetics, since natural wood shrines are much more susceptible than other kinds of structures to the ravages of weathering.

Nearly all Jōmon pottery was in the wide-mouthed *hachi* form and appears to have been used mainly for cooking and serving food. The Yayoi period brought a variety of new pottery forms, including the jar *(tsubo)*, designed for storage, especially of dried rice; the pot *(kame)*, a vessel, similar to the *hachi*, that was also used in cooking; and the pedestaled *takatsuki* for the formal serving of food. All of these new pottery forms emerged to meet the needs of the agricultural society that evolved in Japan during the Yayoi period. Production of pottery for use in the storage of rice is particularly deserving of note. Jōmon had been a classless society primarily because it had no particular commodity that could be accumulated or stored as wealth. In the Yayoi period, however, rice itself became just such a commodity, and as it was accumulated and stored the grain stratified society into differing classes according to wealth as measured primarily by the possession (or nonpossession) of it. For the rest of the premodern period, rice remained the principal standard of wealth in Japan.

In addition to the archaeological record, knowledge of Japan in the early centuries A.D. may be found in the dynastic histories of China. To the Chinese of this age, the Japanese were one of a number of lesser breeds of people existing beyond the borders of their great Middle Kingdom. Accordingly, they relegated the accounts of Japan to the sections in their histories dealing with barbarian affairs.

The Chinese called Japan the land of Wa (which they wrote with a character that means "stunted" or "dwarfed") and, in their earliest account of it, dating from about the first century B.C., described Wa as consisting of "one hundred"—probably meaning a great many—countries or tribes. They recorded that the people of Wa periodically sent missions to China during the first and second centuries A.D., including one that visited the court of Emperor Kuang-wu of the Later Han dynasty in 57 and received from the emperor a gold seal investing Wa as a tribute-bearing state. In the late eighteenth century (1784) a seal fitting the description of the one bestowed by Kuang-wu was found by farmers near Hakata Bay in northern Kyushu. For the great majority of scholars who accept it as authentic, this seal lends important support to the general factuality of the Chinese dynastic accounts of Wa.

In the late second and early third centuries there were disorders in Wa that led to political consolidation and the establishment of a territorial hegemony under a queen named Himiko (or Pimiko). The Chinese observed that

[Himiko] occupied herself with magic and sorcery, bewitching the people. Though mature in age, she remained unmarried. She had a younger brother who assisted her in ruling the country. After she became the ruler, there were few who saw her. She had one thousand women as attendants, but only one man. He served her food and drink and acted as a medium of communication. She resided in a palace surrounded by towers and stockades, with armed guards in a state of constant vigilance.[4]

Himiko's authority was apparently based on her religious or magical powers and probably derived from the shamanism of northeastern Asia that is known to have been widely disseminated in early Japan. She is described in the above account as a mediator (shaman) between the people and their gods, and as such may well have been among the first to perform what later became the most sacred function of the Japanese sovereign. According to the mythology, the ruling dynasty of Japan is descended from the Sun Goddess (Amaterasu), the supreme deity or *kami* of the Shinto pantheon, and only a duly selected sovereign from this dynasty is qualified to perform the rites of communion with her that are essential to governing the country.

The territorial hegemony over which Himiko presided was called Yamatai, and even today scholars hotly dispute where its seat was located. The problem is that the instructions in the Chinese dynastic accounts (specifically, the *History of the Kingdom of Wei*, compiled about 297) of how to get to Yamatai from the continent (Korea) are wrong. The instructions guide us smoothly enough across the Korean Straits to northern Kyushu, but then say to turn south and go a series of distances that, if taken, would lead into the Pacific Ocean. Scholars have long contended that either the instructions should have said to turn east instead of south, thereby leading to the vicinity of modern Nara and Kyoto in the central provinces, or the distances given are wrong and the seat of Yamatai was somewhere in northern Kyushu.

If Yamatai had its seat in the central provinces, it would indicate that, by at least the late 230s, a hegemony had already been established linking this region with northern Kyushu, and Himiko, as Yamatai's titular hegemon, was able to send missions to China on behalf of all of Wa. If, on the other hand, the seat of Yamatai was in northern Kyushu, it would suggest that Himiko's influence probably extended over a much more limited area, possibly only northern Kyushu itself.

Some of the descriptions in the Chinese dynastic histories about the customs of Wa are intriguingly similar to the practices or habits of the Japanese today. For example, the Wa people paid deference to their superiors by squatting or kneeling with both hands on the ground; they clapped their hands in worship; and they placed great store in ritual purification.

Apart from such observations about worshipful clapping and ritual purification, we know little about the evolution of those religious beliefs of ancient Japan that collectively came to be called Shinto (the way of the *kami* or gods) to distinguish them from Buddhism, which was introduced to Japan from Korea about the middle sixth century. In Shinto we can observe a primitive religion of the sort that elsewhere in the world has been absorbed by the universal faiths but that in remote and parochial Japan has been perpetuated into modern times. The central feature of Shinto is its belief in *kami,* a polytheistic host that, on the one hand, animistically inhabits nature and, on the other hand, is intimately associated with people and their most basic units of social organization, such as the family and the farming village (fig. 4). The very word *kami* has the connotation of "upper" or "above," and not that of "transcendent." Probably the most famous definition of it is the one given by the eighteenth-century scholar and Shinto revivalist Motoori Norinaga (1730–1801):

> The word *kami* refers, in the most general sense, to all divine beings of heaven and earth that appear in the classics. More particularly, the *kami* are the spirits that abide in and are worshipped at the shrines. In principle human beings, birds, animals, trees, plants, mountains, oceans—all may be *kami.* According to ancient usage, whatever seemed strikingly impressive, possessed the quality of excellence, or inspired a feeling of awe was called *kami.*[5]

Shinto, which developed no significant notion of the fate of the life spirit after death, has from its origins been overwhelmingly concerned with existence in this world. The *kami,* for the most part, are associated with life as a vital, creative force; and in this sense Shinto contrasts sharply with Buddhism, which takes a darkly pessimistic view of the world as a place of suffering and misery. Shinto also has little concept of the ethical as a means to measure human behavior, but instead considers the misdeeds of people, along with various physical defilements and natural disasters, to be essentially visitations from without that must be handled by special rites, such as exorcism and purification. Purification or lustration (of a kind presumably dating back at least to the time of the Chinese observations on the people of Wa) is particularly important in Shinto; in fact, it is the principal act performed at Shinto shrines both by worshipers and by priests.

There are basically two kinds of purification rituals in Shinto, the external and the internal. External or physical purification *(kessai)* is most commonly done by the worshiper, upon visiting a shrine, by the symbolic act of rinsing his mouth and hands with water. Internal purification or exorcism *(harai),* on the other hand, is exclusively the preserve of the priest, who normally performs it by waving a wand. When a priest thus purifies a person, it is thought that his spirit is restored to its original, pristine and upright nature.

A practice in Shinto that has always been an important feature of the social lives of the Japanese is the *matsuri* or festival. In the most basic of such festivals a *kami* (represented by some object or emblem) is transported in a portable shrine, usually on the shoulders of a team of young men, in a journey through a village or about a locale. The mood is one of joy and celebration: it is an occasion for entertainment and pleasure,

Fig. 4   Wooden statue of a Shinto deity, 12th–13th century *(Honolulu Academy of Arts, Gift of Robert Allerton, 1964 [3311.1])*

and the young men, often well fortified with sake, take their honored guest on an exhilarating ride, shouting and careening along.

Although most *kami* are benign, if not beneficent, there are also malevolent deities and spirits *(tatarigami)* that must be carefully handled and, when necessary, propitiated. The amalgam of folk beliefs about malevolent spirits, however, cannot be ascribed solely to the native religion of Shinto. Such beliefs were also introduced in early times from the continent, perhaps most conspicuously with shamanism. We have already noted that the third-century Queen Himiko was probably a shaman or mediator with the gods. But there are also shamans of a more mundane type who have been used throughout Japanese history to deal with malevolent spirits. Such a shaman, most often a woman, typically enters into an ecstatic state—called *"kami* possession" *(kamigakari)*—and allows an evil spirit to enter her body, where it can be induced to reveal why it is causing trouble and what can be done to appease it. Shamans of this sort have appeared frequently in the historical records and in literature, and in recent times certain of them have even become the founders of new religious sects through the revelations they have made while in states of *kami* possession.

Although Shinto may be said to lack a code of personal ethics, it has always been associated with an idea, *makoto* or sincerity, that has been probably the most important guide to behavior in Japanese history. The three great systems of religion and belief in premodern Japan were Shinto, Buddhism, and Confucianism. Whereas Buddhism and Confucianism were imports from China (from about the mid-sixth century), Shinto was, of course, native. In later centuries, people tended to categorize these systems by observing, rather simplistically, that Buddhism was "other-worldly" or "metaphysical," Confucianism "rational," and Shinto "emotional." Scholars of the late seventeenth and eighteenth centuries went so far as to say that the "original" nature of the Japanese was an emotional, Shinto nature, and that Buddhist metaphysics and Confucian rationality should be rejected as alien. Apart from the beliefs of these Neo-Shinto scholars of later times, we can observe that the Japanese have always placed great store in the emotional side of human nature, and that sincerity of feeling and action has more often than not taken precedence in their minds over other possible values, such as "truth," "justice," or "the good." This is not to suggest that sincerity is necessarily incompatible with these other values, but simply that sincerity, the ethic of the emotions, has been a dominant—if not predominant—strain in the Japanese sentiment throughout the ages.

Shinto has an exceptionally rich mythology, which has been recorded primarily in two works, *Kojiki (Record of Ancient Matters)* and *Nihon Shoki* (or *Nihongi* [*Chronicles of Japan*]) that were compiled in the early eighth century (712 and 720) and are the oldest extant books written by Japanese. These works will be discussed in the next chapter; let us note here some of the principal myths in the Shinto tradition.

The beginning of the mythology, a creation story, was probably composed at a relatively late date, perhaps in the seventh century, under the influence of Chinese ideas of cosmology. We are told that in the beginning the world was in a state of chaos, but gradually, in the manner of Chinese *yin-yang* dualism, the light particles of matter rose to form heaven and the heavy particles settled to become the earth (or, more precisely, an oceanlike body of viscous substance). Deities *(kami)* materialized and, after the passage of seven generations, the brother and sister gods Izanagi and Izanami were instructed to create a "drifting land." Izanagi thereupon thrust his spear into the ocean mass below, and as he withdrew it brine dripping from the tip formed a small island. Izanagi and Izanami proceeded together by means of a heavenly bridge to the island and there begot not only the remainder of the islands of Japan but also a vast number of other deities. In the process of giving birth to the fire deity, Izanami was badly burned and descended to the nether world. The ostensibly gallant Izanagi, in a sequence of the myth startlingly similar to the legend of Orpheus and Eurydice, went to fetch her but was so repelled by the appearance of Izanami's decaying and maggot-infested body that he hastily retreated. To purify himself (in the finest Shinto tradition), Izanagi went to a stream and, as he disrobed and cleansed his body, he produced a new flock of *kami*. Among these were the Sun Goddess, who sprang into being as Izanagi washed his left eye, and Susanoo, the god of storms, who appeared from his nose.

The Sun Goddess was appointed to rule over the plain of high heaven, and thus became the preeminent figure in the Shinto pantheon. Her brother Susanoo, on the other hand, was given dominion over the sea. A fretful and ill-tempered creature, Susanoo insisted upon visiting the Sun Goddess in heaven to say good-bye before taking up his post. Upon arriving in heaven, Susanoo committed a series of offenses against his sister, such as breaking down her field-dividers, destroying her looms, and defecating in her palace. Outraged, the Sun Goddess, in a solar-eclipse type of myth sequence, secluded herself in a cave and plunged the world into darkness. To lure her out, the other deities of heaven prepared a program of riotous entertainment and placed a cock atop a perch, or *torii*, before the cave to signal its commencement. When the Sun Goddess, her curiosity aroused, peeped out, she was seized by a strong-armed deity who pulled her into the open and thereby restored light to the world.

The *torii*, or bird perch, in this so-called "rock cave" story became, it is believed, the entranceway to the Shinto shrine of historical times. The *torii* is the most familiar symbol of Shinto and can be found at all shrines, no matter how small (fig. 5). Many local shrines, indeed, appear to consist of little more than *torii*.

Fig. 5   *Torii* at Miyajima in the Inland Sea *(Consulate General of Japan, New York)*

After securing the submission of certain tribal deities in the "land of luxuriant rice fields" (i.e., Japan), the Sun Goddess dispatched her grandson, Ninigi, to this land, commanding him:

> Do thou, my August Grandchild, proceed thither and govern it. Go! and may prosperity attend thy dynasty, and may it, like Heaven and Earth, endure for ever.[6]

To seal her command, the Sun Goddess bestowed upon Ninigi a sacred regalia, consisting of a Chinese-style bronze mirror, a sword, and a curved jewel *(magatama)*. Objects similar to those of the regalia have been found in gravesites dating from the middle Yayoi period, and appear to have symbolized local tribal rulership. In historical times, however, the mirror, sword, and curved jewel have been used exclusively as tokens of the right of the imperial family to rule. The mirror has been especially treasured because it is believed—or *was* believed, until the end of World War II—to represent the *kami*-body of the Sun Goddess. According to the mythology, it was installed in a Shinto shrine at Ise after an emperor confessed that he felt uneasy about having it nearby in the palace. The supreme sanctity of the Ise Shrine derives from the fact that since that time (or at least from as early as we know) it has housed the sacred mirror of the regalia.

Ninigi descended from heaven to a mountaintop in southeastern Kyushu, but seems to have done little to assert his rule over the "land of luxuriant rice fields." It was his great-grandson Jimmu who, after conducting a campaign to the central provinces, where he destroyed aboriginal enemies, performed rites to his ancestress, the Sun Goddess, that signified his assumption of the status of first emperor of Japan. Sometime in the early historical period (the late sixth or early seventh centuries) the Japanese, under the influence of certain Chinese calendrical considerations, calculated the date of Jimmu's accession to the emperorship to be 660 B.C.;[7] and the authors of *Kojiki* and *Nihon Shoki* established, as part of the mythology, the genealogy of an "unbroken line of sovereigns" which, if accepted, would make the present emperor, Akihito, the 125th in lineal descent from Jimmu. Archaeological evidence, however, suggests that the historical ruling dynasty of Japan dates back only to the early sixth century A.D. and was probably preceded by at least two other "imperial dynasties."

This evidence about earlier dynasties dates from approximately A.D. 300, when Japan entered what scholars call the tomb period because of the earth and stone burial mounds *(kofun)* that were constructed throughout much of the country from this time until the early seventh century. Some of these burial mounds are simply converted hills or knolls of land, but others are truly stupendous in size and must have required great concentrations of labor. The larger tombs, many of them in a keyhole shape possibly taken from similarly constructed tombs on the Asian continent, are in the central provinces and are generally thought to be the graves of rulers—possibly the successors to Queen Himiko of Yamatai—who presided over a hegemony that included much, if not all, of central and western Japan.

From the standpoint of art, the most important objects from the tomb period are terra cotta figurines, usually several feet in height, known as *haniwa*. Implanted on the slopes and tops of the burial mounds, the *haniwa* represent a great variety of things, including people, animals, houses, and boats (fig. 6). The mythology informs us that an emperor in early times was so moved by the agonies of attendants and others buried alive with deceased members of the imperial family that he inaugurated the practice of using clay images in place of people on the occasion of royal funerals. Although often cited to explain the origin of the *haniwa*, this tale seems to have little basis in truth. No evidence has been found that the Japanese actually engaged in this gruesome practice of live burial, even though it was common in ancient China. More important, the images of human beings do not appear until relatively late in the evolution of the *haniwa*. The earlier *haniwa* were simply plain cylinders. Perhaps they were employed to reduce erosion or to mark off certain areas on the burial mounds for ritual purposes. On the other hand, the later

Fig. 6 *Haniwa* shamaness *(courtesy of the Brooklyn Museum, Gift of Mr. and Mrs. Stanley Marcus)*

haniwa, which depict living beings and sundry commonplace objects, indicate a new use of these images to reproduce in the afterlife a world that was familiar to the deceased.

Apart from certain shamanistic female figurines, most of the *haniwa* are entirely secular in appearance: that is, they have no religious or magical aura about them. This may be a commentary on the simple, direct outlook of the early inhabitants of Japan. A number of Japanese scholars have asserted that the *haniwa* possess a quality they call *heimei* —openness and candor—that reflects the native spirit of Japan before it was altered by Confucian rationalism and the complex religious doctrines of Buddhism. Whether or not this is true, the *haniwa* are aesthetically excellent examples of the Japanese preference, which we observed in Yayoi pottery, for naturalness in the use of materials and for plain, uncluttered forms.

Beginning in the early 400s, there was a change in the funerary objects of the burial mounds. Whereas the mounds until then had contained things that were used mainly for ornamental and ritual purposes, including many bronze pieces, the fifth century brought an increasing number of more practical objects, such as tools and weapons of iron. Most striking was the appearance on the mounds of warrior and horse *haniwa*. The Chinese dynastic histories make no mention of the existence of horses in the land of Wa in earlier times, a fact which of course does not necessarily mean that there were no such animals there before the fifth century. But the depiction of horses as *haniwa* has lent support to the theory, advanced soon after World War II, that Japan was invaded in this period by horse-riding warriors who, entering from Korea, conquered the country and established themselves as its new ruling elite.

The horse-rider theory is an intriguing idea, especially when considered in conjunction with the movement of "barbarian" peoples on the northeast Asian mainland during this same period.[8] But it seems that those who have advanced the theory have not paid sufficient attention to all the archaeological evidence. As presented by its originator, Professor Egami Namio, the theory rests squarely on the contention that there was a "sudden" appearance of horse-rider grave goods and warrior and horse *haniwa* in and on the great tombs in the late fourth century. Actually, as noted above, such goods and *haniwa* did not appear until well into the fifth century, and then their appearance was not sudden but gradual. The Japanese did indeed, about this time, receive new knowledge of fighting on horseback as well as the material accoutrements of such fighting, including armor, helmets, and protective gear for horses; but these seem clearly to have been imported by the Japanese themselves and not brought to the islands by continental invaders.[9]

Whether or not it was founded by alien horseriders, a new dynasty seems clearly to have arisen in the central provinces in the early 400s. Judging from the fact that the very largest burial mounds date from this time (the largest is that of the protohistorical "Emperor Nintoku," which covers an area 1,500 feet in length and is situated outside modern Osaka), the new dynasty came into being with considerable force and power. The dynasty's power was used at least in part to pursue a policy of military expansionism in Korea, where three states—Silla, Paekche, and Koguryŏ —were struggling for hegemony. Japan may have established a military colony or outpost called Mimana on the southern tip of Korea,[10] and during the fifth century Japanese rulers made requests of China on at least five occasions for the confirmation of titles related to Japan's involvement in the Korean fighting, including "King of Wa" and "Generalissimo Who Maintains Peace in the East Commanding With Battle-Ax All Military Affairs."[11]

The dynasty of the fifth century appears, in its turn, to have been supplanted in the early sixth century by the ruling family that became the imperial dynasty of historic times. This final dynastic tran-

Fig. 7   Ise Shrine *(Consulate General of Japan, New York)*

sition, which gave rise to the line of the Sun Goddess, occurred on the eve of history—that is, within decades of the period, about mid-sixth century, when the native records become generally reliable as factual accounts.

The principal monument to the Sun Goddess is the Ise Shrine (fig. 7), which houses her image, as noted, in the form of the mirror, the most precious object of the imperial regalia. The Ise Shrine is made of soft-textured, unpainted cypress, and is a splendid example of a shrine maintained in a "natural" state. Since antiquity it has been the custom to rebuild the structures of the Ise Shrine every twenty years in adjacent, alternate sites (the last rebuilding was in 1993). No one knows the reason for this unusual custom, although possibly it derives from the desire to preserve the freshness of the wood and to avoid the warping and sagging to which this kind of material is susceptible. The severely simple buildings of the shrine, with their raised floors, thatched roofs, and crossed end-rafters, show Shinto architecture at its best. Situated in lovely forest surroundings, they give the feeling of great naturalness and tranquility, of a spirit somehow representative of Japan before the introduction of Buddhism in the sixth century.

This style of architecture can be traced back to line drawings on rather oversized bronze bells, known as *dōtaku,* of the mid-Yayoi period and to certain house *haniwa* of the age of burial mounds. The style is sometimes called "granary" *(kura)* construction, because its characteristic structure, as seen in the buildings of Ise, was probably first used to store rice. Later, it is believed, the same kind of structure was adapted to both palace and shrine use.

2

The Introduction of Buddhism

THE SIXTH CENTURY inaugurated an epoch of great vitality in East Asia. After some three and a half centuries of disunion following the fall of the Han dynasty in 220, China was at length reunited under the Sui dynasty in 589. Although the T'ang replaced the Sui in 618, there was no further disruption of national unity for another three centuries.

The period of disunion in China produced conditions favorable to the spread of Buddhism, which had been introduced from India during the first century A.D., and it was largely as a Buddhist country that China entered its grand age of the T'ang dynasty (618–907). Buddhism had not only secured great numbers of religious converts in China; it had come to be regarded as virtually essential to the institutional centralization of the country, and its themes dominated the world of the visual arts.

Under the T'ang, China enjoyed its greatest national flourishing in history. Its borders were extended to their farthest limits, and Chinese culture radiated outward to neighboring lands. In East Asia, both Korea and Japan were profoundly influenced by T'ang China and underwent broad centralizing reforms on the Chinese model.

At mid-sixth century, Japan was divided into a number of territories controlled by aristocratic clans called *uji*. One clan—the imperial *uji*—had its seat in the central provinces and enjoyed a status approximating that of *primus inter pares* over most of the others, whose lands extended from Kyushu in the west to the eastern provinces of the Kantō. In northern Honshu, conditions were still unruly and barbarous.

Even at this time in Japanese history, there was a pronounced tendency for the heads of the non-imperial *uji* to assume, as ministers at court, much if not all of the emperor's political powers. Although there were a number of forceful sovereigns during the next few centuries, Japan's emperors have in general been noteworthy for the fact that they have reigned but have not ruled.

The word "emperor" is actually misleading when discussing this ancient age, for the emperor we find presiding over the loosely associated clans of the Yamato state in mid-sixth century appears, like a *kami* of primitive Shinto, only to have been relatively superior to or elevated above the leaders of the other clans. Not until the next century did the Japanese, under the influence of Chinese monarchic ideas, transform their sovereign into a transcendentally divine ruler, giving him the Chinese-sounding title of *tennō* that is always translated into English as emperor.

Although the Japanese thus created an exalted emperor figure on the Chinese model, they did not adopt the key Chinese Confucian theory of the emperor ruling through a mandate from heaven. A corollary to this theory was that a mandate granted by heaven to a virtuous ruler could be withdrawn from an unvirtuous one, and it was on the basis of this rationale that the Chinese justified or explained the periodic changes of dynasty in their history. In Japan, on the other hand, the native mythological assertion (noted in the last chapter) that the Sun Goddess had granted a mandate to the imperial family to rule eternally was retained, and the emperor line of the sixth century was thus enabled to achieve its extraordinary continuity of unbroken rulership throughout historic times until the present day.

Tradition has it that Buddhism was officially introduced to Japan from the Korean kingdom of Paekche in 552.[1] Since about a third of Japan's aristocracy was by that time of foreign descent, the Japanese undoubtedly already knew about Buddhism as well as the other major features of continental civilization. Nevertheless, it was over the issue of whether or not to accept Buddhism that a larger debate concerning national reform arose at the Japanese court in the second half of the sixth century.

Buddhism was at least a thousand years old when it entered Japan. It had emerged in northern India with the teachings of Gautama (ca. 563–483 B.C.), the historic Buddha, and had spread throughout the Indian subcontinent and into Southeast and East Asia. But it had become a complex, universalistic religion that embraced doctrines far removed from the basic tenets of its founder. Gautama, in his Four Noble Truths, had taught that (1) the world is a place of suffering; (2) suffering is caused by human desires and acquisitiveness; (3) something can be done to end suffering; and (4) the end of suffering and achievement of enlightenment or buddhahood lies in following a prescribed program known as the Eightfold Noble Path (right views, right intention, right speech, right action, right livelihood, right effort, right mindfulness, and right concentration). For most people, following the Eightfold Noble Path probably would not be easy. The doctrine of karma, or cause and effect, held that acts in previous existences were likely to have enmeshed one tightly in the web of desire and suffering and to have predestined one to at least several more cycles of death and rebirth.

These fundamental teachings of Buddhism, which the contemporary West has found appealing as a psychology, were greatly augmented some five centuries after Gautama's death with the advent of Mahayana, the Buddhism of the "Greater Vehicle." The believers in Mahayana deprecatingly called the earlier form of Buddhism Hinayana, or the "Lesser Vehicle," since it was essentially a body of doctrine designed to instruct individuals in how to achieve release from the cycle of life and death.[2] This, the Mahayanists asserted, implied that buddhahood was really open only to those with a special capacity to follow correctly the Eightfold Noble Path. They claimed—and indeed produced ancient scriptures to "prove"—that just before his death Gautama had revealed the ultimate truth that all living things have the potentiality for buddhahood. The Mahayanists, moreover, came increasingly to regard Gautama as a transcendent, rather than simply a mortal, being and gave reverence to a new figure, the bodhisattva or "buddha-to-be," who has met all the requirements for buddhahood but in his great compassion has postponed his entry into that state in order to assist others in their quest for release from the cycle of life and death. In contrast to Hinayana, which could be considered "selfish" because it urged people to devote themselves solely to attainment of their own enlightenments, Mahayana preached universal love, through the ideal of the bodhisattva, for all beings, animal as well as human.

The Mahayana school of Buddhism, which had its greatest flourishing in East Asia, also accumulated a vast and bewildering pantheon of buddhas and other exalted beings, some of whom were taken from Hinduism and even from the religions of the Near East. In an effort to categorize and account for the roles of these myriad deities, the Mahayanists formulated the theory of the "three forms" of the buddha: his all-embracing, universal, or cosmic form, his transcendent form, in which he might appear as any one of many heavenly figures, such as the healing buddha (in Japanese, Yakushi), the buddha of the future (Miroku), and the buddha of the boundless light (Amida); and his transformation form, or the body he assumed when he existed on earth as Gautama. Without knowledge of this theory of the three forms, one cannot understand the interrelationship among the various Buddhist sects that appeared successively in Japanese history.

It is difficult to gauge the precise impact of Buddhism in Japan during the first century or so after its introduction. In China, it had already proliferated into a number of abstruse metaphysical sects, within both the Hinayana and Mahayana schools, that could scarcely have appealed to the Japanese beyond a small circle of intellectuals at court. As others outside this circle gradually became aware of Buddhism, they apparently regarded it at first as a new and potent form of magic for ensuring more abundant harvests and for warding off calamities. They also responded directly and intuitively to the wonders of Buddhist art as these were displayed in the sculpture, painting, and temple architecture brought to Japan. Moreover, the Japanese probably accepted with little difficulty the validity of Buddhism's most fundamental premises: that all things are impermanent, suffering is universal, and man is the helpless victim of his fate. People in many ages have held these or similar propositions to be true, and we should not be surprised to find the Japanese of this period accepting them in the persuasive language of Buddhism.

Possibly the strongest feeling the Japanese of the seventh and eighth centuries came to have about Buddhism was that it was an essential quality of higher civilization. It is ironic that this religion, which in its origins viewed the world with extreme pessimism and gave no thought to social or political reform, should enter Japan from China as the carrier of such multifarious aspects of civilization, including the ideal of state centralization.

It is impossible to explain in a few words, or perhaps even in many, how primitive Shinto managed to survive the influx of Buddhism. Part of the answer lies in the unusual tolerance of Eastern religious thought in general for "partial" or "alternative" truths and its capacity to synthesize seemingly disparate beliefs and manifestations of the divine. In Japan, for example, the principal *kami* of Shinto came to be regarded as Buddhist deities in different forms, and Shinto shrines were even amalgamated with Buddhist temples. Another reason why the Japanese throughout the ages have with little or no difficulty considered themselves to be both Shintoists and Buddhists is that the doctrines of the two religions complement each other so neatly. Shinto expresses a simple and direct love of nature and its vital reproductive forces, and regards death simply as one of many kinds of defilement. Buddhism, on the other hand, is concerned with life's interminable suffering and seeks to guide living beings on the path to enlightenment. It is fitting that even today in Japan the ceremonies employed to celebrate such events as birth and marriage are Shinto, whereas funerals and communion with the dead are within the purview of Buddhism.

The dispute in Japan in the mid-sixth century over whether or not to accept Buddhism, and at the same time to undertake national reforms, divided the Japanese court into two opposing camps. One consisted of families which, as Shinto ritualists and elite imperial guards, felt most threatened by the changes Buddhism portended; the other camp, including the Soga family, took a progressive position in favor of Buddhism and reform. In the late 580s, the Soga prevailed militarily over their opponents and, further strengthened by marriage ties to the imperial family, inaugurated an epoch of great renovation in Japan.

The most important leader of the early years of reform was Prince Shōtoku (574–622), who with Soga blessing became crown prince and regent for an undistinguished empress (fig. 8). Shōtoku has been greatly idealized in history, and it is difficult to judge how much credit he truly deserves for the measures and policies attributed to him. Yet, he seems ardently to have loved learning and probably he was instrumental in ex-

Fig. 8 Lacquered wooden statue of Prince Shōtoku, Edo period *(Honolulu Academy of Arts, Gift of Nathan V. Hammer, 1953 [1804.1])*

panding the relations with Sui China that were critical at this time to the advancement of Japanese civilization. Quite likely it was also Shōtoku who wrote the note to the Sui court in 607 that began: "From the sovereign of the land of the rising sun to the sovereign of the land of the setting sun." The Sui emperor did not appreciate this lack of respect and refused to reply; but the note made an important point. In earlier centuries, rulers of the land of Wa, such as Himiko of Yamatai, had sent missions to China. Henceforth, however, Japan intended to uphold its independence and would not accept the status of humble subordination expected of countries that sent tribute to mighty China.

Formerly, the Japanese had called their country Yamato, but sometime in the seventh century they adopted the designation of Nihon (or Nippon), written with the Chinese characters for "sun" and "source." Apparently they hoped that this designation, derived from the fact that Japan's location in the sea to the east made it the "source of the sun," would give them greater prestige in the eyes of the Chinese. Whether or not it did, eventually it was the Chinese pronunciation of Nihon—Jihpen —that was transmitted back to Europe by Marco Polo in the thirteenth century and incorporated into the European tongues in forms like the English "Japan."

The Japanese dispatched a total of four missions to Sui China during the period 600–614 and fifteen to T'ang between 630 and 838. The larger missions usually consisted of groups of about four ships that transported more than five hundred people, including official envoys, students, Buddhist monks, and translators. Some of these visitors remained abroad for long periods of time—up to thirty or more years—and some never returned. The trip was exceedingly dangerous, and the fact that so many risked it attests to the avidity with which the Japanese of this age sought to acquire the learning and culture of China.

Although there are no replicas or contemporary drawings of the ships used in the missions to Sui and T'ang, we know that their sail and rudder systems were primitive and that they were obliged to rely on the seasonal winds. They usually left in the spring, when the prevailing winds were westward, and returned in the winter, when the winds blew to the east. The shortest route to the continent was across the 115-mile channel that separates Kyushu from southern Korea. But sometimes the Japanese ships were blown off course and drifted far down the Chinese coast. During most of the seventh century, when relations with Korea were poor, the Japanese set sail directly for South China, although the passage was longer and more difficult. The return trip, which almost always began from the mouth of the Yangtze River, was the most treacherous of all. A miscalculation or an accidental alteration in course could carry the ships into the vastness of the Pacific Ocean. Often they landed on islands in the Ryukyu chain and were obliged to make their way home as best they could.

Dangerous as they were, the missions to China from the seventh through the mid-ninth centuries were essential to the establishment of Japan's first centralized state. The Japanese borrowed freely from a civilization that, at least in material and technological terms, was vastly superior to their own. Yet Japan's cultural borrowing was sufficiently selective to bring about the evolution of a society which, although it owed much to China, became unique in its own right.

The influence of Korea in this transmission of Chinese civilization to Japan has not yet received adequate attention among scholars. During the first century or so A.D., Japan's relations with Korea had been close, and various Japanese tribal states had dispatched missions to China via the Han Chinese military commanderies in Korea. Sometime in the late fourth century, as observed in the last chapter, Japan established Mimana on the southern tip of the Korean peninsula; and for the next two hundred years Japanese armies were involved in the endless struggles for supremacy among Korea's three kingdoms of Paekche, Silla, and Koguryŏ. By the sixth century, Japan had come in general to support Paekche— which is credited with officially introducing Buddhism to the Yamato court in 552—against the rising might of Silla. But Japan's efforts were not sufficient to alter the trend of events in Korea. Silla destroyed Mimana in 562, Paekche in 663, and Koguryŏ in 668; it thereby unified Korea as a centralized state on the lines of T'ang China, much like the newly reformed state that was emerging in Japan during the same period.

Koreans and Chinese had migrated to Japan from at least the beginning of the fifth century. But during Silla's rise to power the number of immigrants from the continent—especially refugees from Paekche and Koguryŏ—increased substantially, as we can tell from accounts of how they were given land and allowed to settle in different parts of the country. Throughout the seventh century, which was of course the great age of reform, these Korean immigrants played a vital role as scribes, craftsmen, and artists in the advancement of culture and civilization in Japan.

Prince Shōtoku and other Japanese intellectuals of the early reform period studied not only Buddhism but also the teachings of Chinese Confucianism. Like Buddhism, Confucianism was about a millenium old when it entered Japan and it had expanded greatly beyond the simple humanism of Confucius (551–479 B.C.) and his followers. The early Confucianists were concerned with man in society, and not with metaphysical speculation: they preached the cultivation of virtue and its application to public service. In his famous Seventeen-Article Constitution of 604, Prince Shōtoku, in addition to calling for the reverence of Buddhism, sought also to propagate Confucian values among the Japanese.[3] Indeed, the Constitution is mainly a Confucian document. Although it may appear to be a collection of simplistic maxims—for example, that harmony should be prized (Article I) and that ministers should obey imperial commands (III), behave decorously (IV), reject covetous desires (V), and attend court early in the morning (VIII)—it is the first statement in Japanese history of the need for ethical government. Addressed primarily to Japan's ministerial class, the Constitution, in characteristic Confucian fashion, offers general principles of guidance for rule by moral suasion rather than compulsion, which requires detailed laws with specified punishments.

Scholars have long questioned whether the Seventeen-Article Constitution, which appears in *Nihon Shoki*, a work compiled more than a century later, could truly have been written by Prince Shōtoku, inasmuch as it contains ideas and principles that the Japanese were not likely to have stressed or adopted until the late seventh or early eighth centuries, when state centralization, based on continued borrowing from the continent, was more advanced. Reference to the office of "provincial governor," for example, seems anachronistic, since that office was not established until the late 600s. Also questionable, in the minds of some scholars, is whether the principle of supreme imperial rule as set forth in the following articles of the Constitution could have been articulated and subscribed to by the Japanese as early as 604: "When you receive imperial commands, fail not scrupulously to obey them. The lord is Heaven, the vassal is Earth. Heaven overspreads, and Earth upbears. When this is so, the four seasons follow their due course, and the powers of Nature obtain their efficacy" (III); and "In a country there are not two lords; the people have not two masters. The sovereign is the master of the people of the whole country" (XII).

These are lofty Chinese ideas about emperorship, which hold that the emperor not only enjoyed absolute authority over all the people but, in the proper exercise of his office, was essential to the basic functioning of nature itself. Nor is anything said in these or other articles of the Constitution about the native deities, the *kami*, whose supreme representative, Amaterasu the Sun Goddess, is said by *Kojiki* and *Nihon Shoki*, as we have seen, to have mandated the imperial family's right to rule forever. In other words, the Constitution is silent about what subsequently became the unassailable basis for the legitimacy of single-dynasty rule in Japan: Amaterasu's mandate. During the early and middle seventh century the Japanese appear to have experimented with various ideas, drawn from Confucianism and Buddhism as well as Shinto, to justify imperial rule. Probably not until the late seventh and early eighth centuries did they finally settle on the Shinto interpretation, as reflected in Amaterasu's mandate, and codify it for all future generations in *Kojiki* and *Nihon Shoki*.

Despite Prince Shōtoku's efforts to stimulate central reform, very little of real significance could be achieved so long as the aristocratic clans continued to exercise almost complete autonomy over their lands and the people on them. After Shōtoku's death in 622, the Soga, who had been the progressive advocates of Buddhism and the adoption of Chinese culture a half-century earlier, became the chief obstacles to reform of the decentralized *uji* system. In the early 640s, there formed at court an anti-Soga faction that included an imperial prince, leaders of various ministerial houses, and men who had studied in China. In 645 this group forcibly overthrew the Soga, reasserted the supremacy of the throne (the Soga were accused of having plotted to supplant the imperial family), and instituted the reform of Taika ("Great Change").

The Taika Reform was essentially a land reform patterned on the institutions of T'ang China. Although a paucity of records makes it unpossible to determine just how extensively it was carried out, the intent of the Reform was to nationalize all agricultural land—that is, to make it the emperor's land—and to render all the people of the country direct subjects of the throne. Land was then to be parceled out in equal plots to farmers to work during their lifetimes. Upon the death of a farmer, his plot would revert back to the state for redistribution.

This is a gross oversimplification of the provisions of the Taika Reform, but it will suffice to show the idealistic concept of land equalization upon which the Reform rested. This concept had evolved from Confucian egalitarianism, which held that the equal division of land would render the people content and harmonious. Equality, however, was to apply only to the lower, peasant class of society. Members of the aristocracy were to receive special emoluments of land based on considerations such as rank, office, and meritorious service. In this way, the aristocracy was enabled to remain about as privileged economically as it had been before the Reform.

In practice, then, the equal-field system of the Taika Reform was only equal for some people. Moreover, its conscientious implementation would have required an administrative organization far more elaborate than Japan possessed in this age. Perhaps we should marvel that the system worked as effectively as it did; yet within a century it had begun to decay. The aristocratic families, along with Buddhist temples and Shinto shrines, started to accumulate private estates that were in many ways similar to the territorial holdings of the pre-Taika *uji*. (We may note that the equal-field system fared little better in T'ang China, the land of its birth. After the failure of this system later during the T'ang, China never again in premodern times attempted to nationalize land and parcel it out by allotment at the local level to individuals or families.)

Another major act of reform was the promulgation by the court, in 702, of the Taihō ("Great Treasure") Code, which specified the central and provincial offices of the new government (some of which were already functioning) and set forth general laws of conduct for the Japanese people. Also modeled on T'ang, the Taihō Code provided Japan with an elaborate and symmetrical bureaucratic structure of the sort that had evolved over a millennium or more in China Although it functioned smoothly enough through most of the eighth century, it ultimately proved too weighty and inflexible for Japan in this early stage of its historical development. Beginning in the ninth century, new offices that were opened outside the provisions of the Taihō Code successively became the real centers of national power in Japan.

In 710 the court moved to the newly constructed city of Nara, which remained the capital of Japan until 784. Before this move, the site of the court had often been shifted, usually in and around the central provinces. Some claim that the Shinto view of death as a defilement—and the death of a sovereign as the defilement of an entire community—was the main reason for this constant moving about. But another likely reason is that the loose control of the Yamato court over the territorial *uji* in earlier centuries necessitated its frequent transfer from place to place for strategic purposes. When the Soga became politically dominant in the late sixth century, they established the court at Asuka to the south of present-day Nara, where their seat of territorial power was located.

The epoch from the introduction of Buddhism in 552 until the Taika Reform of 645 is generally known in art history as the Asuka period. Most, if not all, of the Buddhist statuary, painting, and temple architecture of the Asuka period was produced by Chinese and Korean craftsmen. It is therefore not until a later age that we can speak of the true beginnings of Japanese Buddhist art. Nevertheless, the treasures of the Asuka period, which are in the manner of China's Six Dynasties era (220–589), are of inestimable value not only because of their individual merits but also because they constitute the largest body of Six Dynasties-style art extant. Owing to warfare and other vicissitudes, few examples remain in China or Korea.

Although the first Buddhist temples in Japan were constructed by the Soga in the late sixth century, none has survived. Of the buildings still standing, by far the oldest—and indeed the oldest wooden buildings in the world—are at the Hōryūji Temple, located to the southwest of Nara. Originally constructed in 607 under the patronage of Prince Shōtoku, the Hōryūji may have been partly or entirely destroyed by fire in 670 and rebuilt shortly after the turn of the century. Even so, it contains buildings that clearly antedate those of any other temple in Japan.

Buddhist temples of this age were arranged in patterns known as *garan.* Although the *garan* varied in the number and arrangement of their structures, they usually had certain common features: a roofed gallery in the form of a square or rectangle, with an entrance gate in the center of its southern side, that enclosed the main compound of the temple; a so-called golden hall to house the temple's principal images of devotion; a lecture hall; and at least one pagoda, a type of building derived from the

Fig. 9   *Garan* of the Hōryūji Temple *(Consulate General of Japan, New York)*

Fig. 10   Golden Hall of the Hōryūji Temple *(photograph by Joseph Shulman)*

Indian stupa and originally intended to contain the relic of a Buddhist
saint. At the Hōryūji, the golden hall and a single, five-storied pagoda are
located to the right and left inside the entrance gate, and the lecture hall
is to the rear of the compound, actually integrated into the northern side
of the gallery (figs. 9–10). The chief characteristics of the golden hall are
its raised stone base and its hipped and gabled upper roof; as probably
the oldest of the Hōryūji buildings, it is especially representative of the
Buddhist architectural style of the Six Dynasties period.

Among the statuary in the golden hall is a trinity of figures in bronze,
set in relief against flaming body halos. According to an inscription, this
was cast in 623 to commemorate the death of Prince Shōtoku the year
before (fig. 11). It shows the historical Buddha, Gautama (in Japanese,
Shaka), flanked by two attendant bodhisattvas. The Buddha is seated

Fig. 11   Shaka trinity at the Hōryūji Temple *(Asuka-en)*

cross-legged on a dais with his clothing draped in the stylized waterfall pattern of the Six Dynasties period. He also strikes one of the many mudras or special hand positions of Buddhist iconography (the upraised hand here gives assurance against fear and the open palm is a sign of charity); and he has a protuberance on his head and a third eye that indicate extraordinary knowledge and vision and are among some twenty-three bodily signs introduced by the Mahayana Buddhists to indicate Gautama's superhuman qualities. The expression on the faces of all three figures of the trinity is that known as the "archaic smile," whose impersonality and vague mysteriousness contrast strikingly with the unabashed frankness we noted in the countenances of many of the early native *haniwa* figurines of human beings.

The bodhisattvas stand on pedestals of lotus blossoms and are attired in the sort of princely garb that Gautama wore before he renounced the world. In the Buddhist tradition, the lotus, which may be found floating on the surface of the murkiest water, stands for purity. It can also symbolize the universe, with each of its petals representing a separate, constituent world.

Two excellent examples of wooden sculpture from the Asuka period are the figure in the Hōryūji of the bodhisattva Kannon, known as the Kudara Kannon, and the seated image in a nearby nunnery of Miroku, the buddha of the future (figs. 12–13). Both statues have features of the Six Dynasties style—for example, the stiff, saw-toothed drapery of the Kannon and the waterfall pattern in the lower folds of the Miroku's clothing. Yet, there is also in both a suggestion of the voluptuousness and earthly sensuality that were to appear later in the sculpture of the T'ang. The Miroku, whose surface appears like metal after centuries of rubbing with incense, has been particularly admired for its tender, dreamlike expression and for the gentle manner in which the hand is raised to the face. It strikes a mudra characteristic of Miroku statues.

The art epoch from the Taika Reform of 645 until the founding of the great capital city of Nara in 710 is usually called the Hakuhō period after one of the calendrical designations of the age. It was a time of vigorous reforming effort in Japan, directed by the imperial family itself; and some of the more powerful sovereigns in Japanese history ruled during the Hakuhō period. Of these, it was the emperor Temmu (reigned 673–86) who first advanced Buddhism as the great protector of the country and of the imperial family. Buddhism had previously been patronized by individuals, such as Prince Shōtoku and certain chieftains of the Soga family. Under Temmu and his successors, Buddhism received the official patronage of the court, which sponsored the construction of a series of great temples during the late seventh and eighth centuries.

In both sculpture and painting, the Hakuhō period marked the transition in Japan, after a time lag of about a half-century, from the Bud-

Fig. 12   Miroku buddha *(Asuka-en)*

dhist art style of China's Six Dynasties era to that of the T'ang. A bronze trinity (now situated in the Yakushiji Temple in Nara) of Yakushi, the healing buddha, and two attendant bodhisattvas exemplifies the great T'ang style of sculpture as it was produced in Japan (fig. 14). The main elements of this style can perhaps best be seen in the figures of the bodhisattvas: for example, in their sensuously curved and fleshy bodies, their raised hairstyling, and their more naturally hanging draperies.

The finest examples of painting from the Hakuhō period are the frescoes that adorn the interior of the golden hall at the Hōryūji. Although a fire in 1949 badly damaged these frescoes, photographs show how they formerly appeared. An attendant bodhisattva in one of the trinities depicted was especially well preserved and has been widely admired as one of the best examples of T'ang painting (fig. 15). Quite sim-

Fig. 13   Kudara Kannon at the Hōryūji Temple *(Asuka-en)*

ilar in appearance to the bodhisattvas in the Yakushi trinity of bronze statues, it shows the great skill in linear technique of the artist of this age. Its even lines have been called wirelike in contrast to the alternately thick and thin lines, derived from the brushwork of calligraphy, that were later so favored by painters in China and Japan.

Fig. 14   From the Yakushi trinity at the Yakushiji Temple
(Asuka-en)

The site for Nara was chosen by Chinese geomancy, the art of select-
ing suitable terrain on the basis of the favorable arrangement of its surrounding hills and the auspicious character of its "wind and water."
Modeled after the T'ang capital of Ch'ang-an, although on a smaller
scale, Nara was laid out in orderly fashion with the palace enclosure in
the north-center, a grand boulevard running down its middle to the city's
main gate of entrance in the south, and evenly intersecting north-south
and east-west avenues. Unlike the Chinese, the Japanese never constructed walled cities; and although the population of Nara probably
reached two hundred thousand in the eighth century, making it Japan's
first truly urban center, contemporary accounts describe it as a city of
open spaces with many fields interspersed among the buildings.

The orderliness of the original plan for Nara paralleled the balanced
arrangement of the governmental offices and boards elaborated in the
Taihō Code, and reflected the fundamental Chinese taste for symmetry
in such matters. Some have speculated that the Japanese, on the other
hand, inherently prefer asymmetry. In any case, just as they ultimately

Fig. 15 Attendant bodhisattva: detail of fresco in the
Golden Hall of the Hōryūji Temple *(Asuka-en)*

deviated from China's form of a balanced bureaucracy, the Japanese also
failed to develop Nara as planned. The present city lies almost entirely in
the northeastern suburbs of the eighth-century plan, and only recently
placed markers enable us to see where the palace enclosure and other
important sites of the original Nara were located. Kyoto, which became
the seat of the court in 794 after its move from Nara, was also laid out
symmetrically like Ch'ang-an; and it too spread erratically, primarily into
the northeastern suburbs. But, whereas Kyoto was often devastated by
warfare and other disasters during the medieval period and has few
buildings within its city limits that predate the sixteenth century, Nara
has retained substantially intact a number of splendid edifices and their
contents dating from the eighth century.

    Even today, the visitor to Nara can recapture much of the splendor of
the brilliant youth of Japanese civilization. Nevertheless, it is difficult, in
view of the later introversion of Japanese society, to envision how extraordinarily cosmopolitan Nara must have been in the eighth century. The
Japanese of the Nara period were the eager pupils of Chinese civiliza-

tion, and T'ang China was then the greatest empire in the world. The Buddhist art of China, which the Japanese fervently emulated, was an amalgam of many influences, not only from India but also from regions as remote as Persia, Greece, and the Byzantine empire, all of which were in contact with China by means of the overland caravan route known as the Silk Road. *Objets d'art,* many still preserved in Nara, were imported from these exotic places; and the Japanese court of the eighth century welcomed visitors from India and other parts of Asia outside China, visitors of a variety that would not appear in Japan again until modern times.

One unusual aspect of Nara civilization was the degree of dependence of the Japanese on the Chinese written language. There is no archaeological or other evidence to indicate that the Japanese ever independently attempted to devise a script of their own. The apparent reason is simply that, in remote times, they became aware of the sophisticated writing system of China and, as they advanced in the ways of civilization, were content to use Chinese for purposes other than speech, much as Latin was employed in Europe during the Middle Ages.

This could not, however, be a permanently satisfactory arrangement, since structurally the Chinese and Japanese languages are vastly different. Chinese is monosyllabic, terse, and has no grammatical inflections. Tense and mood are either ignored or expressed by means of syntax and word position within a sentence. Japanese, on the other hand, is polysyllabic, diffuse and, like the Indo-European tongues, highly inflected.

After some fumbling starts in the Nara period, the Japanese in the ninth century finally evolved a syllabary of approximately fifty symbols (derived from Chinese characters) called *kana.* Although they could thenceforth theoretically write their language exclusively in *kana,* they had by this time also imported a great number of Chinese words into their vocabulary, words that were most appropriately written with Chinese characters (even though they were pronounced differently in Japanese).

Ultimately, the Japanese came to write in a mixture of Chinese characters and *kana.* In the modern language, the characters are used mainly for substantives, adjectives, and verbal stems, and the *kana* symbols are employed as grammatical markers and for the writing (among other things) of adverbs and foreign names. There is little question that Japanese is the most complex written language in the world today, and the modern man who holds utility to be the ultimate value must sorely lament that the Japanese ever became burdened with the Chinese writing system. Yet, from the aesthetic standpoint, the Chinese characters have been infinitely enriching, and through the centuries have provided an intimate cultural bond between the Chinese and Japanese (as well as the Koreans, who have also utilized Chinese characters) that is one of the most significant features of East Asian civilization.

The oldest extant books of the Japanese, as we have seen, are two works of myth and history entitled *Kojiki* and *Nihon Shoki,* completed in 712 and 720, respectively. Prince Shōtoku supposedly wrote texts a century earlier on both Buddhism and history, but these were destroyed in the burning of the Soga family's library at the time of the 645 Taika coup.

It is fitting that Japan's earliest remaining works, composed at a time when the country was so strongly under the civilizing influence of China, should be of a historical character. In the Confucian tradition, the writing of history has always been held in the highest esteem, since Confucianists believe that the lessons of the past provide the best guide for ethical rule in the present and future. In contrast to the Indians, who have always been absorbed with metaphysical and religious speculation and scarcely at all with history, the Chinese are among the world's greatest record-keepers. They revere the written word, no doubt even more so because of the evocative nature of their ideographic script, and they transmitted this reverence for writing to the Japanese at an early date.

The *Kojiki* consists of an account of Japan from its creation to approximately the year A.D. 500, plus additional genealogical data about the imperial family for the next century and a quarter. Unreliable as history, it is written in a complex style that employs Chinese characters both in the conventional manner and to represent phonetically the sounds of the Japanese language of the eighth century. Because of its difficulty, the *Kojiki* received scant attention for more than a thousand years; not until the great eighteenth-century scholar Motoori Norinaga devoted more than three decades to its decipherment did its contents become widely known even among the Japanese.

The *Kojiki* and *Nihon Shoki* (whose first part covers much the same ground) are, as noted, the principal repositories of Japan's extraordinarily rich mythology, a mythology derived from a variety of materials including ancient songs and legends, word etymologies, professed genealogies, and religious rites. Although the two works contain numerous variant tales, they give essentially the same account of the course of Japan up to the eve of recorded history in the sixth century. Japanese scholars of the twentieth century have proved conclusively that this central narrative of myths, which tells of the descent of the imperial family from the omnipotent Sun Goddess and its assumption of eternal rule on earth, was entirely contrived sometime during the reform period of the late sixth and seventh centuries to justify the claim to sovereignty of the reigning imperial dynasty. Moreover, both books, but particularly the *Kojiki,* have been shaped to give antiquity and luster to the genealogies of the leading courtier families of the same period.

In contrast to the *Kojiki,* the *Nihon Shoki* is written in Chinese and has been read and studied throughout the ages. It is also a much longer work and contains, in addition to the mythology, a generally reliable history of the sixth and seventh centuries. Indeed, as virtually the only written source for affairs in Japan during this age, it became the first of six "national histories" that cover events up to 887.

Nara civilization reached its apogee in the Tempyō epoch of Emperor Shōmu (reigned 724–49). Shōmu is remembered as perhaps the most devoutly Buddhist emperor in Japanese history, and certainly Buddhism enjoyed unprecedented favor during his reign. Yet, this favor seems to have been based more on adoration than understanding. The so-called six sects of Nara Buddhism were highly complex metaphysical systems imported from China that, doctrinally, provided little more than intellectual exercise for a handful of priestly devotees in Japan. Some were never established as independent sects, and none acquired a significant following among the Japanese people.

Judged by the great rage at Nara for the copying of sutras to obtain health and prosperity, Buddhism still held its appeal as potent magic. The particular favor enjoyed by the healing buddha, Yakushi, suggests that the primitive faith-healing instincts of the Japanese were widely aroused by this popular Mahayanist deity.

But by far the most significant role of Buddhism in the Tempyō epoch was as the great protector of the state. Shōmu, who founded a national Buddhist center at the Tōdaiji Temple in Nara and caused branch temples and nunneries to be constructed in the provinces, carried to its climax the policy of state sponsorship of Buddhism inaugurated by Temmu half a century earlier. Ironically, Shōmu's great undertaking so taxed the public resources of the Nara court that, far from strengthening central rule as he wished, it was probably the single most important factor in stimulating a decline in national administration over the next century and a half.

Whatever the long-range effects of its construction on the course of political events, the Tōdaiji became one of the greatest Buddhist establishments in Japan and the focal point for the brilliant age of Tempyō art (fig. 16). Compared to the Hōryūji, the Tōdaiji was laid out on a mammoth scale. It was spread over an extensive tract of land and its central image, housed in the largest wooden structure in the world, was a bronze statue fifty-three feet tall of the cosmic buddha Vairochana (called in Japanese *daibutsu* or "great buddha") that required eight attempts before it was successfully cast (fig. 17). At the *daibutsu*'s "eye-opening" ceremony in 752, when a cleric from India painted in the pupils of its eyes to give it symbolic life, there were some ten thousand Buddhist priests in attendance and many visitors from distant lands. It was by all accounts one of the grandest occasions in early Japanese history.

Shortly before the eye-opening ceremony, Shōmu, who in 749 had abdicated the throne in favor of his daughter, appeared before the *daibutsu* and humbly declared himself a servant to the three Buddhist trea-

Fig. 16   Tōdaiji Temple *(Consulate General of Japan, New York)*

Fig. 17   *Daibutsu* at the Tōdaiji Temple *(Consulate General of Japan, New York)*

Fig. 18   Guardian deity in dry lacquer at the Tōdaiji
Temple *(Charles E. Tuttle Publishing Co.)*

sures (the buddha, the law, and the priesthood). This act was the high
point in the Nara court's public infatuation with Buddhism. Although
many later sovereigns were personally devout Buddhists, none after
Shōmu ever made this sort of official gesture of submission to Buddhism
or to any religion other than Shinto.

Among the many excellent examples of Tempyō art at the Tōdaiji are
statues in two new mediums, clay and dry lacquer. In the unusual technique of dry lacquer sculpture, the artist began with either a clay base or
a wooden frame and built up a shell consisting of alternate layers of fabric
—mainly hemp—and lacquer. The very nature of the material made a
certain stiffness in the trunks and limbs of the finished figures inevitable.
Nevertheless, as can clearly be seen in one of the fierce guardian deities
at the Tōdaiji, the sculptors in dry lacquer were able to achieve much of
the realistic detailing that was so characteristic of the T'ang-inspired art
of the Tempyō period (fig. 18).

The most famous work in dry lacquer is the image at the Tōshōdaiji
in Nara of the blind Chinese priest Ganjin (688–763), who after several
unsuccessful attempts made the perilous crossing to Japan in 754 to
found one of the six Nara sects (fig. 19). This is the oldest surviving
portrait of an actual person in Japanese history. There is a painting from
the late seventh century of Prince Shōtoku and two of his sons, but it

Fig. 19   Statue of Ganjin at the Tōshōdaiji Temple *(Asuka-en)*

was done many years after the prince's death and was drawn in such a stylized Chinese fashion that the artist obviously made no attempt to portray the features of real individuals. The Ganjin statue, on the other hand, is extraordinarily lifelike and shows the priest in an attitude of intense concentration. It was this kind of emotionally moving realism that so greatly impressed Japanese sculptors of later centuries when they looked back for inspiration to the classical art of the Tempyō period.

Near the Tōdaiji and originally part of the temple complex is a remarkable building called the Shōsōin (fig. 20). It has the appearance of a gigantic, elongated log cabin with its floor raised some nine feet off the ground on massive wooden pillars. Actually, the Shōsōin consists of three separate units that are joined together, each with its own entrance-way, and it is a storehouse of world art from the eighth century. It has stood intact for more than eleven centuries and before modern times was opened only infrequently, sometimes remaining sealed for periods of

Fig. 20   Shōsōin *(Asuka-en)*

up to a century or more. Because of its special construction—in addition
to a raised floor, it has sides made of logs that expand and contract to
maintain the temperature and humidity inside at a more even level—the
Shōsōin has preserved its contents in nearly perfect condition.

Of the ten thousand or so items contained in the Shōsōin, more than
six hundred were the personal belongings of Emperor Shōmu; they include books, clothing, swords and other weapons, Buddhist rosaries,
musical instruments, mirrors, screens, and gaming boards. There are also
the ritual objects used in the eye-opening ceremony for the *daibutsu,* as
well as many maps, administrative documents, medicines, and masks of
wood and dry lacquer used in *gigaku,* a form of dance learned from China
that was popular at Buddhist temples during the Nara period.

The imported objects come from virtually every part of the known
world of Asia and Europe—including China, Southeast and Central Asia,
India, Arabia, Persia, Assyria, Egypt, Greece, and Rome—and include a
vast variety of fabrics, household belongings, blown and cut glass,
ceramicware, paintings, and statuary.

The outpouring of visual art in the Tempyō period was accompanied
by the first great blossoming of Japanese poetry. Although there are a
number of simple and artless songs in both the *Kojiki* and *Nihon Shoki*
and although efforts to poetize are very ancient in Japan, the compilation about mid-eighth century of the *Man'yōshū (Collection of a Myriad
Leaves)* marked the true beginning of the Japanese poetic tradition. A

lengthy collection of some 4,500 poems, the *Man'yōshū* is not only Japan's first anthology but in the minds of many the finest, astonishing as this may seem for so early a work. Some of the *Man'yōshū* poems are spuriously attributed to emperors and other lofty individuals of the fourth and fifth centuries, an age shrouded in myth, and a great many more are anonymous. Its poems appear in fact to constitute a sampling of composition from about the middle of the seventh century to the middle of the eighth, although we cannot know how representative this sampling is of all the poems that must have been written in Japan during that period.

Several features of the *Man'yōshū* set it apart from later anthologies. First, it possesses a kind of native freshness and youthful vigor in its verses that was lost in later centuries after Japanese culture had been more fully transformed by the influence of continental civilization. Second, its poems appear to have been written by people from many classes of society, including peasants, frontier guards, and even beggars, as well as the aristocrats who through much of the premodern era completely monopolized poetic composition. Some modern scholars believe that those *Man'yōshū* poems whose authors appear to have been non-aristocratic were, in reality, composed by courtiers who "went primitive." Nevertheless, the poems were at least written from the standpoint of the non-aristocrat, a fact that distinguishes them from virtually all the other poetry composed in Japan for many centuries to come.

A third feature of the *Man'yōshū* is the variety (by Japanese standards) of its poetic forms. Included in it are a number of so-called long poems *(chōka)* that possess a considerable grandeur and sweep. Yet, even at this time the Japanese showed a marked preference for shorter verse, and the great majority of poems in the *Man'yōshū* are in the *waka*[4] form of thirty-one syllables—consisting of five lines of 5, 7, 5, 7, and 7 syllables—that was employed almost exclusively by poets for the next five hundred years or more. Even when poets once again turned to other forms, they usually selected those that were variants of the *waka*. For example, the linked verse that became popular from about the fourteenth century on was composed by three or more poets who divided the *waka* into two "links" (one made up of the first three lines of 5, 7, and 5 syllables and the other of the last two lines of 7 and 7 syllables), which could be joined together endlessly. And the famous seventeen-syllable *haiku* that came into fashion in the seventeenth century consisted simply of the first link of the *waka*.

No complete explanation can be given of the Japanese predilection for brief poetry, but it is certainly due in large part to the nature of the Japanese language. Japanese has very few vowel sounds and is constructed almost solely of independent vowels *(a, i, u, e, o)* and short, "open" syllables that consist of a consonant and a vowel (for example, *ka, su, mo*).

The language therefore lacks the variety of sound necessary for true poetic rhyme: indeed, it rhymes too readily. Moreover, it has little stress, another element often used in prosody. Without recourse to rhyme or stress, Japanese poets have generally found it difficult to write lengthy pieces. The longer the poem, the greater the risk that it will become indistinguishable from prose. Instead, poets have since earliest times preferred shorter poetic forms, usually written in combinations of five- and seven-syllable lines. No one has been able to say with certainty why the five- and seven-syllable line units have been so preferred, although one interesting conjecture is that they are another reflection of the Japanese taste for the asymmetrical.

Precluded by the scope of the *waka* from writing extended narratives or developing complex ideas, poets have concentrated on imagery to elicit direct emotional responses from their audiences. They have also fully exploited the exceptional capacity of the Japanese language for subtle shadings and nuance, and have used certain devices such as the "pivot word" *(kakekotoba)* to enrich the texture of their lines and make possible the expression of double and even triple meanings. Use of the pivot word can be illustrated by the line *Senkata naku,* "There is nothing to be done." *Naku* renders the phrase negative, but at the same time it has the independent meaning of "to cry." Thus, an expression of despair may simultaneously convey the idea of weeping.

During the Heian period (794–1185), when poetry became the exclusive property of the courtier class, strict rules were evolved that severely limited the range of poetic topics and the moods under which poets could compose. Poetry was intended to be moving but not overpowering.

By contrast, the *Man'yōshū* contains poems dealing with many of the subjects that later poets came to regard as unfitting or excessively harsh for their elegant poeticizing, such as inconsolable grief upon the death of a loved one, poverty, and stark human suffering. A "long poem" from the anthology expresses one poet's feelings after the loss of his wife:

Since in Karu lived my wife,
I wished to be with her to my heart's content;
But I could not visit her constantly
Because of the many watching eyes—
Men would know of our troth,
Had I sought her too often.
So our love remained secret like a rock-pent pool;
I cherished her in my heart,
Looking to aftertime when we should be together,
And lived secure in my trust
As one riding a great ship.
Suddenly there came a messenger

Who told me she was dead—
Was gone like a yellow leaf of autumn,
Dead as the day dies with the setting sun,
Lost as the bright moon is lost behind the cloud,
Alas, she is no more, whose soul
Was bent to mine like bending seaweed!

When the word was brought to me
I knew not what to do nor what to say;
But restless at the mere news,
And hoping to heal my grief
Even a thousandth part,
I journeyed to Karu and searched the market place
Where my wife was wont to go!

There I stood and listened
But no voice of her I heard,
Though the birds sang in the Unebi Mountains;
None passed by who even looked like my wife.
I could only call her name and wave my sleeve.[5]

One of the most famous of the *Man'yōshū* poems is the "Dialogue on Poverty," which begins with these lines:

On the night when the rain beats,
Driven by the wind,
On the night when the snowflakes mingle
With the sleety rain,
I feel so helplessly cold.
I nibble at a lump of salt,
Sip the hot, oft-diluted dregs of sake;
And coughing, snuffling,
And stroking my scanty beard,
I say in my pride,
"There's none worthy, save I!"
But I shiver still with cold.
I pull up my hempen bedclothes,
Wear what few sleeveless clothes I have,
But cold and bitter is the night!
As for those poorer than myself,
Their parents must be cold and hungry,
Their wives and children beg and cry.
Then, how do you struggle through life?[6]

The poem cited above on the death of a wife is by Kakinomoto no Hitomaro (dates unknown), the finest poet represented in the *Man'yōshū* and perhaps the greatest in all Japanese literature. Few details remain about Hitomaro's life, although it is known that he was of low courtier rank, held some provincial posts, and served as court poet during the late seventh and eighth centuries. The function of court poet in Hitomaro's time entailed the composition of commemorative poems or encomiums on occasions such as courtly journeys or imperial hunts and of eulogies upon the deaths of members of the imperial family. This use of poetry for the expression of lofty sentiment in response to prominent public events or ceremonies was no doubt influenced by the Chinese practice, but it was not perpetuated in Japan much beyond Hitomaro's time. Japanese poets have always been powerfully drawn to personal lyricism rather than the pronouncement of what may be regarded as more socially elevated, if not precisely moralistic, feelings. The early Japanese language was particularly suited to lyrical expression, and the extent to which Japanese poets went to retain that quality can be seen in how carefully they protected their native poetic vocabulary, consisting mostly of concrete, descriptive terms, from the intrusion of more abstract and complex Chinese loan words. Kakinomoto no Hitomaro was fully capable of writing lyrical poetry, as his deeply felt lament on the death of his wife reveals; but he also composed sustained verse, particularly in the "long poem" form, on topics of public and stately relevance that were not regarded as the proper concern of later poets.

Since it was the *waka* that was to reign supreme in later court poetry, let us examine one of these poems from the *Man'yōshū:*

> I will think of you, love,
> On evenings when the gray mist
> Rises above the rushes
> And chill sounds the voice
> Of the wild ducks crying.[7]

In this poem, which is attributed to a frontier guard, we find a blending of the two main subjects of *waka,* romantic love and nature. We will observe in the next chapter the important qualities of romantic love as they evolved in the courtier tradition. Let us note here some aspects of the Japanese attitude toward nature.

The Japanese seek beauty in nature not in what is enduring or permanent, but in the fragile, the fleeting, and the perishable. Above all, their feelings about nature have from earliest times been absorbed by the changes brought by the seasons. Of the four seasons, spring and autumn are preferred, the former as a time of celebration of the beginning or renewal of life and the latter as a moment signaling the ultimate perishing of all life and beauty. But, whatever the season, it has been the element of change that has mattered most. A courtier of the fourteenth century expressed this sentiment when he wrote that it is precisely because life and nature are changeable and uncertain that things have the power to move us.[8]

Although the Japanese taste for spring and autumn may at first have been nearly equal, autumn, the season when things perish, possessed an inherently greater allure; and with the passing years—and especially the arrival in the late twelfth century of the medieval age of fighting and disorder—autumn (and its portent of winter) assumed supremacy. Then, as we shall see, poets and others sought to press their senses "beyond beauty," and to find aesthetic value in the realm of the lonely, the cold, and the withered.

Underlying the Japanese preference for perishable beauty is an acute sensitivity to the passage of time. Indeed, the "tyranny of time" has been a pervasive theme in literature and the other arts. It is a tribute to the aesthetic and artistic genius of the Japanese that they were ultimately able, as just suggested, to use this theme to extend their tastes beyond the range of conventional beauties to things, such as the withered and worn, that have literally been ravaged by time.

In addition to composing poetry in their own language, the early Japanese also wrote verse in Chinese. The difficulties of writing in a foreign tongue are obviously enormous; yet, Chinese culture was held in the highest esteem by the Japanese, and for a time, especially during the early ninth century, it appeared that the courtiers might cease entirely their literary efforts in the Japanese language and devote themselves exclusively to composition in Chinese. Fortunately for the evolution of a native culture, this did not happen. But Chinese nevertheless continued to hold much attraction for the Japanese, both as a classical language and, in poetry, as a means to express those ideas of a complex or abstract nature for which the *waka* was totally inadequate. The earliest anthology of Chinese poetry by Japanese, the *Kaifūsō (Fond Recollections of Poetry)*, was compiled in the mid-Nara period, about the same time as the *Man'yōshū*. An example taken from this anthology is the following piece, "Composed at a Party for the Korean Envoy":

> Mountain windows scan the deep valley;
> Groves of pine line the evening streams.
> We have asked to our feast the distant envoy;
> At this table of parting we try the pleasures of poetry.
> The crickets are hushed, the cold night wind blows;
> Geese fly beneath the clear autumn moon.
> We offer this flower-spiced wine in hopes
> To beguile the cares of your long return.[9]

3

The Court at Its Zenith

IN 794 THE COURT MOVED to the newly constructed city of Heian or Kyoto, about twenty-eight miles north of Nara. The decision to leave Nara was apparently made for several reasons. Many people at court had become alarmed over the degree of official favor accorded to Buddhism and the manifold opportunities presented to Buddhist priests to interfere in the business of state. Their fears were particularly aroused when an empress (Shōmu's daughter) became closely involved with a faith-healing priest named Dōkyō (d. 772). Before the loss of his patroness, who died in 770, Dōkyō rose to the highest ecclesiastical and ministerial positions in the land and even sought, through the pronouncement of an oracle, to ascend the throne itself. Dōkyō thus achieved notoriety in Japanese history as a commoner who blatantly challenged the imperial family's sacrosanct claim to reign exclusively over Japan. The Dōkyō affair appears to have convinced the court of two things: that Nara, with its many Buddhist establishments and its ubiquitous priesthood, was no longer satisfactory for the conduct of secular affairs; and that henceforth the line of succession to the throne should be confined solely to male members of the imperial family.

Another reason for the move to Kyoto was that Nara, situated in the mountainous southern region of the central provinces, had become too cramped as a location for the court. Kyoto provided much freer access, both by land and water, to the rest of the country. In particular, the court could more readily undertake from Kyoto the expansion and consolidation of its control over the eastern and northern provinces, a region that had until this time been occupied chiefly by recalcitrant tribesmen known as Emishi.

The Emishi, referred to in early accounts as "hairy people," have often been identified with the Ainu, a race of Caucasian-like people who live in Hokkaido, the northernmost of Japan's major islands, and number today only a few thousand. It was long believed that the Ainu occupied all of Japan during the Neolithic Jōmon age—that they were the "Jōmon people"—and, driven steadily eastward and northward by the advance of civilization in Yayoi times, suffered a fate similar to that of the American

Indians. Since the Ainu, like Caucasians, have considerably more body hair than the Japanese, it appeared obvious that they were the very "hairy Emishi" mentioned in the pages of the *Nihon Shoki* and other historical accounts. Yet, there are several reasons to doubt this linking of Ainu and Emishi. For one thing, the expression "hairy people" was loosely and pejoratively applied in both China and Japan to uncivilized people in general—people who were regarded as unkempt, dirty, and uncouth—and did not necessarily imply that such people were racially endowed with a greater quantity of hair. Also, mummified bodies of Japanese warrior chieftains of later centuries in the north, who reportedly had Emishi mothers, have been examined and found to possess none of the bodily characteristics of the Ainu.

There is, then, a strong possibility that the Ainu, whose precise origins remain a mystery, never settled extensively south of Hokkaido; and that the Emishi were in fact ethnically the same as the Japanese, but were not incorporated into the Yamato state when it was established in the central and western provinces during the fourth through the sixth centuries. In any event, after several failures, armies dispatched by the Heian court finally inflicted decisive defeat on the Emishi in the early years of the ninth century and thus eliminated the threat posed by these ferocious tribesmen on the eastern frontier.

After the move to Kyoto, the court attempted to encourage the activities of Buddhist prelates who would devote their attention to spiritual rather than worldly matters. Among the first to receive court patronage was Saichō (767–822), who journeyed to China in 804 and returned to found the Tendai sect of Buddhism at the Enryakuji, a temple he had earlier opened on Mount Hiei northeast of Kyoto. The Enryakuji was in a particularly favorable spot, since it was believed that evil spirits invaded from the northeast and it could serve as guardian of the capital.

Tendai was broadly founded on the teachings of the Mahayana or Greater Vehicle school of Buddhism. Its basic scripture, the *Lotus Sutra,* purportedly contained Gautama's last sermon, in which he revealed to his disciples the universality of the buddha potential. The Buddha asserted that until this time he had allowed individuals to practice Hinayana, the Lesser Vehicle, and to seek their own enlightenments. Now mankind was prepared for the final truth that everyone could attain buddhahood. In the Buddha's words as found in the sutra:

> Those harassed by all the sufferings—
> To them I at first preached Nirvana
> Attainable by one's own efforts.
> Such were the expedient means I employed
> To lead them to Buddha-wisdom.
> Not then could I say to them,
> "You all shall attain to Buddhahood."

For the time had not yet arrived.
But now the very time has come
And I must preach the Great Vehicle.[1]

We noted that the universalistic concept of Mahayana was accompanied
both by a tendency to regard the Buddha as a transcendent, rather than
earthly, being and by adulation for the bodhisattva, or buddha-to-be,
who would assist others on the path to buddhahood.

The *Lotus Sutra* is not only the basic text of Tendai, but the principal
writing of all of Mahayana Buddhism. Drawing within its pages the
entire range of Buddhist thought, both Hinayana and Mahayana, the
Lotus is held to be the "one vehicle," the sole and ultimate source of religious truth. Its influence has been especially great in the countries of
East Asia, where it has been revered not only as a text for religious study,
but also an object of devotion in and of itself. Thus, according to some
Buddhist sects, one need not try to understand the *Lotus*'s contents but
simply to worship it. And believers have through the ages sought religious
merit by copying the *Lotus*, a task requiring considerable effort because
of the sutra's great length.

The Tendai center at the Enryakuji played an extremely prominent
role in premodern Japanese history. It became a vast complex of more
than three thousand buildings, where priests engaged in a wide range of
both spiritual and secular studies. In the best Far Eastern tradition, the
Tendai priests sought to synthesize all known religious truths and practices; and ultimately it was Tendai that, beginning in the late Heian
period, spawned the various popular sects that finally spread Buddhism
to the common people throughout Japan.

Another, and less edifying, way in which the Enryakuji attained distinction in premodern times was as a center for *akusō* or "rowdy monks."
During the Nara period, the court had strictly limited the entry of people
other than members of the aristocracy into the Buddhist priesthood. But
after the move of the capital to Kyoto, entry restrictions were relaxed and
the more important Buddhist temples, which were already in the process
of acquiring great wealth in landed estates, hired increasing numbers of
peasants to serve in their private armies. By the tenth and eleventh centuries, these hordes of *akusō* had become regularly engaged not only in
fighting among themselves but also in intimidating Kyoto into meeting
their demands for such things as ecclesiastical positions at court and titles
to desirable pieces of estate land.

The manner in which the Enryakuji monks commonly made their
demands upon the court reveals something of the ties that had evolved
by this time between Buddhist temples and Shinto shrines. Obtaining the
sacred *kami* emblems of the Hie Shrine located at the foot of Mount Hiei,
the monks placed them in a portable car and transported the car to the
capital, where they deposited it at a busy intersection near the palace.

Since no one dared touch the car, activities simply ceased in that part of the city until the monks, their demands met, condescended to remove it and carry it back to the mountain.

Although the Tendai sect's Enryakuji Temple became a great national center for Buddhist studies in Japan, the particular kind of Buddhism that exerted the strongest influence at court during the early Heian period was Tantrism. Tantrism was a branch of Mahayana Buddhism established independently in India about A.D. 600 and subsequently transmitted to China and Japan. Because of its stress on incantations, spells, and primitive magic, Tantrism has been viewed by many outsiders as a corrupt and decadent phase of Buddhism after the period of its greatest historical flourishing. Insofar as one part of Tantrism became associated with Indian Shakti practices dealing with death, destruction, and living sacrifices, there may be justification for this view. But the form of Tantrism that spread to the Far East did not embrace such grotesque practices. Known also as esoteric Buddhism because of its insistence on the secret transmission of its teachings, Tantrism came to hold a unique appeal for the aristocracy of the Heian court and provided a powerful stimulus to the arts in Japan during the ninth and tenth centuries.

Tantrism was introduced to Japan as the Shingon (True Word) sect by the priest Kūkai (774–835; also familiarly known by his posthumous canonical name of Kōbō Daishi, or Great Teacher Kōbō), who traveled to China in 804 on the same mission as Saichō. Kūkai, who founded a Shingon center atop Mount Kōya near modern Osaka, was without question one of the most outstanding figures in Japanese history. The distinguished British scholar of Japan, Sir George Sansom, has said of him:

> His memory lives all over the country, his name is a household word in the remotest places, not only as a saint, but as a preacher, a scholar, a painter, an inventor, an explorer and—sure passport to fame—a great calligrapher.[2]

Among other things, Kūkai is credited with inventing the *kana* syllabary.[3] Most likely *kana* was more the product of evolution than invention. But it is also believed that knowledge of Sanskrit provided at least some of the inspiration that led to *kana*, and Kūkai is known to have become an avid student of Sanskrit during his three-year stay in China.

Kūkai's scholarly accomplishments were imposing. In a tract entitled *The Ten Stages of Religious Consciousness*, he made perhaps the most famous attempt in Japanese history to synthesize and evaluate various religious beliefs according to their higher or lower "stages of consciousness." At the bottom, Kūkai placed the animal passions, where no religious consciousness at all existed; he then proceeded upward by stages through Confucianism, Taoism, various Hinayana and quasi-Mahayana sects, fully developed Mahayana and, finally, to the ultimate religious consciousness of Shingon itself.

Shingon is centered on belief in the cosmic buddha Vairochana (in

Japanese, Dainichi). All things—including the historical Buddha, Gautama, and such transcendent beings as Yakushi (the healing buddha) and Amida (the buddha of the boundless light)—are merely manifestations of this universal entity. In order to enter into communion with Dainichi and realize the essential oneness of all existence, the supplicant must utilize the Three Mysteries of speech, body, and mind. Proper ritual performance requires the coordinated practice of all three mysteries; but perhaps the most important is that of speech, which calls for the recitation of spells or "true words" (mantras in Sanskrit; *shingon* in Japanese). The use of words as spells has fascinated man throughout his existence, and the mantras of esoteric Buddhism derive from an ancient tradition. Probably the most famous mantra is the Tibetan phrase *Om mani padme hum* ("The jewel is in the lotus!"), but there are a great many others also employed in the religious supplications of esotericism.

The mysteries of the body are based primarily on the hand poses known as mudras. We have seen the use of mudras for iconographic purposes in sculpture and in pictorial representations of buddhas and bodhisattvas. In Shingon ritual, on the other hand, mudras are struck by the *believer* as he addresses himself to these superior beings.

A device used in Shingon as an aid to meditation is the mandala, or cosmic diagram (fig. 21). Mandalas may simply be sketched on the ground and expunged after the completion of a rite; or they may be permanently produced as carvings and paintings. In Japan the most common type of mandala is the hanging scroll, although there are also a number of mandalas carved in relief and painted on temple walls. These diagrams, which usually depict Dainichi surrounded by the myriad lesser figures of the Shingon pantheon, are often superior works of art. And indeed in the Heian period the exceptional visual attraction of the mandalas and other Shingon icons greatly helped to endear esotericism to the Kyoto courtiers, who were finely sensitive to beauty in all its forms.

It was by no means simply the visual delights of Shingon that made it so popular at the Heian court. Despite efforts during the Taika or Great Reform era to create a Confucian-type meritocracy under the throne, Japan's ruling class had remained preponderantly aristocratic: that is, birth almost invariably took precedence over ability or achievement. In the Nara period there was some opportunity for men of modest backgrounds to advance by entering the Buddhist priesthood or by specializing in Chinese studies; but in Heian times the court reverted to a rigid hierarchical ordering of society determined solely by family origins. It is not surprising, then, that the Heian courtiers found congenial a sect like Shingon, which similarly asserted a fixed hierarchy among its pantheon of deities headed by Dainichi. Interestingly, Dainichi is written with the characters for "great sun"; and the Japanese were not slow to identify him with the supreme Shinto deity, the Sun Goddess. Going a step further,

Fig. 21 Mandala *(courtesy of the Brooklyn Museum)*

they were able to liken the gods of Shingon collectively to the community of *kami* from whom all the great courtier families claimed descent.

The exclusive, esoteric character of Shingon also appealed greatly to the Heian courtiers. Although Shingon, like Mahayana Buddhism in general, preached the universality of the buddha potential, in practice it confronted its would-be followers with such complex and time-consuming practices that only priests or leisured aristocrats could hope to master them. And in any case Shingon gave the general populace little chance even to attempt the practices by keeping them secret from all but a favored few. The mysteries of Shingon were theoretically transmitted solely by the teacher, or guru, to his direct disciples. Outsiders might derive some satisfaction from contemplating with awe the dark wonders of Shingon, but as the uninitiated they would forever be denied the highest rewards it promised.

So strongly did the courtiers favor Shingon that, in order to meet the competition, the Tendai sect also evolved a form of esotericism. It is scarcely an exaggeration to say that esoteric Buddhism, particularly during the ninth and tenth centuries, permeated every aspect of the lives of the Heian aristocracy. Its aestheticism, exclusivity, and promise of realizing through arcane practices the buddha nature in this life were irresistible to the courtiers. Yet, esoteric Buddhism, although it may have been established on a high plane by Kūkai and his immediate successors, was particularly susceptible to corruption; and in the late Heian period, it degenerated to the point where its clergy engaged in base practices, accepting fees from the laity to secure direct benefits in health, fame, and prosperity.

An important trend among the new sects of Heian Buddhism was their move away from the busy centers of temporal life and political activity to mountainous, remote regions. Kyoto eventually became as clustered with temples as Nara, but at least the example was set for some temples to locate where the temptations of worldly pleasures were minimal and where monks could truly lead the disciplined and meditative religious life.

Buddhism had entered Japan as part of a great reforming process aimed at centralization, and it was surely a sign of maturity that, after some two centuries, an increasing number of both secular and religious leaders saw the importance of drawing a distinction between the proper spheres of activity of the court (as an administrative body) and the Buddhist church. The Heian sects sought to sustain the idea of Buddhism as the guardian of the nation, and rowdy monks engaged in ugly quarrels over quite mundane issues; but still there was general recognition of the need henceforth to keep church and state separate.

The founding of temples in mountainous regions also brought significant changes in Buddhist architecture. Only two buildings remain from the early Heian period—the golden hall and pagoda of a Shingon temple, the Murōji, situated in a dense forest of towering cryptomeria about forty miles from Kyoto—but we can tell from these, as well as from various reconstructions, what the new trends in architecture were. The orderly, *garan*-type layouts were abandoned by the mountain temples in favor of adapting the shapes and placement of their buildings to the special features of rough, uneven terrain. This kind of architectural integration with the natural environment seems to have been particularly to the liking of the Japanese. It was reminiscent of earlier Shinto architecture and, at the same time, revealed the Far Eastern impulse to merge with—rather than seek to overcome—nature. A keen sensitivity to nature and a desire to find human identity with it in all its manifestations are among the strongest themes in the Japanese cultural tradition.

Fig. 22   Shishinden of the imperial palace in Kyoto *(photograph by Joseph Shulman)*

Other features of Shinto architecture incorporated into both temple and secular buildings in the early Heian—or, to art historians, Jōgan—period were the elevation of floors above ground level and the thatching of roofs with cyprus bark instead of clay tiles. (See the end of Chapter 1 for other remarks about the influence of granary style architecture on both shrine and palace buildings.) These features can plainly be seen in the old imperial palace (Shishinden) in Kyoto (fig. 22). The buildings of the palace compound were frequently destroyed by fire, and the present structures, most of them erected in the nineteenth century, are not even situated in the same part of the city as the original compound. Nevertheless, they are faithful reproductions and, in the absence of other buildings, give us at least some idea of what the capital looked like in early Heian times.

Buddhist sculpture of the Jōgan period showed a marked change from the realistic, often grandly imposing works of the Tempyō epoch. The court had withdrawn its direct patronage of Buddhism and, although many temples became privately affluent through the acquisition of landed estates, there was no further urge to undertake such vast artistic projects as the casting of the *daibutsu,* which had required the concerted effort of many craftsmen. Jōgan statues were generally much smaller than those of Tempyō and were most likely carved by individual sculptors, who made very little use of the materials favored during Tempyō—bronze, clay, and dry lacquer—but preferred, instead, to work chiefly in wood. One reason for the new preference for wood was the interest aroused by the sandalwood statues imported from China about this time and in vogue at court.

Many Jōgan statues were carved out of single blocks of wood, a fact that helps account for their general smallness. They were also left either entirely unpainted or with only the lips and eyes tinted in order not to seal off the natural fragrance of the wood.

An excellent example of Jōgan sculpture in wood is the statue of the healing buddha, Yakushi, at the Jingoji in Kyoto. The rigid stance and stylized clothing of the buddha may appear to signify a reversion to an earlier, less sophisticated method of sculpture. But in fact they reflect the wish, in line with esoteric tastes, to produce figures that were unearthly and mysterious. The statue's facial expression is grim and forbidding, and its body is much heavier and more gross-looking than the typical Tempyō image. The "wave" pattern of its draperies is characteristic of Jōgan sculpture and can be seen even more sharply delineated in the seated image of the historical buddha at the Murōji.

Apart from the mandalas, virtually the only paintings extant from the Jōgan epoch are representations of ferocious and hideous creatures such as Fudō, "the immovable." These creatures, some of which have multiple heads and arms, were in reality the cosmic buddha, Dainichi, in altered forms, and their job was to frighten and destroy the enemies of Buddhism. Fudō is usually shown with a flaming body halo, a sword in one hand and a rope in the other.

Esoteric iconography inspired some Jōgan artists to attempt the first plastic representations of the deities of Shinto. Several of these *kami* figures still remain, but there is little to indicate that any real impetus was given at this time to evolve a new form of Shinto art.

The court of the early ninth century was outwardly perhaps even more enamored of Chinese civilization than its predecessor at Nara a century earlier. Chinese poetry was in particular the rage among Emperor Saga (reigned 809–23) and his intimates, who held competitions in Chinese versemanship, compiled anthologies in the manner of the *Kaifūsō*, and virtually ignored the *waka*. It was also during Saga's reign that Kūkai was first received at court. A brilliant scholar, litterateur, and gifted writer in Chinese, Kūkai has been ranked along with Saga and Tachibana no Hayanari (d. 842), who headed the mission that Saichō and Kūkai accompanied to the continent in 804, as one of the three "great brushes" or calligraphers of the age. Kūkai had visited Ch'ang-an, the wondrous capital of T'ang, and had returned not only with many books and works of art but also with knowledge of the latest Chinese fashions, including the vogue for esoteric Buddhism. A contemporary observer might well have judged, from the preferences of such luminaries at court as Saga and Kūkai, that Japan of the early ninth century had indeed become a miniature model of China.

We can see in retrospect that the Japanese did not slavishly copy Chinese civilization; some important institutions never took root in Japanese soil and others were considerably remolded to suit the native setting. In addition to abandoning the fundamental Confucian principle of government by merit, the Japanese also ultimately rejected the T'ang "equal-field" system of land distribution. Within a few centuries, nearly all agricultural land in the country had fallen into the hands of the aristocracy and religious institutions as private estates. Along with a parallel deterioration of the court's provincial administration, this process created conditions (as we shall see in the next chapter) that gave rise to a warrior class in the provinces in mid- and late Heian times.

The most significant political development at court in the ninth century was the rise of a single clan—the Fujiwara—which was descended from one of the chief architects of the Great Reform and came to dominate the imperial family through marriage even more completely and for a much longer time than the Soga. Insinuating themselves ever closer to the throne, the Fujiwara in 858 assumed the office of imperial regent[4] (held previously only by members of royalty, such as Prince Shōtoku) and within a century became the undisputed wielders of absolute power at court.

Fujiwara mastery over the imperial family was to a great extent made possible by the peculiarities of Heian marriage customs. Usually, although not invariably, courtiers of this age established formal residence in the homes of their wives. From the contemporary literature it appears that the typical courtier kept one or more secondary wives and mistresses and frequently was lax in visiting his principal wife, perhaps not calling upon her more than once or twice a month. Yet, the principal wife's home remained their joint residence and it was there that the children were raised. Although emperors did not actually move in with their Fujiwara wives, the offspring of such unions were reared in the mansions of the maternal relatives. Between the late ninth and late eleventh centuries, emperors without exception were the sons of Fujiwara mothers, and in view of their upbringing no doubt identified themselves as closely with the Fujiwara as with the imperial family.

Even as the Fujiwara began their rise to power, the court reached the decision to terminate official relations with China. One reason for this decision, made sometime after the last mission of 838,[5] was that the T'ang dynasty had fallen into decline and China was no longer a safe place for travel; but perhaps more fundamental was the fact that the Japanese did not feel the same need as before to look to China for guidance and inspiration. The long period of cultural borrowing, begun some two and a half centuries earlier, had at last come to an end.

The Japanese court of the late ninth century not only severed official relations with China; it also gradually withdrew from all but the most necessary dealings with the provinces of Japan itself. In contrast to its cosmopolitanism in the Nara period, the court in the tenth century became isolated to an extraordinary degree from the rest of Japanese society. Of the various causes for this isolation, one of the most decisive was the court's system of ministerial ranking by which infinitely greater luster and prestige was bestowed upon officials in the capital than upon those in the provinces. To accept and occupy a provincial post, the courtier was obliged not only to forsake the comforts and cultural attractions of the Heian capital, but also to suffer diminished status and even risk social opprobrium. For want of opportunity in Kyoto, some courtiers had no alternative; moreover, the possibility of acquiring new wealth in the provinces was tempting. But for a member of the upper nobility, life away from the capital was almost unthinkable. Even if given an important governorship, he would be apt either to send a deputy in his place or simply direct the vice-governor, usually a local magnate, to look after the administrative affairs of the province.

The epoch of the tenth century and most of the eleventh was one of "power and glory" for the Fujiwara regents. It was also an age when the Japanese brought to maturity their classical culture. Although it owed much to its Chinese antecedents, this culture was nevertheless genuinely unique and a true product of the native genius.

Of all the arts that flourished at court during the Fujiwara epoch, the one that most embodied its creative spirit was literature and, in particular, poetry. The ninth-century craze for Chinese verse waned with the trailing off of relations with the continent, and the courtiers turned their attention once again to the *waka*. Before long, their passion for this traditional form of poetic expression was revived to the point of near insatiability and they devoted themselves endlessly to composition both in private and in the company of others at poetry contests, where teams of the right and left were called upon to compose on given themes. The ability to recognize a *waka* allusion and to extemporize at least passable lines became absolutely essential, not only in the more formal tests of poetic competence to which the courtier was put, but also in everyday social intercourse. Probably no other society in history has placed so great a premium on versification.

Inseparable from the revival of interest in the *waka*, and indeed the development of Fujiwara literature in general, was the evolution of the *kana* syllabary. Even at the height of enthusiasm for Chinese poetry at the court of Emperor Saga earlier in the ninth century, this means for writing in the vernacular was being perfected. Kūkai himself, as we have seen, was closely associated with the "invention" of *kana*.

During the time of Saga, three imperially authorized or official anthologies of Chinese poetry were compiled, and in 905 the first official anthology of *waka*, the *Kokinshū (Collection of Ancient and Modern Poems)* was produced at court. Although the earlier, unofficial *Man'yōshū* had been a superb collection, it was the *Kokinshū* that truly set the standards for classical Japanese poetry. The *Man'yōshū* had been written by means of a complex use of Chinese ideographs to represent Japanese phonetics, and the Heian courtiers found it obscure and difficult to read. Moreover, the *Man'yōshū* set forth the sentiments of a quite different age. In the new world of the *Kokinshū*, refinement, taste, and decorum took absolute precedence over candor and vigorous emotional expression. The Heian poet, as we can observe in the following poems from the *Kokinshū*, was expected to versify at the proper time and in the proper mood:

> This perfectly still
> Spring day bathed in the soft light
> From the spread-out sky,
> Why do the cherry blossoms
> So restlessly scatter down?

> Although I am sure
> That he will not be coming,
> In the evening light
> When the locusts shrilly call
> I go to the door and wait.[6]

It was eminently proper to respond sensitively to the charm of a spring day and to reflect wistfully upon the brevity of life as called to mind by the scattering of the cherry blossoms; it was also most fitting for the poet to express loneliness and yearning for a lover, so long as he did not carry his feelings to the point of uncontrollable anger or anguish at being neglected.

A leading poet of the day was Ki no Tsurayuki (868?–946), one of the compilers of the *Kokinshū*. Tsurayuki also wrote the preface to this anthology and thereby produced not only the first important piece of literary criticism in Japanese history but also an excellent statement of the standards that guided the courtly taste in versification. In the opening lines to the preface, Tsurayuki expressed the deep psychological, social, and aesthetic significance that he, as a representative of the Heian courtier class of the early tenth century, attached to poetry:

> The poetry of Japan has its roots in the human heart and flourishes in the countless leaves of words. Because human beings possess interests of so many kinds, it is in poetry that they give expression to the meditations of their hearts in terms of the sights appearing before their eyes and the sounds coming to their ears. Hearing the warbler sing among the blossoms and the frog in his fresh waters—is there any living being not given to song? It is poetry which, without exertion, moves heaven and earth, stirs the feelings of gods and spirits invisible to the eye, softens the relations between men and women, calms the hearts of fierce warriors.[7]

Tsurayuki speaks of poetry in terms of "words" and "heart." The words are the Yamato language—free from the tainting of Chinese—that was established as the classical medium of expression for native poetry by the *Man'yōshū.* But the heart or feelings seen as the proper subject matter for poetry by Tsurayuki and his fellow *Kokinshū* poets are quite different from those of the *Man'yōshū,* some of whose most memorable verses deal with such harsh topics as death, poverty, and hunger. The range of feelings in the age of the *Kokinshū* was greatly narrowed and refined to a high degree. As Tsurayuki puts it, poets should be inspired to verse

> when they looked at the scattered blossoms of a spring morning; when they listened of an autumn evening to the falling of the leaves; when they sighed over the snow and waves reflected each passing year by their looking glasses; when they were startled into thoughts on the brevity of life by seeing the dew on the grass or the foam on the water; when, yesterday all proud and splendid, they have fallen from fortune into loneliness; or when, having been dearly loved, they are neglected.[8]

In all his actions the Heian courtier aspired to *miyabi*—courtly refinement—and it was this quality that became the most enduring aesthetic legacy of Japan's classical age. Even after rough provincial warriors rose to become the new rulers of the land in the late twelfth century, they instinctively responded to and sought to perpetuate the courtly tradition as epitomized in *miyabi.* The turbulent centuries of the medieval age produced many new cultural pursuits that catered to the tastes of various classes of society, including warriors, merchants, and even peasants. Yet, coloring nearly all these pursuits was *miyabi,* reflected in a fundamental preference on the part of the Japanese for the elegant, the restrained, and the subtly suggestive. There is indeed a strong temptation to assert that *miyabi*—as first codified, so to speak, in the poems of the *Kokinshū*—has constituted the most basic theme in Japanese aesthetics. As one Western authority has observed, "Nothing in the West can compare with the role which aesthetics has played in Japanese life and history since the Heian period"; and "the miyabi spirit of refined sensibility is still very much in evidence" in modern aesthetic criticism.[9]

Closely related to *miyabi* was the concept of *mono no aware,* which can be translated as a "sensitivity to things" or, perhaps, a "capacity to be moved by things." *Mono no aware,* or simply *aware,* appeared as a phrase of poetry in the *Man'yōshū* of the Nara period, but did not assume its principal aesthetic connotations until the high age of Heian culture, beginning about the time of the *Kokinshū.* In the discussion of Shinto in Chapter 1, we observed that there has run through history the idea that the Japanese are, in terms of their original nature (that is, their nature before the introduction from the outside of such systems of thought and religion as Confucianism and Buddhism), essentially an emotional people. And in stressing the emotional side of human nature, the Japanese have always assigned high value to sincerity *(makoto)* as the ethic of the emotions. If the life of the emotions thus had an ethic in *makoto,* the evolution of *mono no aware* in the Heian period provided it also with an aesthetic. Ki no Tsurayuki, in his preface to the *Kokinshū,* was the first to describe the workings of this aesthetic. For example, when inquiring (in the opening passage of the preface, quoted above) whether anyone can resist singing—or composing poetry—upon "hearing the warbler sing among the blossoms and the frog in his fresh waters," Tsurayuki said, in effect, that people are emotional entities and will intuitively and spontaneously respond in song and verse when they perceive things and are moved. The most basic sense of *mono no aware* is the capacity to be moved by things, whether they are the beauties of nature or the feelings of people, a capacity that Tsurayuki, at least, believed would directly lead to aesthetic expression.

Because of the particular Japanese liking, already noted, for the perishable beauties of nature and because of the acute Japanese sensitivity to the passage of time, *mono no aware* has always been tinged with sadness and melancholy. Some commentators have sought to convey this sense by translating the phrase as the "pathos of things." But this is misleading, because it suggests that things can inherently possess qualities like pathos or a pathetic beauty. Rather, in the Japanese tradition, such qualities come into being only when people *perceive* them in things. In other words, the Japanese have traditionally tended to the belief that beauty is not in the object but is evoked by the subject (i.e., the perceiver).

In addition to reviving interest in Japanese poetry, the use of *kana* also made possible the evolution of a native prose literature. The origins of the mature prose of the Fujiwara epoch can only be roughly identified, although they seem to lie primarily in two early kinds of works, the so-called tale *(monogatari)* and the private diary *(nikki).* The term *"monogatari"* has been used loosely through much of Japanese history for a wide variety of writings, from purely fictional prose to quasi-historical records. In its earliest usage, however, *monogatari* meant certain supernatural or fantastic tales that derived both from oral folk legends and from Buddhist miracle stories written in Chinese. The oldest extant *monogatari* of this type is *The Tale of the Bamboo Cutter (Taketori Monogatari),* dating from the late ninth or tenth century. It is the story of an old man who finds a princess in a piece of bamboo. The princess, upon growing into comely maidenhood, tantalizes various suitors by refusing to marry them unless they perform hopelessly difficult deeds. Finally, when she is embarrassingly faced with the amorous advances of the emperor himself, the princess flies away to the moon.

The second kind of incipient Heian prose writing was the private diary.

Public diaries or journals, written in Chinese, had been kept in Japan since at least Nara times; but the private diary, if we think of it as an accounting of daily events expressed in an intimate and personal mode, could not truly be undertaken until the development of *kana* enabled would-be diarists to write in the vernacular of their age. The earliest private diary that we have is the *Tosa Diary (Tosa Nikki)* of Ki no Tsurayuki. Written about 935, it recounts Tsurayuki's journey by boat to the capital from the province of Tosa, where he had just concluded a term as governor. The most distinctive feature of this work, as of all literary or artistic diaries of the Heian period, is the inclusion of a large number of poems. Many entries in the *Tosa Diary,* in fact, consist merely of a poem or two with some brief comments about the circumstances that inspired composition. For example:

> *Eleventh day:* After a little rain the skies cleared. Continuing upriver, we noticed a line of hills converging on the eastern bank. When we learned that this is the Yawata Hachiman Shrine, there was great rejoicing and we humbly abased ourselves in thanks. The bridge of Yamazaki came in sight at last, and our feelings of joy could no longer be restrained. Here, close by the Ōōji Temple, our boat came to anchor; and here we waited, while various matters were negotiated for the remainder of our journey. By the riverside, near the temple, there were many willow trees, and one of our company, admiring their reflection in the water, made the poem:
>
>> A pattern of wave ripples, woven—it seems—
>> On a loom of green willows reflected in the stream.[10]

One stimulus, then, to the evolution of Japanese prose seems to have been the need to elucidate the reasons for writing poetry, a need that can be traced back to certain explanatory notes appended to poems in the *Man'yōshū.* In any event, prose has from this earliest time been closely linked to poetry in the history of Japanese literature. In the diaries of the Heian period, poems are presented as the distinct compositions of one person to another and usually serve as a means for the expression of their most strongly felt emotions. On the other hand, in such later literary forms as the *nō* theatre of the medieval age and the bourgeois novels and puppet plays of the seventeenth and eighteenth centuries, metrical lines of seven and five syllables were generally employed for poetically toned renderings of the heightened, climactic passages of otherwise prose narratives.

The opening lines of the *Tosa Diary* state: "It is said that diaries are kept by men, but I shall see if a woman cannot also keep one."[11] Although it is generally agreed that Ki no Tsurayuki wrote this earliest of private diaries, he chose to use the subterfuge that it was kept by his wife. An obvious reason for this was that men regarded Chinese as the only proper and dignified medium for writing. Women, who had far less opportunity to learn Chinese, were the ones who turned most readily to *kana* to express themselves in the vernacular, and it was they who became the greatest writers of prose literature in the Heian period.

The first truly feminine diary was the late tenth century record known as *The Gossamer Years (Kagerō Nikki)*, written by a woman identified only as the "mother of (Fujiwara no) Michitsuna." Unlike the *Tosa Diary*, which was kept on a day-to-day basis and seems to present events as a fairly consistent and balanced chronology, *The Gossamer Years* is a sporadic and uneven account spread over some twenty-one years, from 954 to 974. The entries for some days are exceedingly detailed, but there are also long periods of time during which nothing at all is reported. This loose handling of the diary form (in fact, much of this diary was probably written toward the end of or even after the period it covers), combined with the intensely personal and subjective character of the writing, makes *The Gossamer Years* very much like a kind of autobiography or even an "I-novel"; and indeed the distinction between the diary and the fictional tale was often quite vague in Heian literature.

Whereas the *Tosa Diary* is centered on a journey (a common theme in diaries and other personal accounts), *The Gossamer Years* deals with an equally popular theme, the romance. The mother of Michitsuna was married to Fujiwara no Kaneie (929–90), who eventually became imperial regent at court. Like most high-ranking Heian courtiers, Kaneie was not a faithful husband, and after an affectionate beginning with his wife (who bore him the boy Michitsuna), he began to neglect her for other women. Most of *The Gossamer Years* deals with the author's distress and fretful resentment over the fact that her husband comes to call upon her with less and less frequency. Left alone with little to break the tedium of her sequestered existence (a fate all too common among Heian court ladies), the mother of Michitsuna is driven to a neurotic outpouring of self-pity and absorption with her own grievances to the exclusion of any consideration for the feelings of others.

At the end of *The Gossamer Years* we find these forlorn remarks:

> The weather was fairly good for the rest of the year, with only a few snow flurries. . . . I thought of how quickly the years had gone by, each with the same unsatisfied longing. The old, inexhaustible sadness came back, and I went through the rites for my ancestors, but absent-mindedly.

In the very next, and last, line of the book, however, we are told that "Late on the eve of the new year there was a pounding outside . . ." and realize that Kaneie's interest in the mother of Michitsuna is not entirely exhausted.[12]

Another type of contemporary literature very similar to the private diary was the poem-tale *(uta-monogatari)*, the most celebrated of which is *The Tales of Ise (Ise Monogatari)*, compiled sometime in the early tenth century. *The Tales of Ise* consists of 125 passages or episodes of varying length, loosely grouped together, and each containing one or more poems. Most of the poems deal with love, and particularly with the romantic adventures of a great court lover and poet of the previous century, Ariwara no Narihira (825–80). Quite likely *The Tales of Ise* was compiled by one or more persons who gathered a collection of poems, most of them by Narihira, and then placed them in narrative contexts by drawing on biographical information concerning Narihira's life. To the foreigner, *The Tales of Ise* is apt to seem like a light and even insignificant work, but it has been venerated by the Japanese through the centuries as one of the greatest masterpieces in their literature. A typical passage from *The Tales of Ise* goes like this:

> In former times there lived a young nobleman named Narihira. Upon receiving the ceremony of initiation into manhood, he set forth upon a ceremonial falconry excursion, to review his estates at the village of Kasuga, near the former capital of Nara.
>
> In the village there dwelt alone two young sisters possessed of a disturbing beauty. The young nobleman gazed at the two secretly from the shade of the enclosure around their house. It filled his heart with longing that in this rustic village he should have found so unexpectedly such lovely maidens.
>
> Removing the wide sleeve from the silk cloak he was wearing, Narihira inscribed a verse upon it and sent it to the girls. The cloak he was wearing bore a bold pattern of passionflowers:
>
> > Young maiden-flowers
> > Of Kasuga, you dye my cloak;
> > And wildly like them grows
> > This passion in my heart,
> > Abundantly, without end.
>
> The maidens must have thought this eminently suited to the occasion, for it was composed in the same mood as the well-known
>
> > For whom has my heart
> > Like the passionflower patterns
> > Of Michinoku
> > Been thrown into disarray?
> > All on account of you.
>
> This is the kind of facile elegance in which the men of old excelled.[13]

The crowning achievement in the development of prose in the early and middle Heian period was the completion shortly after 1000 of *The Tale of Genji (Genji Monogatari)*, a massive novel by Murasaki Shikibu (978–1016), a lady-in-waiting at court. In spite of the excellence of much other Heian literature, it is Murasaki's incomparable masterpiece that recreates the age for us, or at least the age as seen through the eyes of the privileged

Heian courtiers. The leading character of this novel, Genji, "The Shining One," was the son of an emperor by a low-ranking concubine and a paragon of all the Heian virtues: he was dazzlingly handsome, a great lover, poet, calligrapher, musician and dancer, and the possessor of impeccable taste in a society that was in a very real sense ruled by taste.

Like most of his peers, Genji, at least in his youth, had little official business to occupy him at court, where affairs were controlled by a few leading Fujiwara ministers. Instead, he devoted himself to the gentle arts and especially to the pursuit of love, an endeavor that involved him in a seemingly endless string of romantic entanglements. In Genji's circle, the typical love affair was conducted according to exacting dictates of taste. Lovers delighted each other by exchanging poems written on fans or on carefully selected and scented stationery, which they adorned with delicate sprays of flowers. A faulty handwriting, a missed allusion, or a poor matching of colors could quickly dampen a courtier's ardor. On the other hand, the scent of a delicately mixed perfume or the haunting notes of a zithern on a soft summer night could excite his greatest passion and launch him recklessly on a romantic escapade whose outcome was more than likely to have embarrassing and even disastrous results both for the lovers and for others among the intimately associated members of Heian courtier society.

In a famous scene that takes place one rainy night, when Genji and his friends informally assess the merits of womanhood, there is this exchange between To no Chujo, a young Fujiwara, and Genji:

To no Chujo: "I have at last discovered that there exists no woman of whom one can say 'Here is perfection. This is indeed she.' There are many who have the superficial art of writing a good running hand, or if occasion requires of making a quick repartee. But there are few who will stand the ordeal of any further test. Usually their minds are entirely occupied by admiration for their own accomplishments, and their abuse of all rivals creates a most unpleasant impression. Some again are adored by over-fond parents. These have since childhood been guarded behind lattice windows and no knowledge of them is allowed to reach the outer-world, save that of their excellence in some accomplishment or art; and this may indeed sometimes arouse our interest. She is pretty and graceful and has not yet mixed at all with the world. Such a girl by closely copying some model and applying herself with great industry will often succeed in really mastering one of the minor and ephemeral arts. Her friends are careful to say nothing of her defects and to exaggerate her accomplishments, and while we cannot altogether trust their praise we cannot believe that their judgment is entirely astray. But when we take steps to test their statements we are invariably disappointed."

He paused, seeming to be slightly ashamed of the cynical tone which he had adopted, and added "I know my experience is not large, but that is the conclusion I have come to so far." Then Genji, smiling: "And are there any who lack even one accomplishment?" "No doubt, but in such a case it is unlikely that anyone would be successfully decoyed. The number of those who have nothing to recommend them and of those in whom nothing but good can be found is probably equal. I divide women into three classes. Those of high rank and birth are made such a fuss of and their weak points are so completely concealed that we are certain to be told that they are paragons. About those of the middle class everyone is allowed to express his own opinion, and we shall have much conflicting evidence to sift. As for the lower classes, they do not concern us."[14]

The Tale of Genji has long been held by Japanese critics to exemplify the aesthetic quality of *mono no aware,* and indeed *aware* appears as an adjective in the book (referring to things that are moving) no less than 1,018 times.

If *mono no aware* is the predominant mood of Heian literature, there is at least one work—*The Pillow Book (Makura no Sōshi)* of Sei Shōnagon (dates unknown)— that exudes a quality quite the opposite, that of *okashi:* "lightness" or "wit." Like her near-contemporary Lady Murasaki, Sei Shōnagon also served as a lady-in-waiting at court. Her book (the title presumably taken from the fact that she kept it close at hand—that is, near or even *in* her wooden pillow) is a miscellany of jottings, listings, anecdotes, aphorisms, and personal opinions. Sei had a keenly observant eye, especially for human foibles, which she delighted in exploiting; and indeed, with her assertiveness and biting tongue, she may be regarded as a kind of forerunner of the militant women's liberationist in her behavior toward men. She records, for example, the following account of what occurred when a courtier named Narimasa, whom she held in low esteem, attempted to visit her secretly one night:

"May I presume to come in?" he said several times in a strangely husky and excited voice. I looked up in amazement, and by the light of the lamp that had been placed behind the curtain of state I could see that Narimasa was standing outside the door, which he had now opened about half a foot. The situation amused me. As a rule he would not have dreamt of indulging in such lecherous behavior; as the Empress was staying in his house, he evidently felt he could do as he pleased. Waking up the young woman next to me I exclaimed, "Look who is here! What an unlikely sight!" They all sat up and, seeing Narimasa by the door, burst into laughter. "Who are you?" I said. "Don't try to hide!" "Oh no," he replied. "It's simply that the master of the house has something to discuss with the lady-in-waiting in charge."

"It was your gate I was speaking about," I said. "I don't remember asking you to open the sliding-door."

"Yes indeed," he answered. "It is precisely the matter of the gate that I wanted to discuss with you. May I not presume to come in for a moment?"

"Really!" said one of the young women. "How unpleasant! No, he certainly cannot come in."

"Oh, I see," said Narimasa. "There are other young ladies in the room." Closing the door behind him, he left, followed by our loud laughter.[15]

The Pillow Book is the earliest example of still another type of literature—the miscellany or "running brush" *(zuihitsu)*—that has enjoyed much popularity in Japanese history. Along with the diary and the poem-tale, the miscellany, like horizontal picture scrolls and linked verse, reflects the Japanese preference for the episodic and loosely joined, rather than the long and unified, artistic form. *The Tale of Genji,* as a great, sustained work, was exceptional. In literature the Japanese have concentrated on polishing short passages, phrases, words, and even syllables—no better proof of this exists than their consuming love for the *waka*—and have been little inclined to think in terms of plot development or the carefully constructed narrative line.

Although written in fifty-four chapters, *The Tale of Genji* is actually divided into two major parts. The first centers on the life and loves of Genji, and the second deals with the generation at court after Genji's death. The Genji chapters, despite their prevailing mood of sadness and melancholy, portray a truly ideal society, a society whose members little doubted that theirs was the best of worlds possible in this life. Genji and his companions were not much given to philosophical speculation but seem instinctively to have accepted the implications of esoteric Buddhism that ultimate truth or reality lay in the very splendor of their own existence. Genji in particular represented the perfection of the Heian courtier, and upon his death, as the opening lines of the book's second part lament, there was no one to take his place.

Among Genji's successors, we find new doubts and psychological uncertainties that alter the tone of the novel: there is almost a presentiment in the book's latter part of the momentous changes that within a century or so were to bring about the decline of courtier society and the rise of a provincial warrior class. Some historians have suggested that Heian aristocratic society, even at its peak, was unbearably stultifying to all but the privileged few—mostly members of the Fujiwara and imperial families—who could aspire to advancement at court; that, despite the idealization of court life in the earlier chapters of *The Tale of Genji,* there was discontent among many courtiers over their lot. No doubt the rumblings of the military in the provinces, which mounted steadily during the eleventh century, were also disquieting to the courtiers in spite of their outward show of aloofness toward provincial affairs.

While the term *monogatari* was applied during the Fujiwara epoch to such differing literary works as poem-tales and novels, it was also used for a new type of historical writing. The *Nihon Shoki* had been produced by the Nara court as the first of what was intended to be an ongoing series of official histories of Japan, much like the dynastic histories of China. As it turned out, six such national histories, covering up to the year 887, were actually compiled. All were written in Chinese and, with the exception of the *Nihon Shoki*, were notably dull, consisting as they did of a dry recitation of the facts and events of court government.

One reason for abandonment of the practice of compiling national histories was the general turning away from Chinese-derived institutions and patterns of behavior that accompanied the cessation of official missions to the continent in the latter part of the ninth century. Also, in the same way that the newly acquired capacity to write in Japanese with the use of *kana* encouraged the keeping of private diaries, people at court were inspired to record the historical events of their age in a more colorful, personally interpretive fashion. Although not precisely the same in structure, the national histories had been patterned on the highly formal dynastic records of the great bureaucratic state of China. Yet Heian Japan had not become a bureaucratic state on the order of China; and the Heian courtiers, lax in matters of national administration, had become ever more introspectively absorbed with their own ceremonially oriented life in the capital. It was only natural that, in history as in literature, they should develop new mediums of composition more suitable to the expression of their sentiments concerning the public and private affairs of Kyoto courtier society.

The new form of history writing that evolved at this time is called the historical tale *(rekishi monogatari);* it was much influenced by the fictional tale, especially *The Tale of Genji.* A product of the blurring of history and literature, or fact and fiction, it can be regarded as a kind of "embellished history." The thinking that brought history and literature together in this form is revealingly suggested in a scene from the *Genji* itself. In this scene, Genji visits Tamakazura, one of the ladies living in his Kyoto residence and the one who is most given to reading romantic tales *(monogatari).* After first teasing Tamakazura about allowing herself to be deceived by stories that she knows perfectly well are not true, Genji, becoming serious, says: "Amid all the fabrication [in *monogatari*] I must admit that I do find real emotions and plausible chains of events. . . . [The *monogatari*] have set down and preserved happenings from the age of the gods to our own. *The Chronicles of Japan (Nihon Shoki)* and the rest are a mere fragment of the whole truth. It is your [*monogatari*] that fill in the details."[16] To Genji, *Nihon Shoki* and the other national histories told only part of the story of the past: the great events and happenings. The details about how people actually lived, felt, and thought had to be filled in by others in a "plausible" manner.

The first of the historical tales was *A Tale of Flowering Fortunes (Eiga Monogatari),* written in the mid-eleventh century by the court lady Akazome Emon (dates unknown), who unabashedly modeled her work, in structure and style, on the *Genji.* Whereas the six national histories were written in Chinese, *Flowering Fortunes* is in Japanese. And the fact that the author of this first historical *monogatari* was a woman is fitting, since women had already taken the lead in writing a new kind of fiction—the fictional *monogatari*—by taking advantage of the capacity to write the Japanese language presented by the invention of *kana*.

Covering the period from about 946 until 1028, *Flowering Fortunes* is a woman's-eye view of events and affairs at the Heian court, including marriages, births, deaths, personal rivalries, and romantic liaisons. Its title refers to the flowering fortunes or flourishing of the Fujiwara, especially under Michinaga (966–1027), who is generally regarded as the greatest of the imperial regents. The awe with which Akazome Emon beholds the resplendent Michizane is well expressed in the following passage:

> Those who prosper must decline; where there is meeting, parting will follow. All is cause and effect; nothing is eternal. Fortunes that prospered yesterday may decline today. Even spring blossoms and autumn leaves are spoiled and lose their beauty when they are enshrouded by spring haze and autumn mist. And after a gust of wind scatters them, they are nothing but debris in a garden or froth on the water. It is only the flowering fortunes of this lord [Michinaga] that, now having begun to bloom, will not be hidden from sight during a thousand years of spring hazes and autumn mists. No wind disturbs their branches, which grow ever more redolent with scent—rare and splendid as *udumbara* blossoms, peerlessly fragrant as the blue lotus, fairest of water-flowers.[17]

Having lyrically described the most fundamental of all Buddhist truths, the impermanence of all things, Akazome Emon asserts that, alone among things, the flowering fortunes of Michinaga will not be governed by this truth but will continue—through Michinaga himself and his progeny—for a thousand years (forever?).

Glorification of the Fujiwara and particularly Michinaga is even more pronounced in the second of the historical tales, *The Great Mirror (Ōkagami)*, which was probably written by a courtier in the late eleventh or early twelfth century and covers the period 850–1025 (the same period as that of *Flowering Fortunes*, but with a century added at the beginning). Whereas *Flowering Fortunes* is written in chronological form, *The Great Mirror* is organized according to "annals and biographies."[18] The annals are the records of emperors and are uniformly brief, occupying only about 10 percent of the entire work. The biographies, on the other hand, are those of the prominent Fujiwara who served at court during the reigns of these emperors and account for the work's remaining 90 percent. In short, *The Great Mirror* is, first and foremost, a history of the Fujiwara leading inexorably to the family's pinnacle of grandeur and glory in the age of Michinaga. In the following passage, the author, elaborating upon the "cult of personality" of Michinaga first propounded by Akazome Emon in *A Tale of Flowering Fortunes*, goes so far as to liken him to two of the greatest culture heroes in early Japanese history, Prince Shōtoku and Kūkai, the founder of Shingon Buddhism, and then to a god or a buddha:

[Michinaga] is in a class by [himself]. He is a man who enjoys special protection from the gods of heaven and earth. Winds may rage and rains may fall day after day, but the skies will clear and the ground will dry out two or three days before he plans anything. Some people call him a reincarnation of [Prince Shōtoku]; others say he is [Kūkai], reborn to make Buddhism flourish. Even to the censorious eye of old age, he seems not an ordinary mortal but an awesome manifestation of a god or a buddha.[19]

Whereas formerly they had scarcely questioned that spiritual fulfillment could be found in this world, the courtiers by the eleventh century increasingly cherished the thought of attaining salvation in the next. Such salvationism was not new to Japan but had been introduced to it as early as the seventh century in the teachings of Pure Land Buddhism. Pure Land Buddhism was based on adoration of the transcendent buddha Amida, who an eternity earlier had vowed to save all beings, provided only that they placed their faith wholly in him. By simply reciting the *nembutsu* (an invocation in praise of Amida),[20] an individual could ensure that upon death he would be transported to the blissful "pure land" of Amida in the western realm of the universe.

Amidism was made particularly appealing to the courtiers of the late Heian period by the popular doctrine of *mappō*, "the latter days of the Buddhist law." This doctrine held that after the death of Gautama, some five centuries B.C., Buddhism would pass through three great ages: an age of the flourishing of the law, of its decline, and finally of its disappearance in the degenerate days of *mappō*. Once the age of *mappō* commenced—and by Japanese calculations that would be in the year 1052—individuals could no longer hope to achieve Buddhist enlightenment by their own efforts, as had the followers of Hinayana and even of the Mahayanist sects of Shingon and Tendai esotericism. There would be no alternative during *mappō* but to throw oneself on the saving grace of another, such as Amida, in the hope of attaining rebirth in paradise.

Eventually, it was the Pure Land sect, with its simple message of universal salvation, that provided the practical means for the spread of Buddhism to all classes of Japanese in the medieval era. But in its first phase of development in Japan, Amidism was embraced—and interpreted in characteristically aesthetic terms—by the Heian courtiers. In the *Ōjō Yōshū (Essentials of Salvation)*, for example, the Tendai priest Genshin (942–1017) urged the practice of the *nembutsu* and vividly pictured the attractions of the pure land:

After the believer is born into this land and when he experiences the pleasures of the first opening of the lotus, his joy becomes a hundred times greater than before. It is comparable to a blind man gaining sight for the first time, or to entering a royal palace directly after leaving some rural region. Looking at his own body, it becomes purplish gold in color. He is gowned naturally in jeweled garments. Rings, bracelets, a crown of jewels, and other ornaments in countless profusion adorn his body. And when he looks upon the light radiating from the Buddha, he obtains pure vision, and because of his experiences in former lives, he hears the sounds of all things. And no matter what color he may see or what sound he may hear, it is a thing of marvel. Such is the ornamentation of space above that the eye becomes lost in the traces of clouds. The melody of the wheel of the wonderful Law as it turns, flows throughout this land of jeweled sound. Palaces, halls, forests, and ponds shine and glitter everywhere. Flocks of wild ducks, geese, and mandarin ducks fly about in the distance and near at hand. One may see multitudes from all the worlds being born into this land like sudden showers of rain.[21]

One of the favorite themes in Fujiwara art was the *raigō*, a pictorial representation of the coming of Amida at the time of death to lead the way to the pure land (fig. 23); and among the most famous *raigō* paintings is a triptych traditionally attributed to Genshin, who was a fine artist as well as a scholar (even though this work was obviously done by someone else a century or more after Genshin's death). Amida is shown descending to earth on a great swirl of clouds in the company of twenty-five bodhisattvas, some playing musical instruments, some clasping their hands in prayer, and still others holding forth votive offerings. The formal way in which the figure of Amida, facing directly frontward, has been inserted into the center of the picture gives it a stiffly iconographic appearance; yet the gentle and even smiling expressions of all the figures— Amida as well as the host of bodhisattvas—are strikingly different from the fierce, unearthly visages of Jōgan art. The Fujiwara epoch, in literature as well as the visual arts, was soft, approachable, and "feminine." By contrast, the earlier Jōgan epoch had been forbidding, secretive (esoteric), and "masculine."

The favor that Amidism came to enjoy among the courtiers in the eleventh century is significantly revealed in the conduct of the regent Michinaga, who in his heyday had joyfully exclaimed in verse his contentment with the world:

> The full moon makes me feel
> That the world is mine indeed;
> Like the moon I shine
> Unveiled by clouds.

Yet, as death approached, Michinaga turned his thoughts ever more to Amida and the hereafter. Following a practice that became common in Japan, he sought in his final moments to facilitate Amida's descent to lead him to the pure land by facing his bed toward the west and holding in his hand a colored string attached to Amida in a *raigō* painting. Later

Fig. 23   *Raigō,* "The Descent of Amida and the Celestial Company" *(courtesy of the Seattle Art Museum, Eugene Fuller Memorial Collection)*

artists, in their desire to emphasize the rapidity with which true believers could expect to be transported to the pure land, painted *raigō* that showed Amida and the heavenly host coming down toward the viewer in great haste (rather than in the gentle, floating manner of the work described above). The *raigō* scene was even reenacted dramatically, and there is at

Fig. 24   Byōdōin Temple *(Consulate General of Japan, New York)*

least one recorded case of a man who, on his deathbed, engaged a group of priests to visit him dressed as Amida and the twenty-five attendant bodhisattvas.

The temple where Michinaga died, the *Hōjōji,* is no longer in existence, but we are told that he had it built with the intent of reproducing on earth the beauties and delights of the pure land. Michinaga's son, the regent Yorimichi (992–1074), also sought to recreate the pure land in the Byōdōin, a temple at Uji, several miles to the south of Kyoto (fig. 24).

Fig. 25   Statue of Amida buddha by Jōchō at the Byōdōin Temple *(Consulate General of Japan, New York)*

Opened in 1052, the first year of *mappō*, the Byōdōin has the finest remaining examples of Fujiwara period architecture, including the much admired Phoenix Hall, a light, elegantly designed structure that was apparently given its name in later times because it is shaped like a phoenix (or, at least, like a bird), with wings extended in flight. Inside the hall is a sculptural representation of the *raigō*, with a central image of Amida and, attached to the upper parts of the walls, small, gracefully shaped figures of the bodhisattvas, adorned with halos and riding wisps of clouds. The Amida image, which is made of wood and has the characteristic gentleness and courtly air of Fujiwara art, is the work of Jōchō (d. 1057), the most celebrated sculptor of his age and one of the first persons in Japanese history to receive distinction and honor from the court as an artist of individuality and not merely as a craftsman (fig. 25).

Although no examples of domestic architecture remain from the Heian period, we know from written accounts and picture scrolls what sort of mansions the courtiers built for themselves during the age of Fujiwara ascendancy. The chief architectural style for aristocratic homes, known as *shinden* construction, consisted in fact of a collection of one-story structures laid out very much like the Byōdōin Temple (fig. 26).

Fig. 26 *Shinden*-style mansion of the Heian period (*drawing by Arthur Fleisher*)

Inasmuch as the courtiers preferred to live within the city limits of Kyoto, they were obliged for want of space to build their homes on fairly small plots of land, usually not more than two and a half acres or so in size. The typical *shinden* mansion consisted of a main building facing southward—the *shinden* or "living quarters" of the master of the family —and three secondary buildings to the east, west, and north. All four structures were raised about a foot above the ground and were connected by covered corridors. There were also two additional corridors leading southward to miniature fishing pavilions that bordered on a small lake with an artificial island in its center. The lake was usually fed by a stream flowing from the northeast, often under the mansion itself, and it was by the stream's banks that the courtiers enjoyed gathering for poetry parties. At such parties, a cup of rice wine was floated downstream and, as it came to each guest, he was obliged to take it from the water, drink, and recite a verse.

Like modern Japanese homes, those of the Heian courtiers had partitions, sliding doors, and shutters that could readily be removed to make smaller rooms into larger ones and to open the whole interior of a building to the out-of-doors. Also, like most homes in Japan today, the *shinden* were sparsely furnished. Although chairs were coming into general use in China about this time, they were not adopted by the Heian Japanese except for certain ceremonial purposes. A few chests, braziers, and small tables were the only objects likely to be left out in the open in *shinden* rooms and not stored away after use.

One item of furniture that was unique to courtier society was the so-called screen of state, behind which ladies ensconced themselves when receiving visitors. Conspicuously depicted in the twelfth-century picture scrolls based on *The Tale of Genji,* the screens of state were wooden frames, several feet in height, with draperies hung loosely from their crosspieces (a screen of state can be observed in the foreground of fig. 27, p. 85). They could be easily moved about, and often came to represent the final fragile barrier to the Heian gallant in his quest to consummate a romantic liaison.

4

The Advent of a New Age

THE *haniwa* FIGURINES of armor-clad warriors and their mounts and the numerous military accoutrements dating from the protohistoric tomb period are plain evidence that the fighting traditions of the Japanese go back to remote antiquity. There is, moreover, the strong likelihood that these traditions were nourished uninterruptedly in the provinces even during the centuries when an elegant and refined cultural life was evolving under continental influence in the central region of Japan.

One of the principal steps taken by the court to strengthen its control as a central government following the Great Reform of 645 was the establishment of a military system of militia units in provinces throughout the country. These units, which were under the control of the provincial governors, comprised foot soldiers conscripted from the peasantry and mounted fighters, drawn from locally powerful families, who served as officers. From the beginning, however, the peasant foot soldiers, who, under Chinese influence, used the crossbow as their principal weapon, proved to be unsatisfactory in battle. This was particularly evident during the fighting in the north against the Emishi tribesmen in the late eighth and early ninth centuries (described in Chapter 3).

In 792, two years before the move of the capital to Heian and even while expeditions, recruited from the militia units, were still being sent against the Emishi, the court abandoned conscription. Thenceforth it sought to use the locally powerful families to provide mounted fighters, when necessary, to deal with rebellions and other disturbances in the provinces. Although court administration of the provinces in general declined during the early Heian period, its provincial governments continued to be important sources of weapons and supplies for these fighters on horseback, who began to take shape as a distinct warrior class from about the late ninth or early tenth century.

The mounted fighter of ancient Japan relied primarily on two weapons, the sword and the bow, of which the latter was by far the more important. We can observe this, for example, in the description of the fighter's profession as the "way of the bow and horse," a phrase that continued to be used to describe the "warrior way" even after the bow was supplanted, centuries later, by other weapons as the primary instruments of war.

The process by which a provincial warrior class emerged in Japan was complex and differed from region to region; yet one area in particular—the eastern provinces of the Kantō—became its true spawning ground. From earliest times the Kantō had been renowned as the source of the country's best fighters. Men of the Kantō, which, along with Mutsu province directly to the north, produced the finest horses in Japan, learned riding and the other military skills, including archery, from infancy. The Kantō was still rugged frontier country, with vast tracts of open fields to draw adventuresome settlers, and the records give accounts of feuding there over land and power. From at least the early tenth century, chieftains arose in the Kantō to form fighting bands of locally bred mounted warriors. At first, the members of these bands were almost exclusively related by blood, but with the passage of time the chieftains also incorporated outsiders, whom they embraced in feudal lord-vassal relationships. Increasingly, the bands engaged in struggles, formed leagues, and established hegemonies; and in time great leaders appeared to contend for military control over ever larger territories, up to one or more provinces.

Warfare in the Kantō and elsewhere, which by mid-Heian times had become virtually the exclusive pursuit of equestrian fighters, probably seldom involved armies of more than a few hundred and was highly ritualized. When armies clashed, warriors from both sides usually paired off and fought one against one, first with bow and arrow and then, upon moving in closely, with swords. The aim of close combat was to unseat one's foe, then leap down and kill him with a dirk. As a trophy of battle and as proof for later claims for reward, the victorious warrior typically took his foe's head.

Even though the provincial warriors never lost their awe and admiration for the culture of the imperial court, their fundamental values were the antithesis of those of the Heian courtiers. They were samurai—men who "served"—and they behaved in accordance with an unwritten code that stressed manly arrogance, fighting prowess, unswerving loyalty to one's overlord, and a truculent pride in family lineage.[1]

Paradoxical though it may sound, the greatest samurai leaders came from a background of courtier society itself. The rise of the Fujiwara to preponderant power in Kyoto stifled opportunity for others at court, including those from the less privileged branches of the Fujiwara and even members of the imperial family. Many of these individuals left Kyoto to accept appointments to offices in the provincial governments. Settling permanently in the provinces after expiration of their terms of office, they took up warrior ways, became the leaders of bands, and attracted members of lesser samurai families as their supporters and vassals. Ultimately, two great clans descended from princely forebears—the Taira and Minamoto—emerged to the forefront of samurai society and became the principal contenders for warrior supremacy of the land.[2]

Although at first there was no clear territorial division of influence, by the late eleventh and early twelfth centuries one of the main branches of the Minamoto came to exert sway over the Kantō, having honed its martial powers in two long, grueling wars fought in the late 1100s against independent-minded satraps in Mutsu and Dewa provinces to the north.[3] Meanwhile, a branch of the Taira from Ise province steadily acquired land and influence in the central and western provinces. Control of the fertile Kantō, a region some ten times greater than the plain of the central provinces, eventually proved decisive in enabling the Minamoto to found the first warrior government in Japan at Kamakura in 1185. But proximity to the court in Kyoto gave the Ise Taira an early advantage over the Minamoto in the protracted competition and conflict that ensured between these two samurai houses from about the middle of the twelfth century.

The Taira benefited especially by an important political development at court in the late eleventh century. During the last years of the regent Yorimichi (990–1074), founder of the Byōdōin Temple at Uji, Fujiwara power in Kyoto began to wane, and the first of a series of abdicated sovereigns arose to reassert the traditional claim of the imperial family to rule in fact as well as in name. The abdicated sovereigns sought further to weaken the Fujiwara monopoly of court government by engaging as their aides and officials members of other houses, including samurai of the Ise Taira. Under the patronage of the abdicated emperors, the Ise Taira became the first noncourtiers to gain ceremonial admittance to the imperial palace. They also received extensive grants in estate lands and appointments to various provincial governorships in the western provinces of Honshu and in Kyushu.

Despite the assertiveness of the abdicated emperors, political conditions in Kyoto steadily deteriorated during the twelfth century. By mid-century, serious divisions had appeared within the Fujiwara and imperial families, and quarrelsome samurai of both the Taira and Minamoto clans were gathering in ever greater numbers in Kyoto. In the 1150s, the tranquility of the "flowery capital" was rudely shattered by two fierce clashes of arms. The first of these, in 1156, found the Taira and Minamoto intermingled on both sides, but the second, in 1159, resulted in a resounding victory of the Ise Taira over their archrivals and the inauguration of some twenty years of Taira ascendancy at court under the leadership of Kiyomori (1118–81).

The age of Ise Taira ascendancy was a transitional period in Japanese history. Although samurai warriors, the Taira attempted to follow in the footsteps of the Fujiwara courtiers by marrying into the imperial family and assuming many of the highest ministerial positions at court. In thus devoting their attention to traditional court politics and ignoring the pressing need for new administrative controls in the provinces, the Taira directly contributed to their own downfall, which occurred in a climactic renewal of struggle with the Minamoto from 1180 to 1185.[4]

One of the chief sources of information about the rise and fall of the Ise Taira is a work entitled *The Tale of the Heike* (another name for the Taira), the finest of a genre of writing known as war tales. The war tales, all of which were anonymously written or compiled, are accounts of warriors and their battles based on actual events that have been embellished, and hence are partly history and partly fiction. The first of the tales was composed sometime in the late tenth century and deals with the rebellion of one Taira no Masakado (d. 940) in the Kantō during 939–40.[5] Tales continued to be produced up to the seventeenth century, but the period of their greatest flourishing was the early medieval age, the thirteenth and fourteenth centuries.

Some of the war tales were composed shortly after the events they describe, while others were put into writing on the basis of an earlier oral tradition. *The Tale of the Heike,* which recounts the rise of the Ise Taira and their eventual fall and annihilation in the Minamoto-Taira war of 1180–85, was probably first compiled as a book in the early thirteenth century. But subsequently the *Heike* was greatly elaborated and expanded by guilds of blind Buddhist monks who, chanting the tale's episodes to the accompaniment of a kind of lute known as the *biwa,* entertained audiences everywhere as they journeyed around the country. From the body of war tales that spans the medieval centuries, those—such as the *Heike*—that deal with the twelfth-century clashes between Taira and Minamoto have remained especially popular among the Japanese through the ages and have been the stuff from which countless plays, dramatic dances, movies, and the like have been fashioned. Perhaps the best proof of the ongoing popularity of the *Heike* in particular lies in the fact that, as we will see in the next chapter, virtually all the warrior plays of the *nō* theatre (an artistic creation of the late fourteenth and fifteenth centuries) are based on characters and stories from it.

The later war tales degenerated into mere recitations of the interminable battles of the middle ages, one often indistinguishable from another. But in the *Heike* and a few others we have a priceless repository of the ethos of the medieval samurai. Despite the apparent lust of the samurai for armed combat and martial renown, much romanticized in later centuries, the underlying tone of the medieval age in Japan was from the beginning somber, pessimistic, and despairing. In *The Tale of Genji* the mood shifted from satisfaction with the perfections of Heian courtier society to uncertainty about this life and a craving for salvation in the next. Yet the very fact that the courtiers conceived of Amida's western paradise as an idealization of their own world, and tried to recreate it in architecture and landscape, reveals that they were far from prepared to discard the temporal values they had long cherished. How different are the sentiments expressed in the opening lines of the *Heike,* a work that in many ways served to announce the advent of the medieval age:

> The sound of the bell of the Gion Temple tolls the impermanence of all things, and the hue of the Sala tree's blossoms reveals the truth that those who flourish must fade. The proud ones do not last forever, but are like the dream of a spring night. Even the mighty will perish, just like dust before the wind.[6]

It is the age of *mappō,* the "latter days of the Buddhist law" (discussed in the last chapter), and the *Heike,* suffused with *mappō* sentiment, tells the story of how the Ise Taira, full of arrogance and hubris, have, under the leadership of Kiyomori, forced their way to the heights of court society, only to suffer grievous failure and destruction in their five-year war with the resurgent Minamoto. In the larger sense, however, the Taira are only the most spectacular example of decline in a time governed by the dark, inscrutable laws of *mappō.* In their years of residence in Kyoto the Taira have become more and more courtier-like; and in the *Heike* they can even be seen as surrogates for the courtiers, who are also in rapid decline and about to lose out historically as Japan's ruling class to the emerging warrior elite represented by the Minamoto.

The courtly qualities of the Ise Taira are highlighted throughout the *Heike:* a flute, for example, is found on the body of a youthful Taira, and his killer, a Minamoto adherent, observes that none among the Minamoto was likely to carry such a thing into battle; another Taira, before going to his death, beseeches a famous poet to include one or more of his poems in an anthology that the emperor has ordered the poet to compile; and still another Taira, certain that he too will die in battle, returns a famous lute, once prized by emperors, that has been entrusted to him because of his uncommon musical talent. As we read the first half of the *Heike,* we may feel that the Taira richly deserve what we know is coming to them in the Minamoto-Taira war of the work's second half; but once the war has started, our sympathies are increasingly drawn to them, largely because they are portrayed as courtier-like, elegantly bewildered, and not at all the military match of the ferocious Minamoto. One of the saddest and most courtier-like passages in the *Heike* describes the Taira flight to the western provinces after they have been driven from Kyoto in 1183. They have stopped for one night at Fukuhara on the Inland Sea before setting out, forlorn, on their westward journey:

As dawn broke, the Taira set fire to the Fukuhara palace and, with the emperor, they all boarded the boats. Departing the capital had been more painful, but still their feelings of regret were great indeed. Smoke at evening time from seaweed burned by fisherfolk, the cries of deer on mountain peaks at dawn, waves lapping the shore, moonbeams bathing their tear-drenched sleeves, crickets chirping in the grasses—no sight met their eyes nor sounds reached their ears that failed to evoke sadness or pierce their hearts. Yesterday they were tens of thousands of horsemen aligned at Ōsaka Barrier; today, as they loosened their mooring lines on waves in the western sea, they numbered a mere seven thousand. The sky was cloudy and the sea calm as dusk approached. Lonely islands were shrouded in evening mists; the moon floated on the sea. Cleaving the waves to the distant horizon and drawn ever onward by the tides, the boats seemed to row up through the clouds in the sky. Days had passed, and they were already separated far from the mountains and rivers of the capital, which lay behind the clouds. They seemed to have gone as far as they could go. All had come to an end, except their endless tears.[7]

The Taira name has come down through the ages as synonymous with the proud and the mighty who "will perish in the end, like dust before the wind." Indeed, they have even given rise to the popular saying "Even the haughty Taira (Heike) will not last long" *(Ogoru Heike wa hisashikarazu)*. But, in truth, the Taira have been to a large extent the victims of the process of literary embellishment that the *Heike* underwent. There is no historical evidence, for example, to suggest that Kiyomori was the cruel, power-mad villain that the *Heike* makes him out to be; the Ise Taira, as a warrior clan, were not nearly as inept militarily as they are depicted in the *Heike;* and the Taira as aristocratized, courtier-warriors reflects not so much historical fact as the artistic tastes of the Muromachi period (the fourteenth century), when what became the most widely disseminated version of the *Heike* was compiled.[8]

Taira ascendancy at court in Kyoto was brief, and contributed little if anything to the improvement of rulership in Japan. But in one of their major pursuits—overseas trade and intercourse—the Taira opened the door to a new flow of influence from China that significantly affected both the direction and the tempo of cultural developments in medieval Japan.

Although official relations with the tottering T'ang dynasty had been terminated in the late ninth century, contacts with the continent were never completely severed, and throughout the tenth and eleventh centuries private traders continued to operate out of Kyushu, particularly the ancient port of Hakata. Moreover, the Heian court, even though it steadfastly refused to dispatch its own missions again to China, kept officials permanently stationed at a commandery near Hakata to oversee the import trade and to requisition choice luxury goods for sale and distribution among the Kyoto aristocrats. When the Taira, with the backing of the abdicated emperors at court, became influential in the western provinces in the twelfth century, they naturally took a keen interest in—and eventually monopolized—the highly profitable maritime trade with China.

China of the Sung dynasty (960–1279) was a changed country from the expansionist, cosmopolitan land of T'ang times that the Japanese had so assiduously copied in their Great Reform several centuries earlier. China could no longer serve as a giant conduit for the flow of world art and culture to remote Japan. From its founding, the Sung dynasty was harassed by barbarian tribes pressing in from the north and northwest. And indeed, just as the Taira assumed a commanding position in Japan's burgeoning overseas trade in the early twelfth century, North China fell to foreign invaders. The Sung—known henceforth as the Southern Sung (1127–1279)—moved its capital from Kaifeng in the north to Hangchow south of the Yangtze delta, where it remained until overthrown by the Mongols of Khubilai Khan in 1279.

Despite political woes and territorial losses, the Sung was a time of great advancement in Chinese civilization. Some scholars, impressed by the extensive growth in cities, commerce, maritime trade, and governmental bureaucratization in the late T'ang and Sung, have even asserted that this was the age when China entered its "early modern" phase. The Sung was also a brilliant period culturally. No doubt most of the major developments of the Sung in art, religion, and philosophy would in time have been transmitted to Japan. But the fortuitous combination of desire on the part of the Sung to increase its foreign trade with Japan and the vigorous initiative taken in maritime activity by the Taira greatly speeded the process of transmission.

One of the earliest and most important results of this new wave of cultural transmission from the continent was a revival of interest in Japan in pure scholarship. The Nara court, following the Chinese model, had founded a central college in the capital and had directed that branch colleges be established in the various provinces. The ostensible purpose of this system of colleges, which by the mid-Nara period had evolved a fourfold curriculum of Confucian classics, literature, law, and mathematics, was to provide a channel of advancement in the court bureaucracy for sons of the lower (including the provincial) aristocracy. But in actual practice very little opportunity to advance was provided, and the bestowal of courtier ranks and offices continued to be made almost entirely on grounds of birth. Before long, the college system languished, and the great courtier families assumed responsibility through private academies for the education of their own children. Moreover, as the courtiers of the early Heian period became increasingly infatuated with literature (that is, belles-lettres), they almost totally neglected the other fields of academic or scholarly pursuit. Courtier society offered scant reward to the individual who, say, patiently acquired a profound knowledge of the *Analects* of Confucius; yet it liberally heaped laurels upon and promised literary immortality to the author of superior poems.

The Sung period in China, on the other hand, was an exceptional age for scholarship, most notably perhaps in history and in the compilation of encyclopedias and catalogs of art works. This scholarly activity was greatly facilitated by the development of printing, invented by the Chinese several centuries earlier.

Japanese visitors to Sung China were much impressed by the general availability of printed books on a great variety of subjects, including history, Buddhism, Confucianism, literature, medicine, and geography, and carried them in ever greater numbers back to Japan. By the time of the Taira supremacy, collections of Chinese books had become important status symbols among upper-class Japanese. Kiyomori is said, for example, to have gone to extravagant lengths to obtain a 1,000-volume encyclopedia whose export was prohibited by the Sung. Some courtiers confided in their diaries that they had little or no personal interest in these books but nevertheless felt constrained to acquire them for the sake of appearances. Yet, the Chinese books brought to Japan about this time, in the thousands and even in the tens of thousands, not only provided the nuclei for many new libraries but motivated the Japanese to print their own books and to a great extent stimulated and made possible the varied and energetic scholarly activities of the coming medieval age.

One of the finest artistic achievements of the middle and late Heian period was the evolution of a native style of essentially secular painting that reached its apex in the narrative picture scrolls of the twelfth century. The products of this style of painting are called "Yamato [that is, Japanese] pictures" to distinguish them from works categorized as "Chinese pictures."

Painting in Japan from the seventh to the ninth centuries, like art in general, had been done almost entirely in the Chinese manner. Portraits of people, for example, showed Chinese-looking features, and even landscapes were mere imitations of noted places in China. The evolution of Yamato pictures from the ninth century on constituted a transition from this kind of copying to more original painting that dealt with Japanese people in Japanese settings.

Nearly all of the early Yamato pictures were painted either on folding screens or sliding doors. Regrettably, like the *shinden* mansions in which they were kept, none has survived. Yet there are abundant descriptions in the records of what they looked like; and in the background scenes of some of the later narrative scrolls—for example, the twelfth-century works based on *The Tale of Genji* (see fig. 27)—we can glimpse screens and doors pictorially decorated in the Yamato style.

Fig. 27　Scene from the Genji Scrolls: Yamato paintings on sliding doors in background; "screen of state" in foreground (*Tokugawa Art Museum, Nagoya, Japan*)

These early Yamato pictures, which reached their peak of popularity in the Fujiwara epoch, depicted either pure landscapes or landscapes in which courtiers were shown at their leisure: viewing the moon, gathering the first blossoms of spring, or simply standing amid the tranquil beauties of nature. The two major themes were the seasons and famous places of Japan.

It is doubtful, as suggested at the end of Chapter 2, that any other people in history has ever been as absorbed as the Japanese, in their literature and art, with the seasons and the varying moods they bring. In works of prose, such as *The Tale of Genji,* there is a constant awareness of the seasons and their intimate association with the life cycle of the Heian courtier; and in *waka* poetry, we find numerous words and phrases that stereotypically identify the time of year, such as the "morning mists" of spring or the "cry of the deer" in autumn. Yamato pictures, as well, came to have many associative subjects linked with each of the seasons: for example, the morning glories, lotus ponds, and Kamo festival of summer, and winter's mountain villages, waterfowl, and the sacred *kagura* dance.

A unique feature of the Yamato pictures of famous places was that they were painted for the most part by people who had never seen these places, except possibly the ones closest to Kyoto. In other words, the Yamato artists produced provincial scenes either as they were traditionally supposed to appear or as the artists imagined them to appear. There could be no more telling proof than this of the extent to which the Heian courtiers had come to conceive of the world outside Kyoto and its environs in almost purely abstract, aesthetic terms.

With development of the *kana* syllabary and the use of *kana* for the writing of *waka,* Yamato artists began to add poems to their pictures appropriate to the particular seasons and settings they were depicting. They thus joined together three forms of art: poetry, calligraphy, and painting. And in the process they contributed a narrative or descriptive element to their works that led from the painting of individual scenes on screens and doors to the use of Yamato pictures as illustrations in books, and finally, about the turn of the twelfth century, to the development of narrative scrolls (perhaps most conveniently referred to henceforth as *emaki* to avoid confusion with the earlier types of Yamato pictures).

Although horizontal handscrolls had long been used for pictorial purposes in China, it was the Japanese who in the late Heian period came to employ them in the creation of a major art form. The oldest, and in many ways the most splendid, of the *emaki* extant from Heian times are the Genji Scrolls, probably painted sometime around the mid-twelfth century (fig. 27). There may originally have been as many as twenty of these scrolls but only four have come down to us. Strictly speaking, the Genji Scrolls are not fully narrative pictures, since they do not possess the horizontal flow of movement and the blending of scenes one into another that became the dominant characteristic of subsequent *emaki*. Rather, the Genji Scrolls consist of separate scenes with sections of text interspersed among them.

A distinctive technical convention used in the Genji Scrolls is the removal of roofs from buildings to provide oblique views into their interiors from above. Another is the drawing of faces with stylized "straight lines for eyes and hooks for noses." This elimination of facial expression seems particularly fitting for the portrayal of members of a society that so admired fixed, ideal types. Like the authors of much of Heian literature, the artists of the Genji Scrolls sought more to create a series of moods than to depict particular individuals and particular situations (although of course we know from the novel who the people are and what they are doing).

Another fine *emaki* of the twelfth century is the Ban Dainagon Scroll, which relates a complex political intrigue of 866 in which a certain Great Councilor Ban was alleged to have caused the destruction by fire of one of the principal gateways leading into the palace compound in Kyoto. Completed about 1175, this work is of a different character from that of the Genji Scrolls. In contrast to the static, stylized beauty of the latter, it is full of action. Moreover, although set chiefly in Kyoto, the Ban Dainagon Scroll is crowded with people from both the upper and lower classes. As we run our eyes from right to left, we see animated figures enacting the continuous flow of narrative: the conspiracy that led to the burning of the palace gateway, the chance discovery that Ban was involved in it, and finally his banishment from the capital.

A particularly unusual set of early *emaki* are the Animal Scrolls traditionally attributed to a Buddhist priest named Toba (1053–1140), although stylistic analysis by scholars suggests that the scrolls were not all painted by the same person and were in fact probably done over a period of some hundred years from Toba's time until the early thirteenth century. The most artistically admirable sections of the scrolls show animals, including rabbits, monkeys, frogs, and foxes, frolicking and gamboling about (fig. 28). The animals are drawn with a marvelously sure and skillful brush stroke and are the product of a technique of playful, caricature-like artwork that can be traced back to certain charcoal sketches done on the walls of the Hōryūji Temple in the late seventh century and to pictures found in the Shōsōin storehouse of the Nara period. The Animal Scrolls are also interesting from the standpoint of social history, for they contain a number of scenes in which animals, representing people, are shown satirizing contemporary life, particularly the corrupt ways of some members of the Buddhist priesthood. One especially blasphemous scene shows a monkey, garbed like a priest, paying ceremonial homage to a giant frog of a buddha who is seated on a temporary outdoor altar (fig. 29).

Fig. 28   Scene from the Animal Scrolls *(Benrido Company)*

Fig. 29   Scene from the Animal Scrolls *(Benrido Company)*

Emaki were produced during the next few centuries on a variety of themes, including battles, the lives of famous priests, and the histories of noted temples. One of the finest of these is the Tale of Heiji Scroll, which deals with the conflict in 1159 (known as the Heiji Conflict) in which the Ise Taira under Kiyomori vanquished their Minamoto rivals and began their rise to power in Kyoto (fig. 30). The scroll is actually in three parts, the first of which is a long, panoramic view of the Burning of the Sanjō Palace, during which the Minamoto kidnaped the abdicated emperor Go-shirakawa (1127–92) and precipitated the Heiji Conflict. This part of the Heiji Scroll was obtained by the American Ernest Fenollosa (1853–1908) in the late nineteenth century and placed in the Boston Museum of Fine Arts, where it remains today, one of the most treasured of Japanese art works held outside Japan.

The Burning of the Sanjō Palace depicts, from right to left (all scrolls are "read" from right to left), three scenes: (1) a great horde of people, including warriors and others, rushing to the Palace; (2) Minamoto wreaking destruction and havoc in the palace, from which smoke and flames billow; and (3) Minamoto escorting the carriage of the abdicated emperor from the palace. Although I speak here of three scenes, the Burning of the Sanjō Palace is, in fact, presented as a single panorama. The scroll's anonymous artist has brought the three separate scenes together in a continuous flow by using the device, found in some scrolls, of showing different moments of time as though they were occurring simultaneously. By means of this device, a person can, for example, appear two or three times in the same panorama.

Stylistically, the Heiji Scroll—particularly its first part, the Burning of the Sanjō Palace—shows the extraordinary skill of Japanese artists of the time (it was painted in the thirteenth century) in capturing people, especially groups of people, in action. From the standpoint of military history, the Heiji Scroll is one of the earliest pictorial records we have of the samurai, their mounts, armor, weapons, and methods of fighting.

There will be occasion in the next chapter to comment on one or two more *emaki* as they appear in the development of medieval culture.

Fig. 30 "Burning of the Sanjō Palace": a scene from the Heiji Scroll depicting fighting between the Minamoto and Taira in 1159 (*Museum of Fine Arts, Boston*)

5

The Canons of Medieval Taste

THE CHIEFTAIN WHO EMERGED during the course of the Minamoto-Taira War of 1180–85 as the supreme commander of Minamoto forces was Yoritomo (1147–99). Unlike Kiyomori, the Taira leader who died in 1181, the second year of the war, Yoritomo deliberately avoided entanglement in court politics in Kyoto. Instead, he remained at Kamakura, his base in the Kantō, throughout the war, treating the pursuit and destruction of the Ise Taira as secondary to the establishment of control over the eastern heartland of samurai society.

The government that Yoritomo founded at Kamakura is known in English as the shogunate, after the title of shogun ("generalissimo") that the Minamoto chieftain received from the imperial court. Creation of this exclusively military organization marked the beginning of the medieval era of Japanese history, an era that lasted until the commencement of early modern times at the end of the sixteenth century.

There is no question that the Kamakura shogunate represented a radically new form of government in Japan, situated far from the traditional seat of courtier authority in the central provinces and staffed by warriors who were related by feudal ties of personal loyalties. Yet the shogunate was in no sense a rebel regime; on the contrary, it was founded and operated in an entirely "legitimate" fashion. Yoritomo, who remained ever deferential in his formal dealings with the court, was careful to secure imperial sanctification both for his own position and for the important administrative acts of the new shogunate, such as the expansion of its power to the national level through the appointment of Minamoto vassals as land stewards and constables to estates and provinces throughout the country.

The fighting between Taira and Minamoto that led to defeat of the former and ushered in the medieval era (the first part of which, 1185–1333, is also designated the Kamakura period) is most vividly retold in *The Tale of the Heike*. But there is another book, written in the early thirteenth century by Kamo no Chōmei (1153–1216), a former courtier turned religious recluse, that is also an important literary account of this pivotal epoch in Japanese history. Chōmei's work, the *Hōjōki (An Account of a Ten-foot-square Hut)*, is a brief miscellany written in essentially the same style of classical Japanese as *The Tale of the Heike*. Like the *Heike*, it has a famous opening passage, which speaks about the insubstantiality of life and about a world that is ever in flux:

> The flow of the river is ceaseless and its water is never the same. The bubbles that float in the pools, now vanishing, now forming, are not of long duration: so in the world are man and his dwellings. It might be imagined that the houses, great and small, which vie roof against proud roof in the capital remain unchanged from one generation to the next, but when we examine whether this is true, how few are the houses that were there of old. Some were burnt last year and only since rebuilt; great houses have crumbled into hovels and those who dwell in them have fallen no less. The city is the same, the people are as numerous as ever, but of those I used to know, a bare one or two in twenty remain. They die in the morning, they are born in the evening, like foam on the water.[1]

Yet, unlike the *Heike*, the *Hōjōki* makes no direct mention of the struggle between Taira and Minamoto waged in the early 1180s but instead describes the series of disasters—some natural, others induced by the war—that struck the capital during these years. (Among the disasters were fire, whirlwind, famine, and earthquake.) The *Hōjōki* also presents in Buddhist terms a pessimistic view of this existence as a place of foulness and suffering that is perhaps even more emphatic than the one given in the *Heike*. The phrase "ten-foot-square hut" refers to the exceedingly modest dwelling on a mountain outside the capital that Chōmei finally constructs for his home in the effort to renounce all worldly attachments and thus prepare himself for entry into Amida's Pure Land paradise upon death. In the end, however, he sadly admits that he has failed to find complete release from earthly things and, in fact, has become attached even to his little hut. As William La Fleur has discussed, the hut recurs throughout the *Hōjōki* as a carefully crafted metaphor for the Buddhist idea of impermanence and, indeed, for life itself, which, in all its aspects, is fleeting and uncertain.[2]

The recluse retiring to a hut in the wilderness or away from areas of human habitation is a familiar figure in Chinese history, literature, and art, found most conspicuously perhaps in the guise of the Taoist who leaves society and seeks to become one with nature. Recluses and huts also appear in earlier Japanese literature, but it was the *Hōjōki* that established them—especially the hut—as medieval ideals. For Kamo no Chōmei, the construction of a hut of absolute minimum size and quality represented his rejection of materialism to make himself ready, as just noted, for Amida's Pure Land paradise. But even in Chōmei we can observe a tendency to transform what is supposed to be a mean hovel into something of beauty based on an aesthetic taste for "deprivation" (to be discussed later in this chapter) that evolved during medieval times. How

Chōmei the poet aestheticized his hut, perhaps unconsciously, can be observed in the following partial description of it from the *Hōjōki:*

> I laid a foundation and roughly thatched roof. I fastened hinges to the joints of the beams, the easier to move elsewhere should anything displease me. . . . Since first I hid my traces here in the heart of Mount Hino, I have added a lean-to on the south and a porch of bamboo. On the west I have built a shelf for holy water, and inside the hut, along the west wall, I have installed an image of Amida. . . . Above the sliding door that faces north I have built a little shelf on which I keep three or four black leather baskets that contain books of poetry and music and extracts from the sacred writings. Beside them stand a folding *koto* and a lute.
>
> Along the east wall I have spread long fern fronds and mats of straw, which serve as my bed for the night. I have cut open a window in the eastern wall, and beneath it have made a desk. Near my pillow is a square brazier in which I burn brushwood. To the north of the hut I have staked out a small plot of land that I have enclosed with a rough fence and made into a garden. I grow many species of herbs there.[3]

The medieval ideal of the hut reached its climax, spiritually and aesthetically, in the tea ceremony, which was created, as we will see, primarily in the fifteenth and sixteenth centuries. Under the influence of Buddhism (especially Zen Buddhism), the tea master built his teahouse on the model of the peasant hut. And even when the teahouse/hut was situated in a city, such as Kyoto or Nara, it was styled as though—and provided with natural surroundings to give the impression that—it was in a remote "mountain village" *(yamazato)*. The tea master assumed the role of one who has withdrawn from the world and, in a minimalist structure far from the bustle of urban society, seeks to achieve spiritual tranquility, if not enlightenment, through the enjoyment of tea. Inasmuch as the tea ceremony was as thoroughly aesthetic as it was spiritual, the master's hut became, in its arrangement and appointments, the principal manifestation of his conception of "deprived beauty."

An event during the war that was especially shocking to contemporaries was the wanton destruction by the Taira of the Tōdaiji Temple in Nara. The Tōdaiji, it will be recalled, had been constructed under imperial auspices in the mid-eighth century to serve as one of the principal symbols of centralized court rule in Japan. Its loss must have struck many as an irrefutable sign that the country had come to final disaster in the age of *mappō*. Yet, tragic though it was, the burning of the Tōdaiji actually stimulated a minor renaissance in the art of the Nara period.

This renaissance came about when, shortly after the end of hostilities between the Taira and Minamoto in 1185, a drive was undertaken to raise funds for rebuilding the Tōdaiji. Generous contributions were acquired from members of both the courtier and warrior elites, including the new ruler of Kamakura, Yoritomo. Before long, Nara was bustling with activity, as work was begun at the sites of both the Tōdaiji and the Kōfukuji, another major temple devastated by the Taira. Jobs were made available to artists and craftsmen, and new attention was focused on the former seat of imperial rule and its art treasures.

The Nara renaissance of the late twelfth century gave particular opportunity for fame to a group of scholars known as the "kei" school (from the fact that its members all used "kei" in their assumed names). The most distinguished member of this school was Unkei (dates unknown), whose familiarity with the Tempyō art of his native Nara is evident in such realistic pieces as the statues in wood at the Kōfukuji of two historical personages of Indian Buddhism. Stylistically, the statues are reminiscent of the dry lacquer image, noted in Chapter 2, of the blind priest Ganjin, who emigrated from China in the eighth century to found one of the "six sects" of Nara Buddhism.

Although not a member of the warrior class, Unkei has been called a samurai sculptor because most of his surviving works seem to be imbued with the vigor and strength of the new military age. No doubt these general qualities of vigor and strength, so different from the softness and even femininity of Fujiwara art, derived at least in part from Unkei's familiarity with the styles of other, earlier art epochs, including Jōgan (early Heian) as well as Tempyō. Yet, in the minds of many critics, Unkei was also deeply influenced as an artist by his exposure to warrior life in Kamakura, which he visited to do work on commission for high officers of the shogunate. Hence, one may well choose to regard as "samurai pieces" such realistically detailed and dynamically postured statues as the two guardian deities at the Tōdaiji (attributed to Unkei and another member of his school, Kaikei [dates unknown]).

Despite the achievements of Unkei, his colleagues, and some of his successors, sculpture—and especially religious sculpture—declined steadily during the Kamakura period and never again became a major art in Japan. Probably the chief reason for this was that some medieval sects of Buddhism strongly de-emphasized iconography and the use of art for strictly religious purposes.

Like Buddhist sculpture, Buddhist painting also steadily gave ground to secular art in medieval times. One of the most significant developments in painting was in the field of realistic portraiture. So far as we know, Heian artists had made no attempt to depict the actual likenesses of real people. Some scholars suggest that this was largely because the deeply superstitious courtiers feared that portraits might be used for the casting of evil spells. In any case, it was not until about the time of the struggles between the Taira and the Minamoto that the earliest portraits were done. Among the best known is one of Yoritomo by an artist of the Fujiwara clan.

The founding of the Kamakura shogunate did not cause the immediate fossilization of the imperial court as a governing body. Indeed, the court retained certain residual powers for at least another century and a half (for example, it continued to appoint governors who operated side by side in the provinces with the military constables); and when the shogunate was overthrown in 1333, an emperor even attempted to restore the throne to a position of absolute rulership in the country.

But the trend during the medieval age was inexorably toward the imposition of feudal control at every level of society. And from the outset of the age we find a despairing awareness among the courtiers that their days of splendor as a ruling elite could never be revived. Increasingly deprived of political power, the courtiers became ever more covetous of their role as the custodians of traditional culture. This can perhaps best be seen in the realm of poetry, long the most esteemed of the gentle pursuits. Some skill in *waka* versification had of course been mandatory for members of the courtier class throughout most of the Heian period. In the medieval age, it became a way of life for its chief practitioners, who formed exclusive cliques and entered into fierce rivalries over issues involving minute differences in style, choice of words, and appropriate poetic topics.

Needless to say, medieval poets never used *waka* to describe the fighting and disorder that accompanied the rise of the samurai to power. But the sentiments they sought to express were nevertheless far darker and more deeply moving than those of their predecessors a century or so earlier. Here, for example, are two poems from the *Shinkokinshū* (New *Kokinshū*), compiled about 1205 and usually regarded as the last of the great imperially authorized anthologies.

> In a tree standing
> Beside a desolate field,
> The voice of a dove
> Calling to its companions—
> Lonely, terrible evening.

> Even to someone
> Free of passions this sadness
> Would be apparent:
> Evening in autumn over
> A marsh where a snipe rises.[4]

These two poems are by Saigyō (1118–90), a leading contributor to the *Shinkokinshū* and, in the minds of many, one of the finest poets in Japanese history. A man of warrior background who became a Buddhist priest, Saigyō is perhaps best remembered as the first of the great traveling poets. During the Heian period, few among the upper levels of Kyoto society aspired to travel into the provinces, and such travel was usually undertaken only when unavoidable. But with the coming of the medieval age there was a reaction against the overly urban-centered culture of Heian times, and poets and other men of the arts like Saigyō, not content with just imagining what the famous sites looked like, set off on journeys to see them with their own eyes. It also became customary for people of this sort to take Buddhist vows and become priestlike *inja* or "those who have withdrawn from society."

In this way a tradition of travel became associated with the arts in medieval times. Poets like Saigyō and the fifteenth-century linked-verse master Sōgi (1421–1502) became particularly renowned as travelers; but there were others, such as the painter Sesshū (1420–1506), a contemporary of Sōgi, whose art was also greatly enriched by travel. To the medieval Japanese, traveling symbolized the Buddhist sense of impermanence *(mujō)* that was felt so deeply during this age; and travelers, conceived as men who leave society behind to wander to distant, lonely places, were thought to experience more fully the true nature of life itself.

In the second of the two poems above by Saigyō, we are informed of the poignant fact that even a person "free of passions" (that is, one who has taken Buddhist vows and renounced worldly feelings) experiences sadness when he views a bleak autumn scene at evening as a solitary snipe rises from a marsh. The word translated as sadness is *aware*, which, as we saw in Chapter 3, connotes the capacity to be moved by things. In the period of the *Shinkokinshū*, when Saigyō lived, this sentiment was particularly linked with the aesthetic of *sabi* or "loneliness" (and, by association, sadness). The human condition was essentially one of loneliness; but, however painful the awareness of that might be, the medieval Japanese were able to realize some consolation in the beauty of *sabi*, which they found in such things as a desolate field or a monochromatic, withered marsh.

The poets of the Kamakura period, as implied in the title *New Kokinshū*, were inclined more and more to look to the past for inspiration. They admired particularly the poems of the tenth-century anthology *Kokinshū*, but were also influenced to a greater degree than before by the monumental *Man'yōshū* of the Nara period. We observed that the *Man'yōshū*, written by means of a complex use of Chinese characters to reproduce the sounds of Japanese, was excessively recondite for the Heian period courtiers. It is estimated that before the medieval age only a few hundred of its more than 4,500 poems could be fully understood.[5] But with the renewal of scholarship in Japan in late Heian times, there was a revival of interest in and study of the *Man'yōshū;* and during the thirteenth century, a Tendai priest named Senkaku (1203–?) produced the first complete *Man'yōshū* commentary.

A principal compiler of the *Shinkokinshū* and, along with Saigyō, one of the most distinguished poets of the age was Fujiwara Teika (1162–1241). Of all the courtiers of the early Kamakura period, Teika is the best known for his desire to escape from reality into the realm of art.

Upon hearing of Minamoto Yoritomo's rising against the Taira in 1180, for example, Teika noted in his diary that, although his ears were assailed by news of military rebellion and chastisement, such events were of no concern to him. The only thing he wished to do was to compose supremely beautiful *waka*.

In at least one respect, Teika was a product of his age: he was an outstanding scholar as well as poet. Moreover, he was instrumental in setting forth and applying the aesthetic principles that were largely to dictate the tastes of the medieval era. We have just remarked the use of *sabi*. Another major term of the new medieval aesthetics was *yūgen*, which can be translated as "mystery and depth." Let us first examine the "depth" element of *yūgen* as it was conceived by Teika and the other *Shinkokinshū* poets.

One of the basic values in the Japanese aesthetic tradition—along with such things as perishability, naturalness, and simplicity—is suggestion. The Japanese have from earliest times shown a distinct preference for the subtleties of suggestion, intimation, and nuance, and have characteristically sought to achieve artistic effect by means of "resonances" *(yojō)*. In the period of the *Shinkokinshū*, the idea of creating resonances or depth of poetic expression through suggestion was praised to the point of making it virtually the supreme consideration of the poet. The thirty-one-syllable *waka* form of poetry was thus extolled precisely because its brevity demanded resonances and the quality of depth. This sentiment was beautifully articulated by the priest Shun'e (fl. ca. 1160–80):

> It is only when many meanings are compressed into a single word, when the depths of feelings are exhausted yet not expressed, when an unseen world hovers in the atmosphere of the poem, when the mean and common are used to express the elegant, when a poetic conception of rare beauty is developed to the fullest extent in a style of surface simplicity—only then, when the conception is exalted to the highest degree and "the words are too few," will the poem, by expressing one's feelings in this way, have the power of moving Heaven and Earth within the brief confines of thirty-one syllables and be capable of softening the hearts of gods and demons.[6]

In addition to his remarks about the power of words that are "too few," Shun'e makes reference to "an unseen world [that] hovers in the atmosphere of [a] poem." It is this unseen world or sense of atmosphere that constitutes the second element of *yūgen:* mystery. The following poem by Fujiwara Teika well illustrates both the mystery and depth of *yūgen.*

> When the floating bridge
> Of the dream of a spring night
> Was snapped, I woke:
> In the sky a bank of clouds
> Was drawing away from the peak.[7]

In Japanese poetry the dream is often used to create the atmospheric (mysterious) quality of Shun'e's unseen world; and, in this particular poem, strong resonances are brought into play by the words "floating bridge" and "dream," which allude to the last chapter of *The Tale of Genji,* "The Floating Bridge of Dreams," and thus conjure up the brilliant world of romance, love, and beauty that the *Genji* exemplified in the tradition of courtly culture.

While certain courtiers like Teika attempted to evade the realities of the new age by devoting themselves single-mindedly to the traditional arts, other individuals were drawn into the great movements of religious conversion that occurred in the late twelfth and thirteenth centuries. There had been a scattering of evangelists from at least the eighth century in Japan who had traveled into the provinces bearing the gospel and helping with the building of bridges, the digging of wells, and other public works. In the Heian period the priest Kūya (903–72) became especially famous as a popularizer of Amidism. He danced through the streets and sang songs such as this:

> He never fails
> To reach the Lotus Land of Bliss
> Who calls,
> If only once,
> The name of Amida.[8]

But not until the Kamakura period was Buddhism finally carried to all corners of the country.

Amidism had appealed to the Heian courtiers in part because of the opportunity it gave them to reproduce in literature and art the blisses of the pure land and the joy of Amida's descent to greet those about to enter it. Yet the *nembutsu,* or invocation of Amida's name, had simply been one of a number of practices followed by the doctrinally catholic adherents of Tendai Buddhism; and Amidism was not established as a separate sect until the time of the evangelist Hōnen (1133–1212).

Like all the great religious leaders of the Kamakura period, Hōnen received his early priestly training at the Tendai center on Mount Hiei. He found himself, however, increasingly dissatisfied with the older Buddhist methods of seeking enlightenment or salvation through individual, merit-producing acts, and came to stress utter reliance upon and faith in Amida as the only one able to save men in the corrupt age of *mappō.* Yet, in actual practice, Hōnen did not insist upon *absolute faith* in Amida's saving grace.

One of the most fundamental doctrinal problems in Pure Land Buddhism was whether the *nembutsu*—the calling upon Amida to be saved— should be recited once or many times. Since, theoretically, Amida had vowed to save all those who acknowledged their own helplessness and who threw themselves upon his infinite mercy, one recitation should have sufficed. But there was an apparently natural tendency for some people to believe that they could make their salvation more certain or even achieve a "better salvation" if they repeated the *nembutsu* over and over. The individual who was thus motivated to recite the *nembutsu* continuously was, of course, either consciously or unconsciously guilty of a certain lack of trust in Amida, since he felt the need to bolster his faith through added personal effort. Moreover, if repetition of the *nembutsu* was indeed helpful in the quest for salvation, then those with the greater leisure to practice it would have the best chance to be saved.

It was Hōnen's disciple, Shinran (1173–1262), who finally resolved this problem by asserting that Amida promised salvation unconditionally to all who sincerely called upon him once, whether or not they actually pronounced the *nembutsu* aloud. With salvation assured by this single act, the individual was free to recite the *nembutsu* as often as he wished, but such recitation would then be simply an expression of thanksgiving to Amida, and would in no way modify the already given promise of rebirth in the pure land.

Shinran spent many years in the provinces, especially the Kantō, where he preached his message of salvation through unquestioning faith in Amida. He had particular success as a proselytizer among the peasantry, who formed the nucleus of what came to be known as the True Sect of Pure Land Buddhism. Through the centuries, this sect has attracted one of the largest followings among the Japanese, and its founder, Shinran, has been canonized as one of his country's most original religious thinkers.

Another evangelist of Pure Land Buddhism, active in the late thirteenth century, was Ippen (1239–89), who urged the practice of the "circulating *nembutsu*" or chanting of praise to Amida with and among people everywhere. Although Ippen cannot be ranked in importance with Hōnen and Shinran in the history of Pure Land Buddhism in Japan, he has been immortalized in one of the finest of all medieval *emaki:* the Scroll of Saint Ippen, painted approximately ten years after the evangelist's death.

This scroll is a narrative record of Ippen's travels throughout the country, during the course of which he purportedly gathered the astounding total of some 2.5 million converts to his sect of Amidism. The Ippen Scroll is not only a work of art, it is also an invaluable document of thirteenth-century social history. Artistically, the scroll is perhaps most admired for its landscape background, which, although purely Japanese in subject matter, is executed in a style that shows the strong influence of Sung China. In the fifteenth and sixteenth centuries, as we shall see, Sung painting served as the inspiration for a distinguished line of landscape artists in Japan.

As a social document, the Ippen Scroll contains scenes of virtually every major aspect of life and social activity in the Kamakura period, including people at work and play in the countryside and towns and gathered to meet Ippen at Shinto shrines, Buddhist temples, and the private homes of the well-to-do. In one particularly lively scene from the scroll, Ippen is shown leading a group of followers in the ecstatic practice of the "dancing *nembutsu*": that is, the singing of praise to Amida while dancing and tapping small hand-drums. The dancers are tightly crowded into a small frame structure, elegant carriages are clustered about on the street outside, and highborn ladies can be seen mingling with the townspeople.

Apart from the proponents of Pure Land Buddhism, the person who most forcefully propagated the idea of universal salvation through faith was Nichiren (1222–82). One of the most exceptional and interesting figures in Japanese history, Nichiren founded the only major sect of Buddhism in Japan that did not derive directly from a religious institution already established in China. The chief factor in determining the nature of Nichiren Buddhism was Nichiren's own extraordinary personality. But, in order to understand how and why the sect arose in the mid-thirteenth century, it is essential also to note the particular political and social conditions under which Nichiren grew to maturity.

When the great founder of the Kamakura shogunate, Minamoto Yoritomo, died in 1199, he was succeeded as shogun by a young and ineffectual son. A power struggle soon arose among the leading vassals of the Minamoto, and in the early years of the thirteenth century the Hōjō family, related by marriage to Yoritomo,[9] emerged as the new de facto rulers of the shogunate. But the Hōjō chieftain, in characteristic Japanese fashion, sought to avoid being stigmatized as a mere power seeker by assuming the rather modest-sounding title of shogunal regent and by designating an infant of the courtier clan of Fujiwara to occupy the high, but now politically impotent, office of shogun.[10]

While the Hōjō were consolidating their position at Kamakura, a certain former emperor in Kyoto organized a plot to overthrow the shogunate, which seemed so torn with internal strife after Yoritomo's death. In 1221 the former emperor branded the Hōjō regent a rebel and called upon people everywhere to rise and destroy the shogunate. But the Hōjō, acting decisively, sent an army to Kyoto that swiftly overran the former emperor's poorly organized troops.[11]

This brief clash of arms was a great blow to the ancien régime in Kyoto, even though many members of the courtier class had refused to join the former emperor's cause. As victors, the Hōjō were able to confiscate thousands of additional estate holdings for distribution among their samurai followers and to appoint many new military officials throughout the country. Moreover, the Hōjō from this time on not only dictated to a far greater degree than before the conduct of affairs at court, but even assumed the right to decide the line of succession to the throne.

Nichiren was born in a fishing village in the Kantō the year after the former emperor's disastrously unsuccessful attempt to overthrow the Hōjō. He went through his formative years in an age when the fortunes of the imperial court and those institutions that supported it, including the Tendai and Shingon churches, were far lower than they had been during the youth of Hōnen or even of Shinran. Nichiren appears, moreover, to have been more profoundly affected by the concept of *mappō* than probably any other religious leader of the Kamakura period. After a number of years of study at the Tendai center on Mount Hiei and elsewhere, he formed an apocalyptic view of the deterioration of Japan from within and its destruction from without. An exceptionally large number of natural disasters appeared during the mid-thirteenth century to confirm his prediction of internal deterioration; and the two attempts of the Mongols to invade Japan in 1274 and 1281, although unsuccessful, seemed to be chilling portents that the country might indeed be overwhelmed by forces from outside its borders.

Nichiren asserted in loudly militant and shockingly intemperate language that Japan was suffering such agonies because of the false doctrines of other Buddhist sects and the vile ways of those who propagated them. Thus, for example, he labeled Kūkai "the greatest liar in Japan" and the adherents to Shingon, Kūkai's sect, "traitors." He regarded Zen as "a doctrine of fiends and devils"; he called the followers of Ritsu, one of the Nara-period sects, "brigands"; and he considered the *nembutsu* "a hellish practice."[12] When asked by the Hōjō regent how Japan might defend against the pending Mongol invasion (the first invasion), Nichiren replied that the shogunate should crush the other Buddhist sects, inasmuch as they had weakened and corrupted Japan to the point that it was vulnerable to invasion. Upon hearing later that Mongol envoys to Japan had been executed, Nichiren said: "It is a great pity that they should have cut off the heads of the innocent Mongols and left unharmed the priests of the *nembutsu*, Shingon, Zen, and Ritsu, who are the enemies of Japan."[13]

Nichiren held that ultimate religious truth lay solely in the *Lotus Sutra*, the basic text of the Greater Vehicle of Buddhism in which Gautama had revealed that all beings possess the potentiality for buddhahood. At the time of its founding in Japan by Saichō in the early ninth century, the Tendai sect had been based primarily on the *Lotus Sutra;* but, in the intervening centuries, Tendai had deviated from the *Sutra's* teachings and had even spawned new sects, like those of Pure Land Buddhism, that encouraged practices entirely at variance with these teachings.

As a result of his virulent attacks on the other sects of Buddhism and his criticism of the conduct of national affairs, Nichiren was often in trouble with the shogunate authorities, was in fact twice exiled from Kamakura, and was even sentenced to death. Still, he continued to insist that salvation for mankind and for Japan could only be achieved through absolute faith in the *Lotus Sutra*. He preached that, for the individual, there was no need to attempt to read and understand the *Sutra;* buddhahood was attainable simply through recitation of the formula, reminiscent of the *nembutsu*, of "Praise to the Wonderful Law of the *Lotus Sutra.*"

Nichiren's name is written with the characters for "sun" and "lotus." Lotus, of course, represents the *Lotus Sutra*, whereas sun stands for Japan. Nichiren came to envision that, when the age of *mappō* reached its cataclysmic end (which he believed was very near), a great new Buddhist era would commence in which Japan would become the central Buddhist see in the world and in which he, Nichiren, would play a founding role in religious history similar to that of Gautama.

This kind of Japan-centered millennial thinking has led a number of commentators to claim that Nichiren was the first nationalist in Japanese history. Although "nationalist" is probably too modern a term to apply to a person of the thirteenth century, Nichiren certainly had a consciousness of country that set him apart from the other Buddhist leaders of the age. Declaring himself "the pillar of Japan, the eye of the nation, and the vessel of the country,"[14] Nichiren seems even to have equated himself with Japan and its fate.

The last of the so-called new sects of Kamakura Buddhism was Zen, which like Amidism had long been known to the Japanese but was not established independently in Japan until the early medieval age. Zen means "meditation," and meditation—particularly in the cross-legged yogic position—is one of the most fundamental practices in Buddhism. Gautama, in fact, is purported to have achieved his own enlightenment while in a deep meditative state. In Zen, enlightenment *(satori)* may be interpreted as the final realization that a person's suffering stems from the striving for such things as wealth and power that appear to be real, but actually are illusory. Unlike the salvationist sects of Pure Land and Nichiren Buddhism, which called upon the individual to escape from suffering by placing faith completely in some other being or thing (Amida or the *Lotus Sutra*), Zen encouraged the seeking of personal enlightenment—that is, the realization of one's buddha nature—through discipline and effort.

Tradition has it that Zen, which is pronounced Ch'an in Chinese, was first introduced to China from India in the sixth century by a priest named Bodhidharma. We are told that when Bodhidharma met the Chinese Emperor Wu, this conversation occurred:

Emperor Wu:	"Since my enthronement I have built many monasteries, had many scriptures copied, and had many monks and nuns invested. How great is the merit thus achieved?"
Bodhidharma:	"No merit at all."
Emperor Wu:	"What is the Noble Truth in its highest sense?"
Bodhidharma:	"It is empty, no nobility whatever."
Emperor Wu:	"Who is it then that is facing me?"
Bodhidharma:	"I do not know sire."[15]

We are further told that Bodhidharma later sat facing a wall in meditation for nine years. To prevent himself from sleeping, he cut off his eyelids; and from the long, uninterrupted sitting, his legs withered and fell off. We see Bodhidharma today in Japan in the popular Daruma doll with its legless, oval shape and huge, staring eyes.

Emperor Wu understandably regarded Bodhidharma's responses to his questions as nonsensical, presumably not realizing that, in fact, they expressed the essence of Zen. In Zen, enlightenment is sought by dispelling delusion, and that which deludes people most is language. Described as "a special transmission outside the scriptures," Zen rejects—or at least seeks to hold to a minimum—the use of words, both spoken and written. It stresses instead the intuitive, calling for "use of the heart (or mind) to transmit the heart (or mind)" and for "direct pointing to the soul of man." Bodhidharma's apparently nonsensical responses to Emperor Wu's questions can be taken to mean that there is no rationally meaningful answer to anything. Like Bodhidharma, a later Zen master was thus likely to reply to an inquiry from a disciple about, say, the nature of *satori* or enlightenment with a phrase such as "Three pounds of flax!" or "Go wash your bowl!"

From such exchanges as the above between master and disciple, there developed the device of the *kōan* or problem presented to the disciple in the form of a question that cannot be rationally or logically answered and is intended to force the disciple to find an "answer" in some other way. In time a series of *kōan* and what were considered their correct answers were worked out to provide uniform training. Here are two *kōan* and their answers:

Q: "In what way do my feet resemble the feet of a donkey?"

A: "When the heron stands in the snow, its color is not the same."

Q: "Everyone has a native place owing to his karma. Where is your native place?"

A: "Early in the morning I ate white rice gruel; now I feel hungry again."[16]

The *kōan* is especially favored by what the Japanese call the Rinzai sect of Zen, which is also known as the school of "sudden enlightenment" because of its belief that *satori*, if it is attained, will come to the individual in an instantaneous flash of insight or awareness. The other major sect of Zen, Sōtō, rejects this idea of sudden enlightenment and instead holds that *satori* is a gradual process to be attained primarily through seated meditation.

Because of its stress on self-discipline and control, Zen seemed particularly appropriate as a creed for the warriors of medieval Japan, and eventually it did exert a strong influence on the molding of the samurai way of life. But there is danger in overestimating the degree to which Zen was embraced as a religion by the medieval samurai. For all its anti-intellectual claims to simplicity and directness of communication, Zen was more attractive to the sophisticated than to the uncultivated mind. The vast majority of medieval samurai were rough, unlettered men engaged in a brutal profession, and they sought their religious solace chiefly in the salvationist sects. Zen appealed primarily to the ruling members of samurai society.

The influence of Zen spread far beyond the realm of religion in medieval times; indeed, it can be argued that its principal role was not in religion but in aesthetics and the arts. In China during the Sung period, Zen (Ch'an) priests had become prominent figures in literature, painting, and the other arts, even though such activity was contradictory to their religious beliefs, especially the conviction that language is the main cause of delusion. In any case, the Zen that was brought to Japan in its medieval age became the carrier for a new wave of borrowing from China that included poetry and prose in Chinese and painting in the Sung monochromatic ink style *(sumi-e)*. In addition, Zen priests imported many works of art and calligraphy as well as articles of craft, such as ceramics and lacquerware. Medieval Zen priests also became the main agents, as we will see in Chapter 7, for transmission of the tenets of Neo-Confucianism, which had been developing in China throughout the Sung period.

The Hōjō regents were particularly enthusiastic patrons of Zen and sought to make Kamakura its center as part of a larger effort to elevate the cultural life of the new military capital. One way in which the Hōjō promoted Zen was by welcoming to Kamakura prominent Zen (Ch'an) priests who fled China as it came under the control of invading Mongols in the thirteenth century (the Sung dynasty was finally overthrown by the Mongols in 1279). These Chinese priests became the leaders of the Zen establishment in Kamakura and served as the founding abbots of such great Zen temples as Kenchōji and Engakuji. In the fourteenth century, when the Kamakura shogunate was destroyed and the seat of military power was shifted to Kyoto upon the founding of the Ashikaga or Muromachi shogunate (1336–1573), Kyoto superseded Kamakura as the country's Zen center. But the Kamakura period remained the time when Zen, emanating from Kamakura, was probably propagated in its purest form. Once Kyoto became its principal home, Zen was strongly influenced by the older Buddhist traditions of the imperial capital, especially Shingon.

On the whole, the Hōjō regents exercised firm and just rule over samurai society through most of the thirteenth century. Unlike Minamoto Yoritomo, who had governed in a highly autocratic way, the Hōjō opened a Council of State to enable chieftains of the other great samurai families of the east to participate in the decision making of the shogunate. Moreover, the Hōjō based their rule on an epochal formulary, the Jōei Code of 1232, which contained detailed provisions dealing with those matters that were of most concern to the members of a warrior class, including the duties of land stewards and constables, the distribution of fiefs, and the settlement of armed disputes.

Even while the Hōjō were thus placing the shogunate on a firm institutional basis, events were occurring on the continent that were to present Japan with its only major foreign threat in premodern historical times. In the early thirteenth century, the Mongols under Chingghis Khan assembled one of the greatest empires in the history of the world, conquering North China and extending their territorial control across Asia and into eastern Europe. After Chingghis's death, the Chinese portion of his empire was inherited by his grandson Khubilai Khan. It took Khubilai until 1279 to destroy the Southern Sung and to unite all of China under the Yüan or "Original" dynasty (1270–1368). But even before this final achievement, Khubilai sought to bring Japan into a subservient, tributary relationship. The other countries of East Asia had long accepted as a matter of course such a relationship with the mighty Middle Kingdom of China, but the Japanese from at least the time of Prince Shōtoku in the early seventh century had steadfastly resisted being drawn into it.

When the Japanese steadfastly refused to submit—indeed, even to respond—to Khubilai's imperious and threatening demands, the Mongol leader launched two great armadas against them in 1274 and 1281. In the first invasion the Mongol force numbered some 90,000, and in the second nearly 140,000. Both invasions took place in northern Kyushu, which was defended by the samurai of that westernmost island, and both failed—the first after only one day and the second after nearly two months

—because of typhoons that forced the Mongols back onto their ships, out to open water, and subsequently, after severe losses (especially during the storm of 1281), back to the continent.[17]

In the second invasion, the Kyushu samurai were better able to defend themselves because they had built a protective stone wall (about three meters high) around Hakata Bay, where the Mongols had landed in the first invasion and were likely to try to land in the second, and because they had prepared a fleet of small boats that they sent out to harass and, in some cases, even board the larger Mongol troop ships. But in the first invasion the discrepancy in fighting methods and power in favor of the Mongols was such that the Japanese would probably have been decisively defeated if a storm had not fortuitously blown up on the very first—and, as a result, only—day of the invasion.

The samurai were accustomed to firing signal arrows to announce the commencement of battle and then to pairing off to fight one against one, all the while shouting out their names and pedigrees. Here, according to a Japanese source, is how the Mongols responded to this style of fighting during the first invasion:

> The Mongols disembarked, mounted their horses, raised their banners, and began to attack. . . . [One Japanese] . . . shot a whistling arrow to open the exchange. All at once the Mongols down to the last man started laughing. The Mongols struck large drums and hit gongs so many times . . . that they frightened the Japanese horses and they could not be controlled. The Japanese forgot about handling their horses and facing the enemy. . . . [The Mongol] general climbed to a high spot and, when retreat was in order, beat the retreat drum. When they needed to race forward, he rang the attack gong. According to these signals, they did battle. . . . Whereas we [Japanese] thought about reciting our pedigrees to each other and battling man to man in glory or defeat as was the custom of Japanese armies, in this battle the Mongols assembled at one point in a great force.[18]

Not only were the Mongols better organized for battle, operating in units and using drums and gongs for signaling, they also employed weapons, including catapults, exploding balls, and poisoned arrows, that were entirely new to the Japanese. The samurai horses, as mentioned in the above passage, were especially frightened by the drums, gongs, and exploding balls. The exploding balls, we may note, provided the Japanese with their first exposure to the use of gunpowder, which had been invented in China.

The colossal force of 140,000 in the second invasion, although it overran several islands, was never able to make a significant landing on Kyushu proper. A major reason for this failure was the lack of coordination between the two units of the Mongol force, one of which set sail from southern Korea and the other from Ningpo in south China; another was the stone wall the Japanese built around Hataka Bay; and still another was the effectiveness of the samurai counterattacks in small boats. Remnants of the stone wall can still be found at Hakata, and we have a splendid representation of it as well as other features of and scenes from the invasions in the famous Mongol Scroll, painted in the late thirteenth century, shortly after the invasions.

One of the most interesting things we learn from the Mongol Scroll is that the Mongols fought mainly on foot: only their commanders appear on horseback in the scroll. Although I speak of the "Mongols," the invading forces also included many Chinese and Koreans. In any case, the image of these invaders presented in the Mongol Scroll is very different from the one we have of the Mongol armies, formed primarily into units of light cavalry, that conquered much of Asia—and even parts of eastern Europe and the Middle East—during the late twelfth and thirteenth centuries.

In the end, it appears to have been the typhoons that defeated the Mongols. To the Japanese, these typhoons were not mere accidents of nature but rather *kamikaze* or "divine winds" sent by the gods to save their country in its hour of greatest peril. Belief in *kamikaze* was part of a great Shinto revival during the Kamakura period, one of the principal claims of which was that the true defenders of Japan were the *kami* of Shinto rather than the deities of Buddhism, as had been maintained by Buddhists for centuries. In later times, the *kamikaze* concept exerted a powerful influence on the Japanese myth—finally shattered in World War II—of national invincibility.

The Mongol threat was an important, but not sole, cause for the decline of the Kamakura shogunate in the late thirteenth and early fourteenth centuries. Another was the emergence in various regions of the country of new warrior bands that the shogunate, organized originally as a military hegemony over the eastern provinces, found increasingly difficult to control. Still another was a succession dispute that erupted between two branches of the imperial family about the time of the invasions.

This dispute appeared at first to be of little significance, since the Hōjō had stripped the imperial family of nearly all political power a half-century earlier; and an agreement by which the so-called senior and junior branches of the family alternately provided candidates for the emperorship worked tolerably well for a number of years. Then, in 1318, Godaigo (1288–1339), a most forceful and headstrong member of the junior branch, ascended the throne and determined not only to transmit the line of succession exclusively to his own descendants but also to restore the throne to real power.

Godaigo's restorationist or loyalist movement was successful in 1333 when the forces that rallied to him, including both courtiers and samurai, overthrew the Kamakura shogunate and gave the emperor the opportunity to rule, as well as reign, that he had long sought. But the Restoration of Godaigo lasted a scant three years and was a generally reactionary and impractical attempt to turn the course of history back to the early Heian period, before power was first taken from the throne by the Fujiwara regents.

Totally unable to meet the real governing needs of the medieval age, the Restoration regime was overthrown in 1336 by Ashikaga Takauji (1305–58), the chieftain of a main branch of the great Minamoto clan. After driving Godaigo and his remnant supporters to refuge in the mountainous region of Yoshino to the south, Takauji placed a member of the senior branch of the imperial family on the throne and established a new military administration in Kyoto, known in history as the Ashikaga or Muromachi shogunate (1336–1573). The first half-century of Muromachi times, 1336 to 1392, is also designated the epoch of the Northern and Southern Courts, inasmuch as Godaigo and his successors maintained an opposition Southern Court at Yoshino during this period that challenged the legitimacy of what it regarded as the puppet Northern Court of the Ashikaga in Kyoto.

The era of the Restoration and of fighting between the Northern and Southern Courts was one of great confusion and deeply divided loyalties. It also marked the last time in premodern history that either the throne or the courtier class played an active role in the rulership of Japan. In 1392 the Ashikaga, promising a return to the earlier practice of alternate succession, persuaded the Southern emperor (Godaigo's grandson) to return to Kyoto and thus brought to an end the great dynastic schism. In fact, the Ashikaga never kept their promise about returning to alternate succession and the southern branch of the imperial family slipped into oblivion. Even the northern branch, although left in possession of the throne, retained no governing authority whatever, and from this time on the emperorship was little more than a legitimating talisman for the rule of successive military houses.

Probably the single most important historical record of the fourteenth century is a lengthy war tale, covering the period from about 1318 to 1368, with the incongruous-sounding title of *Taiheiki* or *Chronicle of Great Peace*. Although unquestionably inferior in literary quality to *The Tale of the Heike*, the *Taiheiki* has in some respects had a more profound influence on the way in which the Japanese have viewed their premodern age of the samurai. Like *The Tale of the Heike*, the *Taiheiki* has also been a rich source for itinerant storytellers and chanters, and in subsequent centuries its most exciting episodes became just as familiar to Japanese everywhere. But whereas *The Tale of the Heike* has been enjoyed purely as a military epic, the *Taiheiki* has become a kind of sourcebook for modern imperial loyalism.

Although the Southern Court lost in its struggle with the Ashikaga-dominated Northern Court, later generations (after the end of the medieval age) came increasingly to feel that Godaigo, for all his ineptitude in governing during the Restoration, had been wrongfully deprived of his imperial prerogatives by the Ashikaga. These later generations were also deeply stirred by the accounts in the *Taiheiki* of the selfless devotion and sacrifice of the courtiers and samurai who fought for the ill-fated Southern cause. And in the modern era, the Japanese have revered the more prominent of these Southern supporters as the finest examples in their history of unswerving loyalty to the throne. (At the same time, they have regarded Ashikaga Takauji and his chief lieutenants as the most unpardonable of national traitors.)

Of all the Southern Court heroes—indeed, of all the samurai heroes in Japanese history—none has been more revered than Kusunoki Masashige (d. 1336), a local warrior of the central provinces, who joined Godaigo's cause at its beginning and eventually gave his life selflessly for it in battle. In the modern age until the end of World War II in 1945, Masashige was held up as the supreme model of loyalty to the emperor: schoolchildren, reading about his exploits in their texts, idolized him; and *kamikaze* pilots set forth on their suicide missions toward the war's end proclaiming themselves modern-day Masashiges.

According to the *Taiheiki*, Masashige appeared first to Godaigo in a prophetic dream and, upon being summoned, advised the emperor in these words:

"The eastern barbarians (i.e., the forces of the Hōjō), in their recent rebellion, have drawn the censure of heaven. If we take advantage of their weakness, resulting from the decline and disorder they have caused, what difficulty should we have in inflicting heaven's punishment upon them? But the goal of unifying the country must be carried out by means of both military tactics and carefully devised strategy. Even if we fight them force against force and although we recruit warriors throughout the more than sixty provinces of Japan . . . , we will be hard-pressed to win. But if we fight with clever scheming, the military force of the eastern barbarians will be capable of no more than breaking sharp swords and crushing hard helmets. It will be easy to deceive them, and there will be no fear. Since the aim of warfare is ultimate victory, Your Majesty should pay no heed to whether we win or lose in any single battle. So long as you hear that Masashige alone is alive, know that your imperial destiny will in the end be attained."[19]

A master of the style of guerrilla warfare developed by Japanese warriors—especially those of the central and western provinces—from about the time of the Mongol invasions, Masashige shrewdly advises Godaigo to ignore the results of particular battles, since final victory in the war is the only thing that really matters. At the same time, Masashige pledges that, so long as he still lives, the emperor's "imperial destiny . . . will be attained."

It is chiefly Masashige, in fact, who keeps the fires of Godaigo's loyalist movement burning in the central provinces until the anti-Hōjō forces swell to a size sufficient to destroy the Kamakura shogunate, and for his achievements he is well rewarded by the emperor. Later, when Ashikaga Takauji turns against the Restoration, Masashige again rallies to Godaigo's side. But this time, the *Taiheiki* tells us, the emperor ignores Masashige's advice about paying no heed to victory or defeat in any single battle (and the advice's corollary of not risking too much in or expecting too much of any battle) and insists instead that Masashige and other loyalist commanders take a do-or-die stand against Takauji at a place called Minatogawa on the Inland Sea near today's Kobe. Masashige goes to the Battle of Minatogawa in 1336 knowing that he will die; and, when the tide of battle turns against them, he and his brother commit suicide by stabbing each other. Before their deaths, the brothers, in words that were destined to stir the souls of imperial loyalists through the ages, including World War II's *kamikaze* pilots, express their wish "to be reborn again and again for seven lives . . . in order to destroy the enemies of the court!"[20] According to the *Taiheiki*, Godaigo's loyalist movement—his "imperial destiny"—is doomed to final failure in large part because of the emperor's foolhardy refusal to follow the strategy of Kusunoki Masashige.

Another important literary work of the mid-fourteenth century is the *Essays in Idleness (Tsurezuregusa)*, a collection of notes, anecdotes, and personal observations by Yoshida Kenkō (1283–1350), a court poet who took Buddhist vows in his later years. Written about the time of Godaigo's Restoration (although without a word concerning the momentous political and military events of the day), the *Essays in Idleness* is structurally very much like the Heian period miscellany *The Pillow Book*. In content, however, the two books clearly reflect the differences between the ages in which they were written. Whereas *The Pillow Book* is biting, witty, and "up-to-date," Kenkō's work is an elegant expression of the tastes and feelings of a medieval man who possessed both a fine sensitivity for the poignancy of life and the perishability of all things and a profound nostalgia for the customs and ways of the past.

Unlike the author of *Hōjōki* in early Kamakura times, Kenkō was not overcome with anguish by the suffering that accompanies the ceaseless flow and change of life. Indeed, he felt that "the most precious thing in life is its uncertainty," and delighted in something precisely because its beauty promised to be brief or because it already showed signs of fading. Moreover, Kenkō never expressed his love for former times in cloyingly sentimental terms, but with such simple eloquence as:

> In all things I yearn for the past. Modern fashions seem to keep on growing more and more debased. I find that even among the splendid pieces of furniture built by our master cabinetmakers, those in the old forms are the most pleasing. And as for writing letters, surviving scraps from the past reveal how superb the phrasing used to be. The ordinary spoken language has also

steadily coarsened. People used to say "raise the carriage shafts" or "trim the lamp wick," but people today say "raise it" or "trim it."[21]

The *Essays in Idleness* has long been revered by the Japanese as a veritable bible of traditional aesthetics, and indeed Kenkō's tastes were firmly grounded in the basic aesthetic values of the Japanese, including naturalness, simplicity, suggestion, and perishability. But Kenkō may be best remembered for his articulation, in the following famous passage from the *Essays in Idleness,* of still another of these basic values, irregularity or asymmetry, which became increasingly important to the medieval sense of beauty:

> Somebody once remarked that thin silk was not satisfactory as a scroll wrapping because it was so easily torn. Ton'a replied, "It is only after the silk wrapper has frayed at top and bottom, and the mother-of-pearl has fallen from the roller that a scroll looks beautiful." This opinion demonstrated the excellent taste of the man. People often say that a set of books looks ugly if all volumes are not in the same format, but I was impressed to hear the Abbot Kōyū say, "It is typical of the unintelligent man to insist on assembling complete sets of everything. Imperfect sets are better."
>
> In everything, no matter what it may be, uniformity is undesirable. Leaving something incomplete makes it interesting, and gives one the feeling that there is room for growth.[22]

The Muromachi period was the most tumultuous age in Japanese history. During its two and a half centuries, there was almost continuous warfare in one part of the country or another. The third Ashikaga shogun, Yoshimitsu (1358–1408), brought order to much of Japan in the late fourteenth and early fifteenth centuries by skillfully imposing his control over a group of semi-autonomous regional barons or daimyos that emerged out of the fighting between adherents of the Northern and Southern Courts. But after Yoshimitsu's death, the shogunate steadily declined; and for its last hundred years or so it was almost completely powerless as a central government.

Yoshimitsu was not only an outstanding military leader but also a generous and discerning patron of the arts. Presiding in nearly regal fashion over both courtier and warrior elites in Kyoto, he was to a great extent personally responsible for the exceptional flourishing of culture that occurred in his age, known as the Kitayama epoch after the location of his monastic retreat, the Golden Pavilion, in the Northern Hills outside Kyoto (fig. 31).

An important stimulus to Kitayama culture was the renewal by Yoshimitsu of formal contacts with China. Trade and exchange between Japan and China had been minimized during and after the Mongol invasions. But, by the early fourteenth century, animosities had subsided on both sides to the point where Japan's military rulers felt secure in dispatching

Fig. 31   Golden Pavilion *(photograph by Joseph Shulman)*

two trading missions to China (in 1325 and 1341) to acquire funds for the repair of one Zen temple and the construction of another.

In 1368, the same year that Yoshimitsu became shogun, the alien Mongol dynasty of China was overthrown and was replaced by the Ming (1368–1644). Shortly after its founding, the Ming made overtures to Japan requesting aid in the suppression of Japanese-led pirates or *wakō,* who had been marauding the coasts of Korea and China in the century following the Mongol invasions. It was ostensibly in response to these overtures for assistance that Yoshimitsu entered into official relations with the Ming, although privately he was no doubt more strongly motivated to establish such relations from his desire to develop a profitable overseas trade.

Later nationalist historians have roundly denounced Yoshimitsu for accepting a tributary relationship with China of the kind that the Japanese had for some eight hundred years steadfastly rejected, even to the point of precipitating the Mongol invasions a century earlier. Viewed impartially, the missions that were sent periodically to China from Yoshimitsu's time until the end of the Muromachi era were not only commercially profitable, they also provided a steady and highly significant flow of culture from the Ming to medieval Japan.

The Zen temples of Kyoto took the lead in the first phase of intercourse with Ming China. These institutions were excellently suited, owing both to their intimate ties with ruling circles of the shogunate and the general interests and training of their priesthoods, to serve as traders and cultural emissaries to China. One important result of their cultural involvement with China about this time was the production of a large body of literature and scholarship that is rather loosely termed Gozan (Five Zen Temples) literature.[23] Composed entirely in Chinese, the poetry and prose of the leading Gozan writers have been judged by many critics as excessively imitative and pedantic (and far removed from the proper activities of a branch of Buddhism that theoretically eschewed intellectualism and the written word). There can be no question, on the other hand, of the great value of the research and pure scholarship undertaken by the Gozan temples. In addition to exegetical studies on Buddhism and Confucianism, they compiled dictionaries, encyclopedias, and other reference-type materials that provided the groundwork for nearly all subsequent scholarly activity in premodern Japan.

By far the most splendid cultural achievement of the Kitayama epoch was the *nō* ("talent" or "ability") theatre. The precise origins of *nō*, a form of drama based on the dance, are unknown; but it is certain that they were highly diverse, and that *nō* derived from influences both foreign and native, aristocratic and plebeian. Among the earliest of such influences were various types of dance, music, and theatrical entertainment —including juggling, acrobatics, and magic—imported from China during the seventh and eighth centuries. One of these Chinese imports was converted and ossified by the Japanese into a solemn and stately court dance called *bugaku* (done to the accompaniment of *gagaku* or "elegant music"), while others enjoyed only a temporary vogue and declined. Still others, merging with miscellaneous native entertainments and ceremonials, ultimately contributed to the development of *nō*.

The two most popular theatrical forms of the early medieval age were "monkey music" *(sarugaku)* and "field music" *(dengaku)*. Nobody knows the exact meaning of the term "monkey music," although possibly it comes from the comic-like acrobatics and mimicry practiced by *sarugaku* actors. *Dengaku*, on the other hand, was a type of entertainment based originally on the singing and dancing of peasants "in the fields" at harvest festivals.

By the Kitayama epoch, *sarugaku* and *dengaku*, though rivals with their own schools of performers, appear to have influenced each other to the point where they were probably quite similar in actual presentation. We know from the records that both were immensely popular with people in the capital and elsewhere. The last of the Hōjō regents, for example, is reputed to have loved *dengaku* and other diversions so much that he completely neglected his duties at Kamakura; and, in 1349, so many people crowded in to see a *dengaku* performance in Kyoto that the stands collapsed and scores were killed.

The fact that *sarugaku*, rather than *dengaku*, was transformed during the Kitayama epoch into *nō* was partially fortuitous. In 1374 Yoshimitsu attended his first performance of *sarugaku* and was so captivated by two of its actors, Kan'ami (1333–84) and his son Zeami (1363–1443), that henceforth he lavishly patronized their art. This was a most significant event in Japanese cultural history, since without Yoshimitsu's backing the geniuses of Kan'ami and Zeami, who were instrumental in the creation and perfection of *nō*, might have been dissipated on a theatrical form that still catered to rather low and earthy tastes. Given entree to the highest social circles in Kyoto, these two men elevated and refined *sarugaku* to a dramatic art of great beauty and sublimity that could appeal to the most aristocratic of sensibilities.

Kan'ami and Zeami were not only actors but also playwrights; and many of the finest plays in the *nō* repertory can either positively or with reasonable assurance be attributed to their brushes. Zeami, moreover, was an outstanding critic of his day and has left invaluable commentaries on medieval aesthetic and dramatic tastes, tastes that he himself was so influential in molding.

When Zeami first met Yoshimitsu in 1374 he had been a mere child of eleven, and quite likely it was his physical beauty as much as anything that first attracted the shogun, who had a particular fondness for pretty boys. After Yoshimitsu's death in 1408, Zeami and his school of *nō* were temporarily forced into eclipse by those in the shogunate who resented the extraordinary privileges he had previously received. But the popularity of *nō* was by this time too firmly established to be readily destroyed. Before long, it was once again in favor with the Ashikaga shoguns and enjoyed their patronage for the remainder of the medieval age.

Donald Keene has defined *nō* as "a dramatic poem concerned with

Fig. 32   Scene from a *nō* play *(Japan National Tourist Organization)*

remote or supernatural events, performed by a dancer, often masked, who shares with lesser personages and a chorus the singing and declamation of the poetry."[24] The main dancer or actor is known as the *shite,* and the lesser personages include the *waki* or "side person," who usually introduces the play and asks the questions that induce the *shite* to tell his story, and one or more *tsure* (companions) (fig. 32).

To the uninitiated, *nō* can seem painfully slow and its plots so thin as to be almost nonexistent. Moreover, there is little if any attempt made in *nō* to be realistic. It is a theatre of symbolism, employing highly stylized, even ritualistic manners of speech and movement. The very suggestion of realism is often deliberately avoided by having, for example, an old man play the role of a young girl or a little boy that of a great general (all performers in *nō,* incidentally, are males). The *nō* actor is in particular expected to cultivate two qualities: *monomane* or the "imitation of things"; and *yūgen. Monomane* does not of course mean the capacity to act realistically, but to perform the various symbolic movements demanded by the roles of the five categories of *nō* plays—god plays, warrior plays, women plays, miscellaneous plays, and demon plays. Although he regarded mastery of *monomane* as essential, Zeami stressed that the supreme measure of the *nō* actor is his ability to convey the mystery and depth of *yūgen,* one of the most treasured aesthetic values of the medieval age.

Earlier in this chapter I discussed *yūgen* in terms of "mystery" and "depth." Zeami, in one of his critical writings, has this to say about *yūgen:*

> In what sort of place, then, is the stage of *yūgen* actually to be found? Let us begin by examining the various classes of people on the basis of the appearance they make in society. May we not say of the courtiers, whose behavior is distinguished and whose appearance far surpasses that of other men, that theirs is the stage of *yūgen?* From this we may see that the essence of *yūgen* lies in a true state of beauty and gentleness. Tranquility and elegance make for *yūgen* in personal appearance. In the same way, the *yūgen* of discourse lies in a grace of language and a complete mastery of the speech of the nobility and gentry, so that even the most casual utterance will be graceful.[25]

Although Zeami has much more to say about *yūgen* elsewhere, and although, like other aesthetic terms, it is far too complex a concept to be neatly defined in a few lines, it is revealing that, in this passage, Zeami virtually equates *yūgen* with courtliness *(miyabi):* that is, the actor in a *nō* play can convey *yūgen* by looking like, behaving like, and speaking like a courtier.

No words can adequately capture the drama and emotional impact of a *nō* play for the reader who has never actually seen one performed; but a brief description of a play—Zeami's haunting *Nonomiya* or *The Shrine in the Fields*—will at least serve to indicate how a work of this form of medieval Japanese theatre is structured and presented.

The *shite* or protagonist in *The Shrine in the Fields* (a woman play) is a fictional figure from *The Tale of Genji*, Lady Rokujō, a proud and jealous lover of Prince Genji. Like so many other plays in the *nō* repertory, it is opened by an itinerant priest (the *waki*), who announces that he has been visiting the famous sites of Kyoto and would like to go to nearby Sagano to see the Shrine in the Fields where each newly appointed vestal virgin of the Great Shrine at Ise temporarily resided before proceeding to Ise. By a mere turn of his body, the priest indicates that he has made the journey to Sagano, and he kneels before the shrine. As he is praying, a girl enters and, upon questioning, tells the story of how, when Lady Rokujō was staying at Nonomiya with her daughter who had been appointed as the Ise virgin, she was visited by Genji. The time of the year was autumn, the season most dearly cherished in the Japanese tradition because of its many reminders of the inevitable passing of all things, and the poetic dialogue of *The Shrine in the Fields* is suffused with autumnal melancholy and loneliness. By the end of the first scene, it has become clear to the priest that the girl is actually the ghost of Lady Rokujō, who is torn between her continuing worldly passion for Genji and her desire to achieve Buddhist salvation. In the second and last scene, the *shite*, who has temporarily exited,[26] reappears in the unmistakable form of Lady Rokujō and dances the *shimai*, an often protracted dance which constitutes the dramatic climax of the play. At the end of her dance, Lady Rokujō steps through the small wooden *torii* or gateway—the only prop used in *The Shrine in the Fields*—and thus symbolically departs the world and achieves salvation.

Perhaps the best-loved *nō* play is *Matsukaze,* also a woman play, which was written by Kan'ami and revised by Zeami. It tells the sad tale of the ghosts of two sisters—Matsukaze ("Wind-in-the-pines") and Murasame ("Autumn rain")[27]—who when alive had spent their days in the lowly occupation of gathering brine to make salt at their native place of Suma on the Inland Sea. Once, many many years earlier, a courtier named Yukihira had spent some time in exile at Suma; and even after his return to the capital and his death shortly thereafter, the girls remained sunk in grief over the love they had both felt for him. In the final scene of the play, as a gale howls and breakers crash at Suma, Matsukaze and Murasame vow that they will continue to await Yukihira's promised return; but, with the aid of prayers by the priest who has visited them, they are finally released from their tormented existence, and in the end all that remains is the memory of their names in the form of "autumn rain" and "wind in the pines":

Matsukaze:	So we await him. He will come,
	Constant ever, green as a pine.
Murasame:	Yes, we can trust
	his poem:
Chorus:	"I have gone away
Matsukaze:	Into the mountains of Inaba,
	Covered with pines,
	But if I hear you pine,
	I shall come back at once."
	Those are the mountain pines
	Of distant Inaba,
	And these are the pines
	On the curving Suma shore.
	Here our dear prince once lived.
	If Yukihira comes again,
	I shall go stand under the tree
	Bent by the sea-wind,
	And, tenderly, tell him
	I love him still!
Chorus:	Madly the gale howls through the pines,
	And breakers crash in Suma Bay;
	Through the frenzied night
	We have come to you

In a dream of deluded passion.
Pray for us! Pray for our rest!
Now we take our leave. The retreating waves
Hiss far away, and a wind sweeps down
From the mountain to Suma Bay.
The cocks are crowing on the barrier road.
Your dream is over. Day has come.
Last night you heard the autumn rain;
This morning all that is left
Is the wind in the pines.
The wind in the pines.[28]

Both *The Shrine in the Fields* and *Matsukaze* are *mugen* or "ghostly dream" plays. Exploiting the "mystery" aspect of the *yūgen* aesthetic, the ghostly dream plays, which were especially favored by Zeami, bring people (both historical figures and characters from fiction) back from the distant past as mysterious, haunting apparitions. Among the finest of such plays are those in the category of women plays, such as *The Shrine in the Fields* and *Matsukaze*. But the ghostly dream format was also wonderfully adapted to warrior plays, nearly all of which are based on episodes from *The Tale of the Heike*. The most affecting of the warrior *mugen* plays are those that recreate the lives of the fate-driven Taira as they are hounded and destroyed by the Minamoto in the Genpei War. We noted that, as portrayed in the *Heike*, the Taira were transformed into courtly warriors during their long residence in Kyoto in the second half of the twelfth century. Some became well-known *waka* poets; others took up court music, mastering such instruments as the flute and the *biwa;* and still others became romantic lovers in the courtier manner. By featuring the courtly side of the Taira in his warrior plays, Zeami deliberately catered to the tastes of the shogun, Ashikaga Yoshimitsu, and the members of his warrior elite who, as residents of Kyoto during the Muromachi period, themselves acquired courtly tastes and became courtier-warriors.

Typical of the *mugen* warrior plays is *Atsumori,* the story of the youthful Taira commander Atsumori, who is killed by the rough eastern warrior Kumagai Naozane as he attempts to escape after the battle of Ichinotani, fought in 1184 on the shore of the Inland Sea near today's Kobe. *Atsumori* adheres closely to the story as it is presented in the *Heike*. After the Minamoto rout the Taira at Ichinotani, Atsumori tries to flee by riding his horse out to boats waiting in the offing. But even as he approaches the boats, he is challenged by and responds to the shouts of Naozane from the shore to return and fight like a true warrior. In the ensuing clash, Atsumori is thrown from his horse and pinned to the ground by Naozane, who tears off his helmet preparatory to taking his head. Naozane, however, is astounded to see that his foe is a handsome young man with teeth blackened in the courtier manner who reminds him of his own son. Although he would spare Atsumori, Naozane must kill him because other Minamoto partisans are riding toward them and would surely treat Atsumori even more harshly than he. After taking Atsumori's head, Naozane discovers a flute in a pouch at his waist and realizes that Atsumori was the one who played this instrument in the Taira camp that morning. Marveling at this evidence of the courtliness of the Taira, Naozane vows to devote himself thenceforth to praying for Atsumori's salvation.

In *Atsumori,* the *waki* who visits Ichinotani is none other than Kumagai Naozane, who has taken vows and the priestly name of Rensei. At Ichinotani, Rensei encounters some reapers, one of whom is playing a flute. After some questioning by Rensei, the flautist reveals that he is the ghost of Atsumori, who is still torn by the anguish of his defeat and death. In the final scene of the play, after Atsumori has threatened to kill Rensei, the two are reconciled by prayers. Atsumori attains salvation and he and Rensei become companions in Buddhism:

> [Reliving the battle of Ichinotani,
> Atsumori] looks behind him and sees
> That Kumagai pursues him;
> He cannot escape.
> Then Atsumori turns his horse
> Knee deep in the lashing waves,
> And draws his sword.
> Twice, three times he strikes; then, still saddled,
> In close fight they twine; roll headlong together
> Among the surf of the shore.
> So Atsumori fell and was slain, but now the Wheel of Fate
> Has turned and brought him back.
> > (ATSUMORI *rises from the ground and advances toward the*
> > PRIEST *with uplifted sword.*)
> "There is my enemy," he cries, and would strike,
> But the other is grown gentle
> And calling on Buddha's name
> Has obtained salvation for his foe;
> So that they shall be re-born together
> On one lotus-seat.
> "No, Rensei is not my enemy.
> Pray for me again, oh pray for me again."[29]

Another type of theatre, which developed in the shadow of *nō,* was *kyōgen* (mad words). One kind of *kyōgen* served as an interlude between the scenes of a *nō* play, during which a rustic or person of the locality appeared and, in words much more understandable than the frequently difficult language of *nō,* gave additional background information about the region and the leading characters of the play.

Other *kyōgen* were written as separate skits of a comical or farcical nature and were often interspersed on the same programs with *nō* plays, partly to provide relief from the unremitting gloom that pervades nearly all of *nō*. The humor of these independent *kyōgen* was very broad and slapstick. Many skits were based on situations in which clever servants outwitted their daimyo masters. Some scholars have sought to interpret such *kyōgen* as proof that the lower members of society held strong class antagonisms against their superiors in medieval times. There were indeed many instances of social unrest in the medieval age, but it is doubtful that the antics of *kyōgen* reflected true "class antagonisms." *Kyōgen* were produced to entertain and, although occasionally attacked by puritans as irreverent in tone, they were appreciated by audiences from all stations of life, including the daimyos and other people derided in them.

Other artistic pursuits of the Kitayama epoch included linked verse, the tea ceremony, and monochrome painting. But these are more appropriately discussed in the context of the second great cultural phase of the Muromachi era, which occurred during the time of Yoshimitsu's grandson, the eighth Ashikaga shogun Yoshimasa (1436–90).

Yoshimasa became shogun in 1443 at the age of seven and at a time when great forces of upheaval, from peasant uprisings to quarrels among unruly daimyos, were at work throughout Japanese society. Even the strongest of shoguns would have been hard-pressed to hold together the delicately balanced Ashikaga hegemony at mid-fifteenth century; and Yoshimasa—young, pampered, and effete—gave no promise whatever of becoming such a shogun. Yoshimasa was an almost inevitable product of the gradual merger of courtier and warrior elites that had occurred in Kyoto since the time of Yoshimitsu. Although the samurai leaders of the shogunate controlled the imperial court politically, they increasingly succumbed to the elegant courtier style of life; and in Yoshimasa we find a scion of the great warrior house of Ashikaga who, though graced with the title of generalissimo, had scarcely any interest in military matters. In the 1460s, after more than twenty years as nominal head of the shogunate, Yoshimasa sought to relinquish his official duties entirely in order to devote himself to what he regarded as the more pleasurable pursuits of life. Yet, far from slipping gracefully into retirement at this time, Yoshimasa helped precipitate a succession dispute between his brother and son that brought on a frightful holocaust of fighting known as the Ōnin War (1467–77).

Actually, the shogunal succession dispute was merely an excuse for two rival groups of daimyos to engage in a struggle for military supremacy, a struggle that the shogunate, under the inept Yoshimasa, was powerless to check. Fought largely in Kyoto and its environs, the Ōnin War dragged on for more than ten years, and after the last armies withdrew in 1477 the once lovely capital lay in ruins.

There was no clear-cut victor in the Ōnin War. The daimyos had simply fought themselves into exhaustion, and many returned home to find their domains in rebellion. Moreover, the Ashikaga shogunate, although it continued in existence until 1573, was from this time a government in name only. It was under such conditions that the country slipped into a century of conflict and disunion known as the "age of provincial wars."

Despite the carnage of the Ōnin War and the widespread disorder that followed in its wake, the time of Yoshimasa was one of marvelous cultural achievement. Yoshimasa finally managed to transfer the office of shogun to his son in 1473—in the midst of the Ōnin War—and a few years after the end of hostilities he began construction on a retreat, called the Silver Pavilion (in contrast to Yoshimitsu's Golden Pavilion), in the Higashiyama or Eastern Hills suburb of Kyoto (fig. 33). Though a dismal failure as a generalissimo, Yoshimasa was perhaps even more noteworthy as a patron of the arts than his grandfather, Yoshimitsu. In any case, his name is just as inseparably linked with the flourishing of culture in the Higashiyama epoch (usually taken to mean approximately the last half of the fifteenth century) as Yoshimitsu's is with that of Kitayama.

In certain cultural pursuits, most notably the *nō* theatre, the Higashiyama epoch added little to what had been accomplished earlier. Yoshimasa and his cronies loved the *nō*, and sometimes they arranged programs that lasted for several days. But the epoch produced no artists of the caliber of Kan'ami or Zeami, whose works proved to be so lofty that they tended to inhibit further development.

One art that was brought to its highest level of perfection in Higashiyama times was linked verse *(renga)*. The idea of two or more people alternately (or consecutively) composing the 5–7–5 and 7–7 syllable links of a *waka* and stringing them together one after another was not new. The Heian courtiers had occasionally engaged in sessions of linked verse composition for their own amusement, and the pastime became even more popular at court during the Kamakura period. But it was not until the fourteenth century that linked verse was given any serious consideration as an art. By this time, the creative potential of the traditional *waka*, upon which countless generations of Japanese had lavished such unstinting love, was at last exhausted. The *waka* cliques at court dictated such rigid rules of composition that they throttled the efforts of even the most imaginative poets. It was partly because linked verse offered freedom from such restrictions that poets and would-be poets turned increasingly to it in the Muromachi period.

Still another reason for the spread in popularity of linked verse from the fourteenth century on was that it stimulated social intercourse. The leisured Heian courtiers had, of course, been quite socially minded and indeed seem to have enjoyed a constant round of parties, including those

Fig. 33   Silver Pavilion *(photograph by Joseph Shulman)*

that featured poetry recitations and competitions. But the other classes of premedieval times were, so far as we can discern, greatly restricted both in their opportunities to socialize and in the range of their social contacts. Peasants, warrior-peasants, townsmen, and others labored long hours, and apart from occasional shrine and harvest festivals probably had little time or inclination to engage in social relations of a purely convivial type with people outside their immediate families.

The medieval age brought a number of changes that greatly increased the socializing opportunities for people of all classes, especially the new ruling elite of samurai and the guilds of artisans and merchants that emerged in such urban centers as Kyoto, Nara, and the port city of Sakai on the Inland Sea. Records from the early fourteenth century reveal that among the pleasures these people enjoyed when they gathered together socially were *dengaku* and *sarugaku* (which we have already noted), communal bathing, the drinking of tea and sake, and the composition of linked verse.

It would be absurd to mistake a popular diversion for art, and we should not suppose that the extemporaneous *renga* poetizing by party-going peasants, tradesmen, or common samurai produced very many immortal lines. Nevertheless, there are strong indications that the popularistic tastes of the lower classes did significantly influence the development of linked verse in the Muromachi period, just as they contributed (through *dengaku* and *sarugaku*) to the evolution of *nō*.

Linked verse was elevated to the status of a recognized art by the courtier Nijō Yoshimoto (1320–88), who in 1356 compiled the first imperially authorized *renga* anthology. But it was the masters of the fifteenth century who raised linked verse to its highest level. Of these, Shinkei (1407–75) is well remembered, not only for his superior poems but also because of his critical writings on *renga*. An active Buddhist priest, Shinkei said much about the essential oneness of pursuing an art, such as poetry, and seeking religious enlightenment. He also spoke, perhaps more feelingly than anyone else in the medieval age, about advancing aesthetics "beyond beauty" into the realm of the cold, withered, and lonely. Here is how he put it in *Sasamegoto* (Whisperings):

> When a master poet of the past was asked how poetry should be composed, he replied: "Grasses on the withered moor/The moon at dawn."

> This was his way of saying that one should concentrate on things that cannot be expressed with words and should become aware of the sphere of cold and loneliness *(hie, sabi)*. The poems of those who have attained the highest level in the art of poetry are invariably in the cold and lonely style.[30]

The most famous of all *renga* masters was Sōgi (1421–1502), a Zen priest of the Higashiyama epoch who rose from very humble origins and drew inspiration from his contacts not only with the courtier and samurai aristocrats of Kyoto but also with the myriad folk he encountered on his frequent travels into the provinces. Sōgi achieved renown as a traveler similar to that of Saigyō in the early Kamakura period. Although he may not have been as brilliant a composer of pure poetry as Shinkei, he was superb in the art of *renga,* which required a special skill in artistic cooperation with other poets for the purpose of linking verses together. In 1488 Sōgi and two other poets (Shōhaku and Sōchō) met at the shrine of Minase, a village south of Kyoto, where they engaged in what is probably the most famous session of linked verse composition in Japanese history. The opening lines of their hundred-verse poem, now known as "The Three Poets of Minase," go like this:

Sōgi: Snow yet remaining
              The mountain slopes are misty—
              An evening in spring.

Shōhaku: Far away the water flows
              Past the plum-scented village.

Sōchō: In the river breeze
              The willow trees are clustered.
              Spring is appearing.

Sōgi: The sound of a boat being poled
              Clear in the clear morning light.

Shōhaku: The moon! does it still
              Over fog-enshrouded fields
              Linger in the sky?

Sōchō: Meadows carpeted in frost—
              Autumn has drawn to a close.[31]

These poets have skillfully constructed their verses to provide flow and continuity from one link to another by the use of various associative devices: when Sōgi, for example, mentions spring, Shōhaku uses the vernal expression "plum-scented"; and when Shōhaku refers to the moon (which is always associated with the fall), Sōchō promptly shifts to the autumntime. Yet, however delightful such devices may be as employed by the Minase masters, their use was indicative of the fact that linked verse, like *waka*, was becoming excessively restricted by conventions; and in time it too ceased to provide a means for truly creative expression.

One of the finest cultural achievements of the medieval age was the tea ceremony *(chanoyu)*. So far as we know, tea was first brought to Japan from China by Buddhist priests in the early ninth century—that is, at the beginning of the Heian period. Tea drinking, which had been elevated to a cultured pastime in China during the T'ang dynasty, became popular at the Japanese court in Kyoto as part of the general enthusiasm in that age for all things Chinese. The drinking of tea also found a place in Buddhist temples, where it was incorporated into various religious rituals. But after the long period of cultural borrowing from China that had begun in the late sixth century came to an end in the mid-ninth century, tea drinking gradually declined and may even have died out in Japan.

Tea was reintroduced to Japan from China in the late twelfth century, about the time of the founding of the Kamakura shogunate, by the Zen priest Eisai (also pronounced Yōsai; 1141–1215), founder of the Rinzai sect of Zen. Following the lead of Chinese devotees of tea, Eisai extolled the beverage's medicinal value, even writing a book, *Kissa Yōjōki (Book on Improving Health by Drinking Tea)*, that recommended tea as an elixir for extending one's life during the age of *mappō*, when "man has gradually declined and grown weaker, so that his four bodily components and five organs have degenerated."[32] As Eisai explains in the *Kissa Yōjōki*,

> The five organs [liver, lungs, heart, spleen, kidney] have their own taste preferences. If one of these preferences is favored too much, the corresponding organ will get too strong and oppress the others, resulting in illness. Now acid, pungent, sweet, and salty foods are eaten in great quantity, but not bitter foods [which the heart prefers]. Yet when the heart becomes sick, all organs and tastes are affected. . . . But if one drinks tea [with its bitter taste], the heart will be strengthened and freed from illness.[33]

Eisai also urged the use of tea, a stimulant, for keeping awake during long hours of seated meditation in Zen temples.

Sometime between the Japanese abandonment of tea in the mid-Heian period and its reintroduction to Japan by Eisai in the late twelfth century there occurred in China two related developments that had a profound influence on the character of the tea ceremony as it was subsequently created by the medieval Japanese: the use of powdered tea and the invention of the bamboo tea scoop (in Japanese, *chasen*) with which to stir powdered tea to dissolve it in hot water. The Chinese themselves later stopped drinking powdered tea; and today, virtually all the tea that is consumed in the world—whether red (fermented) tea, oolong (semifermented) tea, or green (unfermented) tea—is prepared by infusion: that is, by immersing tea leaves in hot water. The only use of powdered tea is in *chanoyu*. (In their everyday lives the Japanese, like everyone else, drink infused tea.)

During the thirteenth and fourteenth centuries tea drinking spread among all classes of Japan, and tea became a national drink. The tea that was prized most was that grown at Toganoo in the mountains to the northwest of Kyoto. Beginning in the fourteenth century, parties held in Kyoto by members of the samurai elite of the Muromachi shogunate featured tea-judging contests *(tōcha)*, the object of which was to distinguish between Toganoo tea and tea grown in other regions of Japan. The extraordinarily high esteem in which Toganoo tea was held can be observed in the fact that it was called "real tea" *(honcha)* and the other teas were dismissed as "non-tea" *(hicha)*.[34]

The tea-judging contests, which became something of a craze, were often accompanied by linked-verse sessions and, afterward, by the drinking of sake, communal bathing, and gambling.[35] In all, the contests and their sequels must have been lively, frequently bawdy, occasions. A certain parvenu daimyo named Sasaki Dōyo (1306–73) became especially conspicuous about mid-fourteenth century for the gala tea parties he threw. In staging these parties, Dōyo ostentatiously displayed his collection of Chinese objets d'art, including ceramics and other articles used in the preparation and drinking of tea, samples of calligraphy, and painted screens and hanging scrolls.

Dōyo's flaunting of his "foreign pieces" was symptomatic of the general passion for all things Chinese among the newly affluent samurai leaders of the fourteenth century. Envoys who went to China on behalf of these leaders eagerly purchased all the works of art they could find, particularly paintings attributed to Sung and Yüan masters. In the process, they exercised very little critical judgment, accepting many pictures simply on verbal guarantees of their authenticity or on the basis of seals that could easily have been forged. As a consequence, many of the most dearly cherished items in the Chinese art collections of men like Sasaki Dōyo were quite likely of dubious value.

Not until the Higashiyama epoch did the Japanese begin to take careful stock of the numerous artworks and antiques they had so randomly imported from China for several centuries. Yoshimasa assigned members of a group called the "companions" *(dōbōshū)* to survey and catalog the shogunal collection, by this time the largest single accumulation of Chinese treasures in Japan. The companions were artistically talented and discriminating men who were on very intimate terms with the shogun and who were entrusted with the general conduct of his cultural affairs. They included the "three ami"[36] (Nōami, 1397–1471; his son Geiami, 1431–85; and the latter's son Sōami, d. 1525); and in tasks such as the cataloging of the shogunal art collection, which was done chiefly by Nōami and Geiami, these men set the standards for subsequent art connoisseurship in Japan.

Chanoyu evolved during the fifteenth century. We cannot trace with historical accuracy each stage in this evolution, but we can hypothesize that the first was the adoption of rules for the preparation, serving, and consumption of tea and that the second was the creation of a setting—the tea room *(chashitsu)*—in which people gathered for tea. In the beginning, tea was prepared in a separate kitchen or outside corridor and then brought into the tea room. By subsequently moving the entire process of preparation, serving, and consumption of tea into a single room, the fifteenth-century creators of *chanoyu* established a microcosmic, self-contained "world of tea."

The tea room *(chashitsu)* was an offshoot of a new style of room—the *shoin* room—that appeared during the fifteenth century. The rooms of the earlier *shinden* mansions of the Heian courtiers had been little more than spaces enclosed by walls, sliding doors *(fusuma)*, and folding screens and other removable partitions. Their floors were of bare wood, and most rooms had no built-in features and little furniture. People sat on mats

Fig. 34   *Shoin*-style of interior architecture: at the right end of the far wall is the writing desk; to the left of it are the asymmetrical overhanging shelves *(chigaidana);* the floor is covered with *tatami* matting, and *fusuma* and *shōji* sliding doors can be seen in the left and right walls *(drawing by Arthur Fleisher)*

placed on the floors as needed. During the medieval age, standardized rush matting *(tatami)* was increasingly used to cover floors entirely, and walls and sliding doors formed the sidings of all rooms. The sliding doors of this age were of two types: the traditional *fusuma* and the newer, lighter *shōji*, which consisted of latticelike wooden frameworks with translucent rice paper pasted on one side.

Derived from the study chambers built for priests in Zen temples, the *shoin* room became the prototype for the main living room of the modern Japanese house. In addition to wall-to-wall *tatami, fusuma,* and *shōji,* the *shoin* room came to have the following installed features: a floor-level writing desk built into one wall (called a *shoin* desk); asymmetrical overhanging shelves *(chigaidana);* and a *tokonoma* or alcove (fig. 34).

The tea room, as a variant of the *shoin* room, evolved primarily in the sixteenth century. All tea rooms featured alcoves for the display of hanging scrolls and flower arrangements, but some lacked the *shoin* desk, the asymmetrical shelves, or both. Tea rooms also usually had special features, such as small, sunken hearths for teakettles, to be used in *chanoyu;* and from the end of the sixteenth century, as we will see in the next chapter, many tea rooms were constructed with *nijiriguchi* or "crawling in" entrance ways.

Chanoyu, as it reached its first important stage of development in the

Fig. 35   Shigaraki-ware water container for the tea ceremony,
early Edo period *(Honolulu Academy of Arts, Gift of Robert Allerton, 1964 [3311.1])*

Higashiyama epoch of the late fifteenth century, was performed in a *shoin*
room of ample size–perhaps six to eight *tatami* mats or larger—and employed only imported "Chinese articles" *(karamono),* including kettles,
bowls, caddies, and water jars, for the preparation and serving of tea.
Before the commencement of a tea ceremony, all these articles (except
the kettle, if the charcoal fire had already been prepared in it) were placed
on the shelves of a Chinese-style black lacquered stand called *daisu.* In
the alcove, the host typically displayed a Chinese painting and perhaps a
flower arrangement.

     But even as this style of tea ceremony took shape in the Higashiyama
epoch, the sprouts of another style also appeared. The originator of this

new style was Murata Shukō (or Jukō; d. 1502), a man of merchant background from Nara who was an earnest student of Zen Buddhism. Shukō said:

> In pursuing this way [of tea], extreme care should be taken to harmonize Japanese and Chinese tastes. This is of great importance and should be given careful attention. How absurd it is these days for those who are inexperienced to covet with self-satisfaction such things as Bizen and Shigaraki wares on the grounds that they possess the quality of being "cold and withered" and to try, even though scorned by others, to show how advanced they are [in the way].[37]

These remarks are included in a letter Shukō purportedly wrote to a disciple and is the only surviving document we have that is attributed to him. Most of what else we know about Shukō as a tea master is contained in writings on *chanoyu* that date from about a century after his death.

Shukō's admonition about taking care to "harmonize Japanese and Chinese tastes" has traditionally been taken to mean that he stood, in the late fifteenth century, at a point of transition from the elegant and "aristocratic" kind of Higashiyama *chanoyu* just described, which featured imported Chinese articles, to a new, Japanese form of the ceremony that used native ceramics, such as the rough-textured, muted, and often flawed wares of kilns such as Bizen and Shigaraki (fig. 35). Aesthetically, this was a significant transition, because it represented a reassertion of such basic native values as naturalness and irregularity. Shukō's description of Bizen and Shigaraki wares as cold and withered is a reflection of the fact that he, like his successors in the sixteenth century, was strongly influenced by the aesthetics of linked verse formulated by Shinkei and others. In *chanoyu*, cold and withered were tastes that pointed in the direction of the *wabi* aesthetic; and indeed, the new kind of tea ceremony originated by Shukō is called *wabicha*, or "tea based on *wabi*." Developed primarily by Shukō's successors during the sixteenth century, *wabicha* is a subject for the next chapter.

Another art that flourished in the Muromachi period was monochrome painting *(sumi-e)* done in the manner evolved several centuries earlier by artists of the Sung dynasty in China. Like their Japanese counterparts of this later age, the Sung monochrome artists painted a variety of subjects, including Zen abbots, folk deities, and flowers and birds. But their primary interest lay in landscapes (known in Japanese as *sansui* or pictures of mountains and water). And indeed Sung monochrome landscapes are among the more striking works of Chinese art. They are, moreover, perhaps the most supremely moving tributes of any people to the grandeur and vastness of nature.

The Sung masters did not attempt to reproduce nature as it really was; rather, they employed bold and even daring brushwork to capture in stylized outline misty scenes of forests, jagged cliffs, waterfalls, and awesome mountains (the most distant of which often seem to be on the point of vanishing into space). Human figures sketched into these landscapes are usually antlike in size. We see them, insignificant figures engulfed by the cosmos, as lone travelers moving slowly along mountain trails or as recluses seated in pavilion-like huts nestled on the sides of towering peaks.

Sung brushwork owed much to the techniques of calligraphy, and it is in fact common to discuss such brushwork in terms of the three main styles of Chinese calligraphic writing, the "standing," "walking"' and "running" styles. The first of these is distinguished by thick, angular strokes, the second by lines that are thinner and more cursive, and the third—the running style—by impressionistic flourishes and splashes of ink. Some artists preferred to paint chiefly in one style or another. But many used all three simultaneously, typically doing foregrounds in the standing style, middle distances in the walking, and backgrounds in the running.

Sung monochrome painting appealed particularly to the medieval Japanese because its medium of black ink was so compatible with the cold, withered, and lonely tastes of the age. In the first phase of painting in the Sung manner during the fourteenth century, Japanese artists devoted themselves primarily to portrait and figure work; but in the fifteenth century they turned increasingly to landscapes.

Among the greatest masters of monochromatic ink work of the fifteenth century was Shūbun (d. 1450), a Zen priest of the Shōkokuji, one of the Gozan or Five Zen Temples of Kyoto. Although Shūbun, who was active during the second quarter of the century, is reputed to have painted many different subjects in a variety of mediums, the only extant works attributed to him are landscapes, mostly on folding screens and sliding doors. A typical Shūbun landscape is "visionary" in that it is a depiction, derived wholly from imagination, of a scene set in China (fig. 36). Like that of other Japanese artists of his time, Shūbun's work is also impressionistic, since space is not clearly differentiated (that is, it is difficult to judge the relative depths of the various sections of a painting) and mountains, cliffs, and other pictorial elements often appear to be suspended or not properly integrated with the rest of the landscape. By contrast, Sung-style landscapes by Chinese artists are notable for the care with which they are constructed: foregrounds, middle distances, and backgrounds are clearly distinguishable and all parts of a picture "fit together" into a coherent reproduction, albeit stylized, of a view from nature.

Thus there appears to have been a fundamental difference in the approach to landscape between the Sung-style Chinese artist and such Japanese painters as Shūbun, a difference that seems to consist in the fact that

Fig. 36 Landscape attributed to Shūbun *(Seattle Art Museum)*

the Chinese artist was as much concerned with philosophy as with aesthetics. Drawing on his Confucian tradition, he sought to portray in nature the kind of harmony and overall agreement of parts that ideally ought to prevail in human society. In other words, the Chinese artist tried to make a social statement; and the greater the sense of structure and depth he could incorporate into his landscapes, the greater the philosophy of his work.

The Japanese, on the other hand, have never dealt with nature in their art in the universalistic sense of trying to discern any grand order or structure; much less have they tried to associate the ideal of order in human society with the harmonies of nature. Rather, they have most characteristically depicted nature—in their poetry, painting, and other arts—in particularistic glimpses. The Chinese Sung-style master may have admired a mountain, for example, for its enduring, fixed quality, but the typical Japanese artist (of the fifteenth century or any other age) has been more interested in a mountain for its changing aspects: for example, how it looks when covered with snow or when partly obscured by mists or clouds.

Shūbun's disciple and successor was Sesshū (1420–1506), who was also affiliated as a priest with the Zen temple of Shōkokuji. Shortly before the outbreak of the Ōnin War, Sesshū journeyed to Yamaguchi in the western provinces of Honshu, where he came under the patronage of the daimyo family of Ōuchi. With Ōuchi backing, Sesshū went to Ming China in 1467 and remained there until 1469. During his two-year stay abroad, he traveled widely and did many sketches and paintings of the Chinese countryside. Curiously perhaps, Sesshū was little inspired by the work of contemporary Ming artists. He professed that his idols remained the venerable Sung monochrome masters and his own countryman, Shūbun.

Nevertheless, we can see a dramatic change in the landscape painting of Sesshū when compared with that of Shūbun. Instead of atmospheric, spatially undifferentiated scenes with " floating" mountains and the like, we find flattened surfaces and often a total disregard for perspective based on depth. "Winter Landscape" (fig. 37) illustrates the major new features of Sesshū's art. Although the scene leads to mountains in the distant background, there is no sense of great depth; and the mountains themselves are not even three-dimensional, but resemble flat cutouts propped against the back of the picture. The most startling part of the winter landscape, however, is its top center, where a jagged black line appears like a tear in the picture and, next to it, there is an abstract mosaic of surfaces that looks startlingly like the work of a modern cubist painter.

By Sesshū's time, it had become standard practice for artists to sign or affix their personal seals to all of their works. Hence, there is little doubt about the authenticity of the many paintings of his that have been

Fig. 37 "Winter Landscape" by Sesshū *(Tokyo National Museum)*

preserved. One of Sesshū's most famous pieces, still owned by the successor family to the Ōuchi in Yamaguchi, is a horizontal landscape scroll some fifty-two feet in length and sixteen inches in height known as the "Long Landscape Scroll." It directs the viewer, as he runs his eyes from right to left, through an ever-shifting but integrated series of landscape settings and changing seasons. Sesshū's special love for the axlike, angular strokes of the standing style of brushwork is particularly evident in this scroll. We can also observe in it—in addition to the inclination, as in the "Winter Landscape," to flatten surfaces—a liking for the decorative placement of objects in a manner that was to become increasingly marked among Japanese painters from the sixteenth century on.

Another outstanding painting by Sesshū is the hanging scroll or *kakemono* that depicts Ama-no-Hashidate, a bay on the Japan Sea coast to the northeast of Kyoto (fig. 38). Sesshū's use of a soft style to reproduce this lovely setting of mountains, water, and an unusual pine-covered sandbar extending nearly across the mouth of the bay seems especially appropriate. More important from the standpoint of the development of Japanese monochrome painting is the fact that he has here drawn an actual site in Japan and not simply an idealized representation of some Chinese-looking scene.

It would be pleasurable to discuss other types of paintings done by Sesshū—including portraits and studies of flowers and birds—that have also contributed to his reputation among many critics as Japan's greatest artist. But space allows only a few comments on still another kind of monochrome landscape in which he excelled, the landscape executed entirely in the running or "splashed ink" style. The best known of these is a hanging scroll in the Tokyo National Museum that Sesshū painted in 1495 (fig. 39). It is an abstract representation of trees on a small island or jut of land with great mountains just faintly visible in the background. Although at first glance this picture may appear to be something that Sesshū simply "dashed off," closer examination reveals how superb a creation it is. One detects, for example, such details as the rooftops of buildings near the water's edge and rowers in a boat just offshore. It is in extremely abbreviated, impressionistic paintings of this sort that one perceives most directly the intense feeling for nature that motivated artists like Sesshū.

A major form of art that was strongly influenced by monochrome ink painting in the Muromachi period was landscape gardening. The origin of the Japanese love of gardens lies, no doubt, in Shinto animism—the belief that *kami* spirits inhabit nature—and was manifested in ancient times by the marking off or enclosure of sacred spaces of ground, sometimes simply with rocks (forming areas called *iwasaka*) and sometimes with rocks joined by loosely hanging ropes *(himorogi)*. Rocks were thought to be especially favored abodes of the *kami* and, as in all subse-

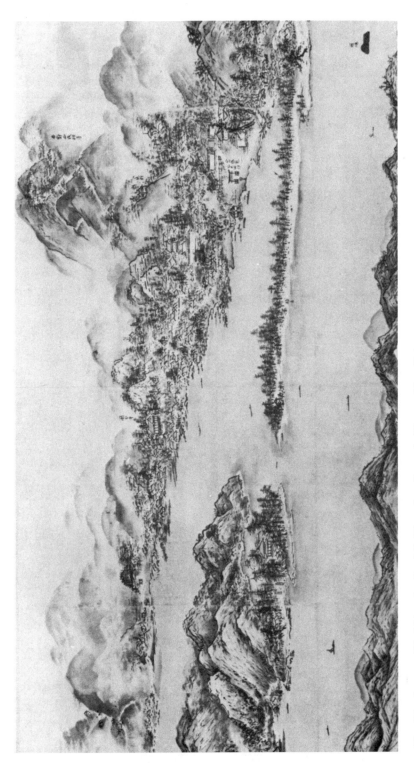

Fig. 38　Ama-no-Hashidate by Sesshū (*Consulate General of Japan, New York,*

Fig. 39　"Splashed ink" scroll of Sesshū *(Tokyo National Museum)*

quent Japanese gardens, those of the *iwasaka* and *himorogi* were used in their natural state and were not sculpted or otherwise altered. Here we see early examples of the aesthetic of naturalness, which has been a fundamental characteristic of Japanese gardens throughout the centuries. Even in its most stylized form, the Japanese garden has always been conceived as a representation of a natural setting. Its antithesis is the geometrically arranged garden, which has often been favored in the West and which is based on the imposition of human concepts of spatial design upon nature.

The chronicles indicate that Japanese aristocrats from at least the mideighth century customarily had gardens near their homes; and during the Heian period, as we observed, a fairly standard type of garden evolved in conjunction with the rambling *shinden*-style of courtier mansion. Situated directly in front of the mansion, the garden was built around a stream-fed pond with a small, artificial island in its center. For the pleasure-loving Heian courtiers, such a garden was both a source of visual delight and an excellent setting for outdoor parties.

Later in the Heian period, with the growth in popularity of Pure Land Buddhism, the *shinden* style of both architecture and garden was adapted to the construction of temples that were conceived as representations on earth of Amida's paradise in thc western realm of the universe. One of the earliest and finest examples of this kind of temple was, of course, the Byōdōin at Uji.

During the medieval age, the Japanese, while still retaining such features of their traditional garden as the pond, stream (often dammed at some point to create a small waterfall), and artificial island, began to experiment in new and abstract ways with the use of rocks. The pioneer in this kind of experimentation was the Zen priest Musō Soseki (1275–1351), designer of the famous moss garden at the Saihōji in Kyoto. Musō and his successors increasingly used rocks of varying shapes and textures to represent both natural formations and man-made structures, such as mountains, cliffs, waterfalls, and bridges. In addition, they employed sand and white pebbles as "water" and thus, in some of their works, eliminated the pond, which for so many centuries had been the central feature of the Japanese garden.

It was during and after the Higashiyama epoch that the finest of the medieval dry rock gardens, known as *kare-sansui* or "withered landscapes," were built, all on the grounds of Zen temples. Some of these gardens, such as the *kare-sansui* at the Daisen'in abbacy of Daitokuji Temple in Kyoto, are reproductions in miniature of scenes from nature. In the Daisen'in garden, for example, we see in the background several large rocks representing towering mountains; and in the middle distance there is a flat, bridgelike rock and, flowing beneath it, a "river" of white sand (fig. 40). This and other *kare-sansui* are very much like three-dimen-

Fig. 40   Garden at the Daisen'in of the Daitokuji Temple *(photograph by Joseph Shulman)*

sional monochrome ink paintings and are based on the same aesthetics as *sumi-e*. Not surprisingly, some of the leading monochrome artists of the age, such as Sesshū and Sōami, were also noted designers of gardens.

Perhaps the most famous Japanese rock garden is the *kare-sansui* at the Ryōanji Temple in Kyoto (fig. 41). Consisting of a flat, rectangular surface of raked white sand with fifteen rocks scattered about singly and in clusters, the Ryōanji garden is ostensibly a representation of the ocean with islands protruding above its surface. The representation of an island or islands in the ocean can be traced back to the early evolution of gardens in historical times, and indeed the pond and island of the garden of the Heian period *shinden* estate derived from this tradition. But the Ryōanji garden, consisting solely of rocks and sand, is so extremely severe in layout that it seems to be an ultimate visual depiction of the medieval aesthetics of the withered, cold, and lonely. As abstract art, it may well be compared to a scroll of calligraphy (black ink on white paper) or to a painting in the splashed-ink style of *sumi-e*.

Many of the major arts discussed in this chapter, including the tea ceremony, monochrome painting, and landscape gardening, have come to be regarded as constituents of a distinctive "Zen culture" of Muromachi Japan. There is no question that members of the Zen priesthood were among the leaders in the development of Japan's medieval culture. Moreover, nearly all of the arts of the middle and late medieval age were

Fig. 41   Garden at the Ryōanji Temple *(Consulate General of Japan, New York)*

governed by aesthetic tastes—such as simplicity, restraint, and a liking for
the weathered, imperfect, and austere *(sabi* and *wabi)*—which, although
not exclusively Zen in origin, certainly came to be associated with the Zen
attitude. The only serious objection to the term "Zen culture" is that it
may be interpreted to mean a religious culture. Obviously one can argue
that all true art must somehow be spiritually or religiously moving. Nevertheless, apart perhaps from certain paintings that portrayed Zen holymen
or depicted scenes associated with the quest for *satori,* the Zen culture of
Muromachi Japan was essentially a secular culture. This seems to be
strong evidence, in fact, of the degree to which medieval Zen had become
secularized: its view of nature was pantheistic and its concern with man
was largely psychological.

The Country Unified

· THE LAST CENTURY of the Muromachi period, following the devastating Ōnin War of 1467–77, has been fittingly labeled the age of provincial wars. Although its first few decades witnessed the blossoming of Higashiyama culture, the age was otherwise the darkest and most troubled in Japanese history. Fighting raged from one end of the country to the other. The Ashikaga shoguns became totally powerless, and the domains of many daimyos were torn asunder either by the internecine warfare of vassals or by great peasant uprisings.

Among those most directly and adversely affected by the Ōnin War were the Kyoto courtiers, so long the bearers of traditional culture in Japanese history. Many courtiers had already departed from the capital during the war for safety elsewhere, and others followed after the end of hostilities. A number of prominent courtiers with special artistic and scholarly abilities accepted invitations to visit the more stable and prosperous provincial daimyos, who wished to infuse some of the cultural brilliance of Kyoto into their domainial capitals.

The cultural interests of the courtiers of the late fifteenth century were overwhelmingly antiquarian. They produced very little literature or art of note but rather devoted themselves to exegetical studies of the glorious poetry and prose works of their Heian predecessors, works such as the *Kokinshū, The Tales of Ise,* and *The Tale of Genji.* Ever more covetous of their role as custodians of the past, they even established secret or arcane interpretations of these classics which, in their increasingly straitened financial circumstances, they eagerly sought to purvey for cash.

Like the courtier class in general, the imperial family also suffered grievously in the age of provincial wars. Emperors, although still theoretically sovereign over the land, had long been mere figures of ceremony at court. From about the time of the Ōnin War they gradually withdrew from participation in all but the most essential courtly functions, and often they found themselves embarrassingly unable even to defray the costs of the latter. The coronation of an emperor of the early sixteenth century, for example, was postponed for more than twenty years for lack of funds.

Still another group whose influence was greatly reduced by the Ōnin War was the Zen priesthood of the Gozan temples of Kyoto. Along with the courtiers, the Gozan Zen priests depended heavily on the patronage of the Ashikaga shogunate, especially the opportunity this patronage gave them to accompany the cultural and trading missions to Ming China. With the collapse of the shogunate as a central governing body in the Ōnin War, initiative in the Ming trade was more and more assumed by certain daimyo houses based in Kyushu and the region of the Inland Sea. We have observed that the Zen priest and artist Sesshū, although formally associated with the Shōkokuji Temple in Kyoto, left the capital during the Ōnin War to take up residence in the Ōuchi domain and subsequently journeyed to China under Ōuchi auspices. Sesshū was simply the most outstanding personality attracted by the Ōuchi during these years in their attempt to make Yamaguchi, their domainial capital, the "Kyoto of the west."

Although the age of provincial wars was a time of great upheaval and seemingly endless disorder, we can see in retrospect that important institutional processes were under way, especially in the evolution of rule at the regional level of Japanese society, that were to make possible a rapid unification of the country at the end of the sixteenth century. Certain daimyos, such as the Ōuchi, had managed to weather the Ōnin War and its aftermath; but most of the other great daimyo houses of the early Muromachi period were destroyed in the final decades of the fifteenth century. Gradually, during the early sixteenth century, a new class of regional barons emerged as the masters of domains which, although generally smaller than the territorial possessions of the pre-Ōnin War daimyos, were more tightly organized as autonomous units capable of survival in a time of constant civil strife.

These new daimyos of the age of provincial wars were a sturdy and in many ways progressive breed of men, who devoted all their energies to strengthening and expanding their domainial rule. They gathered their vassals into more permanent fighting units, compiled legal codes to cover the altered conditions of the age, and adopted a variety of policies to encourage both agricultural and commercial development and even to exploit, through mining operations and the like, the nonagrarian natural resources of their domains.

By mid-sixteenth century, much of Japan had been brought under the control of this new class of daimyos, and the stage was set for a general competition among the more powerful of them to undertake the task of restoring order to the entire country. Unification and the establishment of a lasting military hegemony were ultimately carried out by three great chieftains—Oda Nobunaga (1534–82), Toyotomi Hideyoshi (1536–98), and Tokugawa Ieyasu (1542–1616)—all of whom came from the region of modern Nagoya, midway between the central provinces and the Kantō.

Nobunaga took the first important step toward unification when he led his armies into Kyoto in 1568. Five years later he deposed the puppet Ashikaga shogun and thus officially dissolved the long-moribund Muromachi shogunate. Nobunaga then set about expanding his power outward from Kyoto, dealing in turn with various enemies that included other daimyos, the members of Buddhist sects, and militant peasant bands. A hard and ruthless campaigner, Nobunaga often inflicted savage punishment on those who opposed him. Perhaps the most conspicuous example of this was his attack in 1571 on the Enryakuji Temple of Mount Hiei, whose monks had refused either to join him or to remain neutral in the struggle for control of the central provinces. Circling Mount Hiei, Nobunaga's forces marched up its sides, not only destroying the thousands of buildings that constituted the temple complex but also killing everyone they found from the monks to the many folk who had been drawn from nearby villages for sanctuary on the mountain. Thus, in an orgy of slaughter, Nobunaga virtually obliterated the greatest scholarly and religious center of ancient Japan.

In 1582, while he was in the process of directing his armies against the western provinces, Nobunaga was assassinated at the age of forty-nine by one of his generals. His death was speedily avenged by another general, Hideyoshi, who thereupon assumed the mantle of unifier and, within eight years, brought the remainder of Japan under his control. Hideyoshi, probably the greatest military commander in Japanese history, rose by sheer ability and drive from the ranks of the peasantry to become national overlord, a career record that was exceptional even in this dynamic age.

Although invincible in his march to power in Japan, Hideyoshi ignominiously failed in two attempts to invade Korea in 1592 and 1597. He was apparently motivated to undertake these foreign adventures both from the desire for new lands to conquer and the wish to open by force new avenues of trade with the continent. The first invasion attempt was repulsed by Chinese armies that poured down from the north across the Yalu River, and the second was terminated upon Hideyoshi's death in 1598.

When Hideyoshi died he left an infant son to succeed him, and before long a struggle for power ensued in which two great leagues of daimyos confronted each other. The head of one of these leagues was Tokugawa Ieyasu, a daimyo now based at Edo (modern Tokyo) in the Kantō, who had faithfully served Nobunaga and had later reluctantly submitted to Hideyoshi. The victory of Ieyasu's league over its coalition of opponents in a decisive clash of arms at Sekigahara in 1600 enabled the Tokugawa chieftain to impose a new hegemony over Japan and establish a military government, known as the Tokugawa shogunate, that was to endure until the beginning of modern times in the late nineteenth century.

The age of unification under Nobunaga, Hideyoshi, and Ieyasu was a particularly lively and exciting one in premodern Japanese history, not only because of the spectacular military exploits of these three great unifiers but also because of the arrival of Europeans in Japan. It was the Portuguese who led the European maritime explorations of the fifteenth century down the coast of Africa and into Asian waters. They rounded the Cape of Good Hope and touched India in 1498; and within another fifteen years or so they reached China, where they established a permanent trading station at Macao in 1559. Portuguese traders first set foot on Japanese soil about 1543,[1] landing in a Chinese junk on the small island of Tanegashima off the coast of Kyushu.

Christian missionaries followed shortly in the wake of Portuguese traders to Japan. Europe was at the time aflame with the fervor of the Counter Reformation, and the king of Portugal had undertaken sponsorship of the recently formed and militantly aggressive Society of Jesus. It was, in fact, one of the leaders of the Jesuits, St. Francis Xavier (1506–52), who inaugurated Christian missionary activity in Japan. During his stay there from 1549 until 1551, Xavier developed a strong liking for the Japanese people as well as high optimism for the prospects of conversion among them. Comparing the Japanese to others the Jesuits were then seeking to convert, he observed: "Judging by the people we have so far met, I would say that the Japanese are the best race yet discovered and I do not think you will find their match among the pagan nations."[2] Another of the early Jesuit missionaries to Japan commented: "These Japanese are better disposed to embrace our holy Faith than any other people in the world."[3]

No doubt one reason why Xavier and other European visitors of this age to the Far East felt a certain preference for the Japanese over other Asians they encountered was that the warring, feudal conditions of sixteenth-century Japan reminded them so much of home. The Jesuits in particular, with their special liking for martial order and discipline, could readily appreciate the rigorous lifestyle of Japan's ruling samurai class. Here are some of their observations about the Japanese martial spirit:

"The Japanese are much braver and more warlike than the people of China, Korea, Ternate and all the other nations around the Philippines."
"There is no nation in the world which fears death less."
"I fancy that there are no people in the world more punctilious about their honour than the Japanese, for they will not put up with a single insult or even a word spoken in anger."[4]

Most of the missionary work of the Jesuits in the first decade or so after their arrival in Japan was restricted to those daimyo domains in Kyushu where the Portuguese trading ships made their calls. Not until the rise of Nobunaga were conditions sufficiently settled to allow them to extend their proselytizing activities to other parts of the country, especially to the central provinces. Nobunaga showed himself to be quite well disposed toward the Christian fathers, and on several occasions granted them personal interviews. One apparent reason for his cordiality was his hope that the Jesuits might be useful in combating, at least doctrinally, those Buddhist sects of the capital region that opposed his advance to national power.

Hideyoshi was also friendly toward the Jesuits in his early years as military hegemon. He was keenly interested in foreign trade and, through courtesies extended to the missionaries, sought to lure an ever greater number of Portuguese ships to Japan. Hideyoshi also sent forth his own trading vessels (known as vermilion seal ships from the documents of authorization they carried bearing such seals) and Japanese traders were seen during these years in ports of countries as distant as the Philippines, Cambodia, and Siam.

Portuguese ships had in the beginning dropped anchor in various harbors on the northern and western coasts of Kyushu. More often than not, they selected their ports of call on the basis of whether or not the local daimyos were tolerant of or welcomed Christianity. Undoubtedly the conversion of a number of Kyushu daimyos to Christianity about this time was motivated partly, if not entirely, by their desire to attract Portuguese trade. One of the most prominent of the Christian daimyos was Ōmura Sumitada, who in 1570 opened the harbor of Nagasaki in his domain to Portuguese commerce and ten years later ceded it as a territorial possession to be administered by the Jesuits.

By the late 1580s, when Hideyoshi carried his campaign of unification to Kyushu, Nagasaki had been transformed from a small coastal village into a flourishing port city with a high percentage of Christian converts among its population. The future prospects of both Portuguese traders and Jesuit missionaries in Japan were bright indeed. Then, in 1587, without warning or intimation, Hideyoshi declared the "nationalization" of Nagasaki and ordered the Jesuit missionaries to leave the country within twenty days. Hideyoshi never fully implemented his decree against the missionaries, since he feared that it might drive away the Portuguese traders as well. Yet, the fact that he issued it at all suggests a growing anti-Christian feeling in Japan's ruling circles, a feeling that was to reach great intensity several decades later.

The Portuguese and other Europeans, including Spanish, Dutch, and English, who visited Japan in the late sixteenth and early seventeenth centuries were loosely labeled by the Japanese (in accordance with Chinese practice) as *namban* or "southern barbarians," since they came from the seas to the south. For practical purposes, however, the so-called *namban* culture of this age consisted of the forms of Western technology, culture, and general knowledge introduced to Japan by the Jesuits.[5] By far the leading center of *namban* culture was Nagasaki, which remained strongly under Jesuit and Portuguese influence even after Hideyoshi's nationalization of it in 1587.

Among the first things the Portuguese introduced to the Japanese were Western guns, in particular the muzzle-loading arquebus, a riflelike weapon, somewhat smaller than the musket, that was preferred by the Portuguese and the Spanish. The Japanese set about making these guns immediately and imported as many as possible from Europe. Within ten years the daimyos were using guns in substantial numbers in battles. It is interesting to note that this was the very time, the middle of the sixteenth century, when a military revolution was occurring in Europe because of the widespread use for the first time of hand-held guns in warfare. Astonishing as it may seem, Japan, heretofore a country virtually unknown to—and certainly unvisited by—Europeans and situated in the farthest reaches of the world, underwent a similar military revolution thanks to the introduction of European guns. The leader in this revolution was Oda Nobunaga, who is credited with having organized the first major gun unit in a Japanese army.

Nobunaga divided the infantry of his army into three units by weapons: gunners, bowmen, and spear men. The major problem with the guns of that day, apart from their inaccuracy, was the time required to reload them. During the minutes when the gunners were reloading, the bowmen and spear men had to take up the slack by maintaining the attack against the enemy. The reloading problem could also be dealt with by dividing the gunners into groups and having them fire in relay or volleys. It appears, in fact, that Nobunaga was the first commander in the world to develop such volley fire. Geoffrey Parker, describing the Battle of Nagashino in 1575, in which Nobunaga's guns defeated the finest cavalry in the land (the cavalry of the Takeda family), writes: "The warlord Nobunaga deployed 3,000 musketeers in ranks in this action, having trained them to fire in volleys so as to maintain a constant barrage. The opposing cavalry—ironically of the same Takeda clan which had pioneered the use of the gun—was annihilated. The battle-scene in Kurosawa's film *Kagemusha (The Shadow Warrior)* offers a credible reconstruction, for the action is intended to represent Nagashino."[6] According to Parker, Europeans did not develop the technique of volley fire until the 1590s, some two decades after the Japanese.

It is often assumed that the Portuguese also influenced the Japanese in the construction of castles in the late sixteenth and early seventeenth centuries (fig. 42). Certainly this was the great age of castle building in Japan, but there is little evidence that the Japanese received any direct Portuguese instruction or aid in the building of these fortresses. Rather, the castles of the era of unification appear to have evolved as a natural product of conditions of accelerated warfare and the formation of more firmly and rationally controlled daimyo domains.

In the early centuries of the medieval age, the samurai had apparently felt very little need for strong defensive fortifications. Although occasion-

Fig. 42   Himeji Castle *(Consulate General of Japan, New York)*

ally a force of warriors would attempt to hold a position against great odds, medieval armies usually withdrew when the tide of battle turned against them in order to regroup and fight again another day. In the style of warfare that prevailed until at least the Ōnin War, even the occupation of key cities, such as Kyoto, was seldom regarded as absolutely crucial from the standpoint of overall strategy. Thus, during the war between the Northern and Southern courts in the fourteenth century, the Ashikaga on several occasions temporarily relinquished possession of the capital to the forces of the Southern Court when it seemed impractical or excessively difficult to defend it. Fighting in those days was done almost entirely by the samurai, and few peasants or townsmen were impressed into military service. Since supplies were readily accessible in the countryside, moreover, cities were not essential over the short term even for economic reasons. Hence Kyoto, until the Ōnin War, seldom suffered great physical damage as a direct result of warfare. Armies came and went and the city continued to function more or less as usual.

The new breed of daimyos who emerged in the age of provincial wars expanded their domains by stages and at each stage developed new types of fortifications to meet their military, economic, and administrative needs. In the early sixteenth century the most common fortress or "castle" was a kind of wooden stockade built atop a hill, a site selected solely because of its defensibility. The master, his family, and personal retinue lived at the base of the hill and used the castle only when attacked.

As daimyos spread their hegemonies over larger territories, they began to move their castles to level land. Some picked locations with protective mountains or bodies of water to the rear; but others—particularly the more successful daimyos from about the time of Nobunaga's rise—placed their castles on open land or plains. Daimyos who constructed castles in settings of the latter type obviously felt sufficiently secure in their positions as baronial rulers to sacrifice the military advantages of less exposed terrain in order to make these strongholds the administrative and commercial centers of their domains.

The first true castles, built during the age of unification, were distinguishable from earlier fortresses primarily by their massive stone foundations and their general size and grandeur. A Jesuit priest described the castle that Nobunaga built at Azuchi on the shore of Lake Biwa with these words of wonder and admiration:

> On top of the hill in the middle of the city Nobunaga built his palace and castle, which as regards architecture, strength, wealth and grandeur may well be compared with the greatest buildings of Europe. Its strong and well constructed surrounding walls of stone are over 60 spans in height and even higher in many places; inside the walls there are many beautiful and exquisite houses, all of them decorated with gold and so neat and well fashioned that they seem to reach the acme of human elegance. And in the middle there is a sort of tower which they call *tenshu* and it indeed has a far more noble and splendid appearance than our towers. It consists of seven floors, all of which, both inside and out, have been fashioned to a wonderful architectural design. . . . [Inside], the walls are decorated with designs richly painted in gold and different colours. Some are painted white with their windows varnished black according to Japanese usage, and they look extremely beautiful, others are painted red, others blue, while the uppermost one is entirely gilded.[7]

Hideyoshi built three castles, one in Kyoto, another at Momoyama immediately to the south of the capital, and a third (a particularly massive fortification) at Osaka. Unfortunately, none of the unification-age castles has survived. Indeed, there are few castles remaining in Japan today, and all postdate unification. Warfare and natural disasters, combined with the policy of the Tokugawa shogunate to restrict the possession and repair of castles, have taken their toll over the centuries. In addition to those torn down or allowed to decay in Tokugawa times, a number of fortifications were reduced in the fighting that accompanied the Meiji Restoration of 1868; and an especially splendid castle at Nagoya was demolished during an air attack in World War II.

Although no longer in existence, Nobunaga's castle at Azuchi and Hideyoshi's at Momoyama have given their names to the cultural epoch of the age of unification. The designation of this epoch as Azuchi-Momoyama (or, for the sake of convenience, simply Momoyama) is quite appropriate in view of the significance of castles—as represented by these two historically famous structures—in the general progress, cultural and otherwise, of these exciting years. For castles served not only as fortifications but also as centers of urban growth in the form of castle towns and as the symbols of daimyo authority and material opulence.

Apart from moats and great protective walls of stone, the most conspicuous feature of the Japanese castle was the many-storied keep or donjon (the *tenshu* mentioned in the passage about Azuchi castle). The typical keep had white plastered walls and complexly arranged, hipped and gabled roofs of tile, designed so that each roof was smaller in size than the one directly below it. Although the keeps were relatively safe from attack by incendiary missiles, owing to the composition of their walls and their sloped roofs, they were highly vulnerable to cannon. But Western-style artillery was not introduced into warfare in Japan until the late 1580s, shortly before Hideyoshi completed unification. And, in any case, the keeps of these late sixteenth century Japanese castles were not primarily designed as last-ditch military strongholds. Rather, they were intended to symbolize the power and eminence of their masters. Their exteriors were imposing and their interiors were carefully arranged into private living quarters, decorated according to the prevailing tastes of the age. As we shall see, some of the finest artwork of the Momoyama epoch was done on screens and sliding doors for use and display in castles.

Before examining further the Momoyama epoch of domestic culture, however, let us return to the foreign and exotic *namban* culture of the Portuguese traders and Jesuit missionaries that also flourished briefly during these years.

One of the most noteworthy projects undertaken by Europeans of this age in Japan was the opening of a Jesuit press. During the period from 1591 until 1610, the Jesuits, using chiefly movable type which they introduced to the Japanese, printed some fifty books in Latin, Portuguese, and Japanese (in both the romanized and native orthographies). Most of the

Jesuit publications were Christian religious tracts, but some dealt with language and literature. Among the few examples of literary works that have been preserved are a Japanese translation of *Aesop's Fables* and a rendering into *romaji* or roman letters of the famous medieval war tale *The Tale of the Heike*. The *Heike* and other Japanese narratives, known from the records to have been done in *romaji* at this time, were primarily intended for the use of missionaries as aids in learning the native language.

One of the things for which the Jesuit missionaries became famous was their work in studying the languages of the countries where they proselytized. Of the early Jesuits in Japan who worked in this area, none was more highly regarded than João Rodrigues (1561–1634), who went to Japan as a youth and spent most of the remainder of his life there. Given the sobriquet "Rodrigues the Interpreter," he appears to have attained a greater command of Japanese than any other European of this age, even serving on occasion as interpreter for the hegemon Hideyoshi. In addition to writing a lengthy history of Japan, Rodrigues took the lead in compiling a monumental study in Portuguese of the Japanese language entitled *Art of the Language of Japan (Arte da Lingoa de Iapam)*. In the opinion of C. R. Boxer, Rodrigues' *Art* may be taken as "the starting point of the scientific study of Japanese as a language."[8]

Another cultural activity in which the Jesuits were prominent was the introduction of Western pictorial art to Japan in the form of oil painting and copper engraving. The Jesuits were especially anxious to provide votive pictures for newly established Christian churches and for individual converts to Christianity who wished to display them in their homes. So great was the demand for these pictures that it could not be met solely by the importation of works from Europe, and the Jesuits were obliged to instruct Japanese artists in Western-style painting. All indications are that the Japanese learned the foreign style quickly and soon produced the desired pictures in more than adequate quantity. Yet, regrettably, the great bulk of such pictures by Japanese artists, as well as those brought from Europe, was destroyed in the Christian persecutions of the seventeenth century, and we have only a relatively few works remaining from which to judge Japan's "Christian art" during and after the period of unification.

Although much of *namban* art was either iconographic or religious, there are extant a number of paintings and engravings done in the Western manner of such secular subjects as European cities, landscapes, and nonclerical people. Some of the latter are shown in portraitlike poses, but others are depicted in genre scenes performing everyday activities of work and leisure. These foreign genre pictures are particularly interesting because, as we shall see, it was about this time that the Japanese evolved a new style of genre painting of their own, a style that led ultimately to the famous *ukiyo-e* or "floating world" pictures of the Tokugawa period.

One kind of Japanese genre painting that dates from the late sixteenth century is the so-called *namban* screen. Although designated as *namban* because they depict Europeans in Japan, these screens are actually the creations of Japanese artists working entirely within the native tradition of painting.

The *namban* screens commonly come in pairs and are often very similar in subject matter, one showing the departure of the Portuguese carrack (great ship) from Goa or Macao and the other its arrival at Nagasaki (fig. 43). In the latter, the passengers are usually shown proceeding from the shore toward town, where they mingle with people, both Japanese and Europeans, who have come to greet them. The Portuguese traders are drawn with exceedingly small heads, thin legs, and huge pantaloons, and the Jesuits are shown attired in flowing black clerical robes. In some of the *namban* screens, the Portuguese are accompanied by black servants (who greatly delighted the Japanese) and are leading such animals as Arabian horses, deer, peacocks, and elephants. Also frequently shown in these screens are Christian churches, constructed in the architectural style of Buddhist temple buildings.

It is impossible to date these rather stereotyped *namban* screens precisely, although most of them were probably painted in the early or mid-1590s when the fad for Western things was at its height in Japan. Hideyoshi had established his military headquarters near Nagasaki for the invasion of Korea in 1592, and this proximity aroused a new curiosity about the foreigners and their ways among Japan's samurai leaders. The Jesuits sought to capitalize on such curiosity in the hope of gaining better understanding and offsetting Hideyoshi's anti-Christian acts of recent years. They were fortunate to have available an exceptional "public relations" group of four Japanese Christians from Kyushu who had gone as youths in 1582 on a mission to Europe where they had visited Pope Gregory XIII in Rome. Returning in 1590, these young men possessed not only first-hand knowledge of Europe but also various mementos of their trip, such as artworks, mechanical devices, and maps.

Hideyoshi and his advisers, then planning their invasion of Korea, were much impressed by the foreign maps and techniques of cartography; and the making of maps, many of them painted in bright colors on folding screens and even fans, became as popular about this time as the production of the *namban* pictures showing the arrival of the Portuguese great ship. Most of these *namban* maps were depictions either of the world or of Japan alone, and, apart from a distorted rendering in the world maps of the Americas and the northern and northeastern regions of Asia, they appear to be respectably accurate. The world maps, moreover, make manifestly clear by the varying perspectives from which they were drawn

Fig. 43 *Namban* ("southern barbarian") screen showing the arrival of the Portuguese great ship at Nagasaki (*Cleveland Museum of Art*)

that the earth is round (although the Jesuits in their preaching refused to
endorse the still heretical Copernican theory of earthly rotation around
the sun).

The most frivolous aspect of the craze for things Western in the 1590s
was the aping by Japanese, including Hideyoshi himself, of the Portuguese style of dress and personal adornment. The degree to which these
became fashionable can be seen in a letter written by a Jesuit father about
this time:

> Quambacudono (i.e., the Kwambaku, Toyotomi Hideyoshi) has become so
> enamored of Portuguese dress and costume that he and his retainers fre-
> quently wear this apparel, as do all the other lords of Japan, even the gentiles,
> with rosaries of driftwood on the breast above all their clothing, and with a
> crucifix at their side, or hanging from the waist, and sometimes even with
> kerchiefs in their hands; some of them are so curious that they learn by rote
> the litanies of *Pater Noster* and *Ave Maria* and go along praying in the streets,
> not in mockery or scorn of the Christians, but simply for gallantry, or
> because they think it is a good thing and one which will help them to achieve
> prosperity in worldly things. In this way they order oval-shaped pendants to
> be made containing reliques of the images of Our Lord and Our Lady
> painted on glass at great cost.[9]

But none of the interests the Japanese displayed in *namban* culture and
Portuguese styles was, as we shall see, able to stem the mounting tide of
anti-Christian sentiment that led in the seventeenth century to severe persecutions and, finally, to the expulsion of foreigners and adoption of a
national seclusion policy. Although the Dutch were allowed to trade at
Nagasaki, Christianity and Western ways were in general so thoroughly
rooted out that few traces of *namban* culture were to be found in Japan
after about the mid-seventeenth century. There remained some things,
like firearms, tobacco, and eyeglasses, and a few Portuguese words, such
as *pan* (bread), *karuta* (playing card), and *kappa* (a straw cape used as a
raincoat), to attest to the fact that the Jesuits and their patrons had really
been in Japan for nearly a hundred years. Otherwise, their presence and
cultural influence were to a remarkable extent expunged from the memory of the Japanese until modern times.

Along with architecture, painting was the art that most fully captured
the vigorous and expansive spirit of the Momoyama epoch of domestic
culture during the age of unification. It was a time when many styles of
painting and groups of painters flourished. Of the latter, by far the best
known and most successful were the Kanō, a school that was maintained
by lineal and adopted descendants from medieval until modern times.

The origins of the Kanō school can be traced from Masanobu (1434–
1530), a member of a samurai house who purportedly studied under
Shūbun. Masanobu accepted the post, first declined by Sesshū, of official

artist to the Ashikaga shogunate in the *kanga* or Chinese manner of Sung and Yüan monochrome painting. He thus established the Kanō as a line of professional painters who worked on commission to meet the demands of their warrior patrons.

Although Masanobu founded the Kanō school, it was his son and successor, Motonobu (1476–1559), who was most responsible for defining its character and course of development. Motonobu was by all accounts a true eclectic. He continued the Kanō tradition of *kanga* monochrome painting, which still dominated the attention of nearly all Japanese artists until well into the sixteenth century; but Motonobu also made free use of the colorful Yamato style of native art that had evolved during the Heian period and had reached its pinnacle in the great narrative picture scrolls of the twelfth and thirteenth centuries.

The Yamato style had declined in early Muromachi times with the renewal of trade with the continent and the growing (and finally consuming) interest of Japanese artists, especially members of the Zen priesthood, in Chinese monochrome work. A line of painters called the Tosa school, who were engaged as official artists by the imperial court just as the Kanō were employed by the shogunate, formally sustained the Yamato tradition throughout the Muromachi period. But the Tosa artists produced little work of distinction, and it was not until Kanō Motonobu eclectically blended the Yamato and *kanga* styles that indigenous achievements in the development of painting were restored to the mainstream of artwork in Japan. As if formalistically to seal the merger of the native and foreign ways of painting, Motonobu married the daughter of Tosa Mitsunobu (dates unknown), probably the best of his school in the Muromachi period and the person most responsible for the modest revival of Tosa painting about Motonobu's time.

The greatest representative of the Kanō school in the Momoyama epoch was Kanō Eitoku (1543–90), who, after dissolution of the Ashikaga shogunate in 1573, was successively employed by the new military hegemons, Nobunaga and Hideyoshi. It was a cardinal event in the history of Japanese art when Eitoku was invited by Nobunaga, in 1576, to decorate the interior of his new castle at Azuchi. Although Azuchi Castle no longer stands, we know from the chronicles the great variety of paintings in both monochrome and color it contained, including pictures of flowers, trees, birds, rocks, dragons, phoenixes, Buddhist themes, and Chinese sages.[10]

Probably no other people has sought more assiduously than the Japanese to adapt their art—most notably painting—to developments in domestic architecture. From at least the Heian period on, much of Japanese secular painting had been done on folding screens and sliding doors, the chief devices used for the partitioning of space in the mansions of the Heian aristocracy. Even with the transition from the *shinden* to the *shoin* style of architecture in the Muromachi period, painting was readily adjusted to meet the additional decorative needs of the *shoin* room through the production in greater numbers of vertical hanging scrolls *(kakemono)* for display in the new alcoves or *tokonoma*. But it was not until the Momoyama epoch that the claims of architecture most conspicuously influenced the course of painting in Japan. To decorate the larger wall spaces, sliding doors, and screens of the living quarters of the typical Momoyama castle, the Kanō and other contemporary painters were forced to create a new, monumental style of art.

The practice of painting on folding screens (which in Japan was also adapted to the *fusuma*-type sliding doors) was originally derived from China, and a great number of Chinese-style screen paintings have been preserved from the eighth century in the Shōsōin at Nara. But with the development of Zen-inspired monochrome painting in the Sung period, Chinese artists abandoned the folding screen as a medium for their work. These artists, who were chiefly members of the literati class, saw that the monochrome style of landscape painting could more effectively be rendered on smaller formats, such as hanging scrolls, and by and large they left the decorating of screens to house painters and other lower-class artisans. In medieval Japan, on the other hand, the folding screen remained an extremely popular format for art among both the courtier and warrior aristocracies, and even the most prominent landscape painters, including Shūbun, were obliged to do much of their work on the larger areas of screen panels. This presented considerable difficulty, since the typical subtlety and suggestiveness of landscapes in ink were apt to appear as signs of weakness or insipidity on, say, a six-panel screen that measured some five feet in height and perhaps twelve feet in width.

Sesshū partly solved the problem of painting monochrome landscapes on large surfaces by employing an exceptionally strong brush stroke, a technique that was also adopted by the artists of the Kanō school. In addition, the Kanō turned increasingly from the painting of landscapes to flowers and birds, which provided them greater opportunity for close-up detailing and the decorative placement of objects. Although Sesshū and other Muromachi artists had earlier done scenes of flowers and birds on screens, it was the Kanō and their fellow painters of the Momoyama epoch who most fully exploited this traditional subject category of Chinese art.

But what screen painting really called for was color, and it was this that the Kanō artists, drawing on the native Yamato tradition, added to their work with great gusto during the Momoyama epoch. The color that these artists particularly favored was gold, and compositions done in ink and rich pigments on gold-leaf backgrounds became the most characteristic works of Momoyama art. It has been hypothesized that this extremely free use of gold leaf, which had been known but seldom employed by artists of the Muromachi period, was partly dictated by the need for greater illumination in the dimly lit reception halls of Momoyama castles. In any case, there could hardly be a more striking contrast between the spirits of two ages than the one reflected in the transition from the subdued monochromatic art of Japan's medieval era to the blazing use of color by Momoyama artists, who stood on the threshold of early modern times. The Kanō and other Momoyama artists continued also to paint in black and white, but their greatest and most original contribution to Japanese art was their heroic work in color done on screens.

Many Momoyama screens are unsigned, and it is only from an analysis of their styles or from contemporary accounts that the artists who did them can with any certainty be identified. The most likely reason for this anonymity is that Momoyama screen painters often worked in teams, and no doubt it was regarded as inappropriate for a single individual to take credit for a picture done jointly by affixing his personal signature or seal to it. Tradition has it that when Kanō Eitoku did large projects, like the decoration of Nobunaga's castle at Azuchi, he simply sketched in the outlines of pictures—often using a brush that was like a large straw broom —and left the detailing to his assistants.

Momoyama screen painting developed into a fully decorative style of art in which overall design and the placement of objects were of paramount importance. The boldness with which the Momoyama masters executed their works is readily observable in Kanō Eitoku's composition of a twisting, gnarled cypress tree set against a background of rocks, azure water, and gold-leaf clouds. Later decorative artists of the seventeenth and early eighteenth centuries were to scale down Eitoku's handling of objects and soften his use of color. But they lived in an age when peace and stability were taken for granted in Japan, whereas Eitoku and his contemporaries displayed in their art the tremendous, if often impetuous, energy of the epic Momoyama years of unification (fig. 44).

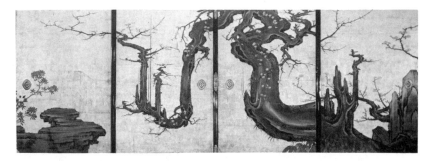

Fig. 44   Kanō Sansetsu's "Aged Plum," a representative work of the decorative screen painting of the Momoyama epoch *(The Metropolitan Museum of Art, The Harry G. C. Packard Collection of Asian Art)*

Another major artist of the Momoyama epoch was Hasegawa Tōhaku (1539–1610). Like all Momoyama painters, Tōhaku worked in a variety of styles, including the colorful decorative manner that was so closely associated with his rivals, Eitoku and the Kanō school. He had a special fondness, however, for the monochrome art of the Muromachi masters and in fact declared himself to be the true successor to the tradition of Sesshū. In several of his major works, including the picture of pine trees on a pair of six-panel screens, Tōhaku demonstrated how a new and imaginative approach to the use of monochrome on large areas could produce extremely satisfying results (fig. 45). His clusters of pine trees, presented without supporting motifs in either the foreground or background, do not seem at all inadequate for the decoration of these multi-paneled screens. Rather, they strikingly enhance, in the best Zen-like tradition, the emptiness of the remainder of the screens' surface.

Apart from the decorative style, the most significant art form to evolve during the Momoyama epoch was genre painting. Genre scenes—that is, portrayals of people in their everyday activities—can be found in Yamato pictures from the Heian period on and are particularly common

Fig. 45   Pine Trees Screen by Hasegawa Tōhaku *(Tokyo National Museum)*

in the later horizontal scrolls of the medieval era. Yet, for the most part, the genre scenes in these scrolls have been placed within the context of running narratives and were not intended to stand alone as depictions of how people of the age characteristically behaved. A major exception is a scroll reputedly painted at the end of the Heian period (although only copies done many centuries later in the manner of the original survive today) entitled "Important Events of the Year" *(nenjū-gyōji)*, which shows Heian aristocrats in the cycle of elegant activities that filled their social calendars. Because the "Important Events" scroll deals only with courtiers, however, its value as social history is limited. True genre art, picturing all classes at work and play, did not appear in Japan until the sixteenth century.

The oldest extant genre painting of the sixteenth century is a work, dating from about 1525, called "Views Inside and Outside Kyoto" *(raku-chū-rakugai zu)*. Done on a pair of six-panel screens, it provides a bird's-eye, panoramic scene of the capital and its environs. Temples, mansions of the elite, mountains, and other famous points of interest in and about the city are clearly distinguishable, and people can be seen everywhere, promenading on the streets, relaxing in courtyards, visiting temples, carrying goods for sale and delivery, and attending the innumerable shops and stalls that stretch in rows along the busy thoroughfares. Because of the picture's obvious stress on the bustling commercial life of the city, a number of scholars have speculated that it was either produced or commissioned by merchants anxious to commemorate the crucial role of trade in the rebuilding of the capital after the devastation of the Ōnin War.

Many other pictures on the theme of "Views Inside and Outside Kyoto," including a particularly detailed one by Kanō Eitoku, were produced during the following two centuries. In addition to their artistic merits, these pictures are invaluable records of the changing features of the ancient capital in an age (at least until 1600) when it was more than ever the vital administrative as well as cultural center of the country (fig. 46)

With the coming of the Momoyama epoch and the general reestablishment of tranquility in the land, genre artists turned increasingly to studies of people at leisure and in the pursuit of pleasure rather than engaged simply in daily chores or as members of a passing scene (as in the pictures of "Views Inside and Outside Kyoto"). Among the great variety of subjects shown in genre works of the Momoyama epoch are picnics, flower-viewing excursions, festivals, horse races, dancing, actors of the popular theatre *(kabuki)*, and women of the pleasure quarters. Of these, the *kabuki* actors and courtesans came especially to attract the attention of artists of the seventeenth-century urban scene, a clear indication of the emergence among them of what may be called a spirit of bourgeois or popular humanism.

Fig. 46 Screen of "Views Inside and Outside Kyoto" (courtesy of the Brooklyn Museum, Gift of W W Hoffman)

Changing techniques in the handling of subjects also indicated the growing humanistic concerns of genre artists of this age. From distant, elevated perspectives that encompassed wide vistas and often huge throngs of people, they gradually shifted to intimate portrayals of small groups of men and women—or even of single individuals—viewed directly from close range. Moreover, by eliminating settings entirely and using stark gold-leaf backgrounds, these late Momoyama and early Tokugawa period genre artists presented their subjects, most of whom were denizens of the demimonde, as directly and candidly as possible.

Although it differs from many of the others, which are frankly erotic, one of the finest of these portrait-type genre works of the Momoyama epoch is the so-called Matsuura Screen (fig. 47). It depicts eighteen women engaged in various casual activities and pastimes, some of which reveal the special fashions and fads of the day. Two women, for example, are playing cards, a game introduced by the Portuguese; another accepts from a companion a long-stemmed pipe containing tobacco, which was

Fig. 47　Matsuura Screen *(Museum Yamato Bunkakan)*

also brought to Japan by Westerners in the sixteenth century; and still another woman plucks the *samisen,* a three-stringed, banjo-like musical instrument of the Ryukyus that first became popular in Japan around the 1590s. Apart from the activities in which its subjects are engaged, the Matsuura Screen is notable for at least two reasons: first, for the skillful manner in which the artist has arranged his women, so that they strike an exceptionally varied and rhythmically interlocking series of poses; and second, for the dazzlingly patterned kimonos the women are wearing. Some authorities have conjectured, on the basis of the studied placement of the figures and the particularly flat appearance of their attire, almost as though it consisted of pieces of material pasted onto the surface of the picture, that the Matsuura Screen was actually produced as an advertisement or a merchant's display poster. In any event, it reveals the great skill that artists of this age were capable of in handling the genre-type portraits that were to serve as forerunners of the famous "pictures of the floating world" (to be discussed in the next chapter).

One of the most prominent people of the Momoyama cultural scene was the noted tea master and arbiter of taste, Sen no Rikyū (1521–91). Descended from a Sakai merchant house, Rikyū became a devoted practitioner of the classical tea ceremony. The putative founder of this ceremony, as noted in the last chapter, was Shukō, a man of the Higashi-yama epoch who died in 1502. During the sixteenth century the ceremony was further developed as *wabicha,* or tea *(cha)* based on the aes-thetic of *wabi.* Haga Kōshirō defines *wabi* as comprising three kinds of beauty: a simple, unpretentious beauty; an imperfect, irregular beauty; and an austere, stark beauty.

Sen no Rikyū himself chose to illustrate the meaning of *wabi* by citing a poem by the Heian-period court poet Fujiwara no Ietaka (1158–1237):

> To those who wait
> Only for flowers,
> Show them a spring
> Of grass amid the snow
> In a mountain village.[11]

Professor Haga's analysis of this poem is itself a noteworthy contribu-tion to our understanding of *wabi:*

> We can imagine a mountain village in the depths of winter when the seven wild grasses of autumn have withered and the brilliant scarlet leaves have scattered. It is a lonely, cold, and desolate world, a world that is even more deeply steeped in the emptiness of non-being than that of "a bayside reed hovel in the autumn dusk." At first glance this may seem like a cold, withered world at the very extremity of *yin.* It is not, of course, simply a world of death. As proof, we have these lines: "When spring comes it turns to bright-ness and amid the snow fresh grass sprouts, here two there three blades at a

time." This is truly "the merest tinge of *yang* at the extremity of *yin.*" Ietaka expressed this notion as a "spring of grass amid the snow." And Rikyū found in it the perfect image of *wabi.* Thus Rikyū's *wabi,* viewed externally, is impoverished, cold, and withered. At the same time, internally, it has a beauty which brims with vitality. While it may appear to be the faded beauty of the passive recluse, or the remnant beauty of old age, it has within it the beauty of non-being, latent with unlimited energy and change.[12]

Sen no Rikyū is noted for having taken the tea ceremony to its farthest extreme. Shukō had suggested that the ceremony be held in a small room, preferably four and a half mats in size, and that it be conducted with a minimum of utensils and decorative accessories (fig. 48). Later *wabicha* masters went so far as to arrange their teahouses to appear like the huts of the most humble of farmers, building them with mud walls and unpainted wood, and eliminating all decoration save a single display of flowers or calligraphy in the *tokonoma.* But Rikyū achieved the ultimate in *wabicha* settings by adopting as his preferred teahouse a stark hut of only two mats in size, which could at most accommodate two or three people in one gathering.

Fig. 48   Interior of the Yūin tea room at Urasenke in Kyoto *(courtesy of Tankōsha Publication Company, by permission of Urasenke)*

The rise of Rikyū was in one respect an indication of the expanded influence, in cultural as well as commercial matters, of the merchant class of the Momoyama epoch. Rikyū, who served both Nobunaga and Hideyoshi, appears indeed as a herald of the coming age of bourgeois culture that flourished under the Tokugawa after 1600. Yet, despite his bourgeois background, Rikyū remained essentially a medieval man. He was not reluctant to take advantage of the new opportunities for social and political advancement that the times presented; but in the realm of culture, Rikyū proved to be a necessary restraining force against the excessive exuberance of the Momoyama spirit.

Momoyama screen art, although bold and showy, was saved from becoming vulgar by its firm grounding in the earlier, more traditional *kanga* and Yamato styles of painting. The tea ceremony, on the other hand, was greatly threatened by the urge to ostentation it aroused among the newly risen military leaders of the age of unification. In their desire to demonstrate their cultural as well as martial grandeur, these swashbuckling chieftains went to extravagant lengths to engage specialists in the "way of tea" and to collect rare and unusual tea utensils and accessories. They frequently purchased these at astronomical prices and greatly coveted them. One daimyo, Matsunaga Hisahide (1510–77), is said on a certain occasion to have saved his life by presenting Nobunaga with a priceless tea caddy. Some years later, after Hisahide had joined a plot against Nobunaga and was faced with imminent destruction, he purportedly smashed to bits another highly treasured piece, a kettle, to prevent its falling into his adversary's hands.

When Nobunaga in his march to power imposed his control over the city of Sakai, then the main port in the lucrative foreign trade with China, he acquired a number of valuable tea pieces from the collections of wealthy Sakai merchants and took into his service several of the better known tea masters of the city, including Sen no Rikyū. In addition to having these masters design the tearoom for his castle at Azuchi, Nobunaga used them to preside over the frequent and elaborate tea parties he held. It became his custom, moreover, to bestow prized tea utensils on his lieutenants for meritorious service; and he even went so far as to make the right of these men to hold formal tea parties a distinction that he alone could bestow. It is recorded that Hideyoshi, when granted this honor in 1578 after an important military victory, was overcome with gratitude toward Nobunaga.

Upon his succession to national overlordship, Hideyoshi displayed an especially strong fondness for mammoth social affairs and is particularly remembered for the great tea party he held at the Kitano Shrine in Kyoto in 1587. The party was scheduled to last for ten days, weather permitting, and everyone, from courtiers and daimyos to townsmen and peasants and even foreigners, was invited. Guests were required only to bring a few utensils to serve themselves and mats to sit on. An outbreak of fighting in Kyushu brought cancellation of the party after only one day; yet it seems to have been thoroughly enjoyed by the great throng of people who attended. Hideyoshi put many of his most valued tea pieces on display and, along with Rikyū and two other tea masters from Sakai, personally served a large number of the assembled guests.

Despite his penchant for the grandiose, Hideyoshi was also a fond admirer of *wabicha* and he and Rikyū became intimate companions. As a result, Rikyū was one of the most influential people in Japanese ruling circles during the late 1580s. Then, suddenly, disaster struck. In 1591, for reasons that remain to this day obscure, Hideyoshi ordered his distinguished tea master to commit suicide. Hideyoshi, who was noted for his impetuosity and who was fully capable of ghastly and capricious acts of tyranny, may have imposed this punishment for some personal slight or because he genuinely feared the power Rikyū had acquired. It is said that Hideyoshi later much lamented having caused the tea master's death. At any rate, the passing of Sen no Rikyū removed from Japan's cultural scene the last great medieval figure and heralded the advent of the already rapidly approaching early modern age.

7

The Flourishing of a Bourgeois Culture

THE GREAT PEACE of more than two and a half centuries that followed the founding of the Tokugawa shogunate in 1600 was made possible largely by the policy of national seclusion which the shogunate adopted during the late 1630s. To many historians this policy, carried out amid fearful persecutions of both native and foreign Christians, has appeared as an arbitrary and extraordinarily reactionary measure whereby the Tokugawa, in order to preserve their national hegemony, terminated a lively century of intercourse with the countries of western Europe and reinstituted harsh and repressive feudal controls over Japan.

The seclusion policy, which was set in place by a series of edicts issued between 1633 and 1636, forbade Japanese to leave Japan and severely resticted Japan's relations with other countries, both European and East Asian. Recent scholars, noting the variety of trade and, in some cases, diplomatic relations that were still maintained—albeit on a very limited scale—with Holland (trade), China (trade), Korea (trade and diplomatic relations), and the Ryukyus (trade and diplomatic relations) have questioned whether the Tokugawa shogunate actually intended to "seclude" Japan from the rest of the world.[1] The most frequently used term for the seclusion policy, *sakoku*, "closed (literally, 'chained') country," certainly suggests a seclusive intent. But, as we will see, this term was not coined until the early nineteenth century, when the West had begun to intrude once more upon Japan. Tokugawa leaders at that time seized upon the term as descriptive of what they believed had always been an immutable "closed country" policy that prohibited further expansion of relations with foreign countries, in particular those of the West. But at the time of its inception in the seventeenth century, the seclusion policy was probably intended more to establish a new international order in East Asia, with Japan at its center, than to seal the country off permanently from all but minimal ties with the outside world.

Yet the fact remains that the seclusion policy did minimize foreign relations, especially with Europe. Of Europeans, only the Dutch were allowed to continue trading with Japan, and from 1640 on their activities were restricted to a small, artificial island in Nagasaki harbor called Deshima (or

Dejima). During the Tokugawa period, there were usually seven or eight officials at the Dutch compound on this island. A Dutch contingent journeyed each year to Edó to meet with shogunate officials;[2] otherwise the Dutch were almost entirely sealed off from contact with the Japanese except for the few who served as trading agents and interpreters.

It has been held that the Japanese paid a tremendous price in progress by cutting themselves off from the West just as it was entering fully into its great age of technological and scientific advancements. No doubt this is in some measure true. Yet, we cannot simply assume that, in the absence of the Tokugawa seclusion policy, Japan would have moved steadily or smoothly into more intimate relations with the West. To the Westerners, Japan still lay at the farthest extremity of the known world; and quite possibly the Western trade of this age with Japan had already passed its zenith. Japan, moreover, was not alone in acting as it did, but was only one of several countries of the Far East—including China, Korea, and Vietnam—that effectively minimized or restricted trade and cultural ties with the West during the seventeenth century. In their first major encounter, the East as a whole thus managed to hold the West at arm's length. Two centuries later when the West, having undergone its industrial revolution, sought once more to intrude into the Far East, its impetus was such that it could not be stopped by unilateral seclusion or restriction policies.

The Tokugawa, of course, did not conceive of participating in a historical movement by which the East rejected the West. They pursued their seclusion policy for essentially two reasons: first, the fear, smoldering since Hideyoshi's day, that Christianity was by its nature antithetical to Japan's traditional social order and religious beliefs; and second, the apprehension that the daimyos of western Japan, who had been the leading opponents of the Tokugawa before the battle of Sekigahara, might ally themselves with the Europeans and attempt to overthrow the Edo regime. Although it is questionable how realistic the Tokugawa concern over Christianity was, there can be no doubt that the presence in Kyushu ports of Europeans capable of providing arms and other military supplies to the western daimyos was a very real threat to national peace. Short of seeking to assert more complete military overlordship of the country than had been achieved at Sekigahara, especially in the western provinces, the Tokugawa actually had no practical alternative other than to impose some sort of seclusion policy if they wished to ensure the security of their regime.

As we saw in the last chapter, Hideyoshi gave a forewarning of the persecution of Christians in 1587 when he abruptly ordered all missionaries to leave Japan. Although the order was not strictly enforced, it was never rescinded; and ten years later, in 1597, Hideyoshi struck with fury against a group of missionaries and their followers and thus inaugurated some four decades of persecutions that led to the virtual extirpation of Christianity from Japan. One of the things that lay behind the 1597 incident was an ugly rivalry between the Jesuit missionaries, supported by the Portuguese, and the Franciscans, who came to Japan in the company of the Spanish (via Manila) in the 1580s. Whereas the Jesuits paid great attention to securing converts from among the ruling samurai class, the mendicant Franciscans devoted their efforts primarily to winning over the poor and lowly. And while the Jesuits regarded themselves as an elite, the Franciscans took pride in flaunting their humility and self-imposed poverty.

In 1596, at the height of the Jesuit-Franciscan rivalry, a Spanish galleon was shipwrecked on Shikoku Island and its cargo confiscated by Hideyoshi's officials. Evidently the pilot of the galleon, angered by the loss of the cargo, warned the Japanese officials that military conquest by Spain would soon follow based on the spy work being done by the Franciscans in Japan. The Franciscan version of the story was that the Jesuits, not the pilot, concocted the story about spying and conquest. In any case, Hideyoshi promptly ordered the rounding up of Franciscan missionaries for execution. Six missionaries of the central provinces were arrested and they, along with twenty of their Japanese converts, were paraded to Nagasaki, where, early in 1597, they were crucified and became the first Christian martyrs in Japan.

Hideyoshi died in 1598 and Tokugawa Ieyasu withheld attacking Christianity because of his desire to increase trade with the Europeans, especially the Dutch and English, who arrived in Japan in 1600. But in 1614 the Tokugawa chieftain, possibly influenced by reports from the Dutch and English Protestants that Catholic missionaries were engaged in subversion, issued an edict strictly banning Christianity. Thereupon began the period of mass persecutions that took the lives of some five to six thousand European and Japanese Christians before it subsided about 1640.

The records will never enable us fully to fathom the conflicting emotions of persecutors and persecuted during this grim phase of Japanese history. But for the interested reader there is an engrossing novel on the subject: *Silence (Chinmoku)*, by the contemporary Catholic writer Endō Shūsaku (1923–96). *Silence* is based on the true story of a Portuguese priest, Christovão Ferreira, who apostatized at Nagasaki in 1633. It is a fictional account of how two other priests, who had been Ferreira's disciples, made their way secretly to Japan to learn the truth about the apostasy. In the book the priests, after being sheltered by Japanese Christian villagers in Kyushu, are forced to separate, and what follows is essentially the story of one of them, Sebastian Rodrigues. It relates how Rodrigues eventually finds Ferreira and how he, too, is driven to apostatize.

Rodrigues first confronts the crisis of faith that leads to his apostasy when, after witnessing the brutal martyrdom of several of the Kyushu villagers, he is asked by another villager, Kichijiro (who is actually an informer), what the Japanese Christians have done to deserve this punishment from God:

> I suppose I [Rodrigues] should simply cast from my mind these meaningless words of the coward; yet why does his plaintive voice pierce my breast with all the pain of a sharp needle? Why has Our Lord imposed this torture and this persecution on poor Japanese peasants? No, Kichijiro was trying to express something different, something even more sickening. The silence of God. Already twenty years have passed since the persecution broke out; the black soil of Japan has been filled with the lament of so many Christians; the red blood of priests has flowed profusely; the walls of the churches have fallen down; and in the face of this terrible and merciless sacrifice offered up to Him, God has remained silent. This was the problem that lay behind the plaintive question of Kichijiro.[3]

Betrayed by Kichijiro, Rodrigues is seized by the shogunate authorities and is accusingly told by one of them that, although he may have come to Japan to save souls, in fact it is Japanese "souls" that are dying for him:

> And whenever a [European priest] is captured it is Japanese blood that will flow. How many times have I told you that it is the Japanese who have to die for your selfish dream. It is time to leave us in peace.[4]

In addition to God's silence, Endō's book deals also with the great issue of how the Japanese adopt or reject elements of foreign cultures. Rodrigues's inquisitors, for example, inform us that even when the Japanese of the late sixteenth century seemed to be accepting Christianity, they were actually transforming the Christian God into a deity of their own, a deity compatible with their religious traditions. Silence is an important intellectual inquiry into cultural borrowing as a major phenomenon in Japanese history.

The Tokugawa held approximately one-quarter of the agricultural land of Japan. In addition, they directly administered a number of the major cities, including Kyoto, Osaka, and Nagasaki, as well as certain important mining sites. The remainder of the country was divided into the domains or *han* of the daimyos. During the Tokugawa period there were two principal kinds of territorial lords: hereditary *(fudai)* daimyos, who had pledged personal loyalty to the Tokugawa before Sekigahara and were raised to daimyo status after this great victory; and "outside" *(tozama)* daimyos, who had been peers of the Tokugawa family head before 1600 and, whether friends or foes at Sekigahara, submitted to him only after he became national hegemon. Because of their long-standing allegiance to the Tokugawa, the *fudai* daimyos were allowed to serve in the shogunal government; the *tozama* daimyos, on the other hand, were barred from all participation in the ruling affairs of Edo.

In theory, the daimyos remained autonomous rulers of the *han*. In practice, the shogunate not only dictated rules of conduct for them but also severely restricted their freedom of action. Daimyos, for example, were not allowed to marry or to repair castles in the domains without permission of the shogunate. Moreover, especially during the first century of Tokugawa rule, the daimyos were frequently shifted from one domain to another or were deprived of their domains entirely for various acts prohibited by the shogunate. But the most important measure by which the Tokugawa controlled the daimyos was the "alternate attendance" *(sankin kōtai)* system, implemented between 1635 and 1642, which required the daimyos to spend every other year in attendance at the shogunate court in Edo (half the daimyos were in Edo one year and the other half were there the next year) and to leave their wives and children behind whenever they returned to their domains. In addition to discouraging any separatist or other seditious thoughts, the alternate attendance system placed a heavy financial burden on the daimyos that further reduced the feasibility of their opposing the shogunate.

Although intended primarily to control the daimyos, the alternate attendance system had other, far-reaching effects, not all of which could have been foreseen by the shogunate. The rapid and vast flow of warriors, their families and servants, and countless artisans, merchants, and others into Edo soon swelled its population to enormous size, perhaps as many as a million, making it one of the largest cities in the world. Meanwhile, the constant shuttling back and forth of daimyo retinues—some numbering in the thousands—from domains to Edo and back contributed greatly to the development of transportation facilities throughout the country. It also proved a great stimulus to the expansion of commerce, since provisioning the retinues and providing for their needs while on the road became big business.

The alternate attendance system also had important consequences in the cultural realm, contributing to the development for the first time of a truly national culture. Thus, for example, the daimyos and their followers from throughout the country who regularly visited Edo were the disseminators of what became a national dialect or "lingua franca" and, ultimately, the standard language of modern Japan.[5] They also fostered the spread of customs, rules of etiquette, standards of taste, fashions, and the like that gave to Japanese everywhere a common lifestyle.

Tokugawa society was officially divided into four classes: samurai, peasants, artisans, and merchants. The main social cleavage, however, was between the ruling samurai class—whose members, from Hideyoshi's time on, had been called upon to leave the countryside (if they had not already done so) and take up residence in the castle towns and cities—and the commoners. The samurai received fixed annual stipends based on the rice harvest of their former fiefs and enjoyed a variety of special privileges, including the exclusive right to wear swords and to cut down on the spot any commoners who offended them.

During the age of provincial wars there had been much social mobility among warriors. By their wits and fighting prowess alone, many men, including some originally from the peasant and merchant classes, rose from obscure positions to high levels of military command. Saitō Dōsan (1494–1556), for example, started as an oil merchant but eventually became daimyo of Mino province, marrying his daughter to Nobunaga; and Hideyoshi, as we have seen, made the unprecedentedly spectacular climb from peasant to national hegemon. Determined to prevent the kind of social upheaval that had made possible the careers of men like Dōsan and Hideyoshi, the Tokugawa instituted a rigid status system among warriors. This system, which prescribed distinctions of the most minute kind for all manner of things, including style of residence, type of clothing, form of transportation, size of retinue, value of gifts given and received, and even, in the case of daimyos, seating positions at the shogun's court in Edo castle, was intended to lock all samurai into place on a social hierarchy that denied the possibility of anyone's rise or fall.

Because they were primary producers of food, the peasants were honored with second place in the official social ordering. But as Sir George Sansom has noted, "[Tokugawa-period] statesmen thought highly of agriculture, but not of agriculturalists."[6] The life of the average peasant was one of much toil and little joy. Organized into villages that were largely self-governing, the peasants were obliged to render a substantial portion of their farming yields—on average, perhaps 50 percent or more—to the samurai, who provided few services in return. The resentment of peasants toward samurai grew steadily throughout the Tokugawa period and was manifested in countless peasant rebellions which, although they never seriously threatened the daimyo domains, much less the shogunate itself, proved increasingly vexatious to the samurai authorities, who were often obliged to accede to peasant demands.

Along with the upper strata of the samurai class, the socially despised artisans and merchants—known collectively as *chōnin* or townsmen— enjoyed the greatest prosperity in Tokugawa times. Although in the long run the seclusion policy undeniably limited the economic growth of Tokugawa Japan by its severe restrictions both on foreign trade and on the inflow of technology from overseas, it also ensured a lasting peace that made possible a great upsurge in the domestic economy, especially during the first century of shogunate rule. Agricultural productivity, for example, increased markedly in the seventeenth century; transportation and communication facilities, benefiting in particular from the alternate attendance system, were extensively improved; urban populations in the key administrative and trading centers of the country, beginning with Edo, rose dramatically; and commerce, stimulated especially by the alternate attendance system and a sharp expansion in the use of money, spread at a rate that would have been inconceivable a century earlier when it had been confined mainly to the central provinces and the foreign entry ports of Kyushu.

It is ironic that the prosperity of the Tokugawa period most greatly benefited that class, the townsmen, that the authorities had emphatically relegated to the bottom of the social scale. Yet this was inevitable. Both samurai and peasants were dependent almost solely on income from agriculture and constantly suffered declines in real income as the result of endemic inflation; only the townsmen, who as commercialists could adjust to price fluctuations, were in a position to profit significantly from the economic growth of the age. We should not be surprised, therefore, to find this class giving rise to a lively and exuberant culture that reached its finest flowering in the Genroku epoch at the end of the seventeenth and the beginning of the eighteenth centuries. The mainstays of Genroku culture were the theatre, painting (chiefly in the form of the woodblock print), and prose fiction, all of which, while drawing heavily on Japan's aristocratic cultural tradition, evolved as distinctly popular, bourgeois forms of art.

Before turning to the *chōnin* arts, however, let us look first at the development of Confucianism during the early Tokugawa period inasmuch as this most Chinese of creeds set much of the intellectual tone for the period. The Japanese had, of course, absorbed Confucian thinking from the earliest centuries of contact with China, but for more than a millennium Buddhism had drawn most of their intellectual attention. Not until the Tokugawa period did they come to study Confucianism with any great zeal.

One of the most conspicuous features of the transition from medieval to early modern times in Japan was the precipitous decline in the vigor of Buddhism and the rise of a secular spirit. The military potential and much of the remaining landed wealth of the medieval Buddhist sects had been destroyed during the advance toward unification in the late sixteenth century. And although Buddhism remained very much part of the daily lives of the people, it not only ceased to hold appeal for many Japanese intellectuals but indeed even drew the outright scorn and enmity of some.

The vigorous and colorful outburst of artistic creativity in the Momoyama epoch was the first major reaction to the gloom of medievalism. With the advent of the Tokugawa period, this reaction spread to the intellectual field and stimulated a great Confucian revival. Interestingly, as we observed in an earlier chapter, it was the Buddhist church—and especially the Zen sect—that paved the way for the upsurge in Confucian studies during Tokugawa times. Japanese Zen priests had from at least the fourteenth century on assiduously investigated the tenets of Sung

Neo-Confucianism, and in ensuing centuries had produced a corpus of research upon which the Neo-Confucian scholarship of the Tokugawa period was ultimately built.

Neo-Confucianism had evolved during the Sung period in China partly as a reaction against Buddhism, which from mid-T'ang times had increasingly come to be criticized as an alien and harmful creed, and partly as an attempt to revitalize native Confucian values and institutions. In the process of its formulation, however, Neo-Confucianism absorbed much that was fundamentally Buddhist, including an elaborate cosmology and metaphysical structure. Of the various schools of Neo-Confucianism that emerged in China, it was the teachings of the great twelfth-century philosopher Chu Hsi (1130–1200) that eventually were accepted as the orthodox doctrine of Confucian learning. From the early fourteenth century until the abolishment of the examination system in 1905, Chu Hsi's brand of Neo-Confucianism was painstakingly studied and rehashed by countless generations of candidates for the degrees of official preferment and entry into the ministerial class that were traditionally bestowed by the Chinese court.

In Japan, too, it was Chu Hsi's Neo-Confucianism that was embraced by the Tokugawa shogunate as an orthodoxy. Although shogunate authorities and Tokugawa-period intellectuals in general had relatively little interest in the purely metaphysical side of Chu Hsi's teachings, they found his philosophy to be enormously useful in justifying or ideologically legitimizing the feudal structure of state and society that had emerged in Japan by the seventeenth century.

Chu Hsi Neo-Confucian philosophy is a dualistic system based on the concepts of *ri,* "principle," and *ki,* a term that seems to defy precise translation into English but has been rendered as "ether" or "substance." The essence of all things lies in their *ri* or principles, which in humans can be conceived as their basic natures. But these natures, which in the orthodox Confucian tradition are regarded as inherently "good," become obscured by the functioning of *ki,* a force governed by the passions and other emotions that produce evil. The fundamental purpose of Neo-Confucian practice is to calm one's turbid *ki* to allow one's nature *(ri)* to shine forth. The person who achieves this purpose becomes a sage, his *ri* seen as one with the universal principle, known as the "supreme ultimate" *(taikyoku),* that governs all things.

Neo-Confucianism proposed two main courses to clarify *ri,* one objective and the other subjective.[7] The objective course was through the acquisition of knowledge by means of the "investigation of things," a phrase taken by Chu Hsi from the Chinese classic *The Great Learning (Ta hsüeh).* At the heart of things to investigate was history, wherein lay knowledge about how the great, sage rulers of the past governed by moral example. Thus rulers and their ministers were in particular enjoined to inquire into the lessons of history in order to chart a proper course of governance. Quite apart from any practical guidance to good rulership it may have provided, this Neo-Confucian stress on historical research proved to be a tremendous spur to scholarship and learning in general during the Tokugawa period;[8] and, as we will see in the next chapter, it also facilitated the development of other, heterodox lines of intellectual inquiry.

Whereas the objective course to the clarification of one's *ri* was fully within the Confucian tradition, the subjective course appeared to have been taken almost directly from Buddhism, and in particular Zen. It was the course of "preserving one's heart by holding fast to seriousness," which called for the clarification of *ri* by means remarkably similar to Zen meditation. This does not mean, of course, that Neo-Confucianism and Zen were in any true sense the same. Whereas Zen and Buddhism in general urged individuals to renounce this world of suffering and per-petual flux and to seek entry to a transcendent realm of bliss (in the case of Zen, through *satori* or "enlightenment"), Neo-Confucianism held that the physical world was based on an inherently perfect moral order that could be known through the illumination of *ri* writ small and the supreme ultimate writ large. In short, whereas Buddhism aspired to perfection in another world, Neo-Confucianism sought it in this world.

Neo-Confucianism's focus on this world harked back to the most fun-damental teaching of Confucius himself, which was his humanism. And from this standpoint Neo-Confucianism, in keeping with all other Con-fucian schools, was primarily concerned with the conduct and affairs of people in the here and now. Social order demanded a strict hierarchical structuring of the classes and conformity by all people with the obliga-tions imposed by the five primary human relationships: the relationships between father and son, ruler and subject, husband and wife, older and younger brothers, and two friends. It can readily be imagined how ap-pealing the rulers of Tokugawa Japan found these highly conservative social strictures that called upon people everywhere to accept without question their lots in life and to place highest value in the performance of such duties as filial piety to their parents and loyalty to their overlords. Tokugawa social hierarchy (based on samurai as rulers, and peasants, artisans, and merchants as ruled) had, in fact, emerged from medieval feudalism. Neo-Confucianism, imported from China, endorsed this hier-archy as based on laws thought to be as immutable as the laws of nature itself.

Much of the credit for establishing and propagating Chu Hsi Neo-Confucianism has traditionally been given to Hayashi Razan (1583–1657), a man of diverse scholarly accomplishments who served four shoguns over a period of more than fifty years. Noted as a Confucian theorist, historian, and specialist in legal precedence, Razan has been thought to have done more than anyone else to gain acceptance of the

Chu Hsi school of Neo-Confucianism as the principal creed of the Toku-gawa shogunate. Recently, however, scholars have called into question not only Razan's role in attracting the shogunate to Chu Hsi Neo-Confu-cianism, but even the dating of when that creed was accepted as the shogunate's orthodoxy.[9]

Neo-Confucianism's first task in the Tokugawa period had been to dis-engage itself from Buddhism, a task that was accomplished by Fujiwara Seika (1561–1619) and Razan, both of whom started their careers as Buddhist priests and only later were allowed to become independent Confucian teachers. But apparently not until much later in the seven-teenth century—long after Razan's death—did the shogunate seriously turn to Neo-Confucianism. In the process, the Hayashi family, in the generations after Razan, became securely fixed as the official Confucian advisers to the shogunate and the hereditary heads of a Confucian acad-emy in Edo.

Although Neo-Confucianism was unquestionably a valuable ideologi-cal tool for the shogunate and a powerful stimulus to learning in the Tokugawa period, it also exerted a certain stultifying influence on litera-ture and the arts in general. Confucianists have always been absorbed first and foremost with morality, and their liking for didactic literature has often led to very dull writing. But perhaps the most telling example of how the Confucian sense of propriety and reserve stifled artistic creativity in the Tokugawa period can be observed in the history of the distin-guished Kanō school of painters.

From the time of Masanobu in the late fifteenth century, the Kanō artists had served the successive military rulers of Japan—the Ashikaga, Nobunaga, and Hideyoshi—and shortly after the founding of the Toku-gawa shogunate they entered into the employ of the country's new war-rior chieftains in Edo. Kanō Eitoku's son, Mitsunobu (1565–1608), who had assisted his father in the decoration of Nobunaga's castle at Azuchi and later did much work for Hideyoshi, was in his later years summoned by Ieyasu to decorate the Tokugawa castle in Edo. But the true founder or "restorer" of the Kanō as the official school of shogunal painters in the Tokugawa era was Eitoku's grandson, Tan'yū (1602–74), who moved permanently to Edo in 1614. In time, there came to be four major and twelve minor branches of the Kanō engaged on a stipendiary basis by the shogunate. Moreover, many other bearers of the Kanō name were employed by daimyos as their official *han* artists. The various Kanō schoolmen thus secured a virtual monopoly of the appointments open to painters among the new Tokugawa military elite. Anxious to please their masters—who were strongly imbued with Confucian moralism—and reluctant to innovate, the Kanō artists after Tan'yū produced little work of real distinction. On the contrary, the best painting of the Tokugawa period was done by others.

The outstanding artist of the early seventeenth century and one of

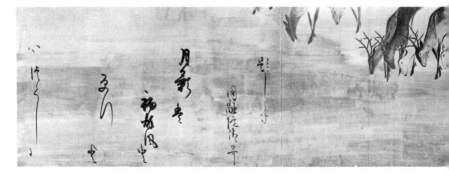

Fig. 49   Poem scroll by Sōtatsu and Kōetsu *(Seattle Art Museum)*

the finest painters in all of Japanese history was Tawaraya Sōtatsu (d. 1643), a man of merchant stock who drew his inspiration from the ancient cultural tradition of the imperial court. Although we know almost nothing about Sōtatsu's personal life, we can deduce some of the influences that worked upon him from his close association with another distinguished craftsman and artist of the age, Hon'ami Kōetsu (1558–1637).

Kōetsu, the son of a Kyoto merchant family that dealt in fine swords, was a person of many skills, including the tea ceremony, the making and adornment of pottery and lacquerware, painting, and—perhaps most notable of all—calligraphy. Indeed, some of the most treasured works of art to come down from this period are "poem scrolls" done jointly by Kōetsu and Sōtatsu, scrolls in which Kōetsu inscribed *waka* (often taken from such admired anthologies of the ancient period as the tenth-century *Kokinshū* and the early thirteenth century *Shinkokinshū*) over the painting of flowers, grass, and animals by Sōtatsu (fig. 49).

Both Kōetsu and Sōtatsu were representatives of the upper merchant class of those cities—especially Kyoto, Nara, and Sakai in the central provinces—that had flourished commercially during the late medieval and Momoyama periods. A number of noted artists and men of culture, from the Higashiyama tea master Shukō to Sen no Rikyū of Hideyoshi's day, emerged from the successful merchant houses of these cities to gain acceptance in the highest social circles of Japan's courtier and warrior elites. The Tokugawa period, of course, witnessed a continuation and expansion of commerce (at least domestically) and the rise of new and even greater urban centers at Osaka and Edo, cities which in the seventeenth century produced a bourgeois culture that catered especially to the great bulk of their middle- and lower-class townsmen. Hence, the art of Kōetsu and Sōtatsu was part of the "higher" or more traditional line of cultural development from pre-Tokugawa times, and the men

themselves were members of a former class of privileged merchants whose influence and status were entering into decline.

Although Sōtatsu employed various styles on many different formats, including horizontal scrolls and folding fans (his family were apparently fan makers), he is noted chiefly for his work in the monumental decorative tradition of Kanō Eitoku and his contemporaries of the Momoyama epoch. Sōtatsu, however, was far more of a "Yamato artist" than his Momoyama predecessors, insofar as he selected the themes for many of his greatest paintings from the Japanese, rather than directly from the Chinese, cultural past. Two of his best-known works are screen paintings based on *The Tale of Genji* and on the *bugaku* form of dance that was popular during the Nara period.

Sōtatsu was a superb master of his craft, not only in his use of a strong and sure brush line and in the matching of colors (including the characteristic gold-leaf backgrounds of the mature decorative style), but also in his sense of design and capacity to exploit to a greater degree than any who came before him the geometrics of screen painting. Such works as the Genji Screen are particularly striking to the modern viewer as studies in form and the placement of objects that seem extraordinarily similar in approach, if not subject matter, to those of Western artists from at least the time of Cézanne and the Post-Impressionists.

Sōtatsu's immediate followers were mere imitators, but the decorative school produced one more great master at the end of the seventeenth century in Ogata Kōrin (1658–1716).[10] Like Sōtatsu and Kōetsu (to whom he was distantly related), Kōrin was the scion of a merchant family that had prospered in Kyoto since the Momoyama epoch and had even had personal and business ties with Hideyoshi and, later, the Tokugawa and imperial families. The Ogata were dealers in textiles, many richly decorated in styles that became popular for clothing during the late sixteenth and seventeenth centuries: no doubt Kōrin's exceptionally powerful sense of design came in part from familiarity with the family wares. In fact, Kōrin himself later became one of the most widely imitated designers of the *kosode* (small sleeve) type of kimono that was a main item of clothing in the Tokugawa period.

Kōrin's great grandfather had married Kōetsu's sister, and his grandfather had participated in the activities of an artists' colony that Kōetsu founded at Takagamine in the outskirts of Kyoto. His father, Ogata Sōken, had also maintained the family interest in the Kōetsu-Sōtatsu school of art. But unfortunately, Sōken was less able than his predecessors to afford the leisure from business that the pursuit of art required, and it was during his time that the Ogata family fortunes declined. Nevertheless, Kōrin was amply provided for during his youth and, by all accounts, became a true Genroku profligate, frequenting the pleasure quarters and pursuing a life of idleness and debauchery.

Not until he ran out of funds sometime about 1693 and was forced to secure a loan from his younger brother Kenzan (1663–1743), who became a distinguished potter and painter in his own right, did Kōrin think seriously about the need to find permanent employment. He began by teaming up with Kenzan—in much the same way that Sōtatsu had teamed up with Kōetsu—and decorating a number of the fine ceramic pieces his brother produced. But although he did this and many other varied kinds of artwork, Kōrin, like Sōtatsu, achieved his greatest fame as a painter of folding screens.

Kōrin was the last of the great decorative artists of early modern Japan and might be said to have brought the decorative style to its highest level of perfection. He much admired the painting of Sōtatsu and even copied a number of the earlier master's work. But whereas Sōtatsu had based works such as the Genji Screen on familiar and easily recognizable themes, Kōrin's best-known paintings are in a purely design-like and decorative manner. This is clearly observable in his Iris Screen, one of the most famous of all Japanese paintings. The screen was actually inspired by an episode from *The Tales of Ise* of the tenth century in which Narihira, who is having a wayside lunch near where some irises are growing, is challenged by a companion to compose a *waka* poem on "A Traveler's Sentiments" and to use the syllables in the word "iris" *(kakitsubata)* to begin each of its five lines. Kōrin made no attempt to reproduce the narrative itself, but simply placed irises in "disembodied" fashion against a stark gold-leaf background. With their blue blossoms and green leaves providing a striking contrast to the dominant golden coloring of the screen, the flowers seem almost to dance before the viewer's eyes (fig. 50).

We noticed that during the fifteenth century a style of residential room, the *shoin* style, evolved from the model of a type of den or library

Fig. 50   Ogata Kōrin's "Iris and Bridge," a painting of the same subject as the more famous Iris Screen *(The Metropolitan Museum of Art, Louisa E. McBurney Gift Fund, 1953)*

found in Zen temples. The principal features of the *shoin* room included *tatami* matting (covering the entire floor), *fusuma* and *shōji* sliding doors, an alcove *(tokonoma)*, asymmetrical shelves, and a low, installed desk called *shoin* (which gave its name to the entire style of room). Not until the Momoyama epoch and early Tokugawa period, however, were all these features fully integrated to form the mature *shoin* style. In the process, three major variations evolved: a grand *shoin* style for the construction of rooms to serve as settings for the public functions and rituals of the samurai elite (shogun and daimyos); an intimate—in many cases, simple and unpretentious—style for use primarily in private samurai residences; and a special style called *sukiya* (literally, "building or room of taste") adapted to the needs of the tea ceremony. Tokugawa law prohibited use of the *shoin* style in the homes of all save samurai, but with the passage of time members of the other classes managed to incorporate *shoin* elements into their rooms. By the time Japan made the transition into the modern age in the late nineteenth century, the *shoin* room was established as the prototypical Japanese residential room. It remains so today.

In addition to serving a variety of interior design and aesthetic tastes, the *shoin* room, through adaptation, also met the demands for social status distinction that were so important in Tokugawa society, especially among the samurai. In earlier times, when residences and most other buildings had floors of polished wood, status was recognized by having some people sit on mats and others directly on the floor or by using mats of different sizes or with different border designs. When *tatami* mats of uniform size (each about six feet by three feet) were used to cover the entire floor in the *shoin*-style room, however, it became necessary to devise new means for showing differences in status, at least between the guest of honor and the others present at a gathering. In private residences, the seat in front of the alcove was established as the place of honor (the records tell us of some cases in which the guest of honor was seated *in* the alcove). In rooms in the grand *shoin* style, the status distinction between the highest-ranking public official present and the others was further reinforced by having him sit in a part of the room's floor structurally raised a step above the rest of the floor.

Probably the best surviving example of a room in the grand *shoin* style is the audience hall at Nijō Castle in Kyoto. One of the most popular stops on tourist itineraries in Kyoto, the castle was built by the Tokugawa as a residence for the shogun when he visited the imperial capital. Used on two occasions by the third shogun, Iemitsu (shogun, 1623–51), it remained unoccupied (at least by shoguns) for more than two centuries, until the last years of the Tokugawa shogunate. The audience hall at Nijō Castle is clearly divided into two parts, an "upper" part for the shogun and a "lower" part for the daimyos in attendance upon him. Although the difference between the upper and lower parts is only a step, the rectangular design of the hall and the use of two rows of friezes (one row about three-fifths up the wall and the other at the edge of the ceiling) to accentuate its horizontality provide a dramatic, imposing setting for anyone seated on the upper part. The setting is made even more imposing by the location of an enormous alcove on the back wall—that is, the wall in front of which, in Tokugawa times, the shogun sat.

Although the second of the three types of *shoin*-style architecture mentioned above was intended by shogunate law, as noted, exclusively for samurai, by far the finest example of it to come down to us from the Tokugawa period—and, indeed, one of the truly great masterpieces of architecture in all of Japanese history—is the Katsura Detached Palace in southwestern Kyoto, built over a period from about 1616 to 1660 by a branch of the imperial family (fig. 51). In the rambling structures of this villa, which has had a profound influence in the twentieth century on both Japanese and foreign architects, are combined those elements of Japanese architecture—including cleanness of line, simplicity of adornment, harmony of buildings to surrounding gardens and ponds, and the flow of space through rooms with readily removable partitions—that will forever be a source of aesthetic wonder and delight.

Two authorities say this about the Katsura Detached Palace: "The Katsura Villa is perhaps the most perfect example in Japan of the integration of architecture and its natural surroundings. The rustic teahouses sequestered in garden corners, the stones leading from the pond up to the Shoin complex, the open verandas and removable exterior screens, all contribute to that interrelation."[11] The reference here to rustic teahouses calls attention to the fact that Katsura, with its several retreats

Fig. 51   Katsura Detached Palace *(photograph by Joseph Shulman)*

for the enjoyment of tea or engagement in the tea ceremony, is also an outstanding example of the third of the *shoin* styles, the *sukiya* or teahouse style.

One final work of Tokugawa-period architecture that must be noted is the Tōshōgū Shrine in Nikkō (fig. 52). Present-day visitors to Japan who take the excursion of several hours by train from Tokyo to Nikkō will be enchanted by its beautiful mountain and forest setting. They will also be dazzled by a shrine comprising brilliantly colored buildings, almost completely encased in a profusion of carvings and other ornamentation, that are marvels of craftsmanship. This great shrine was constructed during the seventeenth century by the shogunate as the permanent resting place of Ieyasu, whom the Tokugawa transformed into a national god with the designation of Tōshō Dai-Gongen (Great Avatar Who Illuminates the East). During the remainder of the Tokugawa period, the Tōshōgū Shrine was visited on countless occasions by shoguns, emissaries of the imperial court, and even foreign (Korean and Ryukyuan) envoys.

The calendrical era of Genroku lasted from 1688 until 1703, but the Genroku cultural epoch is usually taken to mean the span of approximately a half-century from, say, 1675 until 1725. Setting the stage for this rise of a townsman-oriented culture was nearly a century of peace and steady commercial growth. Such growth was, of course, almost en-

Fig. 52   Tōshōgū Shrine at Nikkō *(Consulate General of Japan, New York)*

tirely domestic and, owing in large part to the strict limitations on foreign trade imposed by the seclusion policy, it had begun to taper off markedly even during the Genroku epoch. Nevertheless, the commercial advances of the first century of Tokugawa rule were sufficient to bring to the fore for the first time in Japanese history a numerically significant and prosperous class of merchants who, although still regarded as inferior by their samurai masters, came increasingly to assert their social and cultural independence.

Other factors that contributed to the flourishing of Genroku culture were the rapid spread of learning and literacy among all classes in the seventeenth century and the transformation of warfare from a practical reality, which it had been throughout the medieval age, to little more than a distant memory. The samurai still sported their swords and flaunted their martial ways, but they were generally resigned to the fact that their proper, and apparently permanent, function was to practice the arts of peace rather than those of war.

One result of the great increase in literacy and also of wealth and lei-sure time for many, especially merchants, by Genroku times was a grow-ing demand for knowledge about and instruction in "elegant pastimes" *(yūgei)*, such as the tea ceremony, flower arrangement, incense identifi-cation, the playing of musical instruments, dance, and theatrical chant-ing. During the medieval age many of these "pastimes"—regarded then as "ways" *(michi)*—had been considered very serious pursuits, and knowl-edge about them was frequently transmitted secretly from one person to another (for example, from master to disciple). It was believed by the medieval Japanese that investigation into the way of flowers or the way of incense, to name but two, could even lead to Buddhist enlightenment.

In the Tokugawa period, most of the secrets of the medieval ways were revealed to all who wished to know them in the process of the com-mercialization of the ways and their transformation into elegant pas-times. Books explaining the various pastimes and giving advice about how to pursue them were published in great quantities, and schools big and small were opened to provide personal instruction in them.

The writer Saikaku (discussed below) wrote, "Until age thirteen a person lacks discernment. From thirteen to twenty-four or twenty-five he is under the control of his parents. From then until forty-five he must work for himself and put his family in order. But thereafter he can devote himself without restraint to the quest of pleasure."[12] One avenue to pleasure was the elegant pastimes, and many stories have come down to us about those who threw restraint to the winds in pursuing them. Here, for example, is the story of a merchant who, because of the good fortune of birth, did not have to wait until Saikaku's suggested age of forty-five to enjoy himself:

> From his father's time he had been brought up in style, and so he never had the merchant spirit. He lived in the grand manner and went in for fine tea utensils and tea rooms. . . . He was thoroughly extravagant in his tastes and put up all sorts of buildings and had tea gardens and tea rooms that surpassed those of other people in stylishness. . . . People still talk about him. . . . He took hardly any interest in business and spent his time in amuse-ments.[13]

Here is the story of another merchant devoted to pleasure whose interests, like that of the first merchant, centered especially on the tea ceremony:

Fig. 53   "House of Entertainment" (detail), *ca.* mid-1640s *(Honolulu Academy of Arts, Gift of Robert Allerton, 1960 [2758.1])*

[He] became extraordinarily dissolute and spent money in abandoning himself to promiscuity. . . . Taking up the tea ceremony as his profession, he carried on just as he liked and finally went blind and died at the age of forty-two or forty-three. As his fortune gradually declined in view of these things, he pawned his utensils and so on and crashed when advances to daimyo were not repaid.[14]

The spawning grounds of townsman culture were the pleasure and entertainment quarters that formed, almost like extraterritorial enclaves, within the great cities: the Yoshiwara of Edo, the Shinmachi of Osaka, and the Shimabara of Kyoto (fig. 53). Abounding in brothels, theatres, teahouses, public baths, and sundry other places of diversion and assignation, these quarters were the famous "floating worlds" *(ukiyo)* of Tokugawa fact and legend. *Ukiyo,* although used specifically from about this time to designate such demimondes, meant in the broadest sense the insubstantial and ever-changing existence in which man is enmeshed. To medieval Buddhists, this had been a wretched and sorrowful existence, and *ukiyo*[15] always carried the connotation that life is fundamentally sad; but, in Genroku times, the term was more commonly taken to mean a world that was pleasurable precisely because it was constantly changing, exciting, and up-to-date.

In view of the tremendous pressure that Tokugawa society placed on the individual to conform to the rigid rules of Confucian behavior, sections like the pleasure quarters, offering escape from the heavy responsibilities of family and occupation, were almost essential safety valves against overt social unrest. Although the shogunate always maintained careful surveillance over them, the quarters were to a great extent self-governing. Social distinctions based on birth or status meant little within their precincts: it was money, not pedigree, that usually carried the day in the floating world.

One of the first and greatest chroniclers of townsman life was the poet and author of prose fiction Ihara Saikaku (1642–93). Born into a merchant family of Osaka, Saikaku did not begin to write the fiction that brought him his most lasting fame until he was past forty. His main literary interest during his earlier years was devoted, rather, to the composition of *haikai,* a form of poetry derived from the linked verse of medieval times. As a result of the efforts of various innovating schools (to be discussed later), *haikai* had been freed from the stylistic and topical restraints that had rendered linked verse, like the classical *waka* before it, virtually devoid of the potentiality for original expression. And, in the hands of a facile manipulator of words like Saikaku, it served as an effective device for lively and witty poetizing. Saikaku the poet, however, seems to have been more interested in quantity than quality. Engaging in one-man poetry marathons, he composed the staggering total of 23,500 *haikai* in a single twenty-four-hour period, and thus established a presumably unbeatable, if not necessarily enviable, record for concentrated poetic output.

Frivolous as they appear, the poetry marathons may still be interpreted as an effort by the exuberant and energetic Saikaku to overcome the limitations of even the liberated *haikai* form of poetry, and thus to have been a kind of prelude to the prose writing that took up the last decade or so of his life. Saikaku's firm background in *haikai* is evident in his prose works, which are replete with poetic passages of alternating five- and seven-syllable lines.

Saikaku created a new genre of prose literature called *ukiyo-zōshi* or "books of the floating world," derived from writings known as *"kana* books" *(kana-zōshi)* that had evolved from the late medieval age. As their name implies, these latter writings were done largely in the *kana* syllabary in order to appeal to as wide a reading audience as possible. Advances in printing during the early Tokugawa period also helped increase the circulation of *kana* books, which included purely didactic pieces, adaptations of classics, travel accounts, and supernatural tales, as well as pleasure books on subjects such as loose women and the escapades of lecherous priests and samurai. Yet, by and large, the *kana* books retained a strongly medieval character, either in actual content and style or in the use of outmoded literary devices for presenting moralistic instruction. Saikaku's books of the floating world, by contrast, are realistic and up-to-date and are written in a style that, although occasionally didactic, is essentially detached and analytical.

Most of Saikaku's prose fiction falls into three major categories: erotic *(kōshoku)*, townsman, and samurai books. Since Saikaku was never entirely at home when writing about the samurai class, he did his best work within the erotic and townsman categories. His first book, published in 1682, was entitled *The Life of a Man Who Lived for Love (Kōshoku Ichidai Otoko)*[16] and was an "erotic" work, although the term *"kōshoku"* in its title might more accurately be taken to mean rakish rather than simply erotic. As variously used by Saikaku, *kōshoku* came to have a wide range of meanings, from rakish or romantic on the one hand to lecherous or perverted on the other. In any case, a new form of love—*kōshoku*—was firmly established by Saikaku and others of the Genroku epoch as a major theme in writing and the visual arts. Until this time, love, as conventionalized in the arts, had been based primarily on the principles of courtly love, which had been evolved some seven or eight hundred years earlier by the Heian courtiers and which stressed the aesthetic rather than the erotic.

The Life of a Man Who Lived for Love is the story of Yonosuke, a townsman who commences a long life of sexual adventures by making advances to a maid at the age of eight; at sixty-one, after having enjoyed all the delights that Japanese women can provide him, he sets forth by boat to find an island inhabited only by females. Divided into fifty-four chapters, each of which deals with a year in Yonosuke's life, *The Life of a Man Who Lived for Love* is little more than a collection of spicy episodes brought together as the doings of an indefatigable rake.

In 1686 Saikaku wrote another erotic work, entitled *Five Women Who Chose Love (Kōshoku Gonin Onna)*, which contains five fairly lengthy and well-structured tales that may properly be called novelettes. Whereas *The Life of a Man Who Lived for Love* deals mostly with life in the pleasure quarters, *Five Women Who Chose Love* concerns women of respectable townsman and peasant origins who, because of their excessively passionate natures, become involved in affairs that lead in all cases but one to dishonor and death. In this work, then, Saikaku shifted from accounts of the artificial world of the pleasure quarters to stories, based on real events, of people in everyday life. He also treated one of the most important social themes in all of Tokugawa literature, the conflict between human feelings *(ninjō)* and the heavy sense of duty *(giri)* imposed on the individual by the feudal laws and mores of the age.

In the same year that he wrote *Five Women Who Chose Love*, Saikaku produced still another major erotic work, entitled *The Life of an Amorous Woman (Kōshoku Ichidai Onna)*. This is a tale of the darker side of love, told in the first person, of uncontrolled lust and depravity. The heroine is a nymphomaniac (descended on her father's side from the courtier class of Kyoto) who makes her way through life largely on her own ingenuity and resourcefulness, engaging in a variety of occupations, including those of dancer, parlor maid, seamstress, and calligraphy teacher, as well as courtesan and, finally, common streetwalker. After noting that as a girl she had become intoxicated with love (of the sort she observed being practiced at court) and had come to regard it as the most important thing in life, she recounts her first affair at the tender age of twelve:

> There is naught in this world so strange as love. The several men who had set their affections on me were both fashionable and handsome; yet none of them aroused any tender feelings in me. Now, there was a humble warrior in the service of a certain courtier. The fellow was low in rank and of a type that most women would regard askance. Yet from the first letter that he wrote me his sentences were charged with a passion powerful enough to slay one. In note after note he set forth his ardent feelings, until, without realizing it, I myself began to be troubled in my heart. It was hard for us to meet, but with some cunning I managed to arrange a tryst and thus it was that I gave my body to him.
>
> Our amour was bound to become the gossip of the court and one dawn it "emerged into the light." In punishment I was banished to the neighborhood of Uji Bridge. My love, most grievous to relate, was put to death. For some days thereafter, as I lay tossing on my bed, half asleep, half awake, his silent form would appear terrifyingly before me. In my agony I thought that I must needs take my own life; yet, after some days had passed, I completely forgot about him. From this one may truly judge that nothing in this world is as base and fickle as a woman's heart.[17]

The years take their toll, and in the end the "Amorous Woman," old and destitute, ventures forth yet again in the dark of night with the forlorn hope of attracting unwary customers:

> In these days people have become so canny that, though it be only a matter of ten coppers, they exercise more care in their choice of a harlot from the streets than does a rich man in selecting a high-class courtesan. Sometimes they will wait until a passer-by appears with a torch, sometimes they will conduct the woman to the lantern of a guard box—in either case they scrutinize her closely, and nowadays, even when it is only a matter of hasty diversion, a woman who is old or ugly is promptly turned down. "For a thousand men who see, there are a thousand blind." So the saying goes; but on that night, alas, I did not meet a single one who was blind!
>
> Finally dawn began to appear: first the eight bells rang out, then seven. Aroused by their sound, the pack-horse drivers set forth with a clatter in the early-morning light. Yet I persisted in walking the streets, until the hour when the blacksmith and the bean-curd dealer opened their shutters. But no doubt my appearance and demeanour were not suited to this calling, for during the entire time not a single man solicited my favours. I resolved, then, that this would be my last effort in the Floating World at plying the lustful trade, and I gave it up for once and all.[18]

Saikaku's two great themes were love and money, and in his towns-man books, written mostly after his erotic studies, he examined the *chōnin* ethic of working hard, being clever, and becoming a financial success. *The Eternal Storehouse of Japan (Nihon Eitaigura)*, a collection of stories on the making and losing of fortunes, is perhaps his most celebrated work in this category. Yet, in the same way that he shifted in his erotic works from the romanticization of love to a Defoe-like recounting of the corrupting effect of sexual passion in *The Life of an Amorous Woman*, Saikaku turned his attention in his later townsman writings to the life of the middle- and lower-class merchant, which was generally one of un-ceasing drudgery and the struggle to keep one step ahead of the bill collector.

We observed earlier in this chapter the great emphasis placed on humanism in the Neo-Confucian tradition. But it is important also to note that the kind of humanism that evolved in the Tokugawa period was not at all like the humanism that emerged in the West from the Renaissance on. Whereas modern Western humanism became absorbed with people as individuals, with all their personal peculiarities, feelings, and ways, Japanese humanism of the Tokugawa period scarcely conceived of the existence of true individuals at all; rather, it focused on "the people" and regarded them as comprising essentially types, such as samurai, farmers, and courtesans. We can see this kind of humanistic attitude reflected clearly in the writings of Saikaku and other authors of Tokugawa times, whose fictional characters are invariably drawn either two-dimensionally or simply as stereotypes. For the most part, characters in Tokugawa literature do what we suppose they will do; there is little in the literature as a whole of that quality—character development—that is probably the single most important feature of the modern Western novel.

While Saikaku was perfecting a new kind of prose fiction, two forms of popular drama that had been evolving from at least the early seven-teenth century—the *kabuki* and the puppet theatre—also blossomed into maturity.

Kabuki owed much to both *nō* and *kyōgen*, the main theatrical forms of the medieval age. This is obvious not only in the kind of plays, acting techniques, and musical and narrative accompaniments used in early *kabuki*, but also in the physical staging of these productions. Even more immediate influences, however, can be traced that help explain how *kabuki* became the vigorous and popular type of entertainment it was during its first great flourishing in Genroku times.

The acknowledged originator of *kabuki* was a woman named Okuni, whose background is obscure but who was quite likely a former atten-dant at the great Shinto shrine at Izumo. Sometime in the late 1590s or the early years of the seventeenth century, Okuni led a troupe of female dancers in Kyoto in a kind of outdoor musical entertainment that was labeled (by others) "*kabuki* dancing" and, as a result of its commercial success, soon gave rise to competing troupes. The term *kabuki* was derived from *katamuki*—"slanted" or "strongly inclined"—and was used in this age to describe novel or eccentric behavior. Its application to the dancing of Okuni and her girls is a clear indication that the first *kabuki* company was regarded as a daring and not very proper undertaking.

One thing the Okuni troupe performed was "*nembutsu* dancing" *(nembutsu odori)*, a type of religious ecstaticism (in which people danced around and chanted their praise to Amida buddha) that dated back to the tenth-century evangelist of Pure Land Buddhism, Kūya, but was especially popularized among people everywhere by Ippen during the Kamakura period. By the late medieval age, *nembutsu odori* had become a form of folk dance that was performed more for entertainment than for religious purposes, and it survives in Japan today in the dancing done annually in the midsummer *bon* festival for the dead.

In addition to dances of this sort, the Okuni troupe also performed farcical skits in which they portrayed encounters between men and prostitutes or reenacted assignation scenes in teahouses and bathhouses. (No doubt the girls did these skits very professionally, since they were all apparently practicing harlots on the side.) Shogunate officials sternly disapproved of both the onstage and offstage behavior of female performers such as these, and in 1629, after a period of indecision, they banned their participation in *kabuki* altogether. This had the immediate effect of giving impetus to the rise of another form of entertainment known as "young men's *kabuki*" that had gradually been developing in the shadow of "women's *kabuki*." The performances of these attractive young men included certain kinds of acrobatics and flashing swordplay that were eventually to be incorporated into the mainstream of *kabuki* acting; but, to the dismay of the authorities, the youths were as much of a social nuisance as the female *kabuki* performers since they aroused the homosexual passions that had been widespread in Japan (particularly among samurai and Buddhist priests) from the medieval age on. Finally, in 1652, after a number of unseemly incidents including public brawls in the midst of performances over the affections of the actors on stage, the shogunate also banned young men's *kabuki*. Henceforth, only adult males (or youths who had shaved their forelocks to give the appearance that they were adults) were allowed to perform on the *kabuki* stage.

Throughout the Tokugawa period, *kabuki* was subjected to a greater or lesser degree of official suppression, and this suppression had an extremely important influence on the way in which it developed. Shogunate officials hesitated to ban *kabuki* entirely for at least two reasons. First, they regarded *kabuki*, like the floating world of which it became an integral part, as a necessary outlet for the more elemental drives of the masses, even though these grossly offended their Confucian sensibilities.

And second, they no doubt realized that, like prostitution itself (both male and female), it could never be completely eradicated and might just as well be held to some kind of formal account.

The banning of women from *kabuki* gave rise to the unique personage of the *onnagata*, or male performer of female roles. So special are the acting qualities cultivated over the centuries by the *onnagata* that, even if women were permitted to perform in *kabuki* today, they would have little or no advantage over men in learning the *onnagata* art.

One of the reasons why young men's *kabuki* was not prohibited until as late as 1652 was that the third Tokugawa shogun, Iemitsu (1604–51), had a great fondness for the youthful actors. In finally taking the step after his death, shogunate authorities made clear that, although they could hardly hope to convert the *kabuki* actors and their patrons into puritans, they intended to restrict the extreme promiscuity that had been so blatantly apparent on the *kabuki* stage. At the same time that they banished young men from the stage, the authorities also called upon the people in *kabuki* to devote their attention to becoming real actors instead of just vaudeville-like performers whose main business was illicit sex.

The injunction apparently had some effect, for *kabuki* thereafter was gradually transformed into a truly dramatic art. Actors assumed specialized roles (such as those of *onnagata*), draw curtains were introduced and plays divided into acts, more scenery and stage props were used, and the physical theatre was altered and adapted to the special needs of *kabuki*. Yet, although the particular prohibitions imposed by the shogunate may have helped it to become a more legitimate form of theatre, official treatment of *kabuki* throughout the Tokugawa period as a kind of necessary evil probably also prevented it from rising to a higher level of refinement. *Kabuki* has been and remains a conspicuously plebeian theatre.

In *kabuki*, as it developed from the late seventeenth century, the actor is supreme. The texts of the plays are hardly more than scenarios or guides for the actor, who is expected to embellish or alter them as he sees fit. The typical *kabuki* play consists of a series of dramatic high points or tableaux that are made exciting by the broad gesturing, posturing, and declamations of the actors (fig. 54).

Although *kabuki* prospered in both the Edo and Osaka-Kyoto regions, it was particularly among the citizens of Edo, whose number included a far greater percentage of samurai and whose tastes tended to be more robust and unrestrained, that it enjoyed its greatest patronage. In the early and mid-seventeenth century, *kabuki* had competed for popularity in Edo with the puppet theatre *(bunraku)*, but after a great fire in 1657 had destroyed much of the city and brought about the reconstruction of the Yoshiwara pleasure quarters in the present-day Asakusa section of Tokyo, most of the puppet chanters (who were the principal function-

Fig. 54   Scene from a *kabuki* play *(Japan National Tourist Organization)*

aries in *bunraku*) moved to the Kansai (Kyoto-Osaka region) and left *kabuki* unchallenged in the theatre world of Edo.

The two most famous names in *kabuki* during the Genroku epoch were Ichikawa Danjūrō (1660-1704) of Edo and Sakata Tōjūrō (1647–1709) of the Kansai. Danjūrō, who was influenced by an early form of puppet theatre that dealt with the martial exploits of a semi-legendary hero named Kimpira, developed a style of acting called "rough business" *(aragoto)*. So great were Danjūrō's success and fame that this rough business was widely imitated among Edo performers and became probably the most characteristic feature of that city's brand of *kabuki*. Sakata Tōjūrō, on the other hand, practiced "soft business" *(wagoto)* in his acting and thus demonstrated the Kansai preference for the more intimate and feminine (rather than heroic and masculine, as in Edo), a preference that can be seen even more obviously in the Kansai approach to *bunraku*.[19]

The earliest recorded practitioners of puppetry in Japanese history were groups of people in the late Heian period known as *kugutsu*, who moved about from place to place in gypsy-like fashion and staged entertainments in which the men manipulated wooden marionettes and performed feats of magic and the women sang. In addition, the women apparently also liberally purveyed their physical charms, further proof that from early times prostitution and the theatre (to use the term loosely) were closely linked in Japan. Little is known about puppetry during the next few centuries, although there appears to have been a revival of interest in it during the fourteenth century as a result of the importation of string-operated puppets from China.

The mature art of *bunraku*, as it was developed in the late sixteenth and seventeenth centuries, has been defined by Donald Keene as "a form of storytelling, recited to a musical accompaniment and embodied by puppets on a stage."[20] Of the three main elements of *bunraku*—storytelling, musical accompaniment, and the use of puppets—it is the storytelling (and, to a lesser extent, its musical accompaniment) that is of greatest importance in the history of Japanese culture. Puppetry was a minor theatrical form that was used to supplement the traditionally derived art of the *bunraku* chanters.

Storytelling as performed by itinerant chanters, who were often Buddhist priests, had been popular throughout the medieval age. Among the important literary sources from which the chanters drew their material were the great war chronicles, including *The Tale of the Heike* and *Taiheiki.* For accompaniment, the chanters generally used a lute-like four-stringed instrument called the *biwa.* But by the late sixteenth century, another instrument, the three-stringed *samisen,* which had its origins in China and was introduced to Japan via the Ryukyu Islands, was coming into vogue among chanters. Roughly akin to the banjo, the *samisen* gives off a rather brittle, twanging sound (in contrast to the languid tone of the *biwa*) and is particularly well suited for the accompaniment of the vocal techniques of chanters. During the Tokugawa period, the *samisen* became the principal musical instrument in both the *kabuki* and *bunraku* theatres.

It was thus the adaptation of the *samisen* to the ancient art of chanting and the employment of puppets to depict the narrative action declaimed by chanters that gave rise to *bunraku.* The two men most responsible for effecting the final evolution of *bunraku* to a serious dramatic form in Genroku times were the chanter Takemoto Gidayū (1651–1714) and the playwright Chikamatsu Monzaemon (1653–1724). In 1684 Gidayū, whose distinctive chanting style became the most widely admired of its day, opened a puppet theatre called the Takemoto-za in Osaka and engaged the services of Chikamatsu, a writer of samurai origins from Kyoto who had already achieved some note as the author of plays for the renowned *kabuki* actor Sakata Tōjūrō.

Although Chikamatsu wrote for both the *kabuki* and *bunraku* theatres, his work for the latter won for him the great stature he enjoys in the history of Japanese literature. His *bunraku* plays are of two general types, historical plays *(jidaimono)* and domestic or contemporary plays *(sewamono).* The historical plays are derived from the same kinds of narrative materials that Japanese chanters had used for centuries and are by their very nature rousing tales of derring-do and romantic love. To increase further the excitement of their presentation on stage, Chikamatsu and other *bunraku* playwrights also provided in their scripts for the performance of fabulous tumbling acts and supernatural feats, which their audiences loved and which the puppets, unlike the live actors of *kabuki,* could convincingly do. Chikamatsu's best-known historical play is *The Battles of Coxinga (Kokusenya Kassen),* based on the story of a Chinese loyalist who held out against the Manchus after they invaded China and overthrew the Ming dynasty in 1644.

Chikamatsu did not write his first domestic play, *The Love Suicides at Sonezaki (Sonezaki Shinjū),* until 1703. With this work, derived from actual events that had recently occurred in Osaka, Chikamatsu not only created a new category of puppet plays but also found the precise medium in which he was to do his finest writing. *The Love Suicides at Sonezaki,* which was enormously popular with Genroku audiences, is constructed around a simple plot that Chikamatsu used, with variations and embellishments, as the basis for a number of his subsequent domestic plays. It tells the story of a soy sauce salesman named Tokubei who is in love with Ohatsu, a courtesan of the Osaka pleasure quarters. As the play opens, we learn that Tokubei has quarreled with his employer and must return a sum of money that the employer (actually Tokubei's uncle) had advanced as a dowry for his daughter, whom Tokubei now refuses to marry. The kindhearted although dull-witted Tokubei has temporarily loaned the money to a friend, and, when he seeks to reclaim it, the erstwhile friend not only denies that he ever received any money but even charges that Tokubei has forged his seal. In the ensuing argument, Tokubei is soundly thrashed. Distraught and utterly at a loss what to do, he proceeds to Ohatsu's place where the two lovers, without even considering an alternative course of action, decide to commit double suicide. That night they set forth on a *michiyuki* or "lovers' journey" to their deaths at Sonezaki Shrine.

As a writer of domestic plays for the puppet theatre, Chikamatsu was, like Saikaku, a major chronicler of townsman life during the Genroku epoch. Unlike Saikaku, who in his townsman works examined virtually all aspects of the behavioral patterns and standards of value of the emergent bourgeoisie of Tokugawa Japan, Chikamatsu concerned himself chiefly with the lives of lower-class townsmen and specifically with the conflict between duty or obligation *(giri)* and the dictates of human feelings *(ninjō)* to which the members of all classes were subject in this feudal age.

Even though Chikamatsu is famous for his treatment of this *giri-ninjō* conflict, it is not in fact so strongly presented in his plays as it is in other literary works of the Tokugawa period, such as vendetta stories in which samurai unhesitatingly forsake their own personal interests and even sacrifice their lives to meet the exacting demands of their warrior's code of honor. Tokubei and Ohatsu of *The Love Suicides at Sonezaki,* although in difficult straits, do not seem to be under any unique or overwhelming pressure to act as they do. Rather, they appear to be neurotically obsessed with the "purity" of their love for each other and with the religious urge to perpetuate it through death for Buddhist eternities to come. In later "love suicide" plays, Chikamatsu made the pressure of *giri* more explicit; even so, his favorite theme might better be described as one of "all for love" rather than of fundamental conflict between duty and human feelings.

The literary high point of the love suicide play is the *michiyuki*, the journey of the lovers to their predetermined fate. Chikamatsu's *michiyuki* passages are composed in richly textured and often hauntingly beautiful poetry. Perhaps the most memorable is the one from *The Love Suicides at Sonezaki*, which begins:

Narrator:	Farewell to this world, and to the night farewell.
	We who walk the road to death, to what should we be
	likened?
	To the frost by the road that leads to the graveyard,
	Vanishing with each step we take ahead:
	How sad is this dream of a dream!
Tokubei:	Ah, did you count the bell? Of the seven strokes
	That mark the dawn, six have sounded.
	The remaining one will be the last echo
	We shall hear in this life.
Ohatsu:	It will echo the bliss of nirvana.
Narrator:	Farewell, and not to the bell alone—
	They look a last time on the grass, the trees, the sky.
	The clouds, the river go by unmindful of them;
	The Dipper's bright reflection shines in the water.
Tokubei:	Let's pretend that Umeda Bridge
	Is the bridge the magpies built
	Across the Milky Way, and make a vow
	To be husband and wife stars for eternity.
Ohatsu:	I promise. I'll be your wife forever.
Narrator:	They cling together—the river waters
	Will surely swell with the tears they shed.
	Across the river, in a teahouse upstairs,
	Some revelers, still not gone to bed,
	Are loudly talking under blazing lamps—
	No doubt gossiping about the good or bad
	Of this year's crop of lovers' suicides;
	Their hearts sink to hear these voices.

Tokubei: How strange! but yesterday, even today,
            We spoke as if such things did not concern us.
            Tomorrow we shall figure in their gossip.
            If the world will sing about us, let it sing.[21]

Bunraku enjoyed its greatest prosperity in the half-century after Chika-matsu's death, from about 1725 until the 1780s. An important technical innovation during this period was the introduction in 1734 of the puppet manipulated by three men, one responsible for the back, right hand, head, and eyebrows; another for the left hand; and a third for the feet (fig. 55). So vigorous was the puppet theatre that its influence was strongly felt even in *kabuki* circles, where actors imitated the stiff body movements of the puppets and producers adopted *bunraku* methods of staging and presentation. One sad development, however, was the decline in popularity of Chikamatsu's plays, regarded as too wordy and slow-moving for the new, more lively puppets.

If Saikaku was a realist and Chikamatsu a romantic, the third great literary figure of the Genroku epoch, the poet Matsuo Bashō (1644–94), was something of a mystic. Born into a low-ranking samurai family, Bashō became a *rōnin* or "masterless samurai" at the age of twenty-two upon the death of his lord. Rather than seek similar employment else-where, the young Bashō, who had long been interested in poetry, aban-doned his samurai status and, after studying for a while in Kyoto, moved to the military capital of Edo. Edo remained his nominal home for the rest of his life, although Bashō, like several famous poets of the past (including Saigyō of the early Kamakura period and Sōgi of the Higashi-yama epoch), sought inspiration for his verses in frequent travels into the provinces. He died of illness in Osaka at the age of fifty while on a final journey whose ultimate destination was Nagasaki.

Linked verse, the major form of poetry in the late medieval age, had, as we have seen, suffered the same fate as the classic *waka* from which it was derived by becoming oppressively burdened with rigid sty-listic and topical conventions. In the late sixteenth and seventeenth cen-turies, efforts, motivated by the rise of a townsman culture, were made to liberate linked verse from the shackles of the past. One of the most important figures in this movement was Matsunaga Teitoku (1571–1653), whose Teimon school of poets asserted their right to go beyond the restricted vocabulary of the traditional linked verse and to use more prosaic and even vulgar language in versification. Yet, even though the members of the Teimon school were significant innovators in the lan-guage of their poetry (commonly called by this time *haikai* or "light verse"), they remained staunch traditionalists in their fidelity to the topical dictates of earlier poets and to what they regarded as the invio-lable spirit of the aristocratic linked verse of medieval times. Not until

Fig. 55   Scenes from the puppet theatre *(Consulate General of Japan, New York)*

the meteoric rise in the late 1670s and early 1680s of another group of poets called the Danrin school was *haikai* finally freed, in terms of both language and subject matter, from the heavy hand of the linked-verse masters of the past. It was as a member of the Danrin school that Saikaku poured forth his great and indeed overflowing stream of *haikai* verse.

But the newly risen Danrin movement, despite its importance in making possible the subsequent flowering of *haiku,* was itself seriously restricted by the fact that its followers concentrated mainly on clever wordplays, allusions, and references to current fads and fashions. The Danrin poets soon exhausted the possibilities of such an ephemeral approach to poetry and found themselves left with a corpus of verse that held little prospect of appealing to posterity.

It was Bashō who led Japanese poetry out of the Danrin impasse. Although he never fully abandoned the writing of *haikai,* Bashō adopted as his principal medium of expression the seventeen-syllable *haiku.* Certainly one of the world's briefest verse forms, *haiku* derives from the first phrase or link of the classic *waka* and consists of three lines of 5, 7, and 5 syllables. Since the rules are simple, almost anyone can compose these seventeen-syllable poems, and indeed Japanese of all classes have written *haiku* through the centuries from Bashō's time. But the *haiku* is something like the ultimate in deceptive simplicity, and out of a vast number of acceptable ones only a fraction are apt to be truly fine. Bashō's output of *haiku* was not numerically great (perhaps a thousand or so have come down to us), but it is of such an extraordinary quality as to make him without question one of the greatest of Japanese poets.

With little more than a handful of syllables at his disposal, the writer of *haiku* obviously cannot hope to enter into extended poetic dialogue. He must seek to create an effect, capture a mood, or bring about a sudden and sharp insight into the truth of human existence. Bashō found much of his inspiration in Zen Buddhism, and many of his best *haiku* are the product of his intuitive and profoundly mystical response to life and nature. Bashō's insights are not explicitly presented. His best-known *haiku,* for example, is

> An ancient pond
> A frog jumps in
> The sound of water.

Bashō has not said how wondrous it is to observe the meeting of that which is eternal, as embodied in the ancient pond, and that which is fleeting, as represented by the frog's jump. In the best Zen and *haiku* spirit, he has simply juxtaposed the two images without subjective comment and has left it to the reader to draw whatever meaning or meanings he can from the poem.

Of all Bashō's many journeys, the most famous was one he took with a companion into the remote northern provinces in 1689 and later immortalized in the travel account *The Narrow Road of Oku (Oku no Hosomichi)*. Bashō's travel accounts, of which this is by far the finest example, were not intended to be accurate, diary-like records of his journeys. They are highly poetic evocations of his feelings and sentiments as he visited places famous for their natural beauty, for their association with former poet-travelers, or for their roles in the great events of Japanese history. As Bashō journeyed through the provinces, his fame preceded him and he was often met by people who asked him to write *haiku* or to join them in a round of linked-verse composition. But Bashō did not need others to inspire him, and the most beautiful passages in *The Narrow Road of Oku* are those in which he was moved to compose *haiku* upon encountering some memorable scene or viewing a surpassingly lovely setting:

> We first climbed up to Castle-on-the-Heights, from where we could see the Kitagami, a large river that flows down from the north. Here Yoshitsune once fortified himself with some picked retainers, but his great glory turned in a moment into this wilderness of grass. "Countries may fall, but their rivers and mountains remain. When spring comes to the ruined castle, the grass is green again." These lines went through my head as I sat on the ground, my bamboo hat spread under me. There I sat weeping, unaware of the passage of time.

Natsugusa ya	The summer grasses—
Tsuwamono domo ga	Of brave soldiers' dreams
Yume no ato	The aftermath.

> In the domain of Yamagata is a mountain temple called the Ryūshaku, a place noted for its tranquility. People had urged us "just to take a look," and we had turned back at Obanasawa to make the journey, a distance of about fifteen miles. It was still daylight when we arrived. After asking a priest at the foot of the mountain for permission to spend the night, we climbed to the temple at the summit. Boulders piled on rocks had made this mountain, and old pines and cedars grew on its slopes. The earth and stones were worn and slippery with moss. At the summit the doors of the hall were all shut, and not a sound could be heard. Circling around the cliffs and crawling among the rocks we reached the main temple. In the splendor of the scene and the silence I felt a wonderful peace penetrate my heart.

Shizakasa ya	Such stillness—
Iwa ni shimiiru	The cries of the cicadas
Semi no koe	Sink into the rocks.[22]

Perhaps Bashō's true greatness lay in the fact that, at a time when other Japanese poets (i.e., of the Danrin school) were recklessly rejecting the poetic traditions of the past in the pursuit of artistic freedom and modernity, he sought to bring together the old and the new. His inquiry into Zen brought him into communion with the very essence of the aesthetic spirit of medieval culture. At the same time, as a former member of the Danrin movement, he was fully liberated from the restraining conventions of medieval poetry and was very much a part of the great *haikai-haiku* movement of the seventeenth century, which accompanied and was made possible by the economic and cultural, if not political, burgeoning of the townsman class. He was thus as much a Genroku man as either Saikaku or Chikamatsu. But to a far greater degree than either of his distinguished contemporaries, Bashō dealt with the eternal verities and spoke to all people of all ages.

Still another major art form to emerge from the Genroku epoch— and indeed the form of Japanese art probably best known in the West— was the woodblock print, used to depict *ukiyo-e* or "pictures of the floating world." Any attempt to trace the precise origins of the *ukiyo-e* would necessitate a detailed investigation of the many streams of development in painting in Japan from at least the late medieval era on, and so complex are these streams that the task could probably not be definitively done. But the immediate precursor of the *ukiyo-e* was clearly the genre painting, discussed in the last chapter, that flourished in the late sixteenth and early seventeenth centuries. In fact, it is debatable what criteria should be used to distinguish the earlier genre works from the *ukiyo-e,* although one crucial distinction is certainly the fact that the former were painted (so far as we know) by members of the "aristocratic" schools such as the Kanō, whereas the *ukiyo-e* were done by townsman artists.

The establishment of *ukiyo-e* as an independent art form was, to an exceptional degree, the work of one man, Hishikawa Moronobu (1618– 94). Little is known of Moronobu's background, although he may have been the son of a Kyoto embroiderer. It is certain, in any case, that he grew up in the region of the ancient imperial capital, where he studied the various schools of art still flourishing there. Moronobu probably moved to Edo in the 1660s, at a time when the city was being extensively rebuilt after the great fire of 1657. This was a critical period in the history of Edo, for in the rebuilding of it much of the influence of the older, more traditional Kansai culture was cast off and the city was allowed to assume an appearance and style uniquely its own. It was from about this time, for example, that *kabuki* became the theatre par excellence of Edo; and in Moronobu the newly reconstructed city found an artist who perfectly captured in visual form its vital and engaging spirit. Throughout the Tokugawa period, the art of *ukiyo-e* remained, first and foremost, the art of Edo.

Moronobu possessed two qualities that, apart from his natural artistic ability, made him a successful pioneer in *ukiyo-e*. He had an intimate and personal interest in townsman life, unlike the detached curiosity of most earlier genre painters; and he was sufficiently self-confident and assertive to demand recognition as an independent artist. Much genre painting had been done by unknown people, and in Moronobu's younger years about the only opportunity for aspiring painters, unless they were members of the officially patronized schools like the Kanō and Tosa, was the relatively humble chore of drawing anonymous illustrations for popular books. Moronobu not only insisted upon signing his paintings, he emphatically identified himself on them with such signatures as "The Yamato artist Hishikawa Moronobu." Moreover, he was the first artist of his kind to go beyond the secondary function of illustrating books and to produce both picture albums and "single-sheet" artworks.

But Moronobu's great innovation was to make the shift from painting to woodblock printing. Although he and other *ukiyo-e* artists continued to do some of their work in paint, it was their use of the woodblock print that gave the *ukiyo-e* its special character. Not only did woodblock printing make possible the production of pictures in numbers sufficient to meet the great demand for this plebeian art form; it also provided a medium—that is, pictures printed in ink by means of carved woodblocks —that made *ukiyo-e* unique and instantly distinguishable from all other kinds of Japanese art.

The earliest *ukiyo-e*, done by Moronobu and others, were simply black and white prints known as "primitives" (fig. 56). Gradually, however,

Fig. 56 "Street Scene in the Yoshiwara" by Moronobu *(The Metropolitan Museum of Art, Harris Brisbane Dick Fund, 1949)*

artists began to have colors (usually red or reddish brown and green) painted in by hand on their prints, although these early efforts at the use of color generally added very little to the artistic merit of the *ukiyo-e*. Nevertheless, the urge to employ color persisted, and shortly after the mid-eighteenth century the technique of printing in multicolors and even halftones was perfected. The multicolored print, known as *nishiki-e* or "brocade picture," necessitated close cooperation among three people, the artist, the woodblock carver, and the printer, and thus became in a very real sense a joint artistic endeavor.

From the beginning, *ukiyo-e* artists were primarily interested in two subjects—women of the pleasure quarters and *kabuki* actors—and throughout the Tokugawa period the overwhelming majority of prints they produced were of these two representative types of Edo nightlife, sometimes done with detailed backgrounds but more commonly with few if any background elements. Not surprisingly, the *ukiyo-e* representations of pleasure women and actors usually stress the sensual and erotic, in contrast to the earlier genre paintings in which people were for the most part portrayed objectively and with little infusion of emotion on the part of the artist.

To some lovers of *ukiyo-e,* the early primitive works in plain black and white or black and white with slight coloring are the most vigorous and exciting of all Japanese woodblock prints. But the greatest names in *ukiyo-e* are of artists who flourished after development of the multi-colored "brocade" print, first used in 1765 by Suzuki Harunobu (1725–70). Harunobu achieved widespread popularity not only for his superb use of color but also for his portrayals of beautiful young women in dreamlike settings (fig. 57). Harunobu's women, unlike those of other *ukiyo-e* artists, are more charming than erotic in appearance. In addition, their faces and expressions are almost all identical, reflecting the same kind of humanism based on the concept of people not as individuals but as two-dimensional types or even stereotypes that is found in the characters of Saikaku, Chikamatsu, and other Tokugawa period writers.

Although a number of artists of the *ukiyo-e* school are noted for their depiction of feminine beauty, the most celebrated is Kitagawa Utamaro (1753–1806). Utamaro's typical beauties are long and willowy and have about them a languid and sensual air (fig. 58). Often they are portrayed in great intimacy, with one or both breasts bare and with hair and clothing in casual disarray. To many later—and often unabashedly puritanical —critics Utamaro has epitomized the decadence into which they believe *ukiyo-e* sank at the end of the eighteenth century. It is true that Utamaro lapsed into a kind of mannerism in his final years and that, with the exception of the work of two early nineteenth century artists—Hokusai and Hiroshige, who were in any case unusual in that they specialized

Fig. 57   "Waterfall" by Harunobu *(courtesy of the Brooklyn Museum, Gift of Louis V. Ledoux)*

chiefly in landscapes—the traditional *ukiyo-e* did in fact lose most of its vitality about this time. Nevertheless, Utamaro's art, as observable in his better prints, is clearly of superior quality. In sureness of line, overall composition, and delicacy of handling subject matter, he ranks with the best of the *ukiyo-e* masters.

We may also note that Utamaro, in his celebration of the beauty of the female body, represented something new in the Japanese cultural tradition. Until this age of townsman culture and establishment of the artistic theme of erotic love, the Japanese—in marked contrast, for example, to the Greeks—had devoted little attention to the human body, either male or female, as an object of beauty. Lady Murasaki, the author of *The Tale of Genji*, observed in her diary: "Unforgettably horrible is the naked body. It really does not have the slightest charm."[23] And in the *Genji*, which so wonderfully evokes the high age of court life in the Heian period, we find very little concrete description of what people

Fig. 58   Half-length portrait from the "Studies in Physiognomy: Ten Kinds of Women" by Utamaro *(Cleveland Museum of Art, Bequest of Edward Loder Whittemore)*

looked like. When there are descriptions, they are largely restricted to facial features and, in the case of women, to their hair, which, if long and lustrous, constituted the most important feature of feminine beauty in that age. The court women in the Genji Scrolls are invariably shown in voluminous robes, with only their rather plump, whitened faces and their hands protruding and with hair—body-length or longer—flowing down their backs (see fig. 27). Courtier tastes, and indeed the tradition of courtly love, persisted throughout the medieval centuries; and even though samurai replaced courtiers as rulers, we find no new interest in the arts in the physical beauty of humans. Thus not until the early modern age of the Tokugawa period did the Japanese turn, literally for the first time, to the aesthetic delights of the nude, as we can observe them so finely revealed in the work of Utamaro and other masters of *ukiyo-e*.

One of Utamaro's contemporaries was a mysterious genius named Tōshūsai Sharaku (dates unknown). Almost nothing is known with certainty about Sharaku's identity or activities apart from the astonishing fact that he did his entire corpus of surviving work—some 145 prints, mostly of *kabuki* actors—during a concentrated period of less than ten months in 1794. Whereas Utamaro specialized in pictures of the courtesan, Sharaku was the master chronicler of the actor (fig. 59). Both artists had a penchant for doing close-up, bustlike portraits of their subjects, and both frequently left the backgrounds of their prints blank; otherwise, they had virtually nothing in common. Utamaro's prints are sophisticated and restrained, with composition and coloring precise. Sharaku's, by comparison, are stylistically crude. His colors sometimes clash and he seems to lack the sureness of placement of his subject matter that is so characteristic of Japanese artists. But these ostensible failings seem only to enhance Sharaku's forte: the bursting, elemental energy he has infused into his actors, whose faces and bodies are contorted with dramatic emotion. Unlike most *ukiyo-e* artists, Sharaku sought to portray real people, not simply stereotypes. It has even been speculated that he stopped producing prints so abruptly because actors were outraged at being so unflatteringly drawn. This seems absurd, since no other artist has ever captured the spirit of *kabuki* as Sharaku did, and it seems much more likely that the actors he drew fully appreciated having their dramatic skills depicted in such a vivid, exciting manner.

Before ending this chapter, much of which deals with the lives and pursuits of the denizens of the pleasure quarters, let me say a few words about one habitué of the quarters who not only embodied much of its style and spirit but even today is internationally known as a unique product of Japanese culture, the *geisha* or "person of accomplishment." The *geisha* first appeared in the mid-Tokugawa period (the earliest recorded use of the term *geisha* is 1751). Originally, *geisha* were men,

Fig. 59   Otani Oniji III as Edohei by Sharaku *(Art Institute of Chicago)*

but gradually they became exclusively female. Although most *geisha* worked in the pleasure quarters or "floating worlds," they were also considered to occupy, in a sense, their own realm, called the "flower and willow world" *(karyūkai)*.

Geisha were entertainers, skilled as singers, dancers, storytellers, and conversationalists, who were employed at parties and other social affairs primarily to entertain men. There was supposed to be a clear distinction between *geisha* on the one hand and courtesans and the other, lesser prostitutes on the other. *Geisha* were expected to be strictly entertainers and not engage in the business of sexually gratifying men. But the distinction between entertainment and sex was not always precisely maintained, and some *geisha* even became the concubines or mistresses of men who purchased their contracts from the masters who held them in bondage. Although the Tokugawa government frequently directed the *geisha* not to compete with prostitutes, even seeking to restrict the luxu-

The Flourishing of a Bourgeois Culture

riousness of their style of dressing and encouraging plain and older women to become *geisha,* the problem of *geisha* and the sex business persisted.

Later in the Tokugawa period, free-lance *geisha* pursued their profession outside the pleasure quarters, securing for themselves much greater freedom of movement and activity. Some, like leading courtesans of the pleasure quarters, acquired considerable fame, and some even became the fashion setters for women.

The musical instrument par excellence of the *geisha* was the *samisen,* which, as we have seen, also enlivened the *kabuki* and puppet theatres. Even today, nothing can evoke the feeling and mood of the world of entertainment and pleasure of Tokugawa times like the brittle twanging of the *samisen,* especially as played by *geisha.* Although the profession of *geisha* has declined greatly in modern times, some *geisha* have been successful working in the political world. These *geisha* are engaged to entertain at parties of leading politicians, where the sake flows freely and sometimes important political negotiations are conducted. Although *geisha* are supposed to remain silent about what they hear at these affairs, it is interesting that the leading political parties tend to patronize their own groups of *geisha.*[24]

8

Heterodox Trends

THE TOKUGAWA SYSTEM of rule was shaped by the first three shoguns, who ruled from 1600 until 1651. During this half century the shogunate pursued policies—including national seclusion, alternate attendance, and the confiscation (on the one hand) and transfer (on the other hand) of daimyo domains—that increasingly strengthened its control over both the daimyos and the country as a whole. Some scholars have speculated that if the shogunate had continued on the same course it would have transformed itself from a rather loose, hegemonic government into a centralized monarchy.[1] But, after 1651, what appeared to be a drive toward ever greater centralization of power ceased, and during the remaining two centuries of Tokugawa rule the shogunate in fact allowed many of the powers it had accumulated to slip away.

The post-1651 shogunate became a highly conservative regime, committed to traditional policies and practices and generally unwilling to consider serious or fundamental change to its way of governance. Yet shogunate conservatism, although it led to the meting out of harsh punishments to some dissidents, by no means stifled all diversity and change. The flourishing of a bourgeois culture, for example, brought the modification or alteration of many of the traditional canons of taste in Japanese literature, theatre, and the visual arts. In philosophy, too, scholars expressed much diversity of opinion, often in opposition to Chu Hsi Neo-Confucianism, which, as we have seen, was officially championed as an orthodoxy by the shogunate from at least the late seventeenth century through its patronage of the Hayashi family of Confucian scholars.

The blossoming of philosophy as a field of study was one of the most striking developments of the Tokugawa period. Although the Japanese had contributed much to Buddhist theology before Tokugawa, as observable in the careers and writings of men such as Kūkai, Shinran, and Dōgen, they had done little in philosophy. Indeed, one would be hard pressed to name a single Japanese "philosopher" for the period before Tokugawa. One reason for the advancement of philosophy as a field after 1600 was the quest by the Tokugawa to legitimize their rule—that is, to justify or have recognized as "right" what they had achieved by military "might." After early experimentation with both Buddhist and Shinto rationales for rulership, the Tokugawa settled on Chu Hsi Neo-Confucianism, which provided an ideology that, as we have seen, could be interpreted as sanctifying both the Tokugawa regime and its social class structure as based on laws that were as immutable as those of nature itself. As Hayashi Razan put it:

> Heaven is above and earth is below. . . . [I]n everything there is an order separating those above and those below . . . , [and] we cannot allow disorder in the relations between ruler and subject, between those above and those below. The separation into four classes of samurai, farmers, artisans and merchants, like the five relationships, is part of the principles of heaven and is the Way which was taught by the Sage (Confucius).[2]

The first important scholar to challenge the Neo-Confucian orthodoxy was Nakae Tōju (1608–48). After serving in his youth as a samurai retainer, Tōju denounced the rigidities of such service and retired at the early age of twenty-six to a life of study and contemplation at his birthplace on Lake Biwa in Ōmi Province. As a scholar, Tōju had at first been a keen student of Chu Hsi Neo-Confucianism, but from his observation of people of all classes in Japan he came to question whether certain of its basic tenets were truly meaningful when applied to them. Neo-Confucianism, for one thing, endorsed a hierarchical structuring of society in which all people were expected to accept without question the obligations attendant upon predominantly inferior-superior relations among men. But was it proper for the ruling class of Tokugawa Japan to enjoy its privileges solely on the basis of birth rather than, as in China, on intellectual or scholarly merit?

At an even more fundamental level, Tōju questioned the orthodox Neo-Confucian view of moral perfectibility. According to this view, as we have seen, human nature is basically good and is governed by *ri* or reason. Although there is the danger that one's *ki* (ether or substance) may, through cravings and passions, obscure *ri,* if one's basic nature is properly cultivated through moral training, one will invariably act in a good and upright fashion. Tōju observed that, despite their claim that people should be allowed to act with complete freedom once their inherently moral nature has been cultivated, the orthodox Neo-Confucianists in fact made sure of right action by dictating elaborate rules of social conduct.

Tōju asserted that the most important consideration was man's mind or will to action *(shin).* In other words, whereas the orthodox Neo-Confucianists talked about the *ri*-nature and prescribed how man should behave to prove that he had it, Tōju said that man should act according to the dictates of his mind or "intuition," and should not be fettered by the need to conform to arbitrary norms of social behavior. The creed he thus espoused was formally based on the writings of the Ming dynasty philosopher Wang Yang-ming (1472–1529). The Neo-Confucianism of Wang Yang-ming, which stressed that man had the inherent or intuitive capacity to act morally, held a powerful attraction for many Japanese of the Tokugawa period, especially samurai whose class background and outlook made them logically receptive to a doctrine of personal independence and direct action. Yet, the Wang Yang-ming emphasis on intuition was also close to the spirit of Zen Buddhism and, toward the end of his life, Nakae Tōju became less concerned with social action than with the cultivation of a Zen-like inner tranquility. It remained for others, particularly in the tumultuous final years of the Tokugawa period, to employ Wang Yang-ming Neo-Confucianism as a rationale for political activism.

Another group of scholars who attacked the Neo-Confucian orthodoxy was the so-called School of Ancient Studies *(kogaku-ha)*. The leading members of the *kogaku-ha* had such diverse personalities and viewpoints that it may at first seem inappropriate to group them together as a school. Nevertheless, they were similar at least insofar as each sought to go back beyond Neo-Confucianism—and indeed beyond all the major accretions to Confucianism of the preceding two millennia—to rediscover the original teachings of the Confucian tradition. The Neo-Confucianists in China had started out to do the very same thing and had ended in producing intellectual syntheses that were far removed from the down-to-earth humanism of Confucianism and the sages of early China. The Ancient Studies scholars of Tokugawa Japan also differed widely in their interpretations of what constituted the original teachings of Confucianism and how they should be applied to the conditions of their own country and age.

The first major figure of the Ancient Studies school was Yamaga Sokō (1622–85). Of samurai origin, Sokō earned a reputation as a brilliant scholar, delving into such varied subjects as Shinto, Buddhism, and Japanese poetry, as well as Confucianism, which he studied in Edo under Hayashi Razan. Sokō was also greatly interested in military science, and it was probably this interest as much as anything that eventually led him to attack the Neo-Confucian orthodoxy as irrelevant to Japan in the seventeenth century. He observed that Confucius had lived during an age when conditions in China were far closer to the feudal system of Tokugawa Japan than to the centralized bureaucratic state for which the Neo-Confucianists of the Sung dynasty had shaped their doctrines. Sokō accordingly believed that, rather than the metaphysically based and overly idealistic tenets of orthodox Neo-Confucianism, the practical ethics for everyday living that Confucius had preached should be used for the moral training of the Japanese of his time.

Sokō was also one of the first thinkers of the Tokugawa period to address himself to the problem of justifying the existence of the samurai as a largely idle, stipendiary class. After the founding of the Tokugawa shogunate in 1600, there had been little opportunity for the samurai to pursue their principal calling, and it became a historical anomaly that a class of fighting men should preside over Japan during its longest age of peace. Some samurai became bureaucratic administrators of the shogunate and *han* governments, but others had very little in the way of formal assignments or responsibilities to occupy their time. In the first provisions of its "Laws for the Military Houses," issued in 1615, the shogunate had enjoined the samurai to pursue with single-minded devotion the arts of "peace and war"; and it was in line with this injunction that Sokō formulated his code for samurai conduct. Observing that "the samurai eat food without growing it, use utensils without manufacturing them, and profit without buying or selling," Sokō asked what justified the existence of the samurai as a class. His answer was that "the business of the samurai consists in reflecting on his own station in life, in discharging loyal service to his master if he has one, in deepening his fidelity in associations with friends, and, with due consideration of his own position, in devoting himself to duty above all."[3] Thus, according to Sokō, the samurai was to serve as an exemplar of high moral purpose for Japanese of all classes. Central to this moral purpose was the samurai's commitment to "duty above all." In one sense, this duty or *giri* was the same *giri* we noticed affecting the behavior of townsman characters in the domestic plays of Chikamatsu. When set forth by Yamaga Sokō as a moral imperative for the samurai, however, it implied an absolute loyalty to one's overlord and devotion to duty that far transcended what could realistically be expected of members of the other classes of Tokugawa society.

On the basis of views such as these, Yamaga Sokō is generally credited as the formulator of the code of *bushidō*, or the "way of the warrior."[4] Certainly he was a pioneer in analyzing the role of the samurai as a member of a true ruling elite and not simply as a rough, and frequently illiterate, participant in the endless civil struggles of the medieval age.

Yamaga Sokō is also famous for having been, at one time, the teacher of Ōishi Kuranosuke (1659–1703), leader of the famed "forty-seven *rōnin.*" The story of the forty-seven *rōnin*, probably the best-loved story in Japanese history, has been recreated countless times in many media, including the puppet theatre, *kabuki*, novels, and the cinema (fig. 60). Its "meaning" or "meanings" have been endlessly debated from the time that the *rōnin* carried out their vendetta in 1702 until the present day. One Japanese scholar has even suggested, rather hyperbolically, that "if you study Chūshingura [the *rōnin* story] long enough, you will understand everything about the Japanese."[5] Let us pause to examine the *rōnin* story in some detail.

In 1701 Lord Asano, daimyo of the Akō domain in western Japan, was assigned to perform ceremonial duty at the shogun's court in Edo.

Fig. 60 "View of Loyal Akō Samurai Breaking into Kira's Mansion," by Shirai Toshinobu, depicting a scene from the story of the forty-seven *rōnin* (*Honolulu Academy of Arts, Bequest of Norman D. Hill, 1938 [10,953]*)

On the last day of his duty, Asano attacked a shogunate official named Kira and wounded, but did not kill, him. Having violated a strict rule of the shogunate about drawing a weapon at court, Asano was ordered to commit suicide by disembowelment *(seppuku)* that very afternoon. No one knows precisely why Asano attacked Kira. He said something about a "grudge" before the attack, but after the attack, so far as we know, he went to his death in silence.

Upon Asano's death, all of his vassals automatically became *rōnin* or masterless samurai. Ultimately, forty-seven of them, headed by Ōishi Kuranosuke, joined in a secret pledge to avenge their deceased lord. Late in 1702, nearly two years later, they fulfilled this pledge by attacking and killing Kira at his residence in Edo.

During the long period between Asano's assault on Kira and the *rōnin*'s destruction of him, there had arisen a major division of opinion among the *rōnin* over how to proceed.[6] One group, with Ōishi Kuranosuke as its spokesman, gave first priority to saving the Asano house and its property, holding that the matter could be considered settled—that is, personal revenge against Kira would not be necessary—if the shogunate allowed Asano's younger brother to succeed to his title and estate. But another group was intent from the outset upon avenging their lord by killing Kira. Only when it became clear that the shogunate would not agree to continuation of the Asano house did the two groups come together to carry out their violent act of revenge.

Those among the *rōnin* who all along insisted upon killing Kira did so, according to Eiko Ikegami, primarily because of their determination to remove the stain to their personal honor caused by a clash that resulted in the death of their lord but not the other party. The fact that they did not even know why their lord attacked the other party was immaterial to them. Their determination stemmed from the ancient honor tradition of the samurai.

After a lively debate among officials, intellectuals, and others about how to deal with the *rōnin,* the shogunate decided that they must die because they broke "public" law. The *rōnin* were, however, granted the privilege of dying honorable deaths by *seppuku* (rather than decapitation).[7] Although people at the time may have differed in their opinions about the shogunate's decision to punish the *rōnin* for their "public" behavior, nearly everyone appears to have agreed that their "private" behavior as samurai had been exemplary. Some Japanese even glorified the *rōnin* in death as *gijin* or "men of high moral purpose." Such glorification was in keeping with Yamaga Sokō's idea of *bushidō,* according to which the samurai of Tokugawa times should serve as exemplars of loyalty and morality. But whereas Sokō conceived loyalty and morality in Confucian terms, the revenge-conscious *rōnin* (if we follow Ikegami's analysis) were motivated largely by more particularistic, feudal sentiments of personal honor and loyalty. Their main concern was about *their* honor and *their* loyalty, not about honor and loyalty as universal ideals.

The *rōnin* story was produced on the stage of the puppet theatre within weeks of the attack on Kira; and although the shogunate banned it, it proved to be only the first of an endless stream of theatrical and other versions of the story. Of theatrical versions, the 1748 puppet play *Chūshingura (A Treasury of Loyal Retainers)*[8] established itself as the most popular, and indeed the name "Chūshingura" became, and remains today, synonymous with the entire cultural phenomenon of the forty-seven *rōnin.*

Why, we may ask, did the *rōnin* story become so immediately and lastingly popular? For one thing, of course, it was an inherently exciting, suspenseful story. But to the contemporary Japanese of the early eighteenth century who started the Chūshingura craze, the story of the *rōnin* surely aroused feelings deeper than simply the reactions one might have to an exciting, suspenseful story.

The time was the Genroku epoch. Japan had been at peace almost uninterruptedly for a century. The economy, from its agricultural base to urban commerce, had expanded steadily and, in many respects, dramatically throughout this period. More people had more money and more leisure time than ever before, and Genroku itself became a byword for the cultural flourishing of a consumer society. Peace, prosperity, leisure time, and consumerism had, over the years, eroded the martial spirit of the samurai, who had not had wars to fight for generations. Some people may even have wondered why anyone was still allowed to be a samurai. Then, suddenly, came the astounding news that forty-seven *rōnin* had risked everything—the wrath of the shogunate, their lives, their families—to avenge their lord.

Revenge, in the form of the vendetta *(katakiuchi)*, was a practice that was, in fact, tacitly approved, if not encouraged, by the Tokugawa shogunate, which allowed government agencies at various levels to authorize vendettas. But of the authorized vendettas that have come down to us in the records, virtually all were undertaken by people on behalf of their relatives—for example, the revenge of a son against the murderer of his father. The "revenge" of the forty-seven *rōnin*, as people at the time were quick to point out, was not authorized and, indeed, was not even a vendetta inasmuch as Kira had not killed anyone but had himself been the victim of attempted murder. Nevertheless, whether or not Kira was a proper object of revenge, the *rōnin* were certainly motivated by its spirit and, in the Japanese tradition, came to be idolized as the supreme avengers.

The 1748 puppet play *Chūshingura,* while of course based on the *rōnin* story, is a vastly elaborated and complex tale with many subplots that includes an array of fictional characters in addition to the *rōnin* themselves. Perhaps most striking about this tale is that, despite its complexity of plot, it has been thoroughly cleansed of all the ambiguities of the historical events of 1701–2. The *rōnin* and others who support them are, from start to finish, motivated by only two sentiments: loyalty (for their lord) and revenge. The Kira character[9] is a thoroughly despicable, evil man whose death cannot come too soon, and the *rōnin,* led by the Kuranosuke character, do not for a moment think about saving their lord's house, their personal honor, or anything other than revenge. They plan, moreover, to cap their vendetta—the killing of the Kira character—with the ultimate act of loyalty, their own suicides. The play says nothing about the *rōnin* being arrested by the shogunate and awaiting a decision about their fate. Instead, it ends with them setting off to the temple where their lord is buried to commit suicide before his grave.

I believe that much, if not most, of the popularity of the forty-seven *rōnin* story and the impetus that transformed it into the Chūshingura legend derived from the fact that, at a time (the Genroku epoch) when the samurai spirit was thought to be at its nadir, a group of *rōnin* acted in accordance with what was perceived to be its finest values. Chūshingura, although obviously known to be a largely fictionalized version of the *rōnin* story, removed all the shadings and motivational uncertainties from the story and rendered it a pure celebration of the samurai way.

At least one contemporary of the *rōnin,* however, was not impressed with even their private behavior: Yamamoto Tsunetomo, a samurai from a Kyushu domain whose stories, advice, sayings, and injunctions were compiled and issued in 1716 under the title of *Hagakure.* Tsunetomo's complaint about the *rōnin* was that they did not act immediately after their lord's death, but waited almost two years. For Tsunetomo, delay, either because of hesitation or for the purpose of plotting or scheming, was anathema. The samurai way, he asserts in *Hagakure,* demands immediate action in all crises, action that the samurai should always anticipate—indeed expect—will lead to his death. Here is how Tsunetomo recommends that a samurai carry out revenge:

> The way of revenge lies simply in forcing one's way into a place and being cut down. There is no shame in this. By thinking that you must complete the job you will run out of time. By considering things like how many men the enemy has, time piles up. . . . No matter if the enemy has thousands of men, there is fulfillment in simply standing them off and being determined to cut them all down.[10]

Tsunetomo further expounds on what we might call the rule of immediate action in this passage:

> When the time comes, there is no moment for reasoning. . . . Above all, the Way of the Samurai should be in being aware that you do not know what is going to happen next. . . . Victory and defeat are matters of the temporary force of circumstances. The way of avoiding shame is different. It is simply in death. Even if it is certain that you will lose, retaliate. Neither wisdom or technique has a place in this. A real man does not think of victory or defeat. He plunges recklessly towards an irrational death. By doing this, you will awaken from your dreams.[11]

In speaking about plunging recklessly toward an irrational death, Tsunetomo refers to what he identifies as *shinigurui* or "death frenzy." Death frenzy calls upon the samurai, when faced with a crisis or even an uncertain situation, to enter into what can only be described as a self-induced state of psychosis in which only action—not goals or purpose—matters.

With its radical advocacy of violent irrationality—to the point of psychosis—*Hagakure* has shocked many people. But during Japan's militarist years of the 1930s and World War II, soldiers and others hailed it as something of a bible of samurai behavior, and the postwar nationalist writer Mishima Yukio was even inspired to write a book in praise of its values.[12]

In studying both *Hagakure* and the story of the forty-seven *rōnin,* we should note in particular the distinction, already adumbrated, that we find drawn between the concept of samurai loyalty, on the one hand, and samurai honor, on the other. True samurai loyalty meant total commitment to one's lord, manifested primarily by acting in accordance with what was, or at least could be judged as, best for him. In that regard, Ōishi Kuranosuke and the others among the *rōnin* who wished above all to save the Asano house were surely loyal to the spirit of their dead lord, even though such loyalty might mean a diminution of their honor because they did not take personal revenge against Kira. Yamamoto Tsunetomo was certainly a staunch advocate of loyalty, and says much about it *Haga-kure*. He does not, however, address the question of what the samurai should do if loyalty conflicted with personal honor, as it did in the case of the forty-seven *rōnin* when some of them rejected loyalty if it meant dropping plans to kill Kira (and thus losing honor) in order to save the Asano house.

Tsunetomo's central concern was, in fact, not at all with loyalty but with honor. We can observe this, for example, in the above two quotations from *Hagakure* in which he stresses avoidance of shame, the mortal enemy of honor, above all else. His criticism of the forty-seven *rōnin* was that they did not act immediately. To satisfy him, the *rōnin* should have launched an immediate attack on Kira's residence even though it was then extremely well guarded in anticipation of just such an action. The *rōnin* would all have been slaughtered, the Asano house's hopes would have been dashed, but the forty-seven would, through their death frenzy, have preserved their personal, entirely selfish honor.

Let us return to Yamaga Sokō. In addition to his writings on the way of the warrior, Sokō is also remembered for his stress on another theme, the greatness of Japan, that was to endear him to later nationalists of the modern period.

The study of Confucianism naturally imbued Japanese scholars with a greater or lesser degree of enthusiasm for the civilization of China: some became outright Sinophiles, and although other Confucian scholars of the early Tokugawa period, including Hayashi Razan, had gone beyond their study of Chinese philosophy to investigate Shinto and the Japanese tradition, Yamaga Sokō was the first thinker of stature to claim the superiority of Japanese culture and ethical values over those of China. By exalting the sacred origins of Japan and by claiming that Japan, rather than China, should be regarded as the Middle Kingdom of the world, Sokō gave early voice to an attitude that was to gain wide acceptance after the rise to prominence in the eighteenth century of the Neo-Shintoist School of National Learning *(kokugaku-ha)*.

Another outstanding scholar of the Ancient Studies school was Ogyū Sorai (1666–1728), who went even farther back into Chinese history than Sokō to find the "true" Confucian way in the age of ancient sages who lived before Confucius. Yamaga Sokō had criticized the abstract Neo-Confucian stress on cultivating man's inherently moral nature and had urged the inculcation of more practical, "fundamental" ethics as a means for maintaining social order in Tokugawa Japan. But both Sokō and the Neo-Confucianists were, in the best Confucian tradition, interested chiefly in the subject of morality. Ogyū Sorai, on the other hand, paid less attention to morality than to the legal and institutional controls necessary for governing society.

Although there were antecedents for it in Confucianism, Sorai's greater emphasis on controlling men than on trying to elevate them to the utopian state where they would be sufficiently moral to exist without external controls is generally associated with schools of thought in China other than the Confucian. That Ogyū Sorai should take such a position was in part a response to new social and political problems that beset Tokugawa society about the time of the Genroku epoch and in part simply a reflection of the strongly practical, pragmatic approach of many heterodox thinkers of this age.

Many of the problems that the Tokugawa shogunate encountered as it approached its second century were the result of what today we would call progress. The shogunate, for one thing, was increasingly perplexed about how to deal with the great flourishing of commerce that peace and tranquility brought. While the townsmen enjoyed to the fullest their Genroku prosperity, the shogunate and the samurai class in general, still overwhelmingly dependent on agriculture for income, found themselves more and more financially hard-pressed as the result of market fluctuations and the inflationary drift of the times. In 1695 the shogunate even resorted to the desperate expediency of currency debasement in an attempt to solve its financial difficulties.

Another problem that troubled the shogunate was bureaucratization. The Tokugawa shogunate had been founded on the basis of direct military controls to govern a country that in 1600 had known only warfare for generations. The original structure of the shogunate, although it proved to be remarkably durable, was inevitably altered and expanded with the passage of time to meet changing conditions. One of the most important changes was in the office of shogun. The three great founding shoguns, who ruled until 1651, had been personally dominant figures. But with the growth in complexity of shogunate affairs and the appearance of weak men in the hereditary line of its headship, the shogun's powers often came to be exercised by others, and open struggles over these powers among men and groups within the shogunate became increasingly frequent. Although a particularly strong-willed shogun could still exert his personal influence, the tendency toward a diffusion of power (apparently characteristic of all bureaucracies) can be observed in the history of the Tokugawa shogunate from the late seventeenth century on.

It was precisely to the question of strengthening the shogunate institutionally in order to meet the new demands of the eighteenth century that the Ancient Studies scholar Ogyū Sorai turned his attention. And it is interesting to note that shogunate authorities were not so enamored of the orthodox Neo-Confucianist view of the Tokugawa government as a purely moral agent that they did not lend an attentive ear to the heterodox, legalistic views of Sorai.

Although I have stressed that one of the features common to many heterodox thinkers of the Tokugawa period was their desire to approach things in a more direct and rational fashion, it should be noted that certain scholars who remained within the Neo-Confucian orthodoxy exhibited a similar bent. The best example is Arai Hakuseki (1657–1725), a *rōnin* who served as the personal adviser to two shoguns from 1709 until 1715. Hakuseki was noted for certain bold and forceful policies he initiated, including his efforts to restore the value of the coinage after the currency debasement of 1695, to revise the shogunate's "Laws for the Military Houses," and to restrict the outflow of gold and silver bullion from Japan through the foreign trade with the Dutch and Chinese at Nagasaki. But, from the standpoint of cultural history, Hakuseki's rationalism is best observed in the field of pure scholarship, where he wrote books on such wide-ranging subjects as archaeology, sociology, philology, history, and even conditions in the West.

In all of his scholarly work, Hakuseki exhibited a degree of rationality and a quest for empirical evidence that make his writings valuable secondary reference sources even today. When dealing with Japan's prehistory, for example, he urged the investigation of Chinese and Korean accounts of early Japan and not simply acceptance of the mythical versions of the country's origins as recorded in the *Kojiki* and *Nihon Shoki* of the eighth century. In perhaps his best-known work, *Observations on History (Dokushi Yoron)*, Hakuseki presented a careful analysis in terms of cause and effect of Japanese history from the time of the establishment of the Fujiwara regency in the Heian period until Hideyoshi's unification of the country in the late sixteenth century (with particular emphasis on the rise of the military class to preeminence).

Whereas Arai Hakuseki employed techniques of historical methodology that we would consider quite modern, other scholars of the early and mid-Tokugawa period undertook histories of Japan of a more traditional kind, written in Chinese and based on classical Chinese models of textual organization. One of these was *The Comprehensive Mirror of Our Country (Honchō Tsugan)*[13] of the Hayashi family; another was *The History of Great Japan (Dai Nihon Shi)*, compiled by a school for historical studies established in the Mito *han*. The Mito work, which was not actually completed until 1906, is a chronicle of Japan's imperial line from the time of the mythical founding of the state by the first emperor in 660 B.C. until unification of the Northern and Southern Courts in 1392. Strongly moralistic in tone, it was greatly admired by loyalists of the late Tokugawa period, who attacked the shogunate and urged a restoration of the emperor to power. In fact, the early Mito scholars, whose daimyo was related to the Tokugawa family, had by no means intended their history to be subversive of the shogunate. Nevertheless, *The History of Great Japan*, which stresses the continuity and sanctity of the imperial institution in Japanese history, greatly aroused the nationalistic sentiments of those who finally carried out the Meiji Restoration of 1868.

Another source of inspiration for the loyalists of the Meiji Restoration was the collected writings of the School of National Learning *(kokugaku-ha)*. This school arose in the eighteenth century as an antiquarian literary movement whose members investigated such ancient masterpieces as the *Man'yōshū* and *The Tale of Genji* in the search for a true and original Japanese spirit untainted by those alien systems of thought and behavior, including Buddhism and Confucianism, that had been introduced to Japan from China during the previous thousand years (see the discussion of this in Chapter 1).

Despite its inflammatory appeal to later imperial loyalists, the National Learning movement in its origins was not a radical or aberrant phenomenon at all but a logical development in Japanese intellectual history that owed much to the various schools of Tokugawa Confucianism. The forerunners of the movement, participating in the general upsurge in scholarship stimulated by Confucianism in the seventeenth century, undertook philological studies into the origins of the Japanese language that paved the way for the subsequent work of the two leading National Learning scholars of the eighteenth century, Kamo Mabuchi (1697–1769) and Motoori Norinaga (1730–1801).

Kamo Mabuchi, the son of a functionary at a Shinto shrine who rose to become lecturer to the head of a branch family of the Tokugawa, was much taken with the *Man'yōshū* and asserted that the poems of this eighth-century anthology were imbued with the true spirit of the Japanese. He identified this spirit as one of pure naturalness, spontaneity, and manly vigor, and charged that the influx of Chinese culture into Japan had perverted it to a way of life, exemplified by the courtiers of the Heian period, that was both artificial and effeminate. Mabuchi urged people to compose poems in the manner of the *Man'yōshū* and thereby seek to recapture or "restore" the native temper of ancient times. As we have seen, restorationism—that is, the desire to return to an earlier, golden age in history—was also a strong sentiment among scholars of the Ancient Studies school, although some Sinophiles among them, like Ogyū Sorai, may have wished to revive only the conditions of ancient China. Kamo Mabuchi, on the other hand, insisted unequivocally that the golden age to be sought in the past was a Japanese age.

Although he only met Kamo Mabuchi once, Motoori Norinaga claimed to be his true disciple and never directly challenged Mabuchi's glorification of the *Man'yōshū* as the repository of the original Japanese spirit. But Norinaga's own investigation into courtier literature, especially *The Tale of Genji* and the *Shinkokinshū*, led him to adopt a quite different view of that spirit. Norinaga believed that the most important quality native to the Japanese was their sensitivity, as embodied in the term *mono no aware*. He attacked what he regarded as the excessive rationalism of the Confucianists and claimed that the Japanese were fundamentally an emotional people. To his mind, *The Tale of Genji* was a classical delineation of this emotionalism as it revealed itself in the courtier society of the Heian period. In contrast to Kamo Mabuchi, Norinaga thus extolled the highly refined, indeed effeminate, sensibility that characterized the behavior of individuals in *The Tale of Genji* and the poems of the thirteenth-century *Shinkokinshū* and proclaimed it to be the finest product of Japanese civilization.

Let us look more closely into Norinaga's idea of Shinto emotionalism. In one of his discussions of *The Tale of Genji*, Norinaga describes the basic character of this emotionalism by analyzing the concepts of good and evil in terms of *mono no aware*. But whereas in the conventional use of *mono no aware* as an aesthetic term, as discussed in Chapter 3, its meaning is something on the order of a "sensitivity to things" or a "capacity to be moved by things," Norinaga, in the following passage about the *Genji*, uses it in a more narrow, psychological sense to connote (in the apt phrasing of the translator) "awareness of the poignancy or sorrow of human existence":

> Then what is good or evil in the realm of human psychology and ethics according to the *Tale of Genji?* Generally speaking, those who know the meaning of the sorrow of human existence, i.e., those who are in sympathy and in harmony with human sentiments, are regarded as good; and those who are not aware of the poignancy of human existence, i.e., those who are not in sympathy and not in harmony with human sentiments, are regarded as bad.[14]

Turning to the character of Genji in *The Tale of Genji*, Norinaga notes that, from the standpoint of Confucianism and Buddhism, Genji—the womanizer par excellence—is guilty of "acts of extraordinary iniquity and immorality." But *The Tale of Genji*, rather than developing this theme, instead stresses Genji's "goodness" as one who is profoundly aware of the sorrow of human existence:

> The purpose of the *Tale of Genji* may be likened to the man who, loving the lotus flower, must collect and store muddy and foul water in order to plant and cultivate the flower. The impure mud of illicit love affairs described in the *Tale* is there not for the purpose of being admired but for the purpose of nurturing the flower of the awareness of the sorrow of human existence. Prince Genji's conduct is like the lotus flower which is happy and fragrant but which has its roots in filthy muddy water. But the *Tale* does not dwell on the impurity of the water; it dwells on those who are sympathetically kind and who are aware of the sorrow of human existence, and it holds these feelings to be the basis of the good man.[15]

In an effort to get to the origins of the Japanese tradition, Norinaga also went back beyond Mabuchi's much-esteemed *Man'yōshū* to undertake research on the oldest extant Japanese book, the *Kojiki*. Whereas the *Nihon Shoki* was composed in Chinese and had been studied by courtier scholars through the centuries, the *Kojiki* was so complexly written by means of Chinese characters to reproduce Japanese sounds that it had long been regarded as almost indecipherable. In what was one of the greatest achievements of scholarship in Japanese history, Norinaga devoted nearly thirty-five years to an analysis and annotated translation of the *Kojiki*. The end result is a testament to the exceptionally high standards of scholarly work that had been cultivated in Japan by the eighteenth century.

Although Norinaga approached his translation of the *Kojiki* with an attitude of strict scholarly neutrality, his personal interest in the work went beyond the cultural to the religious. He sought, in fact, to establish the *Kojiki* as a basic scripture of Shinto. Norinaga's own theology was founded on absolute faith in the native *kami* of Japan. Rejecting the various Shinto schools that had emerged in the medieval age and that had absorbed varying amounts of Buddhism, Confucianism, and sundry Chinese lore, Norinaga insisted that the ways of the *kami* were inscrutable and that the accounts of them in such writings as the *Kojiki* and *Nihon Shoki* must be accepted as gospel.

Enriched by the great contribution of Motoori Norinaga, the National Learning movement evolved in several directions during the late Tokugawa period. Some scholars continued to devote themselves to Japanese literature and history; others gave their attention chiefly to the Shintoist elements in National Learning; and still others moved into the field of political activism and became advocates of imperial restoration.

By far the most influential member of the National Learning (or Neo-Shintoist) movement of the early nineteenth century was Hirata Atsutane (1776–1843). Atsutane never had the opportunity to meet Motoori Norinaga, but he deeply venerated the work of the older master and always claimed that he was Norinaga's true successor. Nevertheless, Atsutane was of a very different temperament and outlook from Norinaga. He was, for one thing, a fiery Shintoist and Japanophile, who reviled alien teachings and foreign countries in order to glorify the superiority of Japan and its native learning. Norinaga had combined impeccable scholarship with an abiding religious faith (even though we may regard as excessively naive his acceptance of the mythical accounts of the age of the gods as literally true); Atsutane, on the other hand, seems never to have hesitated to interpret and even to distort things to suit his purposes.

Two examples may be given to illustrate Atsutane's penchant for specious argument. First, he asserted that the reason the ancient Japanese had not articulated a Way of virtuous behavior (that is, a Way like Confucianism), as the early Chinese had, was that they had been inherently virtuous and had felt no need consciously to identify and preach virtue. Second, Atsutane contended that the Japanese failure to develop the art of medicine independently stemmed from the fact that, unlike China and the Western countries, Japan had originally been pure and without disease and hence did not need medicines. Only after contact with the outside world were the Japanese also afflicted with diseases and obliged to seek remedies for them.

Atsutane possessed a wide knowledge of many subjects, including the Western learning of the scholars of Dutch Studies *(rangaku);* in fact, his remarks about medicine were made in spite of (or because of?) a considerable familiarity with Western advances in the field of medicine. Atsutane's religious views may also have been influenced by Christianity, even though that foreign creed had been rigorously proscribed throughout the Tokugawa period. With the rise of Dutch Studies in the eighteenth century, some knowledge of Christianity inevitably filtered once again into Japan despite efforts by the authorities to prevent it. Atsutane's stress on the central importance of a Shinto god of creativity and his belief in a rather pleasant sounding, if vaguely defined, Shinto afterworld may both have been partly or wholly derived from Christianity. His positing of an afterworld was in particular an innovation for Shinto, which had always been notably deficient in such speculation.

The last major movement of heterodox learning in the Tokugawa period was the school of Dutch Studies. We have seen that, although the Japanese had engaged in a century of intercourse with Europeans, particularly the Portuguese, from the 1540s until the late 1630s, much of the Western knowledge they acquired in that period was lost during the anti-Christian persecutions that accompanied implementation of the national seclusion policy. From 1641 on, only the Dutch among Europeans were permitted to trade with Japan; and the Dutch, who shared the limited Japanese foreign trade at Nagasaki with the Chinese, were virtually quarantined from all but a few officials and interpreters who dealt with them at their compound on the small island of Deshima in Nagasaki Harbor.

There was little opportunity under the seclusion policy, therefore, for the Japanese to gain access to Western knowledge. Most of the Dutch at Nagasaki were dour tradesmen who were concerned only with making a profit, and the linguistic talents of the Nagasaki interpreters (both in Portuguese, which remained the lingua franca of communication with the foreigners until the end of the seventeenth century, and in Dutch) were so limited as to make serious exchange with the Hollanders almost impossible. Even so, sufficient information about Dutch superiority in scientific, and especially medical, knowledge did seep out of Nagasaki to stimulate the imaginations of some Japanese scholars. One reason why Western medicine became the object of particular interest among the Japanese was that the doctors regularly assigned to the Dutch contingent at Nagasaki were, unlike the Dutch traders, often men of broad intellectual background and curiosity. One was the German physician Englebert

Kaempfer (1651–1716), who was at Deshima in the early 1690s and twice traveled to Edo with the Dutch party that visited the shogun's court there annually. Kaempfer was a keen student of all aspects of Japan end Japanese life (as he could observe them), and he later published in Europe his *History of Japan,* a book that captured the minds of Europeans just then awakening to an interest in the Far East. It was used by Montesquieu and others in their writings as a primary source for observations on Japan.

By the early eighteenth century, the desire to learn about the West had become increasingly widespread among Japanese scholars and even government officials. The great Confucian rationalist and shogunate adviser Arai Hakuseki, for example, produced a book about conditions in the West based on interviews with an Italian missionary named Sidotti who, after studying Japanese in Manila, had made his way alone to Japan in 1708. One reason for this renewal of interest in the West was the diversity in intellectual inquiry encouraged by the other heterodox schools of scholarship; another was the strong leaning on the part of Tokugawa intellectuals as a whole toward the kind of practical study that Western learning offered.

The actual start of the Dutch Studies movement was made possible by the eighth Tokugawa shogun, Yoshimune (1684–1751), who in 1720 was persuaded by his advisers to lift all restrictions on the importation of foreign books (i.e., Chinese and Dutch books) so long as they did not deal with the still forbidden subject of Christianity. Yoshimune is noted for his efforts to reform the shogunate, including the rather futile policy of reviving the martial spirit of the samurai class. He was also a man who greatly admired learning and was willing to patronize scholars of all schools if he thought their ideas might be useful. He listened, for example, to the views of Ogyū Sorai, even though these were quite at variance with the orthodox Neo-Confucian attitude toward the state; and he agreed to allow the pursuit of Western learning and even sponsored the study of the Dutch language because he hoped they might be of practical value to the shogunate.

Some information about Western science could be garnered through translations of Western books into Chinese by Jesuit scholars of the seventeenth and eighteenth centuries in China; but a working knowledge of Dutch was obviously essential to the new students of Western learning if they wished to go deeply into their studies. It is a tribute to the great zeal of the early pioneers of Dutch Studies that they persisted in the painfully tedious tasks of compiling Dutch-Japanese dictionaries and translating technical books, at first only a few lines at a time, with only the limited help they could obtain from the Dutch and their interpreters at Nagasaki. Nevertheless, by the late eighteenth century, the scholars of Dutch Studies had produced a respectable body of work, including dictionaries, translations, and treatises on Western subjects. And, in 1811, the shogunate gave further impetus to their movement by opening an office for the translation of foreign books in Edo.

The overwhelming interest of the early scholars of Dutch Studies in medical and other scientific matters is attributable not only to the fact that these subjects were practical and safe (that is, unlikely to be connected directly with Christianity), but also, it appears, to the general temperament of the men drawn to study them. The *rangaku* scholars were of a type who had an insatiable curiosity about all manner of things, who loved to experiment simply for the sake of experimenting and, because of their instinctively pragmatic approach to life, were not especially attracted to questions of social or political ideology. Most of the early *rangaku* scholars dabbled in many fields, including medicine, botany, astronomy, and geography. As we shall see, they also practiced painting in the Western style by employing the techniques of realistic perspective and chiaroscuro; but their interest in Western ideas and philosophy was conspicuously slight, even allowing for their wish to avoid the topic of Christianity.

Toward the end of the eighteenth century and the beginning of the nineteenth, however, there appeared a number of scholars of Western learning who devoted their attention increasingly to questions of military preparedness, economics, and foreign affairs, and who also advocated programs of action. Among the reasons for this were the perennial, although ever more pressing, problems of the Tokugawa period: the disequilibrium caused by the growth of commercial markets and a complex monetary system in a state still theoretically based on a natural economy; the inability, because of the seclusion policy, to alleviate domestic economic difficulties by increasing foreign trade; and continuance of the samurai as a largely idle class separated from their main source of income, the soil.

The shogunate attempted to deal with these and other problems by undertaking a series of great reforms, the first of which was conducted by the shogun Yoshimune in the second quarter of the eighteenth century. But apart from some worthwhile programs, such as the encouragement of land reclamation, diversification of crops, and the adoption of more equitable and human penal laws, these reforms were largely traditionalistic and ill-suited to solving difficulties created chiefly by an expanding, dynamic economy. Shogunate reformers, for example, invariably sought to resolve the economic suffering in certain sectors of society by calling upon people everywhere to be more frugal; but, with very few exceptions, they did not consider the possibility of expanding the national wealth through an increase in foreign trade.

The apprehensions of Dutch Studies scholars of the late Tokugawa period were further intensified by the mounting incursion of foreigners, especially Russians, into the regions surrounding Japan. By the end of

the eighteenth century, Russian explorers and traders had pushed eastward across the northern reaches of the world and, in addition to establishing colonies in places such as Kamchatka and the Aleutians, were
making periodic probes into islands closer to Japan, including Hokkaido
(until this time in Japanese history inhabited almost exclusively by the
Ainu) and the Kurils. It is little wonder, therefore, that the Dutch Studies
scholars should turn their eyes northward in assessing the challenges and
opportunities presented by the outside world.

Among the most astute and imaginative of these later scholars of
Dutch Studies was Honda Toshiaki (1744–1821).[16] Raised in one of the
northern domains of Japan, Toshiaki devoted his life to the study of a
wide range of Western subjects from mathematics and astronomy to military science, geography, and navigation. He also traveled widely throughout Japan, observing the social and economic conditions of different
regions, and even went by ship into the northern seas, perhaps as far as
Kamchatka. Toshiaki believed that Japan not only should seek to increase
its foreign trade but also should expand territorially overseas. It was imperative first that Hokkaido, Sakhalin, and the Kurils be colonized to prevent them from falling into the hands of the Russians; then other islands
and territories in Asia and North America could be absorbed to form a
great Japanese empire whose capital, Toshiaki felt, should be situated in
Kamchatka. Toshiaki was particularly fond of likening Japan to England,
the island country of the West that had also founded a far-flung empire.

Toshiaki was perhaps more blatantly imperialistic in his views than
most, but he was certainly not alone among scholars of his age in advocating alteration of the seclusion policy to permit expansion of Japanese
interests abroad. Yet, except for a brief period in the late eighteenth century, the opinions of Toshiaki and like-minded men were not especially
appreciated by the shogunate. This was partly because of a clamping
down on heterodox studies undertaken in 1790 by issuance of an edict
calling upon the Confucian schools conducted by the Hayashi family to
teach only the tenets of the orthodox creed of Neo-Confucianism. This
edict was conceived by shogunate officials who sincerely believed that
the diversity of thinking in the country was having adverse effects upon
society and who hoped to strengthen the moral fiber of the Japanese
people by insisting upon propagation once again of an orthodox philosophical line in officially sponsored schools.

In addition to the various heterodox trends we have been examining in
intellectual circles, the middle and late Tokugawa period also witnessed
what may be called heterodox developments in painting, at least insofar as
the main schools flourishing during this time were influenced to a greater
or lesser degree by Western "scientific" techniques of realistic detailing,
shading, and perspective. When one considers that, by the early Meiji

period (say, the 1870s), the Japanese had become so enamored of Western-style painting that they were prepared almost totally to ignore their own rich artistic heritage, this turning to Western techniques from about the early eighteenth century on constituted a radical heterodoxy indeed.

One of the main schools of painting that arose in the eighteenth century, although under some Western influence, was in fact inspired by the so-called literati artists *(bunjin)* of China (fig. 61). From about the late Han period on, there had developed in China a distinction between professional artists on the one hand and, on the other, amateur artists who were also members of the ruling literati class and regarded painting as a natural and proper function of the cultivated man. In its origins, then, the *bunjin* distinction was a social one; but, from the fourteenth century on, a definite *bunjin* style emerged, distinguished chiefly by the use of soft colors and a thin and delicate brush stroke, and it was this style that was finally introduced to Japan in the eighteenth century. Interestingly, this was the first major school of Chinese painting to be emulated by the Japanese since painters of the early Muromachi period, some four centuries earlier, had succumbed to the beauty of Sung monochrome landscapes.

Unlike their Chinese counterparts, most of the leading Japanese *bunjin* artists painted to earn a living. They seem originally to have been inspired to adopt this particular style because of the influence of Chinese *bunjin* artists who came to Nagasaki in the seventeenth century. The fact that the fashion for *bunjin* art thus emerged from Nagasaki, which had been the center of Portuguese *namban* culture and in Tokugawa times included Dutch as well as Chinese in its foreign community, no doubt helps explain the Western influences that can be seen in much *bunjin* work.

The leading Japanese *bunjin* artists of the eighteenth century were Ike no Taiga (1723–76) and Yosa Buson (1716–83). Taiga, who was born into a peasant family in the outskirts of Kyoto, was an extremely precocious child and, at the age of fourteen, began painting fans in order to support his widowed mother. Although he subsequently became known as the founder of the *bunjin* school in Japan, Taiga's mature painting style is actually quite eclectic and reveals the influences not only of the Muromachi monochrome masters and the Sōtatsu-Kōrin (Rimpa) school but also of Western art (especially in the techniques of perspective and depth perception). Like all *bunjin* artists, Taiga did most of his paintings of Chinese-style landscapes and people. His pictures also often have a delightfully eccentric and witty quality that suggests they were done by one of the more joyous and refreshing personalities of the age.

Taiga's friend Buson was both a noted painter and a master of *haiku*. Like Taiga, he traveled frequently about the country and added much that was Japanese to his essentially "Chinese" landscapes. Also like Taiga,

Fig. 61   "Buddhist Temple among Cloudy Peaks,"
landscape painting in the literati *(nanga)* style
*(Honolulu Academy of Arts, Gift of London Gallery,
Tokyo, 1975 [6162.1])*

Buson did thoroughly charming caricature work that was undoubtedly influenced by the indigenous Japanese tradition of caricature, since Buson is known to have studied the great twelfth-century Animal Scrolls of the priest Toba. In the series of drawings he did to illustrate Bashō's *The Narrow Road of Oku*, Buson, as a writer of *haiku* who also traveled into the northern provinces, has captured the spirit of this great travel account so perfectly that, once having seen his illustrations of it, we have difficulty imagining how they could possibly have been done in any other way. Indeed, Buson's art might well be called the art of *haiku*, and some of his most appealing works are known as *"haiku* pictures" *(haiga)*—that is, pictures used to illustrate *haiku*, the texts of which are usually painted in calligraphic brush style in the upper right-hand corners.

Some comment on Buson as a poet may help to enhance appreciation of Buson the artist. In comparing Buson to Bashō, a Western critic has said, "Bashō was gentle, wise, loving, and mystic; Buson was brilliant and many-sided, not mystic in the least, but intensely clever and alive to the impressions of the world around him. A foreign simile would be to liken Bashō to a pearl, and Buson to a diamond."[17] Two poems will illustrate both Buson's cleverness and his sensitivity to impressions of the world around him:

> Spring rain: and as yet
> the little froglets' bellies
> haven't got wet.
>
> Departing spring:
> with belated cherry blossoms
> shilly-shallying.[18]

Although Taiga and Buson had qualities that were unique and great, many other *bunjin* artists were mere Sinophiles, who turned to this style of painting as part of a greater craving for things Chinese. It is interesting to note that, even at a time when some Japanese were inaugurating a movement of National Learning with strongly xenophobic and nationalistic overtones, others—scholars as well as painters—were giving all their love to China. This is a paradox characteristic of the ambivalence with which the sensitive and highly adaptable Japanese have often confronted the dominant outside world, represented by China in premodern times and the West in the modern era.

A second new school of painting to evolve in the eighteenth century was the realistic or naturalistic school, whose most outstanding practitioner was Maruyama Ōkyo (1733–95). In this school, the influence of Western art was very strong and in fact the followers of Ōkyo were the forerunners of one of the mainstreams of painting in modern Japan. Ōkyo did many sketches and drawings from nature that are extremely detailed and realistic, but his most interesting works are his larger paintings in which he sought to blend traditional Far Eastern and Western artistic styles.

In contrast to the synthesizing efforts of Ōkyo and others of the naturalistic school, the Dutch Studies painters openly attempted to imitate Western models. The best-known, although perhaps also the most extreme, representative of these painters was Shiba Kōkan (1738–1818). Kōkan did not actually study the Dutch language; but, in his diversity of interests and his love of Western scientific and utilitarian methods, he was very much the *rangaku* man. The paintings of Kōkan, who was the first Japanese to produce a copper engraving, are technically excellent and are definitive proof that long before the Meiji Restoration the Japanese had become thoroughly familiar with the mechanics of Western art. Kōkan's work is apt to impress one more for its technique than its inspiration, but there is no denying the great contribution he made to this area of Western learning.

The influence of Western techniques of painting was also felt by the later *ukiyo-e* school of artists. Certain devices, such as realistic perspective, had been employed on occasion by *ukiyo-e* artists from about the early 1700s, but it was not until the great nineteenth-century painters Katsushika Hokusai (1760–1849) and Andō Hiroshige (1797–1858) that the Western influence became pronounced.

Hokusai was a phenomenon even in the prolific world of Tokugawa *ukiyo-e* art. Virtually unknown until he was about forty, Hokusai (who later styled himself "the old man mad with painting") absorbed the main features of all the major art styles, native and foreign, then known in Japan and produced literally tens of thousands of drawings and paintings of a great variety of subjects over an incredibly active career that continued until his death, in 1849, at the age of eighty-nine. Hokusai is best remembered for his landscape prints, especially his "Thirty-six Views of Mount Fuji." Curiously, Fuji, Japan's greatest natural treasure and the object of countless lyrical flights by Japanese poets, had until this time received very little attention from Japanese painters. Possibly this was because Fuji's wonderful symmetry simply was not in keeping with the generally angular, jagged conception of mountains and rock formations in the highly influential Chinese tradition of monochrome landscape work. Significantly, the Western-oriented Shiba Kōkan was also attracted to Fuji and sought to apply scientific techniques to produce a truly realistic painting of the mountain. Hokusai's views of Fuji, on the other hand, are often startlingly conceived, as for example the world-famous glimpse of its snow-capped cone through a huge, curling wave (fig. 62).

Whereas Maruyama Ōkyo self-consciously tried to merge Far Eastern and Western art and Shiba Kōkan imitated Western painting outright, Hokusai, with his boundless energy and enthusiasm, simply absorbed the techniques of Western as well as other art styles and used them to shape

Fig. 62 "The Great Wave at Kanagawa" by Hokusai *(The Metropolitan Museum of Art, Howard Mansfield Collection, Rogers Fund, 1936)*

his own unique style. Hokusai's better landscapes display a superb sense of design and proportion and a compassionately human concern for the figures, often from the lower classes, who inhabit them. Hokusai has enjoyed great favor in the West, and some of his prints, along with those of Hiroshige, have become as well known to Western art lovers as the more famous masterpieces of their own tradition. The case of Hokusai is an excellent illustration of cross-cultural exchange, for here was a Japanese artist who borrowed from the West and at the same time contributed, along with the *ukiyo-e* school in general, a new and exotic inspiration to the French Impressionists and other Western artists of the late nineteenth century.

Hiroshige, although he painted other subjects, was much more of a specialist in landscapes than the extraordinarily dynamic and versatile Hokusai. In a Hokusai landscape, attention is often divided between the setting and the people in it; but in Hiroshige's work, everything is subordinated to the setting and especially to the mood established by season, weather, time of day, and angle of view. Moreover, while Hokusai's figures, as they go about their business, frequently provide an element of genre interest to his landscapes, Hiroshige's are usually mere reminders of the insignificance of man against the vastness of nature (figs. 63–64). In this, Hiroshige would appear to be an inheritor of the spirit of the Chinese and Japanese masters of monochrome landscapes; and even though

Fig. 63 "Cutting a Log" from "The 100 Poems Explained by the Nurse" by Hokusai *(courtesy of the Brooklyn Museum)*

Fig. 64 "Evening Rain at Azuma no Mori" by Hiroshige *(courtesy of the Brooklyn Museum)*

Hiroshige depicts far more dramatic seasonal and weather changes in his prints, there is an underlying tranquility to them that is also very reminiscent of the earlier monochrome work.

Hiroshige achieved his greatest fame in a series of prints entitled "The Fifty-three Stations of the Tōkaidō," depicting scenes along the great highway connecting Kyoto and Edo. By far the most important thoroughfare in Japanese history, the Tōkaidō during Tokugawa times was the scene not only of many great daimyo processions to and from the military capital but also of the coming and going of an unending stream of other people, including merchants, itinerant priests, pilgrims, entertainers, adventurers, and even the Dutch on their journeys to the shogun's court. In response to this bustling traffic, the stations of the Tōkaidō flourished and each accumulated stories and legends about the famous people who had visited its inns, restaurants, brothels, and bathhouses, and about the unusual events it had witnessed. Hence, the Tōkaidō became a fertile source for both writers and artists. Hokusai, among the artists, tried his hand at a series of prints of the Tōkaidō stations, but no painter succeeded in immortalizing the highway and its famous stopping-off places like Hiroshige. To many people around the world who have seen copies of them, these Tōkaidō prints by Hiroshige constitute their most vivid impressions of Japan. And, in truth, they remain even to those long familiar with the country a constant source of delight as extraordinarily effective representations in art of the peculiar qualities of Japan's natural beauties and seasonal moods.

A significant development of the late Tokugawa period was the decisive shift in the center of cultural activity from the Osaka-Kyoto region to Edo. In the seventeenth and early eighteenth centuries, the Kansai had produced such leading figures of the world of art as Sōtatsu, Kōrin, Saikaku, and Chikamatsu. With the exception of Bashō, who moved to Edo, and the painters of the early *ukiyo-e* school, the most outstanding creative artists up through the Genroku epoch were the products of Japan's ancient center of cultural life. But by the Bunka-Bunsei epoch (the end of the eighteenth century and the first quarter or so of the nineteenth), Edo had taken over this central role in culture. It had become the principal home for writers, artists, and intellectuals, as well as the mecca for publishing and scholarship. The cultural primacy of Edo established at this time proved lasting, and indeed has been even more completely asserted in the modern era.

The Bunka-Bunsei epoch was a relatively placid time preceding the final, crisis decades of the Tokugawa period, when the Western powers exerted increasing pressure upon and finally succeeded in forcing Japan to open its doors and enter the modern world. In painting, the epoch was of course distinguished by men such as Shiba Kōkan, Sharaku,

Utamaro, Hokusai, and Hiroshige. But in literature there was no such comparable brilliance. The efforts of late Tokugawa authors were, in fact, polarized rather sharply into the writing either of "witty" and "amorous" books *(kokkeibon* and *sharebon)* or of historical novels *(yomi-hon)*. The distinction between the two categories was essentially one of the overly frothy versus the overly serious, of the pornographic versus the didactic.

Literature dealing with the floating world of the Tokugawa pleasure quarters had reached an early level of excellence in the writing of Sai-kaku. But the subject matter was too narrow in range to be a continuing source for true artistic inspiration and, with few exceptions, the successors to Saikaku produced distinctly inferior work. The examples of this sort of work in the Bunka-Bunsei epoch are interesting as social commentaries on contemporary styles and tastes, and particularly on the meaning of two much-admired qualities of people of fashion in Edo, *sui* and *tsū*, which Sansom has aptly rendered as *chic* and *savoir faire*. Otherwise, the literature of the floating world as observed in its later variants, including the witty and amorous books, was merely a cheap, salacious type of writing that catered to low and vulgar tastes.

The most commercially successful author of this lighter type of literature in the early nineteenth century was Jippensha Ikku (1765–1831), who began his career as the writer of puppet plays in Osaka before he moved to Edo and turned his attention to prose literature. Ikku's most popular work, the picaresque *Hizakurige (A Journey by Foot)*, recounts the adventures of two ribald and devil-may-care rogues as they make their way down the Tōkaidō from Edo. In contrast to the sophisticated inquiries of Saikaku's writings, *Hizakurige*, with its slapstick and its bawdy humor, portrays the world of lusty adventure and the irresistible pleasures of the flesh.

The second major category of literature in the Bunka-Bunsei epoch was the historical novel, whose most noted author was Takizawa Bakin (1767–1848). Like Ikku, but unlike many writers of the epoch, Bakin was able to earn his living solely by his literary efforts. His magnum opus, written over a period of some twenty-eight years and intended to be the longest novel in either Chinese or Japanese, was entitled *Satomi and the Eight Dogs (Nansō Satomi Hakkenden)*. It is the tale of eight men who vow to restore the fortunes of the warrior family of Satomi in the fifteenth century. Against this heroic, medieval background, Bakin set about demonstrating how such ethical values as filial piety, loyalty, chastity, and selflessness actually function in the lives of men. Bakin's didacticism is all-encompassing, and each episode in *Satomi and the Eight Dogs* is designed to show how, inevitably, "virtue is rewarded and vice is punished" *(kanzen chōaku)*. Compared to the literature of the floating world that was predominant through much of the Tokugawa period, this was indeed sober writing. But Bakin's great popular reception suggests that the temper of the times was turning more serious, at least in some circles; and many people were prepared and perhaps even anxious to rekindle Confucian traditions and some of the spirit of the more admirable behavior of the samurai.

Before we leave the subject of heterodoxy during the Tokugawa period, a few words should be said about how heterodoxy spread even into the world of tea. The "orthodoxy" of tea was, of course, the tea ceremony itself, *chanoyu,* which had evolved during the medieval age and which enjoyed great prosperity during Tokugawa times as one of the elegant pastimes *(yūgei)* discussed in the last chapter. *Chanoyu,* as we have seen, is based on the use of powdered tea and is a ritually elaborate procedure whose principal spiritual basis is Zen Buddhism. By the eighteenth century there had emerged a movement, supported especially by literati *(bunjin)* artists, that opposed *chanoyu* and its powdered tea and advocated, instead, the drinking of *sencha* or steeped tea.

The *bunjin* artists were attracted to *sencha* in part because of its association with the literati lifestyle in China, which included the drinking of steeped tea. But these artists, as well as others, also embraced *sencha* as a protest against *chanoyu,* which they viewed as both excessively complex and increasingly debased by virtue of the commercial purveyance of it as an elegant pastime. *Sencha* was a beverage, uncluttered by rules, that could be freely consumed by people coming together in casual social gatherings.

The growing popularity of *sencha* in the second half of the Tokugawa period also benefited from the intellectual trend of the times to look to the past to revive earlier traditions or derive inspiration from them. We have observed this trend, for example, in the School of Ancient Studies of Confucianism and the Neo-Shintoist School of National Learning. *Sencha* advocates rejected powdered tea, a product of the Sung period of Chinese history, and called for a return to the "original way of tea" as it was formulated during the earlier T'ang dynasty, especially in the classic eighth-century writing by Lu Yü, *The Classic of Tea (Cha Ching).*[19]

As the nineteenth century began, incursions by Westerners increased. Not only Russian, but also British and American ships began appearing in Japanese waters. In 1808, for example, the British ship *Phaeton,* on patrol during the Napoleonic wars, entered Nagasaki harbor looking for some Dutch merchants. The Japanese magistrate of Nagasaki ordered the ship to depart, and even began preparations to attack it. But the antiquated weapons of the Japanese could only have mounted a puny offense against the *Phaeton,* which was armed with fifty cannon, and the attack was delayed. Meanwhile, after a few days, the *Phaeton,* having seized and interrogated the Dutch merchants and having demanded and received supplies from the Japanese, departed. It was a brief incident, but it greatly shocked the shogunate and contributed to the mounting xenophobia among shogunate officials and others.

We observed at the beginning of the last chapter that the seclusion policy implemented by the shogunate in the seventeenth century, although it greatly reduced Japan's foreign contacts, was not intended, so far as we can judge, to make Japan a permanently "closed country." But shogunate leaders at the end of the eighteenth century and the beginning of the nineteenth, faced with a new and potentially very dangerous threat from abroad, chose to regard seclusion as the fixed law of the Tokugawa state, even calling Japan *sakoku* (literally, "chained country"), a term first used in 1801.[20] To enforce *sakoku*, the shogunate in 1825 went so far as to declare a policy of "Don't Think Twice" *(ninen naku)* toward unwanted foreigners. If foreigners (meaning Westerners other than the Dutch) should enter Japanese waters or land on Japanese soil, they were to be driven away forthwith.

In that same year, 1825, a scholar of the Mito school, Aizawa Seishisai (1781–1863), published a book, entitled *New Proposals (Shinron)*, that became one of the most influential political writings of its time. The Mito school, as noted earlier in this chapter, had been established by the Mito *han* in the seventeenth century to undertake the research for and writing of *The History of Great Japan*, a lengthy chronicle of Japan covering the period from 660 B.C. to 1392 that focused on the imperial succession. Called the "later Mito scholars" to distinguish them from the early Mito scholars who first undertook work on *The History of Great Japan*, Seishisai and his contemporaries of the Mito school concocted a potent ideology, articulated in *New Proposals*, that they advanced to deal with the foreign threat that then confronted Japan. The basis of this ideology, which was much influenced by the School of National Learning, was belief in Japan as a sacred, divine land. Rejecting the view of Japanese Sinophiles that China was the great Middle Kingdom of the world, the later Mito scholars—like Yamaga Sokō and some others earlier in the Tokugawa period—claimed that status for Japan. But these scholars went far beyond Sokō and the others to claim both a geographical and cultural superiority for Japan that made it the veritable beacon and light of the world. In the words of Aizawa Seishisai in *New Proposals:*

> Our divine Land is where the sun rises and where the primordial energy originates. The heirs of the Great Sun have occupied the Imperial Throne from generation to generation without change from time immemorial. Japan's position at the vertex of the earth makes it the standard for the nations of the world. Indeed, it casts its light over the world, and the distance which the resplendent imperial influence reaches knows no limit. Today, the alien barbarians of the West, the lowly organs of the legs and feet of the world, are

dashing about across the seas, trampling other countries underfoot, and daring, with their squinting eyes and limping feet, to override the noble nations. What manner of arrogance is this![21]

The later Mito scholars, in addition to advocating a policy of forcibly expelling the Western barbarians *(jōi)*, also called upon Japanese everywhere to recognize Japan's sacred character as a nation and, above all, to revere its godlike emperor. Here we see the stirring up of a spirit of extreme reverence for the emperor that was to inspire the imperial loyalists who finally overthrew the Tokugawa shogunate later in the century and that was received as an article of faith by the architects of a modern Japan.

Although reverence for the emperor *(sonnō)* became a loyalist rallying cry against the Tokugawa in the 1850s and 1860s, it was not so used by Aizawa Seishisai and the later Mito scholars of the 1820s. Seishisai, for one, was firmly committed to the Tokugawa state in its existing structure. In calling for reverence for the emperor, he wished to infuse a sense of nationalism in the Japanese people. The first step in doing this was to clarify for the people that Japan was a hierarchically structured state whose head was the emperor but whose actual affairs were handled by the Tokugawa shogunate.

Seishisai did not think that the West posed a serious military threat to Japan; and in fact at the time it did not, since the Industrial Revolution had not yet quite reached the point where Western power could threaten countries big and small everywhere in the world. Rather, Seishisai believed that Western strength lay primarily in Christianity, which he regarded as a pernicious religion that could subvert Japan from within. Only by promoting its own nationalism, which Seishisai associated with the term *kokutai* (usually translated in modern times as "national polity," but meaning here "unity of religion and government"),[22] could Japan defend itself internally against Christianity even as it sought, externally, to drive the Westerners away by force.

Mito thought, as found in Aizawa Seishisai's *New Proposals,* was thus virulently anti-Western, resonating well with the hard-line, *jōi* approach of the shogunate to Western contacts that was reflected in its "Don't Think Twice" policy of 1825. But this was not a policy that the shogunate, in a time of rapidly moving events that included England's defeat of China in the Opium War of 1839–42, would seek to maintain indefinitely, and in 1842 it was abandoned. The Western countries were too insistent; and, out of the milieu of divergent opinions about how Japan should deal with them, an increasing number of voices—many of them those of Dutch Studies scholars—spoke of the need for some kind of accommodation with the West, which would probably mean modifying, at least to some extent, the *sakoku* policy.

Although Japan's "response to the West" in these decades may often have seemed confused and inconsistent, it emerged from a powerful dynamic: to a far greater degree than other non-Western people, the Japanese were both impressed and alarmed by the material superiority of the West. We see this perhaps most clearly in the proclamation of certain scholars in the very last years of the Tokugawa shogunate of the need for a combination of "Eastern morals and Western technology," which aphoristically suggested the central problem that was later to confront a modernizing Japan: how to retain the socially binding ethics of traditional behavior while at the same time resolutely acquiring the material benefits of the Western scientific and industrial revolutions.

Encounter with the West

In 1844 King William II of Holland dispatched a letter to the shogun of Japan warning him that the quickening pace of world events made continuance of the Japanese policy of national seclusion both unwise and untenable. The development of steam navigation, for one thing, now enabled the ships of Western countries readily to penetrate the most distant waters of the world. China, as noted, had already suffered military defeat at the hands of the British in the Opium War, and Japan could not expect to remain aloof from world affairs much longer.

Although they debated it among themselves, Tokugawa officials did nothing concrete in response to the letter of the Dutch king. The shogunate was at the time engrossed in the last of its great traditionalistic reforms, and the failure of this reform, combined with vacillation in the face of the now pressing need to seriously reconsider the seclusion policy, portended trouble for the shogunate. The Edo regime was certainly under no immediate threat in the 1840s of being overthrown, but the political temperature in regard to seclusion was rising and could readily become a challenge of a kind that, in gravity, the shogunate had not faced before.

This challenge became reality with the arrival in Edo Bay in the summer of 1853 of Commodore Matthew Perry of the United States and his squadron of "black ships." Perry had been dispatched by President Millard Fillmore to inquire into the possibility of opening diplomatic and commercial relations with Japan, and in 1854 he achieved the first objective through the signing of a Treaty of Friendship that provided for an exchange of consular officials between Japan and the United States.

The first American consul, Townsend Harris, arrived in Japan in 1856, and it was he who finally secured a commercial pact. This pact, in addition to providing for the opening of certain Japanese ports to trade, contained a set of stipulations, previously worked out by the Western powers in their dealings with China, that became known as "the unequal treaty provisions." These included the principle of extraterritoriality, or the right of the Western signatory to try its nationals by its own laws for offenses committed on Japanese soil; the most-favored-nation clause, which provided that any additional treaty benefit acquired by one Western nation would automatically accrue to all other nations holding similar treaties; and the setting of a fixed customs levy of approximately 5 percent on all goods imported to Japan, a levy that could be altered only with the consent of both parties to a treaty. It was on the basis of the Harris agreement, and especially its most-favored-nation clause, that the principal European powers also acquired commercial treaties with Japan during the next few months.

The coming of Perry and Harris brought to an end Japan's seclusion policy of more than two hundred years, but it did not resolve differences of opinion about the policy. There was the question, for example, of the extent to which Japan should be opened. The Harris treaty specified only that a few ports be made available to foreign trade over a period of years. Should the rest of Japan, even the interior, also be opened to foreign merchants, missionaries, and residents, and if so over what span of time? Some diehards continued to insist that the treaties with the Western "barbarians" be regarded simply as tactical measures valid only until Japan could strengthen itself sufficiently to drive the foreigners once again from the divine land; but other Japanese began to consider more soberly the sweeping and long-term implications of their new relations with the West.

The final, chaotic years of the Tokugawa period are fascinating for the momentous political events that led to the overthrow of the shogunate, but they are not especially important to Japanese cultural history and hence may be briefly summarized here. The first wave of opposition to the shogunate's handling of foreign affairs came primarily from certain of the larger *tozama* or outside *han* of western Japan, especially Satsuma and Chōshū. These great domains regarded as anachronistic the Tokugawa governing system whereby they were theoretically excluded from all participation in the conduct of national affairs at Edo. In the early 1860s, the shogunate sought a reconciliation by bringing some of the more important outside daimyos into its deliberative councils. At the same time, it attempted to strengthen relations with Kyoto by arranging a marriage between the shogun and an imperial princess.

With these developments, the initiative in opposition to the shogunate's policies was assumed by younger, activist samurai from Satsuma, Chōshū, and other domains, many of whom renounced their feudal ties to become *rōnin* and thus free to pursue their own political convictions. These samurai, also known as *shishi* or "men of high purpose," formed the nucleus of the loyalist movement that grew in intensity during the next few years. By the middle of the decade, the loyalists were openly calling for the overthrow of the shogunate on the grounds that, not only had it usurped the rightful ruling powers of the emperor, it had failed militarily to protect Japan against the intrusion of the Western barbarians. For them, "Revere the Emperor!" became a call for imperial restoration and "Expel the Barbarians!" a demand that the shogunate do what in fact was no longer possible: drive the foreigners from Japanese soil.

The climax to the confrontation between the shogunate and the loyalists, more and more of whom were congregating in Kyoto where they aligned themselves with anti-Tokugawa ministers at the imperial court, came in 1866 when the shogunate attempted for the second time in two years to put down the loyalist faction in the most unruly of the domains, Chōshū. At this critical point, Satsuma, whose loyalists had already formed a secret alliance with Chōshū, refused to join the shogunate's expedition, and in the ensuing conflict the shogunate forces were defeated. Encouraged by this demonstration of military weakness on the part of the shogunate, Satsuma and Chōshū loyalists, joined by men from other domains, carried out a coup in Kyoto at the end of the year and proclaimed an imperial restoration. The shogun, realizing the futility of further resistance, capitulated; and, although there was some scattered fighting by stubborn supporters of the shogunate, the restoration was completed by early 1867 with very little loss of blood.

The Meiji Restoration, named after the Emperor Meiji (1852–1912) who ascended the throne in 1867 at the age of fifteen, was a political revolution from above carried out by younger, enlightened members of Japan's ruling samurai class.[1] These men and their supporters had called for a "return to antiquity" *(fukko)*, and, in the early days following the Restoration, there was a certain heady excitement about recapturing the spirit and ways of the past, especially through temporary reinstatement of the ancient institutions of imperial government as originally set forth in the eighth-century Taihō Code. But the new Meiji leaders, who included some Kyoto courtiers along with samurai, were men of the future, not the past. They made this clear from the very outset of the Meiji period by quietly dropping the cry of "Expel the Barbarians!" which they had so recently used to embarrass the Tokugawa shogunate. They may have continued to harbor personal animosities toward the West, particularly for forcing Japan to accede to the unequal treaties; but the Meiji leaders were by and large pragmatic men who respected the material superiority of the West and wished to emulate it by undertaking modernization. Sharing an overriding concern for Japanese territorial independence, they believed that, quite apart from the obvious benefits and enjoyments it would bring, modernization was essential if Japan was to be protected against possible future threats from the outside. Accordingly, they adopted as a general statement of their policy the slogan, taken from Chinese legalist thought, of "Enrich the country and strengthen its arms" *(fukoku-kyōhei)*. Japan was to be enriched through modernization for the primary purpose of strengthening it militarily.

The devotion of the Meiji leaders to modernization can also be seen in the brief, five-article Charter Oath they issued in 1868 in the emperor's name. This may be regarded as a very broad statement of purpose by the new regime, and it is significant that at least two of its articles seem to be explicit commitments to modernization:

Article 4. Evil customs of the past shall be broken off and everything based upon the just laws of Nature.
Article 5. Knowledge shall be sought throughout the world so as to strengthen the foundations of imperial rule.[2]

In line with their determination to make Japan a modern state, the Meiji leaders took a series of steps during their first decade in power that together constituted a radical and sweeping reform of Japanese society. These included abolition of the feudal *han* and the institution of a centrally controlled system of prefectural government; and dissolution of the samurai class and the establishment of basic legal equalities for all people. One of the most severe blows to the old, rigid class system, and particularly to the inflated samurai sense of superiority, was the adoption in 1873 of universal military conscription.

Despite the inevitable stresses caused by social change and the specific grievances of many samurai as they were dispossessed of their traditional privileges, the Japanese by the early 1870s had in general abandoned their dreams of restoring the past and were caught up in an overwhelming urge to join the march of Western progress. This was the beginning of a period of nearly two decades during which the Japanese unabashedly pursued the fruits of Western "civilization and enlightenment" *(bummei-kaika)*. That the government intended to take the lead in this quest for the holy grail of foreign culture can be seen in the dispatch in 1871 of a mission to visit the United States and Europe headed by a distinguished court noble, Iwakura Tomomi (1825–83), and including a number of other leaders of the new Meiji regime. So cherished was the opportunity to journey to the West at this time that one young boy who accompanied the Iwakura Mission in order to study in the United States wrote (years later) that he and his fellow students all fervently believed that one could not become a real human being without going abroad.

Actually, missions abroad to the West were by this time nothing new. The Tokugawa shogunate had send one to the United States in 1860, just two years after ratification of the Harris treaty with Japan. Thereafter, until its overthrow in 1868, the shogunate dispatched missions yearly to both the United States and Europe. In total, more than three hundred Japanese visited the West during the last eight years of Tokugawa rule.[3]

The remarkable thing about the Iwakura Mission was the presence on it of so many ranking officials, who obviously felt that visiting the West at this time warranted their leaving Japan only three years after the convulsion that gave birth to the Meiji government. Scheduled to remain away a year, the mission did not return for nearly two. During that time its hundred or so members, often dividing themselves into smaller groups, visited the United States, England and Scotland, France, Belgium, Holland, Germany, Russia, Denmark, Sweden, Italy, Austria, and Switzerland. The mission had hoped also to visit the Iberian countries of Spain and Portugal, but were prevented by civil war in the former.[4]

The stated aim of the Iwakura Mission was to secure revision of the unequal treaties, but very likely the leaders knew from the beginning that revision was impossible until Japan became stronger and, from a Western perspective, more "civilized." Hence the real purpose of the mission's leaders was to see the West firsthand, learn about its progress and modernization, and set Japan on the course to becoming a modern, progressive nation. Thanks to an official diary of some two thousand pages that was compiled from the mission, we know a good deal about the thinking and impressions of its members during their lengthy travels. In reading the diary we are struck not only with the members' fascination with that great nineteenth-century utopian dream of progress, but also with their discernment in evaluating the various Western countries in terms of their particular strengths (and weaknesses) and their shrewd judgment about how they could borrow selectively from one Western country or another.

The members of the Iwakura Mission clearly perceived that the Western countries had achieved modernization not through mutual cooperation but through a constant struggle for wealth and power that entailed fierce and sometimes violent national rivalries. Of all the ideologies that accompanied the scientific and industrial revolutions and the West's rush into modernity, none exceeded the force of nationalism, and the Iwakura Mission's leaders did not for a moment hesitate to conceive and plan for their own modernization in terms, first and foremost, of Japan's national interests. They understood that, in the age of progress, Japan had to join in its advance quickly and vigorously, lest it be left in the West's historical dust.

Travel to the West became the surest means for advancement among Japanese in the early Meiji period. Of the many youths who went to study in Europe and the United States, the great majority were sponsored by the government as part of its civilization and enlightenment policy. Upon returning home, these youths had virtually unlimited career opportunities. Meanwhile, for those who could not make the trip abroad, the government and other institutions invited a number of foreigners to Japan as teachers and technical advisers. Offering high wages, they were able to attract generally excellent people, who provided knowledge and expertise crucial to the modernization process.

Outward signs of modernity began to appear throughout the country, but particularly in the metropolitan centers like Tokyo and Yokohama: steamships, railroads, telegraph lines, a national postal service, industrial factories, and, especially exciting to the Japanese, gas-burning streetlamps that "made the night as bright as the day." Most of these innovations were, of course, indispensable to modernization; but many others were just marginally important or were even ludicrous fads reflecting the craze among some people to "become Western."

Western-style uniforms were first adopted by the Japanese military before the Restoration and were made standard for policemen, train conductors, and other civil functionaries within a few years after the beginning of the modern era.[5] During the 1870s, Western clothes, deemed more practical and up-to-date, were increasingly worn by men in the cities, often combined amusingly with items of the native costume. Thus, it was not unusual to see men sporting kimonos over long pants or suit jackets and *hakama* skirts. Women and people in the rural areas, on the other hand, were much slower in adopting the sartorial ways of the West. Western shoes, moreover, presented a special problem, for the Japanese foot, splayed from the traditional wearing of sandals, frequently could not be fitted into footgear imported from abroad.

But whereas the shift to Western wearing attire was made erratically, and never completely, the transition to the Western custom of cropped hair for men became something of a national issue. The Japanese are extraordinarily sensitive to ridicule by others. No doubt this sensitivity has been heightened by the minimal contact they have had with foreigners through much of their history. In the early Meiji period, as they sought to "catch up with the West," they also faced the practical problem (already noted in the discussion of the Iwakura Mission) that, so long as the Western nations regarded their ways as barbaric, it would be that much more difficult to secure revision of the unequal treaties and achieve complete independence. Hence, the Japanese government either banned or tried to restrict practices, such as public bathing, tattooing, and the sale of pornography, that they thought the foreigners found offensive. And the wearing of the topknot, which had been the practice of Japanese men for centuries, also came to be looked upon as primitive and unbecoming to the citizens of a modern Japan.

Again, it was the Japanese military who first cut their topknots in order to wear the hats of their Western-style uniforms. By the early Meiji period, all prominent Japanese men, including the emperor, wore their hair cropped (and often grew fine beards and mustaches, like their Western counterparts): indeed, it was very much the sign of the progressive man to wear his hair this way, and a popular jingle claimed: "If you tap a cropped head, it will play the tune of civilization and enlightenment."[6] But the fashion was not immediately accepted by the lower classes, and the Japanese government felt constrained to issue occasional directives urging its adoption. Some headmen in rural villages are said to have walked around reading the directives while still sporting their own topknots; others cut the topknots but let their "hair of regret" hang down their backs. Not until about 1890 did the wearing of cropped hair by men become universal in Japan.

Among the many Western fads, none was more conspicuous or symbolic of the humorous side of foreign borrowing than the eating of beef. Owing to Buddhist taboos and a scarcity of game animals, the Japanese had traditionally abstained from eating red meat. With the coming of foreigners, however, restaurants specializing in beef dishes, especially *gyū-nabe* or beef stew, began to crop up in the cities. A contemporary author of "witty books," Kanagaki Robun (1829–94), even wrote a collection of satirical sketches entitled *Aguranabe (Eating Stew Cross-Legged)* about the conversations of customers in a beefhouse who concluded that a man could not be regarded as civilized unless he ate beef. Kanagaki's description of one customer includes the observation that

> he uses that scent called Eau de Cologne to give sheen to his hair. He wears a padded silken kimono beneath which a calico undergarment is visible. By his side is his Western-style umbrella, covered in gingham. From time to time he removes from his sleeve with a painfully contrived gesture a cheap watch, and consults the time.[7]

Meanwhile, this newly enlightened man commented to his neighbor that "we really should be grateful that even people like ourselves can now eat beef, thanks to the fact that Japan is steadily becoming a truly civilized country." Perhaps it was in celebration of the glory of beef that about this time some students invented sukiyaki, now one of the hallmarks of Japanese cuisine to many foreigners.

In 1872 the Meiji government switched to the Western-style solar calendar from Japan's traditional lunar calendar, which had been inherited from China many centuries earlier. About the same time, the government also adopted the practice of Sunday as a weekly day of rest and, perhaps most intriguing as an example of the infatuation with Western customs, made Christmas one of its national holidays. Even today Japan, a country with only a small Christian population, celebrates Christmas with considerable enthusiasm.[8]

Some of the more fervent advocates of *bummei-kaika* at the height of the Western fever in early Meiji times even went so far as to suggest that Japan should adopt English as its national language. But the most extreme suggestion was that, since Caucasians were observably superior to the people of all other races, the Japanese should intermarry with them as quickly as possible in order to acquire their higher ethnic qualities.

One of the most ultimately profound changes wrought by modernization in Japan was the gradual adoption of Western building materials and architectural styles. Throughout their history, the Japanese had constructed their dwellings and other buildings almost entirely out of wood.

With the growth in recent centuries of great urban centers like Edo and Osaka, this type of construction gave rise to the constant danger—and all too frequent occurrence—of fires that consumed large portions of cities. For example, a devastating fire in 1657 made necessary the extensive rebuilding of Edo. In 1874, after a fire that gutted the Ginza area of central Tokyo, the government took the opportunity to order the construction of a row of some three hundred two-story brick buildings for the use of merchants on this bustling thoroughfare. Contemporary woodblock prints show how grand and exotic these buildings appeared to the Japanese of that day. The government hoped that the Ginza would serve as a model to encourage others to build these new fireproofed buildings; and the newspapers declared that people who walked down the Ginza could enjoy the enchanted feeling of being in a foreign country.[9]

Although more and more public and commercial buildings on Western lines were built in the cities, the construction of Western private homes was undertaken much more slowly. The higher cost of such homes was one reason; another was the continuing, overwhelming preference of the Japanese for their traditional, native-style homes. This was one area in which Westernization made little headway in Japan, and even today many Japanese continue to live, as they have for centuries, in houses consisting chiefly of sparsely furnished rooms with matted floors upon which to sit and sleep.

In intellectual circles, the great national quest for civilization and enlightenment in early Meiji gave rise to a number of study and discussion groups devoted to the question of transforming Japan into a modern state. Of these, the most influential was the Meirokusha or "Meiji Six Society" founded in the sixth year of Meiji, 1873, by some ten of the more prominent Westernizers of the day. The members of the Meirokusha met twice a month to discuss such subjects as politics, the economy, education, religion, the Japanese language, and women's rights. In 1874 they began publication of the *Meiji Six Magazine* for the purpose of publishing articles on their views. A large percentage of the Meirokusha membership comprised men who had engaged in Western learning before the Restoration and had been employed as translators and teachers by the Tokugawa shogunate in its Office for Barbarian Studies, established in 1855 after the arrival of Perry. Hence, the Meirokusha had as its legacy the venerable tradition of Dutch Studies begun nearly a century and a half earlier in Japan.

The leading figure in the Meirokusha, and indeed the most popular and widely read intellectual of the Meiji period, was Fukuzawa Yukichi (1835–1901). Fukuzawa was a low-ranking, but personally ambitious and opportunistic, samurai who began the study of Western gunnery and the Dutch language as a youth under the patronage of his feudal domain. Later, when Fukuzawa visited Yokohama shortly after the signing of the

Harris treaty in 1858 and observed the newly arrived foreigners at first hand, he learned a sad fact that was to cause anguish for all students of Dutch Studies: Dutch was practically useless as a medium for dealing with most Westerners. Fukuzawa, we are told, switched the very next day to the study of English; and, two years later, in 1860, he was selected to accompany the Tokugawa shogunate's first mission to the United States in what was also the first transoceanic voyage of a Japanese-manned ship.

Fukuzawa made two other trips abroad, in 1861 and 1867. In between he published *Conditions in the Western World (Seiyō Jijō)*, a book that established him as one of the foremost interpreters of the West. Fukuzawa was more of a popularizer than a pure intellectual, and as such he made a far greater impact on the people of his time. It is no exaggeration to say that he, more than any other single individual, influenced the minds of a generation of Japanese in the early, formative years of the modern era. His most successful book, *An Encouragement of Learning (Gakamon no Susume)*, written between 1872 and 1876, eventually sold nearly 3.5 million copies. The opening paragraph sets the tone for Fukuzawa's argument:

> It is said that heaven does not create one man above or below another man. This means that when men are born from heaven they all are equal. There is no innate distinction between high and low. It means that men can freely and independently use the myriad things of the world to satisfy their daily needs through the labors of their own bodies and minds, and that, as long as they do not infringe upon the rights of others, may pass their days in happiness. Nevertheless, as we broadly survey the human scene, there are the wise and the stupid, the rich and poor, the noble and lowly, whose conditions seem to differ as greatly as the clouds and the mud. The reason for this is clear. In the *Jitsugokyō* we read that if a man does not learn he will be ignorant, and that a man who is ignorant is stupid. Therefore the distinction between wise and stupid comes down to a matter of education.[10]

Strongly influenced by British utilitarianism and by the then current Western idea of the perfectibility of man through education, Fukuzawa became a staunch advocate of modern education, with the emphasis particularly on practical subjects. He vigorously denounced the social inequities and indignities of Tokugawa feudalism and declared that all men should be free and all countries independent on the basis of "natural reason." The democratic idealism that Fukuzawa thus espoused was concurrently reflected in the new Meiji government's attitude toward education. Dedicating itself to the goal of universal primary education on the American model, the government's 1872 ordinance founding a new public school system contained the vow that "in no village will there be a family without learning and in no household will there be an uneducated person."

In praising Western ways and advocating that Japan adopt them, Fukuzawa heaped withering criticism on his own country's ways and traditions:

If we compare the knowledge of the Japanese and Westerners, in letters, in techniques, in commerce, or in industry, from the largest to the smallest matter . . . there is not one thing in which we excel. . . . Outside of the most stupid person in the world, no one would say that our learning and business is on a par with those of the Western countries. Who would compare our carts with their locomotives, or our swords with their pistols? We speak of the yin and yang and the five elements; they have discovered 60 elements. . . . We think we dwell on an immovable plain; they know that the earth is round and moves. We think that our country is the most sacred, divine land; they travel about the world opening lands and establishing countries. . . . In Japan's present condition there is nothing in which we may take pride vis-à-vis the West. All that Japan has to be proud of . . . is its scenery.[11]

Unlike most of the other members of the Meirokusha, Fukuzawa steadfastly refused to enter the service of the Meiji government and insisted upon the importance of maintaining his independence as a social critic. The sensitivity of the Meiji Six enlighteners in general to changes in government attitude, however, was revealed in 1875 when, as the result of issuance by the government of a restrictive press law, they ceased publication of the *Meiji Six Magazine* and soon terminated the activities of its parent society. Amid the continuing enthusiasm for civilization and enlightenment, the government had found itself faced in the mid-1870s with a newly organized political opposition; and the predominantly government-oriented membership of the Meirokusha deemed it prudent to dissolve an organization that might be viewed as sympathetic to that opposition.

The Meiji Restoration had been carried out under the euphoric slogan of a "return to antiquity"; in fact, the restorationists do not appear to have had any concrete political plan other than to wrest power from the tottering shogunate. As leaders of the new Meiji government, they launched the country on the road to civilization and enlightenment and encouraged aspirations among the Japanese people for "independence," "freedom," and "individual rights," concepts taken from British liberal democracy, which absorbed the thinking of Japanese officials and intellectuals during the first decade or so of the Meiji period. But, although a few extreme Westernizing enthusiasts suggested that Japan establish a republic, no one of importance went so far as to advocate that a "free" people should also have the right to select their own government. The new political and intellectual leadership of Meiji Japan came almost entirely from the samurai class; and, while vociferously attacking the evils of Tokugawa feudalism, they retained the feudalistic attitude that the masses were by nature inert and stupid. It was their purpose to enlighten the people, not to make them politically active but to "enrich the country" and thereby strengthen it vis-à-vis the nations of the West. Even the iconoclastic and utilitarian-minded Fukuzawa was not prepared to encourage a critical attitude on the part of the people toward the government. When political opposition did arise in the 1870s, it was the result not of a movement from without but of a factional dispute within the government itself.

The leaders of the Meiji Restoration were primarily samurai from the domains of Satsuma, Chōshū, Tosa, and Hizen. From the outset, however, the Satsuma-Chōshū men formed a separate clique, based on the pact between their two domains that had been so important in the overthrow of the Tokugawa shogunate, and increasingly they monopolized real power in the new government. The dissatisfaction that this created among the samurai of Tosa and Hizen was transformed into a national issue in the Korean invasion crisis of 1873. The ostensible issue in the 1873 crisis was how to deal with a rebuff by Korea to Japanese overtures to open diplomatic and commercial relations. Most of the Tosa and Hizen leaders in the government urged a hard line, including the possibility of invading Korea; but the Satsuma-Chōshū clique, with the notable exception of Saigō Takamori (1827–77) of Satsuma, counseled restraint on the grounds that Japan was still too weak to risk any foreign involvement. When the views of the "peace" party prevailed, Saigō and other members of the "war" party left the government.

Although the Satsuma-Chōshū clique had won a major victory and had further strengthened its hold on the government, it now had powerful enemies on the outside. Some of these enemies turned to open rebellion, leading armies composed of samurai who were discontented with the progressive policies of the Meiji government. The most serious of these uprisings was the Satsuma Rebellion of 1877, led by Saigō Takamori. More than any other Restoration leader, Saigō felt a continuing attachment to the ideals of the samurai class. His bellicose attitude at the time of the 1873 crisis was based largely on his belief that the samurai of Japan could and should deal with a foreign insult by taking direct military action. In assuming leadership of the Satsuma Rebellion in 1877, Saigō made a last gallant gesture for feudal privilege and became the great romantic hero of modern Japan. At the same time, the failure of the Satsuma Rebellion also marked the last attempt to oppose the Meiji government through force.

Of far greater historical significance was the demand made by other samurai leaders, who had also been members of the war party in 1873, that participation in government be expanded through the establishment of an elected assembly. In 1874 a group of samurai, led by Itagaki Taisuke (1837–1919) of Tosa, submitted a memorial to the throne attacking the absolutist Satsuma-Chōshū regime in the following terms:

> Present political power does not rest with the Emperor, nor with the people. It is monopolized entirely by one group of officials. If the absolutism of these

officials is not corrected, it could mean the downfall of the nation. Moreover the only means of correction would be to establish an assembly elected by the people and to expand discussions concerning the country.[12]

The government replied that it was too soon to consider giving "the people" a voice in political affairs. Actually, it is doubtful that any of the memorialists had in mind an electorate that would include more than a small percentage of the Japanese people. The memorialists were former samurai who espoused ideas of parliamentary democracy at this time primarily as a means to attack the Satsuma-Chōshū oligarchs in the Meiji government. Although the people's rights *(minken)* movement they thus launched eventually became a campaign for full democracy, including universal manhood suffrage, it was by no means a "popular" undertaking in its origins.

One response of the government to the people's rights movement was to issue the press law in 1875 that caused dissolution of the Meirokusha. This law and others repressive of the freedoms of speech and assembly were aimed at curbing the efforts by Itagaki and his allies to form political parties. Nevertheless, the emergent party advocates continued to press their demands, and, in the same year, 1875, Itagaki formed the first national political association, the Patriotic Party (Aikokusha). But it was not until 1881 that the *minken* people received a public commitment from the oligarchs that they would eventually be given the opportunity to participate in government.

In 1881 Ōkuma Shigenobu (1838–1922), one of the last of the non-Satsuma-Chōshū statesmen still in the government, was relieved of his position as the result of disclosures he made about corruption in high office. In the wake of Ōkuma's dismissal, the government secured an imperial edict promising a constitution and the opening of a national parliament within nine years, or by 1890. Although it may appear that Ōkuma thus forced a concession from the Satsuma-Chōshū oligarchs, in fact the latter had for long been considering how and when a constitutional form of government should be established in Japan, and the action of Ōkuma in 1881 probably did not appreciably alter their plans, although they may not have wished to reveal them publicly so soon.

The Meiji oligarchs were, by any criterion, extraordinarily capable and farsighted men who took a strongly pragmatic approach to problems. Once secure in power they did indeed tend toward the authoritarian in consonance with their samurai backgrounds. But one advantage of their functioning as oligarchs was that, immune from the everyday strife of elected politicians, they could concentrate on the pursuit of loftier goals for the betterment of Japan. They were committed to making Japan into a truly modern state, and national constitutions were an integral part of modernist thinking everywhere in this age. The man who assumed chief responsibility for writing the Meiji Constitution was Itō Hirobumi (1841–1909) of Chōshū. In 1882 he went to Europe to study Western constitutionalism, particularly as propounded by German theorists; and, in 1885, he became Japan's first prime minister upon the institution of a cabinet system of government.

Meanwhile, the people's rights advocates were also active, and both Itagaki and Ōkuma formed new political associations—the Liberal Party (Jiyūtō) and the Progressive Party (Shimpotō)—in preparation for the opening of a parliament (or Diet) within the decade. It is difficult to assess precisely the differences between the two major party lines established at this time. The works of Rousseau, Mill, and other Western political theorists had been translated into Japanese and were widely read and admired by the party people. French natural rights democracy seems to have appealed particularly to the Itagaki group, while Ōkuma and his followers espoused British utilitarianism. Moreover, whereas the Liberal Party came in general to represent agrarian interests, the Progressive Party tended to align itself with the emerging class of urban industrialists. Yet, far more than any political creeds, specific issues, or class alliances, it was personal allegiance to the leaders themselves that provided the basis for party unity during this preconstitutional phase of the people's rights movement.

In addition to the political parties, an important source of burgeoning opposition to the Meiji oligarchy was the press. A number of the embryonic newspapers of the early Restoration period had been staffed by former shogunate officials hostile to the new Satsuma and Chōshū leaders in the government. With the continued growth of a modern press, this opposition was taken up by journalists who were largely former samurai excluded from government by *han* cliquism. Many members of the emergent political parties, in fact, first got their start in journalism. Moreover, many newspapers founded in the early Meiji period were intended by their founders to serve as mouthpieces for specific political and social views, almost invariably of an antigovernment tone. Hence, journalism in modern Japan was in its early development distinctly a journalism of protest, and it was to a great extent for this reason that the Meiji oligarchs so readily and frequently attacked journalists through the issuance of restrictive press laws.

The temper of the 1880s in Japan was markedly different from that of the 1870s. For the first decade or so following the Restoration, the Japanese had pursued with great, and often indiscriminate, enthusiasm the remaking of their country on Western lines. In the 1880s, they not only modified their earlier, naive admiration for the West but also began to reassess and find new value in their native traditions. For the oligarchs, it became incumbent to enunciate a coherent ideology for the state they were in the process of constitutionally fashioning. The way in which they did this can be seen most clearly in their policy toward education.

In its act of 1872, the Meiji government had proclaimed the goal of universal primary education, and, during most of the remainder of the decade, it had sought to provide training to Japanese schoolchildren that stressed practical subjects and encouraged Western-style individualistic thinking. But, by the beginning of the 1880s, the official attitude had changed and the government now took deliberate steps both to reinstate traditional moral training in the schools and to redefine the aim of education to serve the state rather than the individual. The culmination of this new policy toward education was the issuance in 1890 of the Imperial Rescript on Education, a brief document that began as follows:

> Know ye, Our Subjects!
> Our Imperial Ancestors have founded Our Empire on a basis broad and everlasting, and have deeply and firmly implanted virtue; Our subjects ever united in loyalty and filial piety have from generation to generation illustrated the beauty thereof. This is the glory of the fundamental character of Our Empire, and herein also lies the source of Our education.[13]

From these few lines it is obvious that, after its earlier flirtation with the ideals of Western liberalism and democracy, the Meiji government in its critical education policy had determined to indoctrinate a social ideology derived mainly from the Shinto-Confucian concepts that had evolved as a new orthodoxy of thought in the late Tokugawa period. Morality was once again to be based on such hierarchical virtues as loyalty and filial piety, and the ultimate object of devotion for all Japanese citizens was to be the throne, described elsewhere in the Rescript on Education as "coeval with heaven and earth." The new Japanese state was, in short, to be conceived as a great and obedient Confucian family with a father-like emperor at its head.

Nor was the government alone in its shift to conservatism in the 1880s. Even the blatant Westernizers like Fukuzawa Yukichi began to have second thoughts about Japan's previously uncritical acceptance of everything Western in its rush to become civilized and enlightened. To a great extent, such second thoughts were simply the result of a more sophisticated view of the West. In their initial, excited response to the utopian ideals of liberal democracy, many intellectuals (although not the leaders of the Iwakura Mission) had failed to temper their pro-Westernism by acknowledging that the Western powers themselves were pursuing baldly self-interested policies of world imperialism. Western theorists sought to justify these policies on the grounds of the social-Darwinist doctrines of Herbert Spencer: before the world could achieve a pacific stage of fully industrialized and enlightened civilization, it must continue to engage in a militant selection process that promised survival to the fittest races and nations.

It is to the credit of the Meiji oligarchs, who were usually far more realistic than their critics, that they always kept in mind the aim of enriching Japan in order to strengthen it militarily. In 1873 they had avoided armed intervention in Korea because it was too dangerous, but even then they envisioned a time when Japan would be able to compete for empire with the West. On the other hand, nongovernmental intellectuals and the public in general did not, for the most part, come to accept the need for more statist-oriented policies and the open pursuit of nationalistic goals until the 1880s.

Overridingly the most important nationalistic goal of the 1880s and early 1890s was revision of the unequal treaties, and the repeated failure of the government to achieve revision contributed not only to growing skepticism about the West but also to the spread of conservative, Japanist sentiments. In one spectacular breakdown of treaty talks in 1888, Ōkuma Shigenobu, who had been drawn temporarily back into the government as a foreign minister, lost a leg when a fanatical member of a right-wing organization threw a bomb into his carriage.

Symbolic to many Japanese of their frustrations and humiliation over treaty revision was a Western-style building in downtown Tokyo called the Rokumeikan or Deer Cry Mansion. Constructed in 1883 for the purpose of entertaining foreign diplomats and dignitaries, the Rokumeikan was the scene of many festive and gala entertainments, the most notoriously memorable of which was a masquerade ball thrown by Prime Minister Itō in 1887. Affairs like the 1887 ball in the Rokumeikan were regarded as the most conspicuous examples of how ludicrously even high-ranking Japanese could behave in their desire to prove to Westerners that they

Fig. 65 "Scene of Constitutional Law Proclamation Ceremony," by Hashimoto Chikanobu (1838–1912), showing gentlemen in Western-style uniforms and ladies in dresses with bustles at the promulgation of the Meiji Constitution *(Honolulu Academy of Arts, Bequest of Normal D. Hill, 1938 [10,953])*

were civilized and knew the social graces (fig. 65). A decade or so earlier, such conduct would probably have been hailed as enlightened and progressive: it was a sign of the changed temper of the times that Itō and his ministers were disparagingly dubbed "the dancing cabinet."

It should not be supposed that the opposition to over-Westernization and the turn to conservatism in the 1880s was either universal or unthinkingly reactionary. Some extremely radical nationalists (like Ōkuma's assailant) did appear on the scene, but many prominent people remained highly committed to Westernization; and even those who most articulately called for a reassessment of traditional values more often than not advocated that Japan discriminately select what was appropriate for it from both East and West. As one of them, speaking about Western civilization, put it:

> We recognize the excellence of Western civilization. We value the Western theory of rights, liberty, and equality; and we respect Western philosophy and morals. We have affection for some Western customs. Above all, we esteem Western science, economics, and industry. These, however, are not to be adopted simply because they are Western; they ought to be adopted only if they can contribute to Japan's welfare. Thus we seek not to revive a narrow xenophobia, but rather to promote the national spirit in an atmosphere of brotherhood.[14]

The debate that emerged in the late 1880s over Westernization versus traditionalism was conducted principally by the members of a new generation whose most impressionable years of intellectual growth had been spent during the epochal, but highly unsettling, period of transition from Tokugawa to Meiji. To a far greater extent than their elders, like the Meiji oligarchs and Fukuzawa Yukichi, they felt the intense cultural uncertainty of being torn between a Japan that had always represented the past and a West that invariably stood for the future.

Among those of the new generation who most fully embraced Westernization was Tokutomi Sohō (1863–1957).[15] The son of a wealthy peasant family of the Kumamoto region of northern Kyushu, Tokutomi received Western training as a youth in his native Kumamoto and later studied at the Christian university, Dōshisha, in Kyoto. In the mid-1880s, Tokutomi moved to Tokyo, where he took up a career as a writer and journalist. He organized a group called the Min'yūsha (Society of the People's Friends) and in 1887 began publication of a magazine entitled *Friend of the People (Kokumin no Tomo)* to express the group's views.

Tokutomi, whose magazine soon achieved an enormous circulation, forcefully advanced his own opinions in books and articles on the progress of modern Japan. He criticized the kind of Westernization advocated by Fukuzawa and other enlighteners of the early Meiji period because it was directed only toward acquisition of the material aspects of

Western civilization and not its underlying spirit. At the same time, Tokutomi pointed out the futility of pursuing the pre-Meiji ideal of "Eastern morals and Western technology," which was precisely what the Meiji government seemed to be doing then in its policy of reinstituting Confucian moral training in the public schools. Under the new policy, Japanese students were expected simultaneously to learn modern, practical things and feudal morality. According to Tokutomi, the only possible choice for Japan, if it was to succeed in modernization, was to reject the Japanese past entirely and pursue wholeheartedly both the material and spiritual aspects of Western civilization.

Tokutomi, who was strongly influenced by the writings of Herbert Spencer, justified his extreme position on the grounds that progress was a universal phenomenon. Hence, Westernization was actually another term for universalization. The features of modern civilization observable in the Western countries were the same that would appear in all countries as they advanced toward modernity. Japan already had many of these modern features and should seek to acquire the remainder as speedily as possible.

The principal challenge to the views of Tokutomi and the Min'yūsha came from the Seikyōsha (Society for Political Education), founded in 1888 by another group of young writers and critics. Publishing the magazine *The Japanese (Nihonjin)* in competition with the Min'yūsha's *Friend of the People*, the Seikyōsha people attacked Westernization and called for "preservation of the national essence" *(kokusui hozon)*. Their general position was perhaps best presented in the book *Truth, Goodness, and Beauty of the Japanese (Shin-zen-bi Nihonjin)* by Miyake Setsurei (1860–1945). Miyake, a student of philosophy who remained a rival of Tokutomi throughout their long, concurrent careers, asserted that although a Spencerian type of struggle among nations was unavoidable during the course of historical progress, the process of modernization did not lead inevitably to a universal kind of state. On the contrary, nations competed best by utilizing those special qualities that distinguished them from others. Like many members of the Seikyōsha, Miyake was much interested in physical geography and placed great store in the effects of geography and climate on the molding of racial characteristics and national cultures. To his thinking, diversity among peoples and nations was fundamental to progress in the world, and any attempt to reject national customs and indiscriminately adopt the ways of others could only be harmful. It was, in any event, clear that the Western countries were clinging tenaciously to their own particularistic national cultures, even while commonly pursuing modernization.

The advocates of preserving the national essence made many effective points in their arguments against the Westernizers, and, in theory, they provided the Japanese with a much-needed feeling of cultural worth after some two decades of breathtaking change within the ever-present shadow of the more advanced and "superior" West. A concomitant to the Seikyōsha movement, for example, was a renewal of interest in Japan's classical literature even at a time, as we shall see, when Japanese writers were first beginning to produce a modern literature under the dominant influence of the West. Ancient works, including collections of *waka* poetry, were reprinted one after another, and especially great excitement was aroused over the rediscovery of Genroku literature. The prose of Saikaku, the puppet plays of Chikamatsu, and the poems of Bashō were resuscitated, annotated, and made available to a wide reading public.

Unfortunately, the concept of preserving the national essence, while emotionally stimulating, did not lend itself to very precise definition, and the Seikyōsha writers were never able to present a convincing program of action. Moreover, even though they were generally reasonable-minded people themselves, their views tended to provide fuel for the xenophobes and extreme nationalists; and, in subsequent years, as Japan embarked upon overseas expansion, preservation of the national essence became synonymous with ultranationalism.

Intertwined with the debate in the mid-Meiji period over such questions as the modern (Western?) spirit and Japan's national essence was the major problem of Christianity. The leaders of the Meiji Restoration had little if any personal interest in Christianity, although some, like Itagaki Taisuke, the pioneer in the people's rights movement, conjectured that it might be an essential element in modernization. On the other hand, many of the intellectuals of the new generation of the 1880s and 1890s, including Tokutomi Sohō, were powerfully, and in some cases decisively, affected by Christian teachings.

The centuries-old ban on Christianity was not immediately lifted at the time of the Restoration. Not until 1873, after the Iwakura Mission observed how highly the Westerners treasured their religion, was it quietly legalized in Japan. Meanwhile, Western missionaries—particularly American and British Protestants—had already entered the country and begun their activities, including the compilation of English-Japanese dictionaries and translation of the Bible into Japanese. One field in which the missionaries performed especially valuable service was education. While the government concentrated on developing a national system of primary education, foreign missionaries and prominent Japanese independently established private schools to provide much of the higher training essential to Japan's modernizing program. Among the well-known private colleges founded about this time were the Christian university, Dōshisha, in Kyoto, and Keiō University and Waseda University in Tokyo, founded respectively by Fukuzawa Yukichi and Ōkuma Shigenobu.

Many of the youths most strongly influenced by Christianity were samurai from domains that had been on the losing side in the Restoration.[16] Restricted in the opportunities open to them in the new government, these youths sought alternate routes to advancement through the acquisition of Western training. When brought into direct contact with foreign Christian teachers, they were particularly impressed with the moral caliber and fervid personal commitment of most of these men. To the young and impressionable Japanese, the foreign teachers appeared to possess qualities of character very similar to the ideal samurai and Confucian scholars of their own traditional backgrounds. Indeed, many Japanese who converted to Christianity in the 1870s and 1880s seem to have viewed it as a kind of modern extension of Confucianism.

For their part, the American missionary and lay Christian teachers who came to Japan in the 1870s also responded with high enthusiasm toward their Japanese students. The faith of these men, who were imbued with the religious spirit of late nineteenth-century New England, was rooted in the belief that God's work on earth was to be carried out by individuals acting in accordance with a high moral code and the dictates of their Christian consciences. They were not particularly concerned with questions of dogma and abstract theology but wished to build strong characters; and they were quick to appreciate the features of good character, derived from the samurai code of conduct, that they detected in many of their students.

Tokutomi Sohō was one of a famous group of thirty-five Japanese youths, known as the Kumamoto band, who in 1875 climbed a hill in their native domain of Kumamoto in Kyushu and pledged themselves to Christianity and to propagation of the faith in order to dispel ignorance and enlighten the people. These youths were students at a school for Western studies in Kumamoto conducted by Leroy L. Janes, a West Point graduate and former military officer in the American Civil War, and several of them went on to become distinguished spokesmen for Christianity in Japan. Although Tokutomi himself later renounced his formal ties with the church, he retained the Protestant Christian belief in "inner freedom" and the individual's duty to use his independent conscience as a guide to social and political behavior. It was on the basis of this belief that he attacked the kind of Confucian morality the Meiji government sought to inculcate in the primary schools from the 1880s on that called upon all Japanese to give blind and unquestioning loyalty to the state.

The influence of Protestant Christianity on Japanese who came to criticize the strongly statist policies of the government in the mid-Meiji period can be seen not only in independent intellectuals like Tokutomi, but also in many individuals who entered the socialist movement after its beginnings in the 1890s. In fact, a number of the most prominent Christians in modern Japan have also been leading socialists. Still other Christians, however, were driven by the unfavorable climate for their views after the commencement of parliamentary government in 1890 to withdraw entirely from the arena of political and social criticism and to devote themselves to the private cultivation of their religion. The best-known example of these Christians was Uchimura Kanzō (1861–1930).

Uchimura, the son of a samurai, attended a Christian-influenced agricultural school in the northern island of Hokkaido and became a student of Dr. William S. Clark, an American lay teacher who, like Janes at Kumamoto, was successful in attracting young Japanese to the faith. Later, Uchimura went to the United States to study at Amherst, and it was there that he was converted to Christianity. In 1891 Uchimura created a sensation back in Japan when, as a teacher at the esteemed First High School in Tokyo, he refused to bow before a copy of the Imperial Rescript on Education. He was branded a traitor by some people, forced to resign his position for the offense of lèse majesté, and became the target of polemical attacks that charged him with possessing allegiances incompatible with the responsibilities to emperor and nation required of subjects in the educational rescript.[17] Uchimura thus became a victim of the shift in attitude, on the part of the Japanese public and many intellectuals, from the open and naive internationalism of the 1870s to an illiberal, virulent nationalism. Although he worked for another decade or so in journalism, Uchimura eventually retired from public view to a life of private teaching and writing on religion.

Contrary to the assertions of his detractors, Uchimura did not embrace Christianity to the exclusion of national loyalty. He steadfastly proclaimed his devotion to the "two J's"—Jesus and Japan—and insisted that, just as Anglicans were essentially English Christians, Presbyterians were Scottish Christians, and Lutherans were German Christians, he was a Japanese Christian. At the same time, he readily acknowledged that trying to be both Christian and Japanese was apt to please neither Christians nor Japanese:

> I do not know which I love more, Jesus or Japan.
> I am hated by my countrymen for Jesus' sake as *yaso* [a Christian], and I am disliked by foreign missionaries for Japan's sake as national and narrow.
> No matter; I may lose all my friends, but I cannot lose Jesus and Japan.[18]

Uchimura even founded a "non-church" *(mukyōkai)* movement in an attempt to deracinate Christianity from its alien institutions and traditions by eliminating its clerical organization and other ecclesiastical trappings, and to render it as much Japanese as Western. For his epitaph he wrote in English:

> I for Japan;
> Japan for the World;
> The World for Christ;
> And All for God.[19]

Even when it enjoyed its greatest popularity in the Meiji period, Christianity could never claim as its own more than a very small percentage of the population of Japan (less than one-half of 1 percent); and after the turn to conservatism in the late 1880s and 1890s, it lost any opportunity it may have had to become a major force in Japanese life. Moreover, even if it had not been seen as a threat to the statist views rendered newly orthodox in the Meiji Constitution of 1889 and the Imperial Rescript on Education, Christianity would have (and indeed has) suffered from sectarianism in Japan, a sectarianism that had been kept to a minimum by American Protestant missionaries in the palmy days of successful proselytizing during the first two decades of Meiji. Apart from its work in such fields as education and medicine and the profound influence it exerted on certain individuals, like the ones we have been examining here, Christianity has been of negligible importance in modern Japan.

The Meiji Constitution was written in secret by Itō Hirobumi and his colleagues and was presented to the Japanese people in 1889 as a gift from the emperor. It was based on a carefully considered mixture of conservative and liberal principles (with the former heavily outweighing the latter) that owed much to the constitutional theories of Germany, the Western country the Meiji oligarchs had come increasingly to regard as most analogous to Japan in historical background and stage of modernization. The conservative character of the Constitution may, for purposes of illustration, be noted in several major areas. First, an appointive House of Peers was given equal lawmaking powers with an elective House of Representatives. Second, the personal liberties granted to the Japanese people were all made "subject to the limitations imposed by law"; in other words, such liberties were not to be inalienable but might be (and often were) restricted by government decree.

But the most strongly conservative feature of the Meiji Constitution was the great power it allowed the executive branch of government. This power derived in large part from omission: that is, from the deliberate failure to specify how the executive was to be formed and what were to constitute the precise limits of its authority. There was no provision at all, for example, for appointment of the prime minister, and no proviso about accountability of the other ministers of state in the cabinet to anyone except the emperor. Clearly, the oligarchs intended to retain firm control of the executive, and, after the opening of the first Diet in 1890, the party members in the House of Representatives found very little prospect that they would in the near future be able to participate significantly in the ruling of Japan. The oligarchs formed an extralegal body known as the *genrō* or "elders," consisting at first entirely of the highest Satsuma and Chōshū leaders in government, and it was they who selected the prime ministers (from among themselves) and continued to dominate the affairs of state.

The sociopolitical orthodoxy that the oligarchs codified in the Meiji Constitution and the Imperial Rescript on Education is commonly called *kokutai,* a term that literally means the body of the country but is usually translated as "national polity." Based on the Shinto-Confucian concept (which we observed in the Rescript on Education) of Japan as a great family-state, *kokutai* held a special appeal for the Japanese people because of its glorification of the mystique of emperorship. The Japanese regarded their line of sovereigns—described in the Constitution as "unbroken for ages eternal" and in the Rescript on Education as "coeval with heaven and earth"—as a unique and sacrosanct institution that gave Japan a claim to superiority over all other countries in the world. For centuries, of course, the emperors of Japan had wielded no political power whatever, and during the Tokugawa period they were held virtual prisoners in Kyoto by the shogunate. Nevertheless, the throne had served as an incomparably effective rallying point for nationalistic sentiment during the difficult and dangerous transition to the modern era. Although perhaps relatively ignored during the liberal euphoria of the 1870s, it inevitably drew the renewed attention of government leaders and conservative intellectuals in the 1880s. For nothing was more venerably Japanese than the imperial institution, and anyone wishing to revive traditional values, whether moral or cultural, was almost perforce obliged to start with recognition of the throne as the font of Japanese civilization. No simple explanation, however, can be given of the throne's role in modern Japan. For the most part the emperor has been held "above politics" and, with few exceptions, his participation in governmental affairs has not been made public. But there can be no question that, as the living embodiment of *kokutai,* he was a potent symbol for radically nationalistic emotions in the period up through World War II.

A corollary to emperor glorification in the *kokutai* ideology was that, of all the peacetime occupations, government service was the most cherished because it meant, in effect, employment by the emperor. Although the Satsuma-Chōshū oligarchs continued to control the highest councils of state, a vast expansion of the bureaucracy during the final years of the nineteenth century created ample opportunities for good careers in government, careers that were avidly sought by youths of all classes. Tokyo Imperial University, moreover, was made a kind of orthodox channel for governmental preferment, further proof of the degree to which Japanese society and the aspirations of its members were subjected to state manipulation in the middle and late Meiji period.

Japanese prose literature by the time of the Meiji Restoration had sunk to an extremely low level. Tedious didacticism, bawdy comedy, and bloody adventure were the stock-in-trade of the authors of these years, and there was little prospect, in the absence of stimulation from outside, that the quality of their work would soon improve. But this remains conjecture, for the fact is that, within a few decades of the Restoration, Western influences had wrought a change in prose literature as profound as in any other area of Japanese culture during the modern era.

The most successful writer in the years immediately before and after the Restoration was Kanagaki Robun, an *edokko* or "child of Edo" who specialized in the traditional genre of "witty books" *(kokkeibon).* One of Robun's post-Restoration works was *A Journey by Foot Through Western Lands (Seiyō Dōchū Hizakurige),* in which he attempted to give a modern twist to Jippensha Ikku's famous story of two rogues frolicking their way down the Tōkaidō from Edo to Kyoto; another was *Eating Beef Stew Cross-Legged,* the parody on the aping of Western customs that we noted earlier in this chapter. A prime example of Robun's irreverent humor can be observed in the title of still another of his books, *Kyūri Zukai.* This title was phonetically the same as Fukuzawa Yukichi's *Physics Illustrated;* but, in the Sinico-Japanese characters used by Robun, it meant *On the Use of Cucumbers.* Such punning was of course frivolous, an adjective that may be applied to much of the work done by Robun and his fellow Edo authors. Although these men continued to hold the center of the literary stage for a while, they produced almost nothing that was memorable. The future of Meiji literature lay clearly in the assimilation of powerful artistic ideas and styles then being imported from the West.

In the first decade or so of Meiji, those Japanese writers and scholars interested in foreign literature devoted themselves mainly to the translation of famous Western works. An adaptation of *Robinson Crusoe* had, in fact, been completed even before the Restoration, and a Japanese rendering of *Aesop's Fables* existed as one of the few products of the old Jesuit press that had survived the attempt by the Tokugawa shogunate to eradicate all traces of contact with the Catholic Christian countries during the century from the 1540s to the 1630s. Among the earliest Western translations to appear in print in the Meiji period was Samuel Smiles's *Self-Help,* a book of success stories whose very title suggests the kind of subject matter that Japan's passionate new devotees of civilization and enlightenment were most likely to appreciate.

One of the first modern Western novels to be translated into Japanese was Bulwer-Lytton's *Ernest Maltravers,* the tale of a modern man's ingenuity and self-motivated drive to succeed (although the translator of this work saw fit to give it the erotically provocative Japanese title of *Karyū Shunwa* or *A Spring Tale of Flowers and Willows* in the hope of boosting its sales). For most of the first two decades of Meiji, Japanese translators of Western fiction concentrated overwhelmingly on the writings of British authors, a clear reflection of the enormous prestige in Japanese eyes of

British civilization compared to that of any other country of the West. In addition to Bulwer-Lytton, prominent British authors translated into Japanese during the early Meiji period included Scott and Disraeli.

The Japanese were especially taken with tales of modern and "scientific" adventures, as can be seen in the popularity of Jules Verne's *Around the World in Eighty Days* and *A Trip to the Moon*. And from about the early 1880s on, largely in response to the movement for parliamentary government, they became infatuated with political novels. The translated writings of Disraeli and Bulwer-Lytton helped make respectable the practice of prose writing, which members of the ruling samurai class of the Tokugawa period had for the most part eschewed as vulgar; and during the 1880s many prominent members of the embryonic parties tried their hands at politically oriented novels. A good many of these novels dealt with the present, but others were set in such disparate times and places as ancient Greece, Ming China, France during the Revolution, and even a hypothetical Japan in the 173rd year of Meiji (A.D. 2040, one hundred fifty years after the opening of the first Diet in 1890).

Some idea of the growing consciousness in the 1880s of Japanese achievements and the anticipation that Japan would assume a more assertive international role can be seen in a passage from one of these political novels entitled *Strange Encounters of Elegant Females (Kajin no Kigū)*, written in 1885 by Shiba Shirō under the nom de plume of the Wanderer of the Eastern Seas. Far from being an account of romance and passion, as the title would seem to suggest, *Strange Encounters* is the story of the Wanderer's investigation into revolutionary activities throughout the world. At the outset, he meets two strikingly beautiful European ladies, one Spanish and one Irish (although both graced by the author with Chinese names), at the Liberty Bell in Philadelphia. The three enter into serious discussion about matters of political repression and revolution and, even after the Wanderer departs for other foreign lands, the ladies periodically reappear to meet him on his travels. Although they are obviously in love with him, the Wanderer can think only of the need for promoting freedom and justice in the world. At one point, the Spanish lady encourages him by saying:

Now that your country has reformed its government and, by taking from America what is useful and rejecting what is only superficial, is increasing month by month in wealth and strength, the eyes and ears of the world are astonished by your success. As the sun climbs in the eastern skies, so is your country rising in the Orient. Your August Sovereign has granted political liberty to the people, the people have sworn to follow the Imperial leadership. So the time has come when, domestic strife having ceased, all classes will be happy in their occupations. Korea will send envoys and the Luchu Islands will submit to your governance. Then will the occasion arise for doing great things in the Far East. Your country will take the lead and preside over a confederation of Asia. The peoples of the East will no longer be in danger. In the West you will restrain the rampancy of England and France. In the South you will check the corruption of China. In the North you will thwart the designs of Russia. You will resist the policy of European states, which is to treat Far Eastern peoples with contempt and to interfere in their domestic affairs, so leading them into servitude. Thus it is your country and no other that can bring the taste of self-government and independence into the life of millions for the first time, and so spread the light of civilization.[20]

A major problem for both translators of Western books and writers of Western-inspired political novels was that of style. Tokugawa authors had employed several methods of writing, from the poetic use of alternating metrical lines of five and seven syllables to a style derived from Sinico-Japanese. The gap between these classical styles and the colloquial language of everyday speech was enormous, and the difficulty of devising a means to reproduce in Japanese the vernacular novels of the modern West taxed the ingenuity of the most dedicated of Meiji translators. As a result, most of the renditions of Western novels in the early Meiji period were not true translations at all, but rather were free adaptations of the original works. During the 1880s, a movement was begun to "unify the spoken and written languages" *(gembun-itchi)*, but it faced formidable difficulties, as the following comments of an aspiring novelist of the time suggest:

> Ever since someone argued that the correspondence between spoken and written languages was a good proof of civilization, people have begun to worry about the style of our language. But we still have a great enemy in habit and inertia. Any new and unfamiliar style provokes people preoccupied only with the surface of things and invites their negative comments like "vulgar" and "inelegant." In the face of these charges, no one dares to try the colloquial style exclusively. . . . Some people seem to be giving up the idea of matching spoken and written styles as hopeless in present-day Japan. But they are too impatient. Of course, the elegant style may have something that colloquialism does not; but in the hands of a skilled writer, colloquialism can offer an indescribable gracefulness with a discipline all its own, which is in no sense inferior to the elegant written style.[21]

Toward the end of the decade, Futabatei Shimei (1864–1909), author of Japan's first truly modern novel, was also the first successfully to bridge the gap between speech and writing. With continuing progress in education, growth of the mass media, and acceptance of the Tokyo dialect as the standard form of speech, the modern Japanese vernacular or *kōgo* was finally evolved, although it was not used widely by novelists until after the Sino-Japanese War of 1894–95, by the authors of primary school textbooks until 1903, or by newspaper reporters in general until a decade after that.

The man who more than any other made possible the writing of a modern prose literature in Japan was Tsubouchi Shōyō (1859–1935).[22] A graduate of Tokyo Imperial University and translator of the collected works of Shakespeare, Tsubouchi published an epochal tract in 1885 entitled *The Essence of the Novel (Shōsetsu Shinzui)*. In it he attacked what he regarded as the deplorable state of literature in Japan during his day:

> It has long been the custom in Japan to consider the novel as an instrument of education, and it has frequently been proclaimed that the novel's chief function is the castigation of vice and the encouragement of virtue. In actual practice, however, only stories of bloodthirsty cruelty or else of pornography are welcomed, and very few readers indeed even cast so much as a glance on works of a more serious nature. Moreover, since popular writers have no choice but to be devoid of self-respect and in all things slaves to public fancy and the lackeys of fashion, each one attempts to go to greater lengths than the last in pandering to the tastes of the time. They weave their brutal historical tales, string together their obscene romances, and yield to every passing vogue. Nevertheless they find it so difficult to abandon the pretext of "encouraging virtue" that they stop at nothing to squeeze in a moral, thereby distorting the emotion portrayed, falsifying the situations, and making the whole plot nonsensical.[23]

Tsubouchi insisted that the novel must be regarded as art, to be appreciated solely for its own sake. He urged that Western, and particularly English, literature be taken as the model for a new kind of novelistic prose writing in Japan free of didacticism and devoted to the realistic portrayal of human emotions *(ninjō)* and the actual conditions of life. Even the supposedly enlightened authors of contemporary political novels dealt only with stereotypical characters who were motivated by the desire to "reward virtue and punish vice." Writers of the new fiction must seek to penetrate the wellsprings of individual behavior and reveal it, with candor, in all its manifestations.

Unfortunately, Tsubouchi, although a first-rate critic, was himself unable to produce the kind of modern novel that he so vigorously advocated. His book *The Character of Present-day Students (Tōsei Shosei Katagi)*, written in conjunction with *The Essence of the Novel*, deals with the lives and loves of students at Tokyo Imperial University in the early 1880s; but, despite Tsubouchi's efforts to delineate the psychological complexities of the students he was portraying, the work is very similar to the superficial character sketches and witty books of Tokugawa authors.

The kind of modern novel Tsubouchi had in mind was in fact written by his friend and disciple, Futabatei Shimei (1864–1904). Futabatei, born in Edo the son of a samurai a few years before the Meiji Restoration, studied Russian from 1881 until 1886 at a school for foreign languages sponsored by the Meiji government. His extraordinary talent for languages enabled him to excel at the school and gave rise to his decision to become a full-time translator and writer. Futabatei's translations from the

Russian of such authors as Turgenev, begun in the mid-1880s, were of prime importance in the literary history of the Meiji period; for they were the first renderings of Western literature into Japanese that can truly be called translations. In the free adaptations of other early and mid-Meiji translators, large sections were often either omitted or added and sometimes only the most essential plot of a book was retained. Beginning with Futabatei, Japanese translation of the literature of the West became a genuinely professional pursuit.

Immediately after finishing his studies at the foreign language school in 1886, the still unknown Futabatei boldly called upon Tsubouchi to discuss the literary matters raised by the latter in *The Essence of the Novel*. Thus began a warm and lasting friendship between the two men that provided, among other things, the conditions necessary for Futabatei to embark upon the writing of the first modern Japanese novel, *The Drifting Cloud (Ukigumo)*, published in installments between 1887 and 1889.

The Drifting Cloud is a realistic novel, written in a colloquial style, that has a unified and sustained plot and probes the feelings and psychological motivations of its principal characters. It is the story of Bunzō, a government clerk who lives in the home of his aunt and who loves and hopes to marry his cousin, Osei. As the story opens, Bunzō has lost his job, much to the disgust of the aunt, who has never been particularly fond of him and is now convinced that he is a failure. Bunzō's apparent inability to get ahead in a generation of Japanese striving madly to achieve the fame and fortune promised by modernity stands in sharp contrast to the prospects of Noboru, a colleague who has received a promotion just as Bunzō is fired. Clearly, Noboru is the new Meiji man, while Bunzō is a pathetic example of those who inevitably fall the victims of progress. When Noboru visits the aunt's home, he predictably causes new difficulties, for the aunt sees in him the ideal match for her daughter, and Osei herself, a flighty and superficial person, responds by rejecting Bunzō and entering into a flirtation with Noboru. Unfortunately, Futabatei's handling of the later stages in the plot of *The Drifting Cloud* is clumsy and unconvincing. The Osei-Noboru flirtation peters out and, in the end, Bunzō, who has been immobilized by events, is encouraged by a mere smile from Osei to anticipate a reconciliation with her. For all its faults, however, *The Drifting Cloud* remains an epochal work that inaugurated realistic fictional writing in modern Japan.

While Tsubouchi Shōyō and Futabatei Shimei were thus taking the pioneer steps in creating a new fiction on Western lines, other writers, motivated in part by the strongly conservative, nativistic trend of the 1880s, sought to revitalize Japanese literature by means of its own tradition. The most influential of these writers emerged from a group called the Ken'yūsha (Society of Friends of the Inkstone), founded in 1885 by Ozaki Kōyō (1867–1903) and others, who were at the time still students at Tokyo Imperial University. Issuing a magazine with the facetious title of *The Literary Rubbish Bin (Garakuta Bunko)*, the members of the Ken'yūsha called for a literary renaissance through rejection of the styles of writing and themes, including the didactic and the "witty," that had held sway in Japan from the Bunka-Bunsei epoch earlier in the century, and restoration of the great prose standards of Genroku, particularly as found in the works of Saikaku.

Like the contemporary scholars of the "national essence" movement, the Ken'yūsha writers were not simply blind reactionaries. Ozaki, for example, thoroughly agreed with Tsubouchi's dictum (presented in *The Essence of the Novel*) that literature should be regarded as an independent art, not requiring justification on moralistic or other grounds. Ozaki believed, moreover, that the realism Tsubouchi sought in modern Western fiction was more readily and appropriately accessible to Japanese in the realistic writing of Saikaku. Ozaki's own novels, written in the style of Saikaku, were enormously popular and helped stimulate the rediscovery of Genroku literature that we have already noted. Yet Ozaki and the other Ken'yūsha writers, despite their appeal to readers in the 1880s and 1890s, contributed virtually nothing to the development of the modern novel in Japan. They were almost unchallengeably powerful in the literary world of the late 1880s and early 1890s, even to the point of controlling many of the most important outlets for fictional publication; but, upon the untimely death of Ozaki in 1903, their brand of "renaissance literature" quickly gave way to other kinds of modern fictional writing whose growth had been prefigured by the earlier work of Tsubouchi and Futabatei.

Japanese poetry, while subject to much the same pull between traditional and modern (i.e., Western) influences that afflicted prose literature and nearly all other aspects of culture in the Meiji period, had its own special problems. First, poetry had always been the most "serious" of Japanese literary pursuits and hence brought an infinitely more weighty tradition to the modern era than the slightly regarded practice of prose writing. Second, although constricting rules of diction and vocabulary could be broken, the special qualities of the Japanese language that so fundamentally determined what could and could not be done poetically (for example, rhyme could not be used as a prosodic device) prevented Japanese poets from emulating much of Western poetry. And finally, in Japan as in the West, poetry could not hope to compete in popularity with the novel as the dominant literary form of modernization.

To many early Meiji poets, the classical *waka*—or *tanka* (short poem), as it has been more commonly called in modern times—was so buried in the past that there was little sense in even trying to exhume it. And, at any rate, both the *tanka* and the *haiku* were forms so limited in scope as to be useless for the expression of modern ideas and sentiments. Poets should instead turn their attention to the translation of Western poetry and to the development of new kinds of verse based on Western models. The first major step in this direction was the publication in 1882 of the *Collection of Poems in the New Style (Shintaishō)*, compiled by three professors of Tokyo Imperial University and consisting of nineteen translations from English and five original pieces by the compilers themselves. Like the political novels of the same time, much of the poetry written in the new style during the next few years dealt with the subjects of governmental and social reform.

Meanwhile, as a result of the conservative winds that had begun blowing forcefully by the middle and late 1880s, devotees of the older poetic modes, and especially the *tanka,* were given something of a new lease on life. The hidebound members of the traditional *tanka* schools, who had continued composing as though the Meiji Restoration had not happened, are of no particular interest to us; but other *tanka* poets actively sought to reform and reinvigorate their art. Perhaps the most noteworthy of these reformist poets (who first came to prominence during the 1890s) was Masaoka Shiki (1867–1902), a practitioner of *haiku* who did not seriously take up the *tanka* until about this time. Shiki was employed as a reporter on the staff of *Japan (Nihon)*, a magazine devoted, like Miyake Setsurei's *The Japanese,* to "preservation of the national essence"; and it was in large part because his editors began publishing *tanka* composed by members of the traditional schools as examples of a native art worth preserving that Shiki decided to speak out on *tanka* reform.

In addition to calling for freedom of poetic diction and the use of modern language, Shiki championed the concept of *shasei* or "realistic depiction." Furthermore, he deplored the fact that the *tanka*, from the time of the standard-setting tenth-century anthology *Kokinshū,* had been infused with an artificiality of wit and a fragility of emotion unsuited to the true spirit of the Japanese. Strongly endorsing the views of the Tokugawa period scholar of National Learning, Kamo Mabuchi, Shiki lauded the merits of the *Man'yōshū.* He saw in the poems of this earliest of anthologies such qualities as masculine vigor, directness of expression, and "sincerity" *(makoto)* that were in particular likely to be appreciated by his fellow countrymen in the expansive, imperialistic mood following Japan's startling military victory over China in 1894–95.

Much like the novelist Ozaki Kōyō, Shiki tried to find realism—apparently the most valued of "modern" aesthetic qualities—in the Japanese literary tradition. In fact, Shiki's advocacy of "realistic depiction" was, as Robert Brower has observed, "a quasi-scientific principle directly influenced by conceptions of illusionist realism in Western-style painting."[24] Here is an example of one of Shiki's *tanka* in the mode of realistic depiction that, in fact, is very much like a *haiku* in its poetic effect:

At the verandah's edge
The tightly curled young plantain
Unfolds its leaves,
And five feet of green
Cover the wash basin.[25]

It appears that, with Shiki, we have still another example of the strong impulse on the part of so many modern Japanese scholars and artists (indeed, probably all of them during at least one phase or another of their careers) either consciously or unconsciously to relate to their own national past those features of modern culture that emerged in the West and that they admire or wish to utilize. But history is cruel to this impulse, for the unalterable fact is that the West evolved such things as modern realistic literature first and the Japanese will never know whether they could have done it independently.

In contrast to their relatively recent exposure to Western literature (that is, belles-lettres), the Japanese had had a rather long historical acquaintanceship with the visual arts, particularly painting, of the West. Unencumbered by a language barrier, the visual arts are obviously more amenable to cross-cultural transmission, although in the case of Japan this in fact meant simply that the inevitable clash between Japanese tradition and Western modernity could be precipitated even more readily and with greater abandon than it could in literature. At the same time, as Sansom has suggested, it is also possible that in the visual arts Japan's aesthetic heritage was better prepared than it was in literature to stand up against Western intrusion.[26]

The Jesuits had first introduced Western visual arts to Japan in the sixteenth century and had even trained Japanese artists in contemporary painting techniques. But the anti-Christian measures of the Tokugawa shogunate had, of course, eliminated this and almost all other Western influences from the country during the mid-seventeenth century. Not until the rise of Dutch Studies about a hundred years later did knowledge of Western art again make its way into Japan. Subsequently, nearly all of the major, vital schools of painting in the late eighteenth and early nineteenth centuries were influenced to a greater or lesser degree by Western techniques. Some painters, like Shiba Kōkan, went over entirely to the foreign medium and learned to paint in precise technical imitation of the Western manner. Curiously, however, the work of Kōkan and other pioneer Western-style painters seems to have fallen into obscurity, and some artists in the last years of the Tokugawa shogunate, after Japan had been opened by Perry, laboriously set about to learn Western painting on their own from the few foreign-language manuals they could acquire without being aware of what Kōkan and his fellow proponents of Dutch Studies had already accomplished.

The most prominent person in the late Tokugawa and early Meiji efforts to develop and popularize Western art in Japan was Kawakami Tōgai (1827–81).[27] A moderately skilled artist in the *bunjin* or literati style of painting, Kawakami took up the study of the Dutch language sometime about the 1850s and soon turned his attention also to European painting. In 1857 he joined the shogunate's Office for Barbarian Studies, the organization that also employed a number of the later members of the Meiji Six Society, and within a few years was appointed to head its newly established section on the study of painting. After the Restoration, Kawakami, who was primarily interested in the practical, scientific side of Western painting, was engaged by the Ministry of Education to develop teaching methods and prepare training manuals on art for use in public schools. Among the innovations he sponsored was instruction in realistic drawing with pencils, rather than painting with the traditional Japanese ink-brush.

In 1876 the Meiji government, continuing its policy of encouragement of Western-style art, opened the Industrial Art School (Kōbu Bijutsu Gakkō) and invited several Italian artists to provide training in painting, sculpture, and general methods of art. The most important of these was Antonio Fontanesi (1818–82), who during his stay of approximately two years in Japan made a profound impression on the students he taught, several of whom became outstanding Western-style painters in later years. So popular was Fontanesi that when he left for home in 1878, at least partly owing to a difference of opinion with his employers in the Japanese government, a number of students withdrew from the school and founded a society for the furtherance of Western art, thereby inaugurating the first independent art movement of the modern era in Japan.

Fontanesi's departure was undoubtedly related to the beginning of a trend in the late 1870s and 1880s away from Western art to a revival of interest in the traditional art of Japan. Coincidentally, in the very same year that Fontanesi left, 1878, another foreigner, the young American Ernest Fenollosa (1853–1908), arrived in Japan to begin a remarkable career as one of the two leading figures in the great resurgence of native art appreciation.

Fenollosa, a recent graduate of Harvard, was originally engaged to teach philosophy at Tokyo Imperial University, but before long he became an outspoken (and highly opinionated) admirer of Far Eastern, and particularly Japanese, art. Eventually, Fenollosa evolved a grand philosophical concept along the lines of "Eastern morals and Western technology," according to which he prophesied a Hegelian-type dialectical synthesis between the spiritual East and the material West that would advance the world to a new cultural plane. On a more immediate and practical level, Fenollosa, along with one of his students, Okakura Ten-shin (1862–1913), began to take stock of Japanese art and to advocate ways in which it could be repopularized and perpetuated.

Traditional Japanese art and artists had unquestionably fallen on bad times during the early Restoration period. The two leading practitioners of the ancient Kanō school of painting, for example, were reduced to menial occupations in order to earn their livings. It was also because of the almost total lack of interest in native work in these years that Fenollosa and others were able to buy up at very low prices the vast number of art pieces that still constitute the core of many major Japanese collections in foreign museums today.

Fenollosa gave lectures to private groups in Japan extolling the glories of Japanese art and even pronouncing it to be superior to the art of the West. He and Okakura also founded a Society for the Appreciation of Painting (Kangakai) and urged the Meiji government to sponsor training in the native artistic styles. Two results of their lobbying were the discontinuance of the Western-oriented Industrial Art School in 1883 and the substitution of brush painting for pencil drawing in public school art courses. But the greatest achievement of Fenollosa and Okakura was their role in the creation in 1889 of the government-backed Tokyo Art School (Tōkyō Bijutsu Gakkō), devoted exclusively to training in Far Eastern art. In 1886–87, Fenollosa and Okakura had traveled to Europe to study methods of art education and museum administration, and within a few years after their return, Okakura became head of the Tokyo Art School.

Of these two dynamic men who led the return to Japanese art in the 1880s, Fenollosa was by far the more inflexible. A transparent Japanophile so far as art was concerned, he also sought to impose on others his personal biases within the realm of Japanese art. For example, while he admired the Kanō school of painting, he viewed with distaste the literati movement of the middle and late Tokugawa period. Largely because of this preference on the part of a foreigner, it appears, no study of the *bunjin* painters was included in the curriculum of the Tokyo Art School.

Okakura, on the other hand, was very similar in sentiment to a number of his contemporaries who have been noted in this chapter, including the "national essence" intellectuals, the novelist Ozaki Kōyō, and the *haiku-tanka* poet Masaoka Shiki. All of these men were participants in the Japanist reaction of the 1880s and 1890s; and, although not all of them may have succeeded very well in their aims, they mutually aspired to revitalize Japanese culture and art by incorporating modern Western (or "international") elements into the native tradition and not by trying simply to reverse the course of progress. The tragedy for most of them was that this was no easy thing to do. A little Western "materialism" could rapidly dissipate a lot of Eastern "spiritualism."

In the case of the visual arts, the return to tradition led by Fenollosa and Okakura had been too radically launched, and within a few years the pendulum began to swing back to a position where both Western-style and Japanese art could coexist in Japan in an atmosphere of relative tranquility and equal competition. The fiery Fenollosa returned to the United States in 1890, and paintings in the Western manner were prominently displayed along with Japanese works in an industrial fair held the same year. More important, it was about this time that a number of highly promising artists returned from periods of study in France, Italy, and other Western countries. Among these, the one who was to have the greatest influence in art circles and who may rightly be regarded as the true founder of modern Western-style art in Japan was Kuroda Seiki (1866–1924). An Impressionist who had studied for ten years in Paris, Kuroda caused a minor furor by publicly exhibiting a painting of a nude for the first time in Japan (fig. 66). His influence and popularity spread rapidly, and in 1896 he was invited to join the faculty of Okakura's Tokyo Art School, a clear recognition—however reluctantly given—that Western-style art was in Japan to stay.

Since very little specific attention has thus far been given to the development of traditional Japanese music, some general remarks should be made before examining the impact upon it of Western music following the Meiji Restoration.

To a great extent Japanese music evolved through the centuries in conjunction with—or, perhaps more precisely, as an auxiliary to—literature. This was particularly true from the medieval age on, when music was used as an accompaniment both to plays of the *nō* theatre and to the recitations of itinerant storytellers, who strummed their lutelike *biwa* as they chanted excerpts from such works as *The Tale of the Heike*. Music, of course, also became an essential ingredient of the two major dramatic forms of the Tokugawa period, *kabuki* and *bunraku*. Like the earlier *nō*, *kabuki* and *bunraku* were presentational rather than representational theatres and hence readily incorporated not only music but also miming, stunt-performing, and, in the case of *kabuki*, dancing. Although some purely instrumental, nonvocalized music was naturally performed (perhaps most notably on the *samisen* and the zitherlike *koto*, an instrument of refined taste dating from very early times), much of the music of premodern Japan was quite clearly subordinated to lyrical singing, acting, and dancing, and to the recitation of libretti that possessed independent literary merit.

Probably the first public performance of Western music in Japan in modern times was the playing by Perry's naval band during its visit to Edo in 1853.[28] And as in the case of the conversion to Western-style clothing, it was the Japanese military that led the way in the adoption of Western music. Military units of the early Meiji period initially formed bands simply as part of their general reorganization along Western lines.

Fig. 66　"Morning Toilette" by Kuroda Seiki *(Heibonsha)*

But before long, these army and navy bands began giving frequent public concerts, and they became familiar fixtures at the ballroom dances and other Western-style social affairs held at the Rokumeikan in the 1880s.

In addition to military music, Christian church music was also prominently introduced to Japan in the early Meiji period. By far the most important form here was the Protestant hymn; and, as one authority has pointed out, many Japanese songs of the Meiji period tended to have a strongly "Christian" sound, just like the early nationalistic songs of missionary-influenced countries in twentieth-century Africa.[29]

It was in the public schools, however, that the most important measures were taken to advance knowledge and appreciation of Western music among the Japanese, and the pioneer figure in implementing these measures was Izawa Shūji (1851–1917). After a period of study in the United States, Izawa was engaged by the Ministry of Education in 1879 to prepare songbooks and to plan for the teaching of music in the public school system. Izawa's principal aim was to find some way of blending traditional and Western music in order to produce a new kind of national music for modern Japan. To accomplish this, he worked chiefly with an American, Luther Mason of Boston, and with members of the *gagaku* school of ancient court musicians. The choice of *gagaku* musicians as the Japanese specialists in the composition of "blended" music is particularly interesting, since it meant that Izawa and his associates chose to bypass the more recent and vital forms of "vulgar" music that had evolved in the Tokugawa period and to draw instead upon the rigidly conventionalized, albeit "elegant," musical tradition of at least a millennium earlier in Japanese history.

One notable product of the mixing of music in early Meiji (although not by Izawa) was the Japanese anthem, "Kimi ga Yo" ("His Majesty's Reign"), composed in response to the desire to have a national song like the Western countries. The words for "Kimi ga Yo," taken apparently from the tenth-century poetic anthology *Kokinshū*, were first put to Western music by an English bandsman in the 1870s but were later adapted to a melody by a *gagaku* musician that was in turn harmonized and arranged for orchestra by a German, Franz Eckert.

However we may judge the efforts of Izawa to synthesize traditional and Western music, the most important result of musical training in public schools from his time on was to accustom successive generations of Japanese students to Western harmonies and modes, and thus to make possible Japanization of the classical repertoire of Western symphonic and chamber music. Today, Bach, Mozart, and Beethoven belong as much to the Japanese as they do to anyone else in the world.

Since the main orchestrated styles of native Japanese music were so closely associated with the theatre, the fate of the traditional theatrical forms after the Meiji Restoration has quite naturally determined their course as well. The *nō* theatre, a remnant of the medieval age, was antiquated even during the Tokugawa period and, despite the authorship of new plays by certain contemporary writers, remains a drama engulfed in history and aesthetic tradition to be admired primarily by connoisseurs and by students of the classical arts. Similar patronage continues to support the bourgeois puppet theatre. After a period of great flourishing in mid-Tokugawa times, *bunraku* declined steadily in popularity and, with the coming of the modern era and new demands for realistic portrayal, has had little hope of regaining any mass following.

Of chief theatrical interest in the early Meiji period was the development of *kabuki*. Much of the success of *kabuki* after the Restoration was owing to the efforts of the impresario Morita Kanya (1846–97) and the playwright Kawatake Mokuami (1816–93). After the overthrow of the Tokugawa regime brought to an end the many restrictions that the shogunate had imposed on *kabuki* over the years, Morita moved his theatre from the outlying Asakusa (formerly the Yoshiwara) region to the central Tsukiji area of Tokyo. Built first in 1872 and reconstructed in 1878 after destruction by fire,[30] Morita's theatre gave rise to a new era in which *kabuki* enjoyed social respectability and was amenable to up-to-date, modernizing ideas.

One step taken to advance *kabuki* was the production of *sangiri* ("cropped hair") plays, especially by Mokuami, that dealt with current fashions and fads (although, apart from greater topical relevance, the *sangiri* plays were structurally much like the domestic pieces—*sewamono*—of traditional *kabuki*). Another type of new play was the *katsureki* or "living history," created after the rise of the people's rights movement in the 1870s. In the politically conscious atmosphere of the times, these plays represented an effort to stage realistic historical drama rather than the fancifully distorted quasi-history of earlier *kabuki*.

An even more significant innovation to emerge from the political ferment of the second and third decades of the Meiji period was *shimpa* or the "new school" of theatre, whose founders were actual participants in the political party movement. Chief among them was Kawakami Otojirō (1864–1911), a former *kabuki* actor and fervid political liberal of the day. Using current events and material from recently written political novels (including the *Strange Encounters of Elegant Females* discussed above), Kawakami attempted to present plays of topical interest, which he further enlivened with special sound and lighting effects. The war with China in the mid-1890s provided a particularly fine opportunity for Kawakami, who was able to capitalize on heightened patriotic feelings by staging *shimpa* extravaganzas dealing with the fighting then in progress on the continent.

10

The Fruits of Modernity

JAPAN WENT TO WAR with China in 1894–95 over the issue, to put it euphemistically, of Korean independence. Korea had traditionally been tributary to China, a relationship that gave the Chinese a kind of protectorate over the foreign affairs of the peninsular, "hermit" kingdom. Victorious in 1895, Japan received, among other rewards, the colonial possessions of Taiwan and the Pescadore Islands. Moreover, by fully exposing the weakness and ineptitude of the Manchu government, it helped precipitate an odious round of concession grabbing by the powers in China during the late 1890s that has been described as "the carving of the melon." The country that took the largest slice of the melon was Russia, whose increasing assertiveness from this time on in northeast Asia led to a serious clash of interests and, finally, war with Japan. In its surprising triumph over Russia in 1904–5, Japan not only extended its empire through acquisition of the Liaotung Peninsula and Korea (formally annexed in 1910) but also vaulted into the ranks of the world powers. Thus, within a half-century, the "Meiji miracle" of modernization—made indubitable by the fine criterion of Japan's proven capacity to beat other major countries in war—had been spectacularly accomplished.

In the year Japan went to war with China, 1894, it also secured revision (effective in 1899) of its unequal treaties with the Western nations, thereby achieving a foreign policy goal that had become a national obsession. This achievement, along with Japan's many other advances in modern technology and the spectacular military victories that were soon forthcoming over China, fostered a universal sense of pride among the Japanese people. Despite the growing differences of opinion among intellectuals and government leaders (discussed in the last chapter) about methods of modernization and the cultural values proper to it, the Japanese were still capable in the mid-1890s of a remarkable unanimity of attitude toward national goals. No one, for example, vocally opposed the Chinese war; on the contrary, virtually all Japanese who spoke out publicly extolled its glories. That candid old Westernizer, Fukuzawa Yukichi, observed, for example, that one thing Westerners "[never] expected, thirty or forty years ago, was the establishment of Japan's imperial prestige in a great war. . . . When I think of our marvelous fortune, I feel as though in a dream and can only weep tears of joy." And Tokutomi Sohō, carried away with national pride, proclaimed, "Now we are no longer ashamed to stand before the world as Japanese. . . . Before, we did not know ourselves, and the world did not yet know us. But now that we have tested our strength, we know ourselves and we are known by the world. Moreover, we *know* we are known by the world."[1]

Even the devout Christian Uchimura Kanzō called the war a righteous undertaking. It seemed, indeed, to be almost a logical necessity for Japan, having become civilized and enlightened, to assume the responsibility for spreading the fruits of modernity to the still backward-thinking peoples elsewhere in East Asia.

One somber result of the Sino-Japanese War was China's further decline as a source of higher culture in Japanese eyes. Although the Meiji Restoration had rather abruptly shifted Japan's attention from China to the West as its chief foreign mentor, China's traditional prestige was still very high in Japan in the early 1890s, especially among many members of the conservative "national essence" movement. But the rhetoric of wartime propaganda, combined with growing contempt for Chinese ineffectuality in the field of battle, led most Japanese intellectuals and leaders to give less and less consideration to their millennia-old cultural ties to China. In the years following the war, some Japanese even conceived of a modern Japan benignly repaying its cultural debt to a decrepit China by aiding Chinese reformists and revolutionaries in their struggle against the alien and antiquated Manchu dynasty.

At the same time, the almost joyful unanimity of attitude with which the Japanese had entered the war with China was shattered in its aftermath. The "triple intervention" in 1896 of Russia, France, and Germany, forcing Japan to retrocede to China one of its main territorial booties from the recent fighting, the Liaotung Peninsula,[2] incensed many Japanese and made them more aggressively nationalistic than before. Other Japanese, appalled by the ugly spectacle of concession grabbing that soon ensued in China, recanted their previous endorsement of war as a valid tool for civilizing and enlightening and became in varying degrees pacifistic. Observing, in addition, the factory layoffs and other economic dislocations and hardships that followed in the wake of the war, some of the latter also came to reject the capitalistic system of economic modernization that was evolving in Japan and espoused the doctrines of socialism.

It was thus in the period following the war with China that Japan was first truly exposed to those harsh ideological divisions of viewpoint that seem inevitably to accompany modernization. Yet, for better or worse in the long run, Japan as it entered this early phase of empire building was spared much actual divisiveness by the authority of the oligarchs, who continued to hold a uniquely superior position within the Meiji government.

The process by which the advocates of political parties gradually acquired power after the opening of the first Diet in 1890 can only be briefly sketched here. In the beginning, they could do little more than seek to harass the oligarchs by adopting obstructionist tactics. Not until after the turn of the century were the party people regularly taken into cabinets; and not until 1918 was a true party leader made prime minister. By then, most of the great Meiji leaders were dead and those few still alive, like Yamagata Aritomo (1838–1922) of Chōshū who, along with Itō Hirobumi, had been the most powerful of the oligarchs, enjoyed only a fraction of their former influence.

Scholars continue to debate whether the kind of party government that had evolved in Japan by the 1920s, ostensibly resembling in its major features the British political system, was or was not democratic. Even if regarded as democratic, the pre–World War II form of party government was certainly extremely fragile, as was demonstrated by the relative ease with which it was crushed by the militarists in the early 1930s. Recent studies by Western scholars strongly suggest that, whatever else it may have been, "Taishō democracy"[3] was not populistic. In order to secure a measure of power from the Meiji oligarchs, the party leaders adopted what has been called the politics of compromise. In other words, they worked much harder at establishing a modus operandi with the oligarchs and other leading bureaucrats than at gaining popular support among the masses. By 1925, when universal manhood suffrage was finally adopted in Japan, there were two major parties. Both naturally sought to secure as large majorities in elections as possible; but there was in fact very little philosophical difference between them, and few if any party leaders were ever really motivated to "take the issues to the people." They were the members of a new kind of ruling elite who stood at the top of a still highly structured and even traditionalistic society, and in many ways they appeared as remote and unapproachable to the common man as rulers always had in Japan.

Although the socialist and other left-wing movements had very little practical success in the period before World War II, they constitute an important subject of study not only for an understanding of the origins of the left wing in Japan today but also because they have, quite understandably, always exerted a powerful influence on Japanese writers, artists, and intellectuals in general. One reason for the left wing's poor showing in the prewar period was the frequent governmental suppression to which it was subjected. For example, the first Socialist Party, founded in 1901, was banned on the very day that it declared its existence. Such treatment by the authorities soon led some socialist leaders to despair of ever achieving their goals by parliamentary means and to embrace more radical ideologies, such as syndicalism and anarchism. Interestingly, the split that occurred about the time of the Russo-Japanese War between those socialists who wished to continue their efforts to reform society from within and those who increasingly rejected legal, parliamentary tactics coincided roughly with the division between the Christians and non-Christians among them. By and large, the Christian socialists of this period, most of whom were fortified by the strong sense of moral purpose imparted by Protestant missionaries and teachers of the late nineteenth century, were unwilling to adopt revolutionary measures, but remained convinced that their programs could and should be implemented through the constituted governmental structure of Japan.

Probably the single most shocking event to the Japanese before World War II was the revelation in 1910 of an anarchist plot to assassinate the Meiji emperor. Scores of arrests were made and twelve men, most of whom were not actually privy to the plot, were executed. The severity of the government's "anti-radical" action at this time effectively stifled all left-wing activities, and it was not until after World War I that they were resumed.

Japan's participation in World War I on the side of the Allies was minimal; yet, as a result, it was able to enlarge its empire through the acquisition both of Germany's island possessions in the Pacific and of the former German interests in North China. World War I also brought an unprecedented economic boom to Japan, which took over most of the Far Eastern markets temporarily abandoned by the European belligerents. Many economists, in fact, judge that it was about this time that Japan finally achieved economic modernity. However such modernity may be defined, Japan by World War I had obviously become a capitalist state of a highly monopolistic character. Much of the country's industry and commerce was controlled by a small number of financial combines or *zaibatsu,* whose managing families were plutocratically associated through marriage and other ties with leading members of the Japanese bureaucracy and political parties.

The Allies claimed to have fought the war "to make the world safe for democracy." And although Wilsonian idealism was largely ignored by the authors of the Versailles Treaty, who were mainly intent upon punishing Germany and furthering their own national interests, the postwar period was a time when Western-style democracy seemed clearly to be in the ascendant in the world. At the same time, the successful Communist revolution in Russia gave new hope to radicals and revolutionaries everywhere. Partly in response to this, and even as Taishō democracy flourished, the long-dormant left wing became once again active in Japan.

Probably the leading theoretician of Taishō democracy and what it might have been was Yoshino Sakuzō (1878–1933). An early convert to Christianity, Yoshino studied in Europe and the United States before assuming a full-time position in political thought on the faculty of Tokyo Imperial University in 1913. He persuasively expressed his aspirations for

Japanese democracy in a series of articles for the magazine *Chūō Kōron (Central Review)*, the most famous of which was "On the Meaning of Constitutional Government," published in 1916.

In essence, Yoshino sought to advance the cause of liberal democracy in Japan against oligarchic or plutocratic rule. He not only advocated universal manhood suffrage (which, as we have seen, was finally adopted in 1925) but also urged reform of the House of Peers and other appointive bodies in order to strengthen the power of the elective House of Representatives. Furthermore, Yoshino attempted to deal with the delicate question of the compatibility of democracy with the *kokutai* concept, which held the emperor to be theoretically the source of all state authority and power. While expressing his personal opinion that the emperor was quite unlikely to go against the sentiments or welfare of the people, Yoshino sought to clarify Japan's particular brand of democracy (within the outward form of a constitutional monarchy) by suggesting that the best Japanese word for "democracy" was *minpon*—literally, "the people are the foundation (of the state)"—rather than the more commonly used *minshu*, "the people are sovereign." Yet Yoshino's idea of the people as the foundation of the state, along with his frequent references to the "people's welfare," also had a strongly Confucian ring to it. Traditional Confucianists had always insisted that government be for the people, without for a moment considering the moral propriety of its also being of and by them.

In addition to the inspiration of the Russian revolution for the exceptionally radical-minded, specific developments in Japan during and after World War I appeared particularly favorable to the left wing as a whole. *Zaibatsu* exploitation and worsening labor conditions, for example, had brought on large-scale and militant industrial strikes in the cities, while in the countryside, where social conditions were little better than they had been before the Meiji Restoration, absentee landlordism had reached nearly the 50 percent level. Moreover, the return of the European powers to competition for the Far Eastern markets, combined with poor governmental planning, precipitated a sharp recession in the postwar period. The fall of silk prices was particularly distressing to farming families, many of which were greatly dependent on supplementary income from sericulture to make ends meet.

The reasons why, despite seemingly propitious conditions, the socialists and others on the left were able to achieve so little in practical terms following World War I deserve more attention than can be given here. But, for one thing, the structure of Japanese society was not conducive to their activities. The majority of Japanese were still farmers engaged in family-oriented, intensive agriculture and were highly conservative in outlook. Reverence for the emperor, and thus for the established order, was particularly strong among them. Even in the urban, industrial sector of the economy, many workers were held in paternalistic thrall by their employers and were simply not as socially and politically incitable as the members of a truly alienated proletariat. Despite occasional outbursts of anguish in such forms as strikes and riots over rises in the price of rice, the great staple of food consumption, both peasants and industrial workers by and large accepted their subordinate positions in life and obeyed the ostensibly unassailable authority of those above them.

This is not to suggest that the masses of prewar Japan were merely ignorant and docile. They were, in fact, almost universally literate, although their moral education, as we have seen, was heavily weighted in favor of the traditionalistic *kokutai* values. And any apparent docility was, I believe, actually a manifestation of how little revolutionary potential there was in prewar Japanese society. If the people were to be spurred into collective action, the appeal would have to come from the nationalistic, emperor-revering right and not from the left wing, which was primarily internationalist in outlook and opposed in particular to those elitist privileges protected by the *kokutai* ideology.

We observed in the last chapter that the most powerful literary force in the late 1880s and early 1890s was the group of Ken'yūsha (Society of Friends of the Inkstone) novelists centered about Ozaki Kōyō, who believed that modern, realistic writing in Japanese should be modeled on the Genroku style of Saikaku. Although Ozaki and his companions remained popular favorites among the reading public through much of the 1890s, as Japan entered its age of parliamentary government and imperialist expansion, their prominence served largely to obscure the great diversity of creative activity and ferment of ideas among other writers in the literary world during this decade.

The danger in any survey of Japanese literature from the 1890s on is the temptation to classify writers according to various schools, such as the romantic and the naturalist, and thereby not only fail to do justice to the individuality of major authors but also give the impression of a more orderly progression of literary trends than actually occurred. In literature, as in other cultural and intellectual pursuits, the achievement of modernity by Japan at the end of the nineteenth century and the beginning of the twentieth brought with it a complexity of outlook and activity that defies precise categorization. Even though it is helpful to apply labels to certain groups of writers because of important characteristics they shared, such labels should not be interpreted as fixed pronouncements on their places in modern Japanese literature.

One characteristic manifested by virtually all Japanese authors from Tsubouchi until at least the end of the Meiji period was their desire to describe man and his behavior as accurately and truthfully as possible. In this sense, all presumably regarded themselves as "realistic" writers, although obviously they differed greatly in their conceptions of what constituted realistic writing. Certain authors of the 1890s, often loosely called romantics, insisted, for example, that an accurate and truthful depiction of man could only be achieved through analyses of the psychological motivations and feelings of individuals and not simply by portrayals of certain types or categories of people. Behind this attitude lay the vexing problem of individualism in modern Japan. It is significant that many of the leading prose writers, poets, and critics of the most prominent journal of Japanese romanticism, *Bungakukai (The Literary World*, published from 1893 until 1898), were either converts to or strongly influenced by Protestant Christianity, the only creed in late Meiji Japan that gave primacy to the freedom and spiritual independence of the individual. The absolutism embodied in the Meiji Constitution demanded strict subordination of the interests of the individual to those of the state; and the hopes of many intellectuals and artists that the people's rights movement might provide a legitimate channel for personal dissent were severely reduced, if not entirely dashed, when, from about the time of the Sino-Japanese War, the political parties began to abandon their strong opposition to the oligarchs and to pursue instead the "politics of compromise."

The feeling of frustration engendered by a society that placed such preponderant stress upon obedience to the group, especially in the form of filial piety toward one's parents and loyalty to the state, no doubt accounts for much of the sense of alienation observable in the works of so many modern Japanese writers. These writers have been absorbed to an unusual degree with the individual, the world of his personal psychology, and his essential loneliness. In line with this preoccupation, novelists have perennially turned to the diary-like, confessional tale—the so-called I-novel—as their preferred medium of expression.

Among the leading figures of late nineteenth century romanticism in Japan was Mori Ōgai (1862–1922), although his participation in this trend constituted only one phase of a long and varied career as writer, translator, and critic. A graduate of the medical school of Tokyo Imperial University, Mori spent the period 1884–88 studying medicine in Germany under the sponsorship of the Japanese army. Even after entering the literary field upon his return to Japan, he remained an army doctor, rising to the rank of surgeon-general before his retirement from active service in 1916.

Mori was the first major Japanese novelist to study the literature of a Western country at its source, and not surprisingly the dominant foreign influence on his writing was German. He produced the earliest quality translations from German literature in the late 1880s, shortly after Futabatei began his translations from the Russian, and, in 1890, he published his first novel, *The Dancing Girl (Maihime)*. Based on Mori's personal experiences and labeled by him an *ich Roman*, or I-novel, *The Dancing*

Girl is the story of a Japanese student in Germany, Toyotarō, who has an affair with a German girl but ultimately abandons her in order to return home and accept a position in the Meiji officialdom. In some ways, Toyotarō represents the exact opposite of Bunzō, the pathetic hero of Futabatei's *The Drifting Cloud*. Whereas Bunzō, a failure in the competition to get ahead in a rapidly modernizing Japan, also finds his hope for happiness in love threatened, Toyotarō rejects love for personal ambition.

Romanticism, which influenced many novelists and poets in the period up to the Russo-Japanese War, gave way shortly thereafter to the more clearly identifiable movement of naturalism. Stimulated in particular by the writings of Zola and Maupassant, the naturalists took their stand on the premise, derived from the philosophical positivism of nineteenth-century Europe, that man and society could be portrayed with scientific realism through careful observation and clinical recording of the most minute, mundane aspects of human behavior. The Japanese naturalist writers have been strongly criticized, however, for at least two major reasons: first, unlike the European naturalists, they concentrated almost entirely on the individual and made little attempt to relate him to the larger concerns of society; and second, by relying heavily on their own personal experiences to describe life as it really is, they were guilty of immense egoism. Yet, however much they may be criticized for their approach and methods, the naturalists certainly addressed with vigor the theme that has held greatest fascination for modern Japanese novelists: the innermost psychological and emotional life of the individual.

The Broken Commandment (Hakai) of Shimazaki Tōson (1872–1943), published in 1906, is generally regarded as the first naturalistic novel in Japan. Shimazaki, a convert to Christianity, had earlier been a contributor of romantic poetry to *Bungakukai,* and his emergence as a pioneer novelist of the naturalist school suggests that, despite the great differences between the two movements in the context of their historical development in Europe, romanticism and naturalism tended to merge in Japan, particularly in their mutually intense, egocentric concern with the individual. *The Broken Commandment* tells of Ushimatsu, a member of Japan's pariah class of *eta,* who has vowed to his father that he will never reveal his class origins. Even after he completes school and becomes a teacher, Ushimatsu maintains the secret in spite of a growing feeling of guilt that he should speak out and join others who are struggling to achieve social equality for the *eta.* In the end, Ushimatsu decides to reveal his identity; but, rather than join the fight for minority rights in Japan, he accepts the offer of a job on a ranch in Texas owned by another, expatriate *eta.* Unlike most other naturalistic novels, *The Broken Commandment* deals with a significant social problem, although any message that might be derived from Shimazaki's handling of it is largely vitiated by the improbable ending he has contrived.

Tayama Katai (1871–1930) was the second major writer of the naturalist school, and his 1907 novel *The Quilt (Futon)* was the earliest purely autobiographical work of the I-novel genre. Dealing with the unhappy love affair between a novelist and his young female pupil, *The Quilt* was for its time an especially daring revelation of the intimate relations between a man and a woman. To Tayama, personal confession was the most scientifically valid and "sincere" of literary techniques; and in his conscientious application of it throughout his career he, more than any other novelist, epitomized the real spirit of Japanese naturalism.

Although other authors began to react against naturalism shortly after it was established and popularized as a movement by Shimazaki and Tayama in the years immediately following the Russo-Japanese War, they in fact shared with the naturalists the important common desire to be free of the restraints of imposed moralism in Japanese society and to investigate at their will the sources of human behavior. One group of these authors, including Nagai Kafū (1879–1959) and his disciple Tanizaki Junichirō (1886–1965), became known as "aesthetes" or "decadents." Whereas the naturalists proclaimed a scientific interest in all aspects of life, no matter how trifling, such aesthetes as Kafū and Tanizaki were expressly concerned with the more unwholesome, hedonistic, and even bizarre patterns of conduct observable in man.

Nagai Kafū spent the years 1903–8 in the United States and France. His chief reaction to the United States seems to have been a mild distaste for the materialistic character of American life as he saw it. In France, on the other hand, the pleasures of Parisian life only intensified the sentiment that was to be the most persistent in Kafū's writings: nostalgia for the gracious and aesthetically cultivated ways of the past.

Back in Japan, Kafū's natural habitat was the demimonde and his guiding urge was to recapture what he could of the former life style of the floating world of Edo. Like the other Japanese aesthetes, he was preoccupied with women—especially the *samisen*-playing geisha type—and with the voluptuous delights they could provide. Ever nostalgic and sensual, Kafū appears constantly to have sought escape from the realities of modern Japanese society. Although he privately expressed outraged shock at the severity of governmental suppression of the anarchists accused in 1910 of plotting against the life of the Meiji emperor, it is doubtful that his escapism stemmed from any deeply felt despair over the restriction of personal freedoms in Japan. Rather, Kafū was drawn by temperament to seek his ideals and pursue his fantasies in the past. As Edward Seidensticker has put it: "Buildings had to be decaying, cultures ill and dying, if not dead, before he could really like them."[4]

One of Kafū's loveliest tributes to the disappearing world of old Tokyo is the elegiac novelette *The River Sumida (Sumidagawa,* 1909). This is the story of Chokichi, a boy growing up. To Kafū, growing up was by its nature sad because it could be accomplished only with the passage of time. Chokichi's great sorrow during the passing of his youth is the loss of his sweetheart, who is sold—not entirely against her will—into the life of a geisha. Chokichi himself yearns to become an actor in the classical *kabuki* theatre and to re-create in life the fantasies of the traditional tales of the past. Here is a passage that movingly evokes not only the intensity of Chokichi's yearning but also Kafū's own peculiar sensitivity to the city that absorbed all of his affection:

> Chokichi noticed by chance on one of the houses of the neighborhood a sign with the name of the street. He recalled at once that this was the very street mentioned in *The Calendar of Plum Blossoms*, which he had avidly read not long before. Ah, he sighed, did those ill-starred lovers live in such a dark, sinister street? Some of the houses had bamboo fences exactly like the ones in the illustrations to the book. The bamboo was withered and the stalks were eaten at the base by insects. Chokichi thought they would probably disintegrate if he poked them. An emaciated willow tree dropped its branches, barely touched with green, over the shingled roof of a gate. The geisha Yonehachi must have passed through just such a gate when, of a winter's afternoon, she secretly visited the sick Tanjiro. And it must have been in a room of such a house that the other hero, Hanjiro, telling ghost stories one rainy night, dared to take his sweetheart's hand for the first time. Chokichi experienced a strange fascination and sorrow. He wanted to be possessed by that sweet, gentle, suddenly cold and indifferent fate. As the wings of his fancy spread, the spring sky seemed bluer and wider than before. He caught from the distance the sound of the Korean flute of a sweet-seller. To hear the flute in this unexpected place, playing its curious low-pitched tune, produced in him a melancholy which words could not describe.[5]

But Chokichi's widowed mother (the teacher of a classical form of dramatic recitation) and his uncle (a *haiku* master)—both of whom are relics of the past—seek to persuade him not to enter the theatre but to remain in school. In despair, Chokichi allows his health to decline and contracts typhoid fever. It is in this melancholy state of affairs that the book ends, though we are given hope that the uncle will now help Chokichi to become an actor. Reflecting on his own past, the uncle realizes that for Chokichi, as for himself, the pursuit of one of the classical arts, such as *haiku* or *kabuki*, is infinitely preferable to the modern alternative of entering into a life of drudgery in business.

Tanizaki Junichirō was a far more powerful and versatile writer than Nagai Kafū. Unlike Kafū, who was obsessed with the vanishing life of Edo, Tanizaki produced books on a great variety of subjects. Some, for example, are set in Japan's distant past, while others are intimately personal accounts, often of a highly erotic nature; still others, like his masterpiece, *The Makioka Sisters*,[6] are evocations of Japanese society. To many readers, Tanizaki was the most decadent of the decadent writers, a view

they formed from the extraordinarily masochistic, sexually perverse behavior of so many of his characters. Nagai Kafū's heroes had, for the most
part, simply used women or had taken what pleasures they could from
them; but, in the writings of Tanizaki, men willingly debase and sacrifice
themselves to the glorification of feminine beauty. This is perhaps best
seen in the recurrent theme of foot fetishism. Tanizaki's last—although by
no means best—novel, *The Diary of a Mad Old Man* (*Fūten Rōjin Nikki*,
1961), deals exclusively with the passion of a sickly, withered, and impotent old man for his daughter-in-law, a former cabaret girl who humors
him in return for monetary favors. The old man is particularly enamored
with the girl's feet and even schemes to have imprints made of them on
his tombstone so that he can lie in eternal abjection beneath them.

Another central theme in Tanizaki's work is the familiar conflict between East and West. For other Japanese, this was a conflict of philoso-
phies or of an Eastern spiritualism as set against a Western materialism;
but for Tanizaki it seems to have been primarily aesthetic. In his earlier
writings he was, as he himself later lamented, excessively infatuated with
the West and its modernity. As he approached middle age, he began to
reassess and to appreciate anew the attractions of traditional Japan. In
keeping with his ever-constant absorption with women, Tanizaki dealt
most effectively with the pull of East and West in such novels as *Some
Prefer Nettles* (*Tade Kuu Mushi*, 1928),[7] where an ostensibly Westernized
man, unhappy in his marriage and accustomed to seeking physical grat-
ification with a Eurasian prostitute, finds himself increasingly drawn to
the old-fashioned, endearing femininity of the Kyoto beauty who is his
father-in-law's mistress. To the man, Kaname, the mistress O-hisa,
though barely beyond adolescence herself, represents the timeless tranquility of the past, which might well be used to dissolve the perplexities
and uncertainties of modern life. One of the current passions of the
father-in-law (referred to as the "the old man") is the puppet theatre,
and comparison is constantly made between the "doll-like" O-hisa and
the *bunraku* puppets. For example, while attending the theatre with the
old man and his mistress early in the book, Kaname "looked at O-hisa.
Her face was turned a little so that the line of her cheek showed, round,
almost heavy, like that of a court beauty in a picture scroll. He compared her profile with [the puppet] Koharu's. Something about the slow,
sleepy expression made him think of the two of them as not unlike each
other."[8] Later, as Kaname's marriage continues to deteriorate, he is invited by the old man to join him and O-hisa on a pilgrimage to the island
of Awaji in the Inland Sea, famous for its provincial puppet theatres. The
old man is intent not only on following the pilgrims' path and attending
the plays but also on acquiring a puppet, the product of a dying craft.
Kaname, the modern man, succumbs completely to the antique charms
of Awaji and to the equally antique ways of his companions:

l man had with some regret come back early from *Mount Imose*, the
ay, and he and O-hisa had spent the evening from nine to twelve
d in canticles and sutras. The canticle floated into Kaname's mind
ly with the image of O-hisa as she started out that morning, the inn-
...ᴄᴘer helping her into straw sandals, her wrists and ankles bound in shiny
white silk after the fashion of pilgrims. He had come along with them for one
evening, and the one evening had grown to two and then to three. Partly of
course it was the puppet plays that had kept him on, but doubtless it was
partly too his interest in the relationship between the old man and O-hisa. A
sensitive woman, a woman with ideas, can only get more troublesome and
less likable with the years. Surely, then, one does better to fall in love with the
sort of woman one can cherish as a doll. Kaname had no illusions about his
ability to imitate the old man; but still, when he thought of his own family
affairs, of that perpetual knowing countenance and of the endless disagree-
ments, the old man's life—off to Awaji appointed like a doll on the stage,
accompanied by a doll, in search of an old doll to buy—seemed to suggest a
profound spiritual peace reached without training and without effort. If only
he could follow the old man's example, Kaname thought.[9]

One of the greatest writers of the late Meiji and early Taishō periods,
who was not associated with any particular movement or school, was
Natsume Sōseki (1867–1916). Sōseki majored in English literature at
Tokyo Imperial University and studied in England from 1900 until 1903.
He subsequently lectured for a brief period at the university as the successor to Lafcadio Hearn, but devoted most of his time during the remaining years of his life to the prolific output of novels that have earned
him the lofty position he holds in modern Japanese literature.

Natsume Sōseki's great theme was the loneliness and isolation of man,
particularly the Japanese intellectual of his age, whose society had in
recent decades rejected so much of the native tradition and taken on so
much of the scientific and industrial facade of the West that it had
plunged itself into a great spiritual abyss. It is from Sōseki that we hear
the most anguished cry over the failure of "Eastern morals" to keep pace
with "Western technology" in the course of Japan's modernization. Man
is by nature an isolated creature, yet how much more agonizing is his
ordeal of loneliness when an impersonal and alien technology has
destroyed the very fabric and continuity of his society.

In dealing with the subject of the solitary human ego, Sōseki used the
familiar confessional technique of "fictional" self-analysis so favored by
modern Japanese authors. In his finer novels, like *Kokoro* (1914), the impact of such self-analysis is one of almost overpowering intensity. *Kokoro*
is a story of friendship between a youth and an older man (referred to by
the respectful Japanese title of Sensei or "Teacher"). As the friendship
between the two unfolds, we learn that some dark tragedy lies in Sensei's
past, a tragedy that has left him with an utterly despairing, misanthropic
view of life. The second half of the book is actually a novel within a novel,

presented in the form of a letter that Sensei writes to the youth confessing the story of his past. It is the tale of a triangular love affair in which Sensei is overwhelmed with guilt for, in his mind, having betrayed his friend and rival and for having driven him finally to suicide. Later, however, Sensei considers the possibility that his friend (identified only as K) had some even more desperate reason for his ghastly act than failure in love:

> I asked myself, "was it perhaps because his ideals clashed with reality that he killed himself?" But I could not convince myself that K had chosen death for such a reason. Finally, I became aware of the possibility that K had experienced loneliness as terrible as mine, and wishing to escape quickly from it, had killed himself. Once more, fear gripped my heart. From then on, like a gust of winter wind, the premonition that I was treading on the same path as K had done would rush at me from time to time and chill me to the bone.[10]

In fact, Sensei does commit suicide after completing the confessional letter to his young friend. And he does so at a time, in the year 1912, of particular poignancy both for him and for the Japanese people:

> . . . at the height of the summer Emperor Meiji passed away. I felt as though the spirit of the Meiji era had begun with the Emperor and had ended with him. I was overcome with the feeling that I and the others, who had been brought up in that era, were now left behind to live as anachronisms.[11]

Even as the Meiji emperor's funeral cortege was leaving the imperial palace in Tokyo, the country was jolted by sensational news. General Nogi Maresuke (1849–1912), hero of the Russo-Japanese War, had committed suicide along with his wife. What made the news sensational was that Nogi had disemboweled himself in the ancient samurai tradition of *junshi* to follow his lord (the emperor) in death. In the words of Carol Gluck, "On first hearing it did not seem possible that one of the best-known figures in Meiji national life had committed *junshi.* . . . In a nation in the midst of a solemn celebration of its modernity, its foremost soldier . . . had followed a custom that had been outlawed by the Tokugawa shogunate as antiquated in 1663."[12]

To some, Nogi's act was deserving of highest admiration as a dramatic reminder of values of the past that may have been lost in the headlong drive to modernize. Among the most profoundly affected was Mori Ōgai, who from this time on devoted himself chiefly to writing works that dealt with Japanese history. And in the popular culture Nogi soon took his place at the forefront of the pantheon of Japan's youth heroes along with the fourteenth-century loyalist fighter Kusunoki Masashige and the forty-seven *rōnin*. Some, on the other hand, regarded Nogi's *junshi* as a national humiliation that went against everything that had been achieved during the Meiji period. To the novelist Shiga Naoya (who will be discussed shortly) Nogi was a "stupid fool" *(baka na yatsu)*.[13] Very likely many Japanese were ambivalent in their feelings about Nogi. As one journalist put it, "[W]hile emotionally we express the greatest respect [for General Nogi], rationally we regret that we cannot approve. One can only hope that this act will not long blight the future of our national morality."[14]

It should not be thought that all writers of the late Meiji and early Taishō periods were pessimistic or skeptical about the values of a modernized Japan. On the contrary, a new group of authors, known as the "White Birch" writers from the title of the magazine *Shirakaba* that they began publishing in 1910, had already appeared on the scene to voice cheerful and idealistic sentiments about the course of Japanese society, sentiments that were more in keeping with the advent of Taishō democracy. The White Birch writers were for the most part younger men from excellent families; indeed, their nominal leader, Mushanokōji Saneatsu (1885–1976), was descended from the Kyoto aristocracy. They regarded themselves as cosmopolites whose interests were in the furtherance of international, rather than simply national, art. Mushanokōji was another who was singularly unimpressed with the purported significance of Nogi's suicide as a reaffirmation of the vital spirit that had traditionally permeated Japanese life and culture.

The White Birch writers took particular exception to what they regarded as the excessively gloomy outlook and plodding ways of the naturalists. Instead, they affirmed their own faith in the positive value of individualism and the expectation that it would thrive in Japan as elsewhere. They also tended to preach a Tolstoian kind of humanism, and dabbled to varying degrees with ideas of social leveling. Mushanokōji even went so far as to establish in Kyushu in 1919 a "new village," whose inhabitants were expected to live in idyllic tranquility and communal brotherhood. But, by and large, the humanism of the White Birch writers, who were secure in their own elitist social status, was more intellectual than practical. The most powerful advocacy of radical social change in this period came from the group of proletarian writers who emerged in the early 1920s along with organized Marxism in Japan.

In addition to their purely literary pursuits, the White Birch writers were active, through their organ *Shirakaba,* in the advancement of the visual arts in the Western manner. This was a time of radical new art movements in the West, ranging from Expressionism to Fauvism and Cubism, end Japanese artists returning from study in France and elsewhere in Europe duly introduced each movement to their country, though not necessarily in any coherent order. Western-style art was by this time firmly implanted in Japan, and even centered on an official establishment located in the branch of the Ministry of Education responsible for the sponsorship of national art exhibitions. One of the pillars of this establishment was Kuroda Seiki, the Impressionist-influenced painter who, as noted, was active in introducing Western art to Japan during the last years of the nineteenth century. Like their contemporary European counterparts, the establishment artists of Japan were startled and shocked by the extreme radicalism of, for example, the Fauvist use of raw, "barbaric" colors and the Cubist reduction of art to geometric lines and planes, and they sought to exclude work based on such techniques and principles from the national exhibitions sponsored by the Ministry of Education. The response of the Japanese avant-garde artists was to withdraw from affiliation with the establishment and to go their private ways by forming societies for joint study and exhibitions.

In the history of Western art the critical transition stage between nineteenth-century Impressionism and these radical movements that branched into the modern art of the twentieth century was the painting of the Post-Impressionists—Cézanne, Van Gogh, Gauguin. These men had recognized the limitations of Impressionism, which was concerned primarily with optical problems and with rendering nature "as it is really seen," and they sought, in their own individualistic ways, new content or meaning in art other than purely pictorial representation. Thus Cézanne's work led to Cubism, Van Gogh's to Expressionism, and Gauguin's to various forms of Primitivism (including Fauvism).[15] The Japanese avant-garde artists and intellectuals of the early twentieth century were, in fact, not very sensitive to the distinctions between one school or movement of modern Western art and another. They appear to have responded more to particular works of art and, especially in the case of the Post-Impressionists, to the artists themselves. The uncompromising individualism of men like Van Gogh and Gauguin and their willingness, for the sake of personal ideals, to flout all artistic and social conventions profoundly impressed their Japanese admirers. Such individualism—unusual in the West and almost totally alien to the Japanese tradition—appealed particularly to the White Birch writers, with their cosmopolitan sentiments, and was one of the themes most vigorously promoted in essays on art that appeared in *Shirakaba*.

A writer of major importance associated with the White Birch group —although he really had little in common with someone like Mushanokōji, apart from the fact that they were lifelong friends—was Shiga Naoya (1883–1971). Shiga's great fame rests on a rather meager literary output, consisting mostly of short stories and one full-length novel, *A Dark Night's Passing (An'ya Kōro)*.[16] The latter, however, is a masterpiece, and is probably the most successful work in the Japanese category of the I-novel.

Shiga's principal subject was invariably himself. As a well-known Japanese critic has remarked: ". . . no one has adhered so scrupulously as he has to the approach of the personal novel [*shishōsetsu* or I-novel], in which the logic of everyday life becomes the logic of literary creation."[17] This idea of the logic of everyday life can be observed in *A Dark Night's Pass-*

ing, which has no plot in the proper sense of the word but is simply a narrative of several years in the life of a young writer, Kensaku. The circumstances and events of the book are not identical with those of Shiga's own life, but they are similar; and the personage of Kensaku, as William Sibley discusses in his monograph *The Shiga Hero,* is the prototype of the main male character in all of Shiga's writings.

Like Shiga himself, Kensaku is not particularly intellectual. Rather, he is a person absorbed with his emotions—with his fears, forebodings, and fantasies. He has dark suspicions, for example, about his birth, suspicions that prove to be well founded when his brother informs him that his supposed father is not his real parent; he has incestuous recollections of his mother, who died when he was a child; and he is assailed with anxieties when his wife, almost inadvertently, has a brief love affair with her cousin. The anxieties over the wife's infidelity lead to a shocking incident at a railway station. Naoko, the wife, causes them to be late for a train, and Kensaku, his anger rising uncontrollably, charges ahead and leaps aboard the train as it is pulling away:

> . . . Naoko ran alongside the train toward the doorway where Kensaku was standing. The train was moving no faster than a man walking.
> "Idiot!" shouted Kensaku. "Go home!"
> "But I can get on! If you take hold of my hand, I can get on without any trouble!" She had to run faster now to keep up with the train. She looked at Kensaku with pleading eyes.
> "It's too dangerous! Just go home!" . . .
> Naoko, refusing to give up, got hold of the handrail. Half-dragged along by the train, she at last managed to get one foot on the step, then pulled herself up. Just at that moment Kensaku's free hand shot out, as in a reflex action, and hit Naoko's chest. She fell backward on the platform, rolled over with the momentum, then lay still, once more face up.[18]

Naoko is only slightly hurt, but Kensaku is left to wonder what kind of demon possessed him and caused him to do such a ghastly thing:

> He could find no answer, except that he had had some sort of fit. That he had done Naoko no serious physical injury was fortunate. But he dared not contemplate what his action had done to their future relationship.[19]

The Taishō period in general, and the years following World War I in particular, witnessed the emergence of a truly mass or popular culture in Japan. Further advances in public transportation, communication, higher education, publishing, and journalism were among the factors that contributed to the widening of opportunities, especially for middle-class urban dwellers, to participate in a new kind of up-to-date "cultural life." Like much of the movement for civilization and enlightenment in the early Meiji period, many aspects of this post-World War I pursuit of a cultural life appear to have been little more than frivolous imitations of

Fig. 67   Portrait of a "modern girl" *(moga)* of the Taishō period, by Wada Seika, *ca.* 1930s *(Honolulu Academy of Arts, Purchase 1994 [7544.1])*

Western habits and fads. The addition of one or two rooms decorated and furnished in the Western manner could, for example, transform a mere house into a "cultural home." And, while "modern girls" could be seen strolling the Ginza with permanent waves and shortened hemlines, "modern boys" sported "all back" hairdos and dark-rimmed, Harold Lloyd glasses (fig. 67). Even the great earthquake that wrought a holocaust of destruction in Tokyo in 1923 ironically helped to advance the popular culture; for in the process of the city's reconstruction it was provided with a greatly increased number of bars, cafés, and other places of leisure and entertainment where the "modern" generation could meet and socialize.

Unlike the age of civilization and enlightenment, when the West represented an exciting but bewildering kind of utopia and only a relatively few people could really partake of it, the evolution of a mass culture in the 1920s not only affected (by definition) virtually all Japanese, but also engendered in them a more cosmopolitan outlook and a stronger sense of internationalism than they had ever had before. Perhaps the greatest spur to this newly internationalist sense was the boom in foreign sports that occurred about this time. American baseball became the national mania that it still is today in Japan, and such leisure sports as golf and tennis also gained steadily in popularity. Japanese athletes, moreover, became increasingly prominent in Olympic competition. The good showing of Japanese swimmers at the Paris Olympics in 1924 even set off a round of pool building in public schools.

Although not always used for edifying purposes, the phonograph and the radio both contributed greatly to the new spread of culture, particularly in making available for the first time to all Japanese the sounds of Western music. Among the *interi* or "intelligentsia," it became fashionable to discuss the merits of, say, the playing of Kreisler or the singing of Caruso.

Literature also shared in the expanding vistas of a mass culture, and writing in the period following World War I was notable for its diversity. If there was any common sentiment among writers of the 1920s, it was an even more explicit concern than before with individualism.[20] For this was the heyday of Taishō democracy and Western liberal ideology in Japan, and many writers sincerely sought to address themselves to basic questions about the individual in a modernist society. Yet Japanese society itself remained highly nonindividualistic, and most writers—like their precursors of the naturalist school—appear to have been concerned more with individuality *(kosei)* than with true individualism *(kojin-shugi)*. The dominant I-novel form was still primarily a means for inquiring into the individual's (usually the author's own) ego and eccentricities rather than into his relationship with society as a whole.

From early times the Japanese have shown a keen liking for tales of the weird and macabre, and they have accumulated a rich literature of such tales drawn from many sources, including legends of China, Buddhist miracle stories, and their own native fables. In the modern era the author who has made most important use of the genre of weird and macabre tales is Akutagawa Ryūnosuke (1892–1927). A sickly but intellectually precocious youth, Akutagawa compiled a brilliant academic record throughout a school career that led to graduation from the English Literature department of Tokyo Imperial University in 1916. So extensive was his knowledge of the literature and scholarship (especially philosophy) of Japan, China, and the West that one of his contemporaries even declared him to be the best-read man of his generation.[21] Akutagawa published his first short story in a literary journal in 1914, and for the remainder of his brief life concentrated almost exclusively on the short-story form. A recent commentator has suggested much about Akutagawa's writing in asserting that the European artist who could best have illustrated his stories was Aubrey Beardsley. Like Beardsley, Akutagawa had a "superlative technique," provided an "abundance of decorative detail," and had a great "love of grotesques."[22]

The fascination of Akutagawa's handling of ancient tales as the material for his stories lies not only in the powerful narrative style in which he presents them but also in his exceptional ingenuity in probing the psychological forces—often bizarrely surprising—that may have lain behind the tales. Akutagawa is best known in the West as the author of *Rashōmon,* which will be discussed in the next chapter in the context of Kurosawa's post–World War II cinematic version of the story. Here I would like to illustrate Akutagawa's literature with *Kesa and Moritō (Kesa to Moritō,* 1918), the medieval tale of a warrior, Moritō, whose passion for the already married court beauty Kesa led to the horrifying act of his unknowingly murdering her.[23] Akutagawa's piece deals with the climax of the story, in which Moritō, blinded by his love, has forced Kesa to agree to arrange things so that he can kill her husband while he sleeps at night; in fact, Kesa herself occupies the husband's bed and thus solves her ghastly dilemma by allowing Moritō to kill her in his stead. But Akutagawa raises the possibility that the thoughts of the two lovers on this fateful night may have been far different from what we might imagine:

Moritō: I was driven by sheer lust. Not the regret that I'd never slept with her. It was a coarse lust-for-lust's sake that might have been satisfied by any woman. A man taking a prostitute wouldn't have been so gross.

   Anyway, out of such motives I finally made love to Kesa. Or rather I forced myself on her. And now I come back to my first question—no, there's no need for me to go on wondering whether or not I love her. Sometimes I hate her. Especially when it was all over and she lay there crying . . . as I pulled her up to me she seemed more disgusting than I was. Tangled hair, sweat-smeared make-up—everything showed her ugliness of mind and body. If I'd been in love with her till then, that was the day love vanished forever. Or, if I hadn't, it was the day a new hatred entered my heart. To think that tonight, for the sake of a woman I don't love, I'm going to murder a man I don't hate! . . .

   I despise the woman. I'm afraid of her. I detest her. And yet . . . perhaps it's because I love her.

Kesa: . . . at last I yielded my corpselike body to the man—to a man I don't even love, a lecherous man who hates and despises me! Couldn't I bear the loneliness of mourning my lost beauty? Was I trying to shut it out that delirious moment when I buried my face in his arms? Or, if not, was I myself stirred by his kind of filthy lust? Even to think so is shameful to me! shameful! shameful! Especially when he let me go, and my body was free again, how loathsome I felt! . . .

   On the pretext of sacrificing myself for my husband, didn't I really want revenge for the man's hatred of me, for his scorn, for his blind, evil lust? Yes, I'm sure of it. Looking into his face I lost that queer moonlight exhilaration and my heart froze with grief. I'll not die for my husband—I'll die for myself. . . .

   Is that the wind? When I think all these torments will end tonight, I feel an immense relief. Tomorrow the chilly light of dawn will fall on my headless corpse. When he sees it, my husband—no, I don't want to think of him. He loves me but I can't return his love. I have loved only one man, and tonight my lover will kill me. Even the lamplight is dazzling . . . in this last sweet torture.[24]

Akutagawa's suicide in 1927 by means of an overdose of sleeping pills was one of the most sensational news events of its time. He had long suffered from various physical ailments and from fits of mental depression, and he may even have been schizophrenic. Still, the apparent care and deliberateness with which he planned his death chillingly implied to many people a far more profound intellectual and emotional despair. In his suicide note Akutagawa referred only to a feeling of "vague anxiety," but others have chosen to interpret his act, on the one hand, in broadly social terms (for example, as a protest against the moral vacuity of Taishō–early Shōwa[25] life) and, on the other hand, as an inevitable end result of the predominantly negative aspect of creativity observable in so many modern Japanese writers. If one accepts the latter thesis, Akutagawa may be seen as setting the model for the suicides in the post–World War II period of Dazai Osamu and Mishima Yukio.

If there was any general sense of moral vacuity in the literary world at the time of Akutagawa's death, one group of writers that should at least be credited with trying to fill it was the Communist-oriented proletarians. The Japanese Communist Party, founded in 1922, had its roots in the radical, anarchosyndicalist branch of the socialist movement that had sprung into notoriety in the first decade of the century and had been crushed after the alleged 1910 plot to assassinate the Meiji emperor. We have seen that despite ostensibly favorable conditions for the growth of radicalism after World War I, the left wing as a whole was able to accomplish little in Japan. The Communist Party in particular found itself from the start beset with great difficulties. Not the least of these was the inability of its members to agree on ideological matters. Some Marxists, for example, asserted that, because the Japanese government was a fully bourgeois-dominated, capitalistic regime, efforts should be made to precipitate its overthrow by the proletariat. Others insisted that Japan had still not experienced a bourgeois revolution, and that it would be necessary to eliminate the many feudal elements in Japanese society before any consideration could be given to a proletarian takeover. Still another critical issue of interpretation for Japanese Marxists was the role of imperialism in East Asia. In his East Asian thesis, designed primarily for China, Lenin identified imperialism as the principal enemy of Asian peoples and called for the Communists among them to cooperate with the nationalist movements of bourgeois democrats (for example, Chiang Kai-shek's Kuomintang in China) to expel foreign imperialists. But because the Japanese were themselves by this time among the major imperialists in East Asia, Lenin's thesis had little applicability to their country.

Even if there had been ideological agreement, the Communist movement stood virtually no chance in prewar Japan, for popular sentiment was hostile and the authorities were unrelentingly harsh. With the approach of the 1930s and mounting Japanese involvement in military adventurism on the continent, the movement was ruthlessly destroyed.

Despite the failure of the Communist movement before World War II, Marxism as a creed held a powerful intellectual appeal for the Japanese. Indeed, one of its major difficulties appears to have been that it was largely monopolized by intellectuals and was not effectively presented in a practical, programmatic way for workers. During the late 1920s and early 1930s, the proletarian writers formed the dominant school in literature, and though we may regard this as a commentary on the low state of writing in general during these years, it is also proof that this school was successful in firing the imaginations of some people with both the Marxist doctrine that social relations can be analyzed in scientific, material terms and the Marxist dream that a workers' utopia lies in the future.

Kobayashi Takiji's *The Cannery Boat* (*Kani Kōsen*, 1929) is regarded as one of the finest works of proletarian literature, and an excerpt from it will show the kind of crude propagandizing that inevitably emerged from writing stimulated by such ideological zeal. The book tells of a commercial craft operating in the waters off Kamchatka and commanded by a fiendishly oppressive captain who cares nothing for the welfare and lives of his crew. When the boat is washed ashore on Kamchatka, the crew encounters a group of Russians, one of whom addresses it through a Chinese interpreter speaking broken Japanese:

"You, for sure, have no money."
"That's right."
"You are poor men."
"That's right too."
"So you proletarians. Understand?"
"Yes."

The Russian, smiling, started to walk around. Sometimes he would stop and look over at them.

"Rich man, he do this to you" (gripping his throat). "Rich man become fatter and fatter" (swelling out his stomach). "You no good at all, you become poor. Understand? Japan no good. Workers like this" (pulling a long face and making himself look like a sick man). "Men that don't work like this" (walking about haughtily).

The young fishermen were very amused at him. "That's right, that's right," they said and laughed.

"Workers like this. Men that don't work like this" (repeating the same gestures). "Like that no good. Workers like this!" (this time just the opposite, swelling out his chest and walking proudly). "Men that don't work like this!" (looking like a decrepit beggar). "That very good. Understand? That country, Russia. Only workers like this!" (proud). "Russia. We have no men who don't work. No cunning men. No men who seize your throat. Understand? Russia not at all terrible country. What everyone says only lies."[26]

One of the most popular mediums of mass culture in the 1920s was the motion picture. The first foreign movie was shown in Japan in 1894; a few years later, the Japanese began making movies of their own; and by the post–World War I period Japanese studios were producing a steady flow of films to meet the increasing demand for them by the movie houses that were proliferating throughout the country. The earliest commercial movies made in Japan were little more than records on film of stage productions of *kabuki* and its modern variant, *shimpa*. In the absence of any innovative methods, much of the popularity of these movies with audiences depended on the emotive skills of the *benshi* or "narrators," who described the stories on the screen.

Although their art appears to be little remembered by Japanese today, the *benshi* of the silent-screen era were in their day regarded as major performers, and some even achieved star status comparable to the cinema's leading actors. There are no analogs to the *benshi* in Western cinematic history. Western film exhibitors in the early years of motion pictures experimented with narrators posted near the screen, but the practice of live narration for silent pictures never proved popular with Western audiences.

Characterized as "poets of the dark" by one scholar of their role in the history of Japanese film,[27] the *benshi* were charged with explaining the events and action of the stories of silent films and, most important, with infusing the films with emotion to "bring them alive." A great *benshi* could, in the language of the theatre, upstage the film itself, attracting audiences that were more intent upon hearing him than viewing the screen.

Most of the films produced to meet the demands for mass entertainment in the 1920s were, needless to say, of very little artistic merit; a great many were of the bombastic *chambara* or samurai "swordplay" type, the equivalent of the stereotyped American Western. Still, some people sought to do original work and became pioneers in a tradition of serious filmmaking that has earned much international recognition in recent years, particularly for the way in which Japanese directors have used the motion picture as a means to express their native, highly refined aesthetic tastes.

The most fundamental characteristic of the cinema is, of course, its visuality, and the history of film is to a great extent the story of how directors evolved methods for exploiting to the fullest the unrelentingly realistic "eye of the camera." For the Japanese, with their exceptional sensitivity to nature and to the life of man *within* rather than *against* it, the

cinema proved to be a uniquely congenial artistic medium. This is nowhere more apparent than in the early use of film by Japanese directors
for the purpose of social observation in the *shomin-geki* (popular, or home,
dramas) that deal with the everyday lives of ordinary, typically lower
middle-class people. Unlike most other audiences, which would not
regard such lives as interesting unless they were enmeshed in significantly
dramatic happenings, the Japanese appear to be fascinated simply with
the pulse and movement of the lives themselves. There need not be great
crises; it is enough for the Japanese taste to be shown how people truly
behave together, most characteristically within the context of family relations. This theme of the home drama will be more fully discussed in the
next chapter along with the films of Ozu Yasujirō, its finest master. But
we can see here how ideally suited the cinema, rather than the stage, is
to the presentation of the *shomin-geki*. For the *shomin-geki* is above all a
form of drama about people's lives unfolding within their natural settings,
settings that the stage cannot adequately reproduce. Ozu's films have
been criticized by some Westerners as overlong and boring. Yet it is precisely the leisurely, unhurried survey of things that appeals most to his
Japanese audiences, making them feel they are seeing life as it really is
and not merely in disjointed glimpses. Time passes, the seasons change,
there is a minimum of struggle: herein lies the essence of life.[28]

In contrast to the flourishing of motion pictures in Japan, efforts from
the early years of the twentieth century to establish a modern Japanese
theatre or drama *(shingeki)* achieved nothing comparable to the great distinction and commercial success of contemporary theatre in the West.
The two main streams of the *shingeki* movement date from the founding
in 1906 of the Literary Association (Bungei Kyōkai), one of whose orga-
nizers was the novelist and critic Tsubouchi Shōyō, and in 1909 of the
Liberal Theatre (Jiyū Gekijō) of Osanai Kaoru (1881–1928). Tsubouchi
regarded *shingeki* as part of the overall attempt made from at least mid-
Meiji times on to reform Japanese literature and theatre in general, and
is remembered, in this phase of his career, primarily for his experiments
in combining scenes from Shakespeare on the same programs with *kabuki*
plays. Osanai and his supporters, on the other hand, completely rejected
traditional Japanese theatrical forms, with their characteristic mixture of
music, dance, and acting, in favor of the representational, essentially
"spoken" theatre of the modern West. As one scholar has observed:

> The enthusiastic followers of Osanai, who eventually assumed almost exclu-
> sive leadership in the *shingeki* world of the following decades, considered
> Shakespeare and the Western classics before Ibsen at the same level as *nō* and
> *kabuki*. They considered these to belong to a world without any connection
> with the vital problems of modern man—a world where dance, music, the

stylization and professionalism of the actors could provide entertainment on a commercial basis for nonintellectuals, but not the discussion and the message of a new world to come needed by intellectuals for a rapid modernization of the country.[29]

Osanai and the avant-garde of *shingeki* fervently subscribed to the literary movement of naturalism, which was at its peak of popularity in Japan when they began their activities and which, they believed, would enable them to reproduce life as it was actually lived with almost scientific accuracy. The novelist Tanizaki Junichirō, himself an antinaturalist, made this observation about the naturalist boom of the time: "the tyranny of Naturalism was so fierce . . . that any common hack could obtain literary recognition just so long as he wrote a naturalism story."[30] And one *shingeki* actor said that naturalism meant so much to him and his fellow performers that they were prepared to die for it.[31]

To Osanai, naturalism was equatable with modernism, and in his overriding desire to break with the theatrical past of Japan he called upon the people of *shingeki* to "ignore tradition" and devote themselves to the naturalist (that is, modernist) theatre of the West. He even suggested that the Japanese, at least for the time being, give their attention entirely to translating and producing contemporary Western plays, especially those of Ibsen, Chekhov, and Gorki. Above all, it was Ibsen who became the god of Osanai's *shingeki;* and at meetings of a club devoted to the study of Ibsenian theatre, the members, we are told, proclaimed that for the "love of Ibsen, even Shakespeare was [to be] dismissed as a block-head."[32]

In addition to the efforts of Osanai and others to develop a modern, legitimate theatre, the early twentieth century also witnessed steps taken to bring modern musical theatre and opera to Japan.[33] The first Western opera staged in Japan was Gluck's *Orfeo et Euridice,* performed at Tokyo's Imperial Theatre in 1911. Shortly thereafter, the Italian choreographer Giovanni Vittorio Rosi was hired to help promote opera for Japanese audiences. But his efforts and the efforts of others ran into a steady stream of difficulties, one of the most serious of which was the lack of good, trained voices. For a while, a group of companies known as the Asakusa Operas (because they centered their activities in the Asakusa amusement quarter of Tokyo) enjoyed success in presenting operas that were rewritten and reshaped to appeal to Japanese tastes. But the companies' fortunes waned in the 1920s as audiences became more knowledgeable about Western music (thanks in large part to the beginning of radio broadcasting) and also had greater opportunity to attend performances of real opera by the Western troupes that, by then, were regularly visiting Japan. The advent of "talkies," including musicals, also contributed to the decline of the Asakusa Operas.

Another major effort in the development of musical theatre in Japan was launched with the founding in 1913 of the Takarazuka Girls Opera troupe—also called the Takarazuka Revue—by the prominent business-man and lifelong theatre enthusiast Kobayashi Ichizō (1873–1957). In part, the Takarazuka Revue was an effort to appeal to movements under way in the late Meiji and early Taishō periods to advance the rights of women and to bring women into activities that had previously been vir-tually all male, such as the theatre. Kobayashi, who aspired to produce a wholesome and modern musical theatre "for the people" *(kokumin-geki)*, sought to blend Western music with traditional Japanese theatrical ele-ments, drawing upon themes, for example, from *The Tale of Genji* and *Madame Butterfly*. Some of the Takarazuka performances were modeled on Hollywood-style musicals; others were revues that included operatic arias, internationally popular tunes of the day, and Japanese folk songs.

At first, the Takarazuka performances were amateurish, but Kobayashi steered the troupe toward professionalism with the establishment in 1919 of the Tokyo Music Academy to provide his girls with formal training in singing and dancing. In the early years, the revue maintained a strong ensemble spirit and avoided having some of its performers emerge as stars. But in the late 1920s a star system did evolve, along with a special eroticism in its performances reminiscent of *kabuki* (although centered on women rather than men), as the Takarazuka troupe was divided into those who played male roles *(otokoyaku)* and those who played female roles *(musumeyaku)*. The "male" performers in particular became pop-ular stars as "beauties in men's clothing."[34] Kobayashi wanted to bring men into the troupe, but his attempts to do so were unsuccessful. Re-maining all female, the Takarazuka Revue became a fixture of Japanese theatre and continues to be popular today.

We have noted that in the field of literature Japanese naturalist writers concerned themselves almost entirely with analysis of the individual and failed, for the most part, to follow the lead of European naturalists by moving also into the realm of social observation and commentary. Natu-ralist participants in the *shingeki* movement, on the other hand, quickly made society, rather than the individual, the focus of their attention, and tended to lean strongly to the left in their social thinking. This became especially apparent in the late 1920s and 1930s, when *shingeki* became so openly "proletarian" that it eventually came under attack from the newly emergent militaristic leaders of Japan. The relative lack of success of *shingeki* before World War II may be attributed, therefore, to several reasons: its failure to produce a significant repertoire of original plays, its tendency to use the stage for ideological propagandizing, and the offi-cial suppression that this propagandizing incurred.

The early and middle 1920s were a time of general tranquility in East Asia, when the Western imperialist powers and Japan pursued cooperative policies in exploiting the commercial potentialities of their holdings and interests in China. But by the end of the decade the Japanese, in particular, found their position on the continent increasingly threatened both by Chinese nationalist aspirations and by Russian pressures from the north. The world market crash in 1929–30 heightened demands that Japan abandon its unproductive policy of cooperation with the Western powers and act independently and forcefully in foreign affairs. It was the military that spoke out most stridently for action, and in September 1931 the army provoked an incident in Manchuria (the bombing of tracks north of Mukden, which the Japanese railway guards falsely blamed on the Chinese) that led within a year to the founding of the puppet state of Manchukuo and, in 1933, to Japan's withdrawal from the League of Nations.

As the army embarked on aggression abroad, right-wing ultranationalist groups in Japan—both in and out of the military—began terrorist and putchist activities against capitalists, party leaders, and others whom they held responsible for the country's critical state of affairs. In traditional manner, these ultranationalists called for a Shōwa Restoration— that is, destruction of the bad ministers of state and the return of power to the emperor. The emperor himself was an exceedingly mild-mannered man who was institutionally shielded from all but his closest aides and advisers and who could not plausibly have assumed the real powers of government. In fact, most of those who plotted and entered into coup attempts against the government in the 1930s seem to have given little thought to what should actually be done if their destructive efforts succeeded. As Professor Maruyama Masao has observed:

> . . . the content of their ideology was extremely vague and abstract, being the principle of accepting the absolute authority of the Emperor and submitting humbly to his wishes. One of the reasons that the participants' plans covered only the violent stage of the operation and were not concerned with the aftermath is that their thoughts were based on the principle of the absolute authority of the Emperor. In other words, any attempt at formulating plans of reconstruction would be tantamount to surmising the will of the Emperor and thus an invasion of the Imperial prerogative. This leads to the mythological sort of optimism according to which, if only evil men could be removed from the Court, if only the dark clouds shrouding the Emperor could be swept away, the Imperial sun would naturally shine forth.[35]

In May 1932 a group of young naval officers assassinated the prime minister, and with dramatic swiftness the era of democratic, party governments came to an end in Japan. The two major parties continued to win Diet elections until they were dissolved in 1940 in the name of national unity, but the prime ministership from 1932 on was held either directly by military men or by bureaucrats who cooperated with them. This marked the beginning of what the Japanese regard as the phase of fascism in their country that led to the Pacific War and, ultimately, to crushing defeat in 1945. Although most Western scholars are reluctant to apply the essentially European concept of fascism to developments in Japan during this period, it is clear that, under the pressure of international and domestic crises, the form of parliamentary democracy that had gradually evolved in Japan from the mid-Meiji period disintegrated rapidly before the rise of the military, who succeeded in establishing an oppressive police state by the late 1930s.

The fascists in Europe were inspired by "heroic leaders"—Hitler and Mussolini—and came to power through mass party movements that intruded themselves into the political systems from the outside. Japan, on the other hand, had no Hitler or Mussolini, and the military advanced to power not by organizing mass support for an attack on the government but simply by replacing the parliamentarians (that is, the political parties) as the dominant elite in the national polity. The myriad ultranationalist groups that engaged in political violence during the early and middle 1930s acted mostly in secret without popular backing and were more of a symptom than a cause of the military's rise.

In intellectual and emotional terms, the military came increasingly to be viewed as the highest repository of the traditional Japanese spirit that was the sole hope for unifying the nation to act in a time of dire emergency. The enemy that had led the people astray was identified as those sociopolitical doctrines and ideologies that had been introduced to Japan from the West during the preceding half-century or so along with the material tools of modernization. Such identification was made part of a newly articulated interpretation of the orthodox creed of state *(kokutai)* in a tract published in 1937 entitled *Kokutai no Hongi* or *The Fundamental Principles of Our National Polity:*

> . . . it can be said that both in the Occident and in our country the deadlock of individualism has led alike to a season of ideological and social confusion and crisis. We shall leave aside for a while the question of finding a way out of the present deadlock, for, as far as it concerns our country, we must return to the standpoint peculiar to our country, clarify our immortal national entity, sweep aside everything in the way of adulation, [and] bring into being our original condition.[36]

Japan was a sacred land, ruled by a godlike (though isolated and nonacting) emperor. Its citizens were the members of a great family headed by the emperor, and they were expected to serve the state with unquestioning loyalty. The military, in particular, was not to be criticized, for it had the holy mission of expanding Japanese influence abroad and it was, in any case, answerable only to the emperor (which meant, for practical purposes, that it was answerable to no one).

The suppression in the 1930s not only of proletarian authors and playwrights but even of professors with scholarly views that were deemed incompatible with the national polity effectively muted much of the literary and academic worlds. The cause célèbre in the elimination of freedom of expression was the attack in 1935 on Professor Minobe Tatsukichi (1873–1948) and his so-called Emperor-Organ theory of the Meiji Constitution. Years earlier, Minobe, a scholar of constitutional law at Tokyo Imperial University, had advanced the interpretation that the emperor should be regarded, under the Meiji Constitution, as the highest organ of state, an organ analogous to the head of the human body. Although strongly criticized by some other scholars at the time for presuming to define an emperor whose august authority was beyond definition and who should be mystically regarded as one with the state itself, Minobe's theory was generally accepted in academic circles, and later he was even honored by appointment to the House of Peers. In 1935 a fellow member of Peers attacked Minobe in a speech in the House, claiming that the Emperor-Organ theory, about which the average Japanese knew nothing, was a grave offense against the imperial institution. The following week Minobe, also in a speech to the House of Peers, readily exposed his accuser's argument as nonsensical and was warmly applauded by the House. The matter seemed closed, but before long there arose a ground swell of opposition to Minobe from veterans' organizations and other groups throughout the country. Army leaders and politicians took the lead in demanding a "clarification of the national polity." The issue raged in the press throughout 1935, and by the end of the year Minobe was formally charged with lèse majesté. He resigned from the faculty of Tokyo Imperial University and was drummed out of the House of Peers; his books were banned and, the following year, he was wounded in an attempt on his life.

To a great extent this era of mounting militarism, domestic suppression, and impending cataclysm was a time when most Japanese manifested an intense passion for escapist entertainment that was labeled by its critics as a conglomeration of "the erotic, the grotesque, and the nonsensical." Included within this category were dance halls and girlie revues, the yo-yo, miniature golf, crossword puzzles, and mahjong. Interestingly, despite growing chauvinism and xenophobia, nearly all of these escapist entertainments were imports from the West.

An exception to the depressed state of the arts during the militarist era was the rise to prominence of one of Japan's finest modern novelists, Kawabata Yasunari (1899–1972), who in 1968 became the first Japanese recipient of the Nobel Prize for literature. Kawabata began writing professionally in the mid-1920s as a member of a group of authors known as Neoperceptionists or Neosensualists (shinkankaku-ha), who attacked the excessively scientific, clinical approach to literature of both the naturalist and proletarian schools and called for a return to purely artistic values and emotional sensitivity in fiction writing. The Neoperceptionists regarded themselves as the avant-garde movement of literary modernism and professed an interest in all manner of contemporary European art credos, including Dada and Surrealism. But the movement never established a distinctive identity, and Kawabata, its most important member, eventually located his deepest artistic wellsprings in the native literary tradition, rather than in the essentially Western ideas of Neoperceptionism.

Speaking of the native literary tradition in terms of "*haiku* and *waka* —those arts of suggestion and evocation, reversal and juxtaposition, so deeply rooted in the alogical, intuitive, and 'irrational' sensibility of the East,"[37] Masao Miyoshi observes that Kawabata, in his novels,

> just lets his language flow in time, lets it weave its own strands, almost come what may. The "shape" of the novel is thus not architectural or sculptural, with a totality subsuming the parts, but musical in the sense of continual movement generated by surprise and juxtaposition, intensification and relaxation, and the use of various rhythms and tempos. The *renga* form is often mentioned in connection with Kawabata and for good reason: it too is characterized by frequent surprises along the way and only the retrospective arrangement of the parts into a totality as they approach a possible end.[38]

Kawabata published his prewar masterpiece, *Snow Country (Yukiguni)*, serially between 1935 and 1937, and made further additions and revisions in the early and late 1940s. Even among Japanese authors, accustomed to preparing their works for serial publication in magazines and newspapers, this is an extreme case of novel writing in fragments. Yet Kawabata seems to have found the procedure congenial because it allowed him to feel his way carefully with his material and provided maximum opportunity to extend or, whenever he should wish, terminate the narrative line. *Snow Country* is the story of a love affair between Shimamura, a world-weary dilettante, and Komako, a geisha in a hot-springs resort. The setting for the affair is suggested in the opening lines: "The train came out of the long tunnel into the snow country. The earth lay white under the night sky." Shimamura is on his way to visit Komako, and Kawabata reveals much of the man's character with the startling device of his reactions to reflections in the train window:

> In his boredom Shimamura stared at his left hand as the forefinger bent and unbent. Only this had seemed to have a vital and immediate memory of the woman he was going to see. The more he tried to call up a clear picture of her, the more his memory failed him, the farther she faded away, leaving him nothing to catch and hold. In the midst of this uncertainty only the one hand, and in particular the forefinger, even now seemed damp from her touch, seemed to be pulling him back to her from afar. Taken with the strangeness of it, he brought the hand to his face, then quickly drew a line across the misted-over window. A woman's eye floated up before him. He almost called

out in his astonishment. But he had been dreaming, and when he came to himself he saw that it was only the reflection in the window of the girl opposite. Outside it was growing dark, and the lights had been turned on in the train, transforming the window into a mirror. The mirror had been clouded over with steam until he drew that line across it. . . .

In the depths of the mirror the evening landscape moved by, the mirror and the reflected figures like motion pictures superimposed one on the other. The figures and the background were unrelated, and yet the figures, transparent and intangible, and the background, dim in the gathering darkness, melted together into a sort of symbolic world not of this world. Particularly when a light out in the mountains shone in the center of the girl's face, Shimamura felt his chest rise at the inexpressible beauty of it.[39]

Shimamura had begun his career as a critic of Japanese dance, but when he was urged to become actively involved in the revival of this traditional art form, he abruptly shifted his attention to Western ballet. Even as he became an authority on the ballet, he never attended a performance, nor did he wish to. Shimamura much preferred to fantasize than to participate in art or even in life; for him the world of fantasy and imagination seemed somehow to be more real than reality itself. His only clear recollection of Komako lies in the tactile sensitivity of a single finger, and he is far more enthralled in observing the girl on the train as a transparent, almost otherworldly image superimposed on the dark landscape rushing by the window than in looking directly at her. He is attracted to Komako precisely because she is a *geisha,* a person professionally trained to evoke fantasy worlds and a person "somehow unreal, like the woman's face in that evening mirror."[40]

Before the international Military Tribunal in Tokyo after World War II, the Allied prosecution charged those Japanese arrested as war criminals with participating in a great and sustained conspiracy for world conquest, beginning with the Manchurian incident of 1931. Certainly the Japanese military was guilty of much aggression in East Asia during the decade and a half from 1931 until final defeat in 1945. But the charge that it pursued—diabolically and step by step—a policy of virtually unlimited foreign conquest vastly oversimplified and distorted the complexity of international events that led Japan to war with China in 1937 and into World War II in 1941. Japan actually blundered into the China war when shooting broke out between Chinese and Japanese troops at the Marco Polo Bridge in northern China on July 7, 1937. Once committed to fighting, the Japanese found themselves in a quagmire from which there was no withdrawal without great and intolerable loss of face. Although the Japanese army won battles and seized large expanses of territory, the Nationalist government of Chiang Kai-shek simply withdrew farther and farther into the Chinese hinterland and continued fighting. As the war dragged on, it became a fearful economic drain upon Japan, and victory became a chimera.

Far from facing the harsh reality that the China war was interminable, Japan schemed even more grandly and in November 1938 proclaimed a New Order in East Asia to signal that henceforth China should be regarded, along with Manchukuo, as an integral part of the Japanese sphere of influence. And in 1940, when Japan moved southward in quest of oil and other resources, the New Order was expanded into a Greater East Asia Co-Prosperity Sphere (Dai Tōa Kyōeiken) that was aimed at drawing not only Southeast Asia but also Australia and New Zealand into an economically self-sufficient regional zone under Japan. The German victories in Europe, including the fall of France in June 1940, buoyed the Japanese into believing that alliance with Germany could help in achieving their goals in East Asia, and in September of that year Japan signed a tripartite pact with the Axis powers. But alliance with Germany and Italy proved of negligible value and had the opposite effect of stiffening the anti-Japanese attitude of the United States. As Japan continued to press into Southeast Asia, the United States reacted by freezing Japanese assets in America and by joining Britain and Holland in imposing an embargo on all exports to Japan.

The intractable American opposition to Japanese aggression in 1941 made Pearl Harbor all but inevitable. President Roosevelt stigmatized December 7, 1941, as a "day that will live in infamy," but the fact is that the United States was simply unprepared for war in the Pacific. This unpreparedness enabled the Japanese to score a series of spectacular victories that seemed to accomplish Japan's dream of founding a Greater East Asia Co-Prosperity Sphere. The Japanese hegemony over the western Pacific and much of Southeast Asia was not seriously challenged for more than a year. One reason was the time necessary for the United States to gear itself to a full-scale war effort; another was the fact that the Allies gave priority to the European theatre of war. But the tide turned at the Battle of Midway, westernmost island in the Hawaiian chain, in June 1942. In one of the first naval battles in history conducted by the carrier-based planes of fleets that never saw each other, the Americans scored a smashing victory, sinking four Japanese aircraft carriers. After Midway, the Japanese Navy was forced entirely onto the defensive.

By the end of 1942, after months of ferocious fighting by American and Australian ground forces in appalling, disease-infested conditions in the jungles of the Southwest Pacific—especially in New Guinea and the Solomon Islands—the Allies began gradually, but inexorably, to push the Japanese back toward their home islands. This was accomplished primarily by a series of "island-hopping" invasions in the Gilbert, Marshall, Caroline, and Mariana chains. These invasions were carried out by American forces employing firepower capable of annihilating the Japanese defensive positions. In many cases the Japanese chose, in fact, to fight to the last man rather than surrender, thus inviting the Americans to engage in annihilation. With the capture of Saipan in the Marianas in June 1944, the United States obtained a base within striking distance of Japan. For the next—and last—year of the war, American bombers mercilessly pounded Japan's cities, large and small. The ghastly results of this bombing are vividly suggested in this description of the final months of the war:

> [The United States] adopted area fire-bombing by night, at relatively low altitude for greater concentration . . . from March 9 [1945], when over three hundred B-29s struck [Tokyo]. Sixteen square miles were burned out in one of the very worst bombardments in history; at least eighty thousand (probably far more; nobody knows) were killed and a million made homeless. Worse was to follow as up to eight hundred bombers pounded all the main Japanese industrial and urban centers.[41]

To the Americans, led by President Roosevelt, the surprise attack on Pearl Harbor, in which more than two thousand Americans died, was an unspeakably dastardly act that inspired a thirst for revenge ("Remember Pearl Harbor!") that may account for much of the brutality with which the United States subsequently conducted the Pacific War. To the Japanese, on the other hand, there was nothing "infamous" or dastardly about Pearl Harbor. On the contrary, they regarded it as a brilliant victory. The Japanese public was ecstatic, and, as Donald Keene has discussed, many prominent writers promptly and publicly expressed their great satisfaction —in some cases their delirium of happiness—that the anticipated war had finally begun and that Japan had delivered a devastating blow at the enemy, identified primarily as the United States and England (the British colony of Hong Kong and Pearl Harbor were attacked simultaneously on December 7 or, by Japanese time, December 8). One writer, for example, chortled, "I never thought that in this lifetime I should ever know such a happy, thrilling, auspicious experience"; and another exclaimed, "The war has at last begun, with a great victory. A people which believed that its ancestors are gods has triumphed. I felt something more than mere wonder." Choosing the classical *waka* form of verse, a poet proclaimed that "The time has come, To slaughter America and England." And another poet grandly pronounced:

> Remember December eighth!
> On this day the history of the world was changed.
> The Anglo-Saxon powers
> On this day were repulsed on Asian land and sea.
> It was their *Japan* which repulsed them,
> A tiny country in the Eastern Sea,
> Nippon, the Land of the Gods
> Ruled over by a living god.[42]

Although the Japanese government was pleased to report Japan's startlingly successful early victories, it concealed the defeats once they started coming. The government, for example, proclaimed a Japanese victory at Midway even though it was not only a defeat but, indeed, one of the most decisive setbacks in the history of naval warfare. With the media under its strict control, the government thus kept the Japanese public largely in the dark about the true course of the war after Midway. But when the systematic bombing of Japan began in late 1944, the truth gradually became clear to everyone. A member of the air defense headquarters in Tokyo during that terrible time said this about the bombing:

> It was the raids on the medium and smaller cities which had the worst effects and really brought home to the people the experience of bombing and a demoralization of faith in the outcome of the war. . . . It was bad enough in so large a city as Tokyo, but much worse in the smaller cities, where most of the city would be wiped out. Through May and June [1945] the spirit of the people was crushed. [When the B-29s dropped warning pamphlets,] the morale of the people sank terrifically, reaching a low point in July, at which time there was no longer hope of victory or draw but merely the desire for ending the war.[43]

11

Culture in the Present Age

AFTER MORE THAN three and a half years of fighting, unconscionably prolonged in the last stages by the fanatical unwillingness of its rulers to recognize that further resistence was futile, Japan finally acceded to the ultimatum of the Allied powers from Potsdam in July 1945, and in August surrendered unconditionally. The last agonies of the war produced, on one side, the horror of suicidal air attacks by *kamikaze* pilots—who were exhorted to re-create the glorious defense of the homeland by "divine winds" directed against the Mongol invaders of the thirteenth century—and, on the other side, the unspeakable holocaust of atomic destruction in the American bombings of Hiroshima and Nagasaki.

In an unprecedented radio broadcast on August 15 (August 14 in the United States), the emperor informed his subjects that "the war situation has developed not necessarily to Japan's advantage, while the general trends of the world have all turned against her interest." In fact, Japan's war-making capacity had been reduced to a pitiful remnant, many of its cities lay in charred ruins, and thousands of its citizens faced starvation. There remained no practical alternative to surrender or, in the words of the emperor, no alternative but "to endure the unendurable and suffer what is insufferable."[1]

Although the emperor's forebodings proved excessively dire, one cannot minimize the suffering the Japanese were forced to endure in the first few years following defeat, despite the vigorous efforts of the Occupation regime—monopolized by the United States through General Douglas MacArthur (1880–1964) as Supreme Commander of the Allied Powers (SCAP)—to reestablish order. People were not only hungry and homeless, they were also spiritually exhausted; jobs were scarce and in some sectors nonexistent; inflation raged and black markets sprang up everywhere.

By contrast, GIs strolling the streets of Tokyo and elsewhere and patronizing military post exchanges seemed to be blessed with undreamed of material prosperity. The Japanese could observe this prosperity not only among GIs in Japan but also through American movies. For once movies became widely available again, some 38 percent of the theatres throughout the country were devoted exclusively to the showing of films from America in which capacity crowds saw, day after day, "the refrigerators, cars, modern houses, highways and all the other accoutrements of the 'Good Life.' "[2]

As in other war-torn countries, luxury commodities such as cigarettes, chocolate, chewing gum, and nylon stockings were coveted in Japan in gross disproportion to their intrinsic values. Prostitution and other forms of fraternization between GIs and Japanese girls became commonplace and highly conspicuous. It was also a time when Americans arrogantly believed that their civilization, if not they themselves, had been proved superior in the modern world. To the Japanese, ever sensitive to matters of face, the swaggering of some GIs must have seemed almost intolerably humiliating.

Yet the Occupation was a considerable success, at least if judged by the extraordinary cooperation between occupiers and occupied and by the new, extremely favorable national attitude the Japanese came to hold toward Americans and the United States. This attitude can be observed, for example, in postwar popularity polls in which for years the Japanese identified the United States as their favorite foreign country or the country they most admired.

The stated goals of the Occupation were to "demilitarize and democratize" Japan. In the name of the former goal the country was stripped of the overseas empire it had painstakingly acquired during the preceding half-century; its army and navy were demobilized and its remaining war machinery dismantled; war criminals—including former Prime Minister (and General) Tōjō Hideki (1884–1948)—were brought to trial; and militarily tainted people were extensively purged from government, business, and other sectors of society. In keeping with MacArthur's utopian vision of making Japan the Switzerland of the Far East, a provision was even incorporated into the SCAP-imposed Constitution of 1947 that declared, "the Japanese people forever renounce war as a sovereign right of the nation. . . . The right of belligerency of the state will not be recognized."[3]

Meanwhile, the democratization phase of Occupation policy was implemented in a series of sweeping political, social, and economic reforms. Of these the most radical (and, in retrospect, probably the most lastingly successful) was the land reform, whereby tenantry was virtually eliminated through the expropriation of most absentee landholdings. Other reforms were directed toward decentralization of the national police force and the education system, elimination of morals training in public schools based on the prewar *kokutai* ideology, encouragement of labor unions, and dispersal of the economic combines through a process of *zaibatsu*-busting.

The new Constitution, written by SCAP Headquarters and presented to the Japanese government in 1946, was premised on the emperor's renunciation of his putative divinity (after the decision not to prosecute him as a war criminal) and on the converse assertion that the people of Japan were now sovereign. Henceforth the emperor was to be a symbol of state, and the state itself was to be representative of the people through a system of responsible party government. A thoroughly Anglo-American type of document, the Constitution dramatically reversed what SCAP regarded as the most illiberal and oppressive features of the Meiji Consititution. Probably most conspicuous and most in keeping with the democratizing zeal of the Occupation authorities was the inclusion in the new Constitution's provisions of an American-style Bill of Rights.

Even before promulgation of the new Constitution and its Bill of Rights, SCAP had abolished the wartime Japanese Propaganda Ministry and Board of Censors (although the Occupation authorities did their own censoring) and released all political prisoners. Some of these prisoners were Marxists who had been in jail since the late 1920s, when prewar Communism was brutally suppressed. One concomitant to the release of such prisoners and the guarantee of basic political freedoms was reestablishment of the Japan Communist Party, which soon acquired about 10 percent of the voting electorate. Japanese intellectuals rushed with eagerness to the previously forbidden fruit of Marxist ideology, and during the first decade of the postwar period, when there was a marked abandonment of the more simplistic doctrines of historical determinism in the West, Japanese scholars and other intellectuals vociferously proclaimed that history had already progressed and would eventually turn out exactly as Marx (and perhaps also Lenin) had said it would.

Even some of the more vocal critics of the United States and its postwar policies agree that the early, New Deal phase of the American occupation of Japan was an exceptionally progressive undertaking. But rapidly changing world conditions in the late 1940s—the advent of the Cold War and the fall of China to the Communists—exerted pressures that brought policy shifts on the part of SCAP to the point where the second half of the Occupation (from about 1948 until 1952) has been labeled a time of undisguised reaction or a reverse course. Clearly the revised aim of SCAP during these years was to transform Japan from an occupied enemy country into a revitalized bastion of the Free World in its struggle to contain the spread of Communism in Asia.

One aspect of the reverse course of the Occupation was a general relaxation of the *zaibatsu*-busting program in the hope of stimulating the Japanese economy, which had remained largely dormant after its devastation during the war. Although they are alleged no longer to have the potential for regaining their prewar stranglehold on national affairs, such combines as Mitsui and Mitsubishi certainly have in the intervening years once again become pervasive entities in Japanese business and commerce. But undoubtedly the single most important boost to the economy was American military spending in Japan during the Korean War (1950–53). Partly because of this spending and the freedom attained through national independence when the Occupation was ended in 1952 (in accordance with the San Francisco Peace Treaty of 1951), Japan was launched upon one of the most vigorous and sustained periods of economic growth of any country in modern history. With its gross national product expanding by about 10 percent annually from the mid-1950s, Japan became, by the late 1960s, the third largest economic power in the world.

Despite the devastation of war and the chaos of defeat (or perhaps because of them), the postwar period brought an immediate, unprecedented expansion in literary output. Released from the severe restrictions of wartime controls, writers rushed to complete manuscripts and get them into print. Newspapers and magazines, traditionally among the most important media for the publication of literature in modern Japan, fought fiercely to acquire the most promising manuscripts and thereby to expand their circulations. Established writers such as Nagai Kafū, who had remained silent during the war in protest against the militarists, received fees for their stories that seemed astronomical.

The alacrity with which some Japanese perceived the potentialities for a postwar publishing boom in all kinds of printed matter can be illustrated by the example of the head of Seibundō Company who, after listening at a provincial railway station to the emperor's August 15 broadcast announcing the surrender and after purportedly shedding tears with others gathered at the station, got the idea on the train back to Tokyo that night of publishing a new Japanese-English dictionary. Completed and issued a month to the day after the emperor's speech, the dictionary, helped by a flood of advance orders, surpassed the three-million mark in sales within a brief period of time. Such was the demand for reading material of every kind that printers and publishers sought frantically to obtain paper—then very scarce—wherever it could be found, and before long there appeared a flourishing black-market trade in this commodity, most of which seems to have come from surplus Japanese army and navy supplies.

One especially strong demand that arose in reaction to the nationalistic exclusivism and xenophobia of the militarist years was for new translations of Western literature, both classical and contemporary. Before the war, Western literature in Japan had been represented chiefly by French, English, German, and Russian writings, but owing to the United States's dominant role in the war and Occupation, American literature was for the first time also comprehensively explored by the Japanese. Major writers such as William Faulkner and Ernest Hemingway drew the most serious and sustained attention, while current American best-sellers about the war, such as John Hersey's *Hiroshima* and Norman Mailer's *The Naked and the Dead,* enjoyed great popularity. In addition to American literature, the writings of Jean-Paul Sartre, Albert Camus, and their philosophic precursor Sören Kierkegaard attracted considerable readership among Japanese intellectuals who, spiritually adrift, discerned a new truth in the doctrines of Existentialism.

In assessing the native postwar literature, Japanese critics commonly discuss it in terms of an explosion in mass communications. Referring to a process much more dynamic than the prewar exposure to mass culture, they speak of reaching out to a truly mass audience and of a heightened sensitivity to the need to deal with mass social problems. Among the organizations calling for the expansion of literary horizons in a spirit of postwar liberation and renovation was the Shin-Nihon Bungakkai (Society for a New Japanese Literature). Attracting some of its membership from the suppressed prewar movement of proletarian writers, the society pronounced democracy to be the highest literary ideal, implying thereby a rejection of most prewar movements in literature, including naturalism, Neoperceptionism, and even the so-called social realism of the earlier proletarian writers.

Among the most dramatic of the authors to emerge to prominence in the Occupation period were those loosely referred to as *burai-ha* or "dissolutes." Profoundly influenced by the doubts, uncertainties, and sense of crisis that had permeated their formative years as writers before and during the war, the *burai-ha,* whose most famous representative was Dazai Osamu (1909–48), viewed the world as a place of existential chaos, distorted values, and universal hypocrisy and tried to find humanity in it even as they drowned their anxieties in lives of debauchery and dissoluteness. Claiming a debt to Camus and Sartre, the *burai-ha* writers rose meteorically for a brief period in postwar letters and left a legacy of romantic self-destructiveness that continues to hold a powerful attraction for the Japanese.

Dazai Osamu was born in 1909 into a wealthy landowning family in northern Japan and began what proved to be an exceptionally prolific writing career in the early 1930s. A chronically unstable person, Dazai had already attempted suicide four times before the postwar period, including one effort with a bar maid in which she died and he survived. His fifth attempt, in 1948, a suicide pact by drowning with his mistress at the time, was successful and brought his life to a pathetic end at the age of thirty-nine.

Like the other *burai-ha* writers, Dazai loudly disparaged the narrow egoism, especially of the prewar naturalist school, that constituted the main theme of the persistent Japanese I-novel tradition. Yet Dazai himself relied overwhelmingly on his own life experience for subject material in his writing—many of his stories are diary-like, autobiographical accounts —and may even be regarded as the last great I-novelist.[4] The difference, as Dazai would contend, was that, whereas the I-novelists of the naturalist school were unremittingly self-centered, the aberrant behavior he portrayed with examples of his own life represented an anguished *cri de coeur* against the falsity and deceit of others (if not of mankind as a whole). At times—for example, in the following passage from *No Longer Human* (*Ningen Shikkoku*, 1948), the story of a man who despairs of living "the life of a human being" and who eventually descends into the abyss of drug addiction—Dazai's attitude is misanthropic:

> Society. I felt as though even I were beginning at last to acquire some vague notion of what it meant. It is the struggle between one individual and another, a then-and-there struggle, in which the immediate triumph is everything. *Human beings never submit to human beings.* Even slaves practice their mean retaliations. Human beings cannot conceive of any means of survival except in terms of a single then-and-there context. They speak of duty to one's country and suchlike things, but the object of their efforts is invariably the individual, and, even once the individual's needs have been met, again the individual comes in. The incomprehensibility of society is the incomprehensibility of the individual. The ocean is not society; it is individuals. This was how I managed to gain a modicum of freedom from my terror at the illusion of the ocean called the world. I learned to behave rather aggressively, without the endless anxious worrying I knew before, responding as it were to the needs of the moment.[5]

Dazai's most celebrated novel is *The Setting Sun* (*Shayō*, 1947), an account of an aristocratic family, much reduced in circumstances, in the immediate postwar period. A widowed mother and her divorced daughter appear to be all that is left of the family, but before long a Dazai-like son, thought lost in the South Pacific, returns home. Addicted to drugs, the son promptly renews the life of dissolution and self-destruction he had charted before entering the army and in a short time commits suicide, leaving a final testament—representing the kind of confessional Dazai so much favored—in which he reveals his alternating fear of and disgust toward the world and the personal yearning for love that actually underlay his appalling outward conduct:

> I wanted to become coarse, to be strong—no, brutal. I thought that was the only way I could qualify myself as a "friend of the people." Liquor was not enough. I was perpetually prey to a terrible dizziness. That was why I had no choice but to take to drugs. I had to forget my family. I had to oppose my father's blood. I had to reject my mother's gentleness. I had to be cold to my sister. I thought that otherwise I would not be able to secure an admission ticket for the rooms of the people.[6]

The decline of Japan's old order is a major theme in *The Setting Sun*, and the death of the mother before her son's suicide may be interpreted as symbolizing the fate of that order after defeat in war. But, to millions of fervid readers, what seemed more importantly to have set was the sun of Japan itself, and perhaps no other novel of the period so effectively evokes the sense of spiritual disintegration that engulfed the Japanese at the war's end. Only through the character of the sister, Kazuko (the book's narrator), does Dazai suggest a glimmer of hope for the future. Determined to have a child by a tubercular, drunken artist friend of her brother's, Kazuko proclaims with a ferocity of will totally lacking in Dazai himself:

> I must go on living. And, though it may be childish of me, I can't go on in simple compliance. From now on I must struggle with the world. I thought Mother might well be the last of those who can end their lives beautifully and sadly, struggling with no one, neither hating nor betraying anyone. In the world to come there will be no room for such people. The dying are beautiful, but to live, to survive—those things somehow seem hideous and contaminated with blood. I curled myself on the floor and tried to twist my body into the posture, as I remembered it, of a pregnant snake digging a hole. But there was something to which I could not resign myself. Call it low-minded of me, if you will, I must survive and struggle with the world in order to accomplish my desires. Now that it was clear that Mother would soon die, my romanticism and sentimentality were gradually vanishing, and I felt as though I were turning into a calculating, unprincipled creature.[7]

If the *burai-ha* writers represented an extreme of overreaction to the social devastation of defeat and occupation, some of the more noted authors from the prewar period, at the other extreme, began writing again after the war almost as though nothing had happened. For example, Nagai Kafū, though distinctive for having remained silent while so many other writers spoke out to one degree or another in favor of the war, began immediately to publish the same kind of pleasure-quarter stories he had always favored. To the *apure (après-guerre)* generation of writers, the most infuriating symbol of continuity with the outmoded literary past was Shiga Naoya. As we saw in the last chapter, Shiga was associated with the patrician White Birch school of writers who made their debut about 1910, and devoted himself as a writer to a minute analysis and re-analysis of his emotional life and psyche and of his relations with his father, his wife, and others close to him. There was no one else who continued to be so thoroughly naturalistic—and thus, according to his critics, so egoistical—in his approach to writing as Shiga, and when he had the temerity to express his distaste for the work of one of the darlings of the new age, Dazai Osamu, the latter insultingly denounced him: "A certain Literary Master feigns distaste for my writings. But what of this Literary Master's own writings? Do they presume to impart 'truth'? What do they claim to be?"[8]

Other famous writers who flourished once more in the postwar period were Tanizaki Junichirō and Kawabata Yasunari. Tanizaki had begun to publish *The Makioka Sisters* serially during the war but was forced to stop by the military authorities, and publication was completed after the war.

The Makioka Sisters is the story of the decline of a once affluent merchant house as revealed in the lives of four sisters after the death of their father, the head of the family. Perhaps Japan's finest modern novel, the book is exceptional because of its considerable length and its plot construction. Most Japanese novels are quite short and structurally loose; many so-called novels are really novellas. This appears to reflect, on the one hand, the native taste for the suggestive instead of the fully delineative—the "art of silence," as one authority[9] has put it—and, on the other hand, the classical tradition whereby the author of prose tended to write episodically and to devote much more care to the transitional elements or passages in a work than to its overall structure. The reader of *The Makioka Sisters* is drawn into a highly complex and detailed narrative of the interwoven lives of the sisters as they seek collectively to find a proper husband for one, to deal with the independent and headstrong ways of another, and above all to grapple with the vicissitudes that have so altered their lives since their father's death. Although Tanizaki informs us only in passing that the time is the advent of the China war in the late 1930s, the reader is absorbed with a powerful sense—intensified by his own knowledge of the coming of World War II—that he is witnessing the decline not only of a single family but of the entire way of life of prewar Japan.

This sense of decline is intense, for example, in the passage where Sachiko, the second sister and central figure in the novel, visits her elder sister as she is about to move out of the main family residence in Osaka. With the dwindling of the Makioka family business, the elder sister's husband—the titular head of the family—had returned to his former position in a bank. The bank has transferred him to Tokyo, and the Osaka house must be sold:

> The house was built in the old Osaka fashion. Inside the high garden walls, one came upon the latticed front of the house. An earthen passage led from the entrance through to the rear. In the rooms, lighted even at noon by but a dim light from the courtyard, hemlock pillars, rubbed to a fine polish, gave off a soft glow. Sachiko did not know how old the house was—possibly a generation or two. At first it must have been used as a villa to which elderly Makiokas might retire, or in which junior branches of the family might live. Not long before his death, Sachiko's father had moved his family there from Semba; it had become the fashion for merchant families to have residences away from their shops. The younger sisters had therefore not lived in the house long. They had often visited relatives there even when they were young, however, and it was there that their father had died. They were deeply attached to the old place. Sachiko sensed that much of her sister's love for Osaka was in fact love for the house, and, for all her amusement at these old-fashioned ways, she felt a twinge of pain herself—she would no longer be able to go back to the old family house. She had often enough joined Yukiko and Taeko in complaining about it—surely there was no darker and more unhygienic house in the world, and they could not understand what made their

sister live there, and they felt thoroughly depressed after no more than three days there, and so on—and yet a deep, indefinable sorrow came over Sachiko at the news. To lose the Osaka house would be to lose her very roots.[10]

The military authorities objected to *The Makioka Sisters* primarily because it was given over so completely to a portrayal of the private (i.e., selfish) affairs of a single family at a time of international crisis, when all citizens were expected to devote themselves wholeheartedly to the nation. Nevertheless the book, with its delicate handling of the nuances and shadings of human relations, was based on a venerable native tradition —the tradition of *mono no aware* (a sensitivity to things)—that dated back at least to the literature of the middle Heian period and such masterpieces as *Kokinshū*, *The Tales of Ise*, and *The Tale of Genji*. Tanizaki, who, as noted in the last chapter, became more and more absorbed from mid-life on with the Japanese past, translated *The Tale of Genji* into modern Japanese in the late 1930s, during the time when he began writing *The Makioka Sisters*. In many ways, *The Makioka Sisters is* a "tale of Genji" set in the present age.

One of Tanizaki's most extraordinary pieces of writing is the essay entitled *In Praise of Shadows*. Reminiscent of the fourteenth-century *Essays in Idleness* by Yoshida Kenkō, it is a miscellany of comments about the traditional tastes and ways of the Japanese as set against those of the modern West. The essay is full of nostalgia for the passing of these older tastes and ways; and so beautifully has Tanizaki pleaded for them that *In Praise of Shadows* has powerfully inspired contemporary architects and others not simply to preserve the past but to use it as a source for art in the present. The meaning of the essay's title is made clear in this passage on the special qualities of the traditional Japanese house:

A Japanese room might be likened to an inkwash painting, the paper-paneled shoji being the expanse where the ink is thinnest, and the alcove where it is darkest. Whenever I see the alcove of a tastefully built Japanese room, I marvel at our comprehension of the secrets of shadows, our sensitive use of shadow and light. For the beauty of the alcove is not the work of some clever device. An empty space is marked off with plain wood and plain walls, so that the light drawn into it forms dim shadows within emptiness. There is nothing more. And yet, when we gaze into the darkness that gathers behind the crossbeams, around the flower vase, beneath the shelves, though we know perfectly well it is mere shadow, we are overcome with the feeling that in this corner of the atmosphere there reigns complete and utter silence; that here in the darkness immutable tranquility holds sway. The "mysterious Orient" of which Westerners speak probably refers to the uncanny silence of these dark places. And even we as children would feel an inexpressible chill as we peered into the depths of an alcove to which the sunlight had never penetrated. Where lies the key to this mystery? Ultimately it is the magic of shadows. Were the shadows to be banished from its corners, the alcove would in that instant revert to mere void.

This was the genius of our ancestors, that by cutting off the light from this empty space they imparted to the world of shadows that formed there a quality of mystery and depth superior to that of any wall painting or ornament.[11]

Kawabata Yasunari expressed perhaps more poignantly than anyone the shattering despair felt by so many Japanese at war's end when he wrote: "I have the strong, unavoidable feeling that my life is already at an end. For me there is only the solitary return to the mountains and rivers of the past. From this point on, as one already dead, I intend to write only of the poor beauty of Japan, not a line else."[12] Even though he asserts that the defeat in war has driven him to it, Kawabata was by artistic temperament drawn to write about the "poor beauty of Japan," both the land and its people. In spite of his Neoperceptionist and modernist dabblings in the late 1920s and the 1930s, Kawabata is probably more Japanese in what is generally understood as the traditional sense than any other modern novelist. As we saw in the last chapter, he is often regarded as a writer of *haiku*-like prose who uses the spare, aesthetically polished language of poetry to sketch his settings and evoke his moods. One is, for example, always keenly aware in a Kawabata novel, as in the poetry by ancient courtier masters, of nature and the seasons, or more precisely, of the particular nature and seasons of Japan that have shaped the temperament of its people.

In 1968 Kawabata became the first Japanese recipient of the Nobel Prize in literature. In his acceptance speech, entitled "Japan the Beautiful and Myself" ("Utsukushii Nihon no Watakushi"), Kawabata dispelled any doubts there may have been about how thoroughly rooted and immersed his art was in the traditional culture of Japan. The speech is one of the finest and most moving paeans to Japanese culture ever composed. Although it deserves to be reproduced in full in a book of this kind, a few brief passages must suffice:

> *The Tale of Genji* in particular is the highest pinnacle of Japanese literature. Even down to our day there has not been a piece of fiction to compare with it. That such a modern work should have been written in the eleventh century is a miracle, and as a miracle the work is widely known abroad. Although my grasp of classical Japanese was uncertain, the Heian classics were my principal boyhood reading, and it is the *Genji*, I think, that has meant the most to me. For centuries after it was written, fascination with the *Genji* persisted, and imitations and reworkings did homage to it. The *Genji* was a wide and deep source of nourishment for poetry, of course, and for the fine arts and handicrafts as well, and even for landscape gardening.
>
> . . .
>
> In the Oriental word for landscape, literally "mountain-water," with its related implications in landscape painting and landscape gardening, there is contained the concept of the sere and wasted, and even of the sad and the threadbare. Yet in the sad, austere, autumnal qualities so valued by the tea

ceremony, itself summarized in the expression "gently respectful, cleanly quiet," there lies concealed a great richness of spirit; and the tea room, so rigidly confined and simple, contains boundless space and unlimited elegance.[13]

It is remarkable that, even as Japan was rising phoenix-like out of the ashes of war to scale almost unbelievable heights of economic success, Kawabata, its premier novelist, spoke rhapsodically to the world about another, exquisitely beautiful Japan—a Japan that might be too fragile to survive the profit-seeking, commercial exploitation, and physical and cultural pollution that helped make such success possible.

Kawabata's postwar work *The Sound of the Mountain* (*Yama no Oto,* 1949) illustrates the characteristically loose-flowing Japanese novel to which *The Makioka Sisters* stands in such contrast. To Kawabata, the natural world and life within it have their own ways of moving and functioning; the things that happen to us and around us are infinitely varied and ever changing, and any effort to impose too much rationality upon them is bound to fail and is in itself a false or dishonest act on the part of an artist. Such an attitude enabled Kawabata to exhibit a striking "sensitivity to things," and in the larger sense joined him to the aesthetic tradition of *mono no aware* that permeated the classical literature with which he, like Tanizaki, was so intimately familiar. But whereas Tanizaki had, in *The Makioka Sisters,* explored chiefly the intimacies of human relations, Kawabata in his writings also used *mono no aware* to deal with the subtle responses of people to the natural settings within which they lived.

An example of Kawabata's poetic handling of perceptions—like the linking of verses in a *renga* sequence—is the following passage from *The Sound of the Mountain:*

The moon was bright.

One of his daughter-in-law's dresses was hanging outside, unpleasantly gray. Perhaps she had forgotten to take in her laundry, or perhaps she had left a sweat-soaked garment to take the dew of night.

A screeching of insects came from the garden. There were locusts on the trunk of the cherry tree to the left. He had not known that locusts could make such a rasping sound; but locusts indeed they were.

He wondered if locusts might sometimes be troubled with nightmares.

A locust flew in and lit on the skirt of the mosquito net. It made no sound as he picked it up.

"A mute." It would not be one of the locusts he had heard at the tree.

Lest it fly back in, attracted by the light, he threw it with all his strength toward the top of the tree. He felt nothing against his hand as he released it.

Gripping the shutter, he looked toward the tree. He could not tell whether the locust had lodged there or flown on. There was a vast depth to the moonlit night, stretching far on either side.

Though August had only begun, autumn insects were already singing. He thought he could detect a dripping of dew from leaf to leaf.[14]

The perceiver in this scene is the main character of the novel, Shingo, a man in his sixties who is engulfed in the unhappiness of himself and those around him—a wife he has long ceased to love, a son who callously ignores his own wife for a mistress, and an embittered daughter just returned home from a disastrous marriage. In the midst of this turmoil of personal relationships, Shingo increasingly senses the specter of his own death. His forgetfulness, at first seemingly attributable to age, leads to a blurring of his awareness between consciousness and dreaming, between things that happened long ago and events as they unfold in the present.

To Kawabata the world is a whole and man and nature are one, and he brilliantly handles Shingo as a perceiver both of human relations and of nature and its phenomena. In mood, *The Sound of the Mountain* is very much part of what appears to be the enduring Japanese tradition of sad beauty that is also connoted by *mono no aware*.

A category of writing that inevitably made its appearance in the postwar period was that of books dealing with the war itself. Virtually without exception they were harshly critical of the war (indeed, all wars) and of Japan's military establishment that conducted it. Perhaps the most terrifyingly stark depiction of the collapse of the once triumphant Japanese Imperial Army is Ōoka Shōhei's *Fires on the Plain* (*Nobi*, 1952), the story of a soldier who is expelled from his unit in the last days of the campaign in the Philippines because the unit, far from having a capacity to continue fighting, no longer possesses even the means to attend to the barest needs of its members. Wandering through the forests of Leyte with only the vaguest hope of eventually reaching a place from which he can be evacuated, the soldier comes upon a deserted village where he finds the corpses of Japanese soldiers piled at the steps leading to a church and, without pausing to consider his act, murders a defenseless Filipino woman who has returned to the village with her lover in search of salt. Upon leaving the village, the soldier encounters other soldiers similarly separated from their units and hears ominous rumors that famine is so widespread within the Japanese army that some men have even resorted to cannibalism. Later he comes across a dying officer who, in a last stage of delirium, raises his arm and exclaims: "When I'm dead, you may eat this." The climax of the novel is reached when the soldier meets two former companions and partakes with them of "monkey meat." It is not long before the soldier has occasion to learn the true source of his food when he witnesses one of his companions on a "monkey"-hunting excursion:

> There was a bang in the distance.
> "He's got one!" shouted Yasuda.
> I rushed out and ran through the forest in the direction of the shot. Presently I reached a spot where the trees grew sparsely and from where I could see across the river bed. A human form was flying over its sun-drenched sur-

face! His hair was in disorder and he was barefoot. It was a Japanese soldier in a green uniform. And it was not Nagamatsu! Again there was the report of a gun. The bullet went wide of its apparent mark and the crouched figure continued running. He ran steadily along the river bed, now and then glancing back over his shoulder. Then, evidently confident that he was out of range, he gradually straightened his back and slowed down to a walking pace. Finally he disappeared into a clump of trees. Now I had seen one of the "monkeys."[15]

Whereas *Fires on the Plain* describes the degradation of the Japanese soldier in the field,[16] *Zone of Emptiness* (*Shinkū Chitai*, 1952) by Noma Hiroshi reveals a scarcely less extreme form of brutalization and degradation of the military man in camp at home. A young soldier, Kitani, has just returned from the prison stockade, where he has spent two years for the falsely alleged theft of a lieutenant's wallet. Japan's "holy war" has entered its final stage of deterioration and disillusionment, and men of all ranks are now engaged in a bestial struggle to secure rations and to avoid the certain death implicit in overseas assignment. But Kitani is fired only with the determination to avenge himself against those responsible for his conviction and unusually harsh sentence and to see once again the prostitute he loved, but who may also have betrayed him. As the true story of Kitani's case is gradually revealed, we are shown the horror-filled inner workings of a totally corrupt system of military life whose every official act is shrilly justified in terms of military reverence for, and selfless devotion to, emperor and nation. In the confessional words of his chief accuser, the lieutenant, whom Kitani finally tracks down:

The army is cruel. . . . There's nothing to keep me from saying it now. The army of the interior is rotten to the core, to the very core. When I was overseas, I used to hear it said that the army of the interior had preserved the old traditions of honor and dignity. . . . Unfortunately, when I returned I realized that this was completely untrue, that everything was worse than I could ever have imagined. At first, I did what I could, as an officer, to maintain standards. That's what caused my downfall. I loved the army with all my heart. It was impossible for me to tolerate the people who jeered at it and besmirched it, but then I found myself coming up against powerful obstacles, colonels, majors . . . the regiment . . . the division. . . . It's all a matter of pleasing your superiors. And not only the officers, but even, if I may say so, their families. . . . I once knew a quartermaster sergeant who was regarded as the most level-headed noncommissioned officer in the entire corps. . . . Well, his wife was unable to leave the house of the battalion head . . . because her presence was indispensable to her husband's advancement. . . . That kind of thing filled me with shame. . . . The supplies that are delivered go straight to the commanding officer, who uses them for making personal gifts. . . . You know Lieutenant Shimorai, don't you? He had a house built for himself, the one he now lives in. I was unable to put up with such corruption. I tried to do something about it, but I was beaten. It's too big a job for one man . . . I was kicked out. I got sick. I no longer count. Kitani . . . I thought that you had been bought by Lieutenant Nakabori. That was why I let you be brought up before the court-martial. When I realized the truth, it was too late.[17]

In *Zone of Emptiness* Noma, a leftist writer from prewar days and himself a veteran of the army, attempts once and for all to demolish the most sacred sustaining myths of emperor worship and the *kokutai* ideology.

A third book of major importance that deals with the war is Ibuse Masuji's *Black Rain (Kuroi Ame)*, an account of the dropping of the atomic bomb on Hiroshima. Based on actual records of the material destruction and human agony caused by the bomb, *Black Rain* is the story of many people, but especially of Shigematsu and his niece Yasuko. In a narrative consisting largely of diary accounts of Shigematsu and others, we meet the inhabitants of Hiroshima and its environs on the day of the bomb, observe their fate with horror at the moment of the bomb's detonation, and then join the survivors as they wander in bewilderment through the nightmarish labyrinth of a devastated city. The present of the novel is set several years after the war's end, and the tale of the bomb and its aftermath is recounted by Shigematsu essentially in the wish to set the record straight about Yasuko who, because of her exposure to the bomb's radiation, is unable to find a husband. In fact, Yasuko is seriously ill with radiation sickness, and the description of her suffering once the symptoms of the sickness become manifest is heartrending.

The semidocumentary material contained in this long book could easily have been presented in an exploitative and sensationalistic way; but the author has exercised considerable artistic restraint, and has thereby fashioned *Black Rain* into a devastatingly effective indictment of the evil futility of war. It should not be supposed, however, that *Black Rain* is all darkness and grief. There runs through it the theme, although it is sometimes only dimly perceivable, of hope and the will to survive. This is made symbolically explicit at the end when, as others listen indoors to the emperor's broadcast announcing surrender, Shigematsu wanders aimlessly around outside and, upon gazing into a stream, makes a surprising discovery:

> How had I never realized there was such an attractive stream so near at hand? In the water, I could see a procession of baby eels swimming blithely upstream against the current. It was remarkable to watch them: a myriad of tiny eels, still at the larval stage, none of them more than three or four inches in length.
> "On you go, on up the stream!" I said to them encouragingly. "You can smell fresh water, I'll be bound!" Still they came on unendingly, battling their way upstream in countless numbers. They must have swum all the way up from the lower reaches of the river at Hiroshima.[18]

Along with translated novels, film became one of the most important media for the transmission of Japanese culture to the West in the postwar period, which soon developed into a golden age of cinema.[19] The main impetus for this was the excellence in cinematic work already achieved in a remarkably short time by prewar Japanese filmmakers. The film industry was also able to expand its activities rapidly after the surrender because the facilities of the major studios—Shōchiku, Tōhō, and Daiei—had suffered no serious war damage and because SCAP adopted a policy of encouraging the reconstruction and building of movie theatres to provide entertainment for the people. At the same time, despite its generally liberating attitude toward freedom of speech and expression elsewhere, SCAP saw fit to impose a fairly wide-ranging censorship on the themes that could be treated in movies. Among those forbidden were nationalism, revenge, patriotism, the distortion of historical facts, racial or religious discrimination, feudal loyalty, suicide, the oppression of women and degradation of wives, antidemocratic attitudes, and anything that opposed the provisions of the Potsdam Declaration and the directives of SCAP.

In their efforts to live with the censorship—or, when possible, to circumvent it—Japanese producers and directors were forced to resort to stratagems and persuasive arguments. For example, in order to secure permission to make *Utamaro and His Five Women* (*Utamaro o Meguru Gonin no Onna,* 1946), its director, Mizoguchi Kenji (1898–1956), pointed out to SCAP that the late-Tokugawa-period woodblock artist Utamaro was not only a cultural hero to the common man in Japan, he was even a kind of prototype of a modern democrat! Mizoguchi also hinted that he would like to take up the theme of female emancipation in a subsequent film.[20]

Inundated by American culture, customs, and fads, Japanese filmmakers began experimenting with new practices and techniques of acting that, if not revolutionary, were at least attention-getting. One of the most widely heralded of these practices was the kiss, an act strictly banned from Japanese films before the war and even deleted from foreign imports. To the prewar Japanese the kiss had been "an act reserved solely for the privacy of the bedroom, if not indeed something of an occult art."[21] Even after the kiss became generally accepted, it was often faked by having the actors angle their heads away from the camera and merely touch cheeks. Some actors apparently even sought to avoid pollution while kissing by covering their mouths with gauze and applying an extra layer of makeup to conceal it.

Among the most popular postwar films, both in Japan and abroad, have been those of Kurosawa Akira (1910–98), including *Rashōmon* (1950), *Ikiru* (*To Live,* 1952), and *Seven Samurai* (*Shichinin no Samurai,* 1954). Kurosawa has been called the most Western of Japanese film directors, and it is true that in content his films, particularly those that are highly action-oriented (such as *Seven Samurai*) or deal with events by means of an Existentialist kind of psychological probing (such as *Rashō-mon*), are more readily and universally comprehensible than the films of many other Japanese directors. Yet Kurosawa, a consummate cinematic craftsman by any international standard, was also a master of those tech-niques—the creation of moods and settings that perfectly blend people and their natural environments, the meticulous attention to the details and textures of life and things—that are the stylistic glories of the Japa-nese film.

Based on a story by Akutagawa Ryūnosuke, *Rashōmon* recounts an incident set in ancient times involving a lord and his wife who, while journeying through a forest, are confronted and set upon by a bandit. At least two facts in the ensuing series of events are undisputed: the bandit violated the wife, and the husband was killed. Otherwise we are presented with a startling set of contradictory interpretations of what truly hap-pened, as the story is told and retold through the eyes of the wife, the bandit, the dead lord (speaking through a medium), and a woodcutter who chanced to witness the incident. Depending upon which version one believes, the husband was killed in a duel with the bandit to uphold his wife's honor, or he killed himself in mortification over the ravishment of his wife, or he was killed when incited to duel with the bandit by the wife after first seeking to disassociate himself from her behavior.

Seven Samurai, an action film of enormous vitality, tells the story of a group of *rōnin,* or masterless samurai, who are hired by a farming village in the sixteenth century to protect it against marauding bandits. It is one of the finest war films ever made, and as such it shows men in the most extreme circumstances faced with choices that must be irrevocably made —choices that openly, even brutally, call into question the most firmly held values and perceptions, however dimly sensed, relating to the mean-ings of their lives. Much of the humanism that forms the basis of the story is exemplified in the conduct in life and in death of the last samurai (really a peasant masquerading as a warrior), who is played in a grandly swash-buckling manner by Mifune Toshirō (1920–97), the quintessential Kuro-sawa hero. But *Seven Samurai* is much more than simply a war film. It is a visually and aesthetically magnificent work of art presented in a setting that, in the most venerable native tradition, reveals the eternal Japanese sensitivity to the flow of time, especially as experienced in the passage of the seasons, and to the finite quality of man *in* nature and not opposed to it. There could be no more eloquent statement of this sensitivity than the ending of the film when, after the bandits have been repulsed for good, the villagers must turn their attention to spring planting and the surviving samurai are obliged, after briefly paying their respects at the graves of their comrades, to move on. Thus they resume the status of *rōnin*—a status that implies social uncertainty and, once again, an absence of direction or meaning in life.

In *Ikiru* Kurosawa dealt, in a contemporary setting, with the crisis of a man who is informed that he is terminally ill with cancer. A petty bureaucrat nearing retirement, the man realizes that for years he has led a joyless and robotlike existence, his private life a void and his public vision restricted to his own worm's-eye view of the functioning of government. He determines to do one socially meaningful, good thing before he dies, and he thereupon embarks upon a campaign to bring about the construction of a small park after the petition for it by a group of neighborhood people has been interminably delayed and misdirected through a maze of bureaucratic offices, including his own. *Ikiru* is an uncompromising critique of officialdom and the world of bureaucratic inertia.

If Kurosawa is to be regarded as the most Western of Japanese film directors, then his polar opposite is Ozu Yasujirō (1903–63), the most Japanese of all directors. A leader in film since the prewar period, Ozu focused his attention almost entirely on the conflict between the traditional and the modern as seen through changing relationships in the Japanese family. The historical antecedents of films on the family (the *shomin-geki* discussed in the preceding chapter) were the domestic plays *(sewamono)* of the puppet and *kabuki* theatres of Tokugawa times and the I-novels of naturalist and other writers in the modern age. The classic dilemma that confronted the individual in the Tokugawa domestic play, it will be recalled, was between the demands of duty *(giri)* and the pull of human emotions *(ninjō)*. In the stylized plots of the period—for example, the prototypical story of the passion of a merchant, who is already married and has children, for a prostitute—the dilemma was characteristically resolved by double suicide *(shinjū)*. Social pressures after the war, of course, were much less severe, and double suicide was no longer common; but the domestic dilemma remained, with *giri* often taken to mean the demands of the traditional Japanese family and *ninjō* the pull of modern ways.

To understand why this should represent a specially Japanese, rather than universal, problem, we must note that there are few analogues to the Japanese family and the enormous importance it has held in Japanese society. It is simply a fact, as outsiders constantly observe, that the Japanese are overwhelmingly group-oriented: they work in groups; they play in groups; they seem happiest in groups. Such extraordinary feeling for collective behavior has its origins in the family, and any rejection of, or failure to conform to, the family raises for the Japanese the most serious questions about his role in society as a whole.

In Ozu's films, such as the powerful and moving *Tokyo Story* (*Tōkyō Monogatari*, 1953), the clash between the traditional and the modern is commonly portrayed in generational terms—that is, in the conflict between a traditional parent and an independent-minded modern child. But the social implications of such a clash are far greater in the Japanese setting than they would be in the Western. Whereas the Western child would most likely think of his parent merely as too conservative or old-fashioned, the Japanese youth is intensely conscious that the parent represents a traditional and still precisely understood pattern of conduct that continues to call all Japanese, to one degree or another, to account.

Ozu preferred scripts constructed less in narrative than in chronicle form, providing dialogues that are closer to the way people normally speak and scenes that are extremely natural in feeling (fig. 68). He also used almost exclusively a single camera shot taken from the eye level of a person seated on *tatami*. As Donald Richie observes, "This traditional view is the view in repose, commanding a very limited field of vision but commanding it entirely. It is the attitude for watching, not listening; it is the position from which one sees the Noh, from which one partakes of the tea ceremony."[22]

The message typically conveyed by an Ozu domestic or popular drama is that life (which is suffused with the same kind of sadness derived from the sense of *mono no aware* that we find in the novels of Kawabata) will go on pretty much as it has. Young people will still be drawn to the modern, and their elders will continue to find contentment, if not total solace, in the carefully defined world of tradition. Other directors, however, have by no means shared Ozu's timeless, almost fatalistic view of things. An important example is the work of Naruse Mikio, another established director from the prewar period, whose postwar films include *When a Woman Ascends the Stairs (Onna ga Kaidan o Agaru Toki,*

Fig. 68 Scene from *Tokyo Story*, directed by Ozu Yasujirō *(New Yorker Films)*

1960) and *Flowing (Nagareru)*. Naruse sees the traditional family-oriented ways as even more binding than Ozu implies and seems to doubt that few Japanese, if any, can fully escape them. In *When a Woman Ascends the Stairs*, the still young and attractive proprietress, or *mama-san*, of a walk-up bar in Tokyo's Ginza section accepts, in violation of her professional code, the advances of a patron and agrees to marry him. In fact, the man is already married, and when the woman meets his wife she realizes that, despite what she had regarded as her own modern and even liberated views, she cannot be responsible for the destruction of a family. In the end she once again ascends the stairs alone to her bar, resigned to resuming the role of a *mama-san* who banters with and flatters her patrons but does not get seriously involved with them.

The contemporary Japanese cinema is of such rich diversity that discussion of the films of a few directors, no matter how important they may be, obviously cannot cover the subject adequately. But, along with Ozu and Kurosawa, the greatest master of film has been Mizoguchi Kenji (1898–1956), director of the incomparably beautiful *Ugetsu* (*Ugetsu Monogatari*, 1953).[23] Viewed from different perspectives, Mizoguchi can be seen as the most romantically traditional of Japanese directors and also as an artist concerned with modern social issues. His traditional side was essentially aesthetic and was probably most fully revealed in his ability to create and sustain atmosphere, particularly in films of the past or some mythical age long ago, such as *Ugetsu,* the tale of a craftsman in the medieval age of civil wars who journeys to a city to sell his pottery and is drawn into an affair by a lovely patroness (fig. 69). In this atmospherically most perfect of films, much of the sense of wonder derives from our uncertainty about what is real and unreal. The craftsman discovers that his affair with the lovely patroness is part of an enchanted spell under which he has fallen; yet when he seeks to return home to his wife, he finds that she also no longer exists but has been dead for many years.

Mizoguchi's modern side is to be found mainly in his treatment of women, including the themes of the importance of their love to men and the fearful way in which they were victimized in traditional, feudal Japan. The latter theme is starkly drawn in *Sansho the Bailiff* (*Sanshō Dayū*, 1954), an overpoweringly tragic story of the wife, son, and daughter of a provincial official in ancient times who are kidnapped by outlaws and sold into slavery, the son and daughter to one group and the wife to another. Upon growing to manhood the son escapes, thanks to his sister, who sacrifices her life to delay his pursuers. The son soon becomes an important official himself, but he abandons his position in order to search for his mother. When he finally finds her, she is a blind old woman who has been used over the years as a prostitute and has even had the tendons of her legs cut to prevent her from running away.

Although in *Sansho the Bailiff* Mizoguchi introduced social criticism

Fig. 69   Scene from *Ugetsu*, directed by Mizoguchi Kenji *(Janus Films)*

into a historical setting, he remained—like his compeers Ozu and Kurosawa—strongly sentimental about the old Japan and its traditional ways.
Other directors, such as Kobayashi Masaki, have rejected what they
regard as this all too easy sentimentalism and have instead focused uncompromising attention on the cruelty and crushing inequities of traditional society. In *Harakiri* (*Seppuku*, 1962) Kobayashi presented the
story of a Tokugawa period *rōnin* who visits a domain to request suste-
nance and vows that he will disembowel himself if it is refused. Regarding the *rōnin* as a mere nuisance, officials of the domain summarily reject
his request and order him to make good his vow by performing *harakiri*
in their presence. As he prepares for the grim ceremony, the *rōnin* speaks
to the officials about another masterless samurai who had called upon
them a short while before with a request identical to his and who had
been forced to perform *harakiri* with a bamboo sword, the only weapon
he carried. The *rōnin* reveals that the earlier samurai was his son, who
had been driven in desperation to come to the domain to obtain food for
his starving wife and child. Informing his captors that he has already
taken the topknots (the symbols of samurai manhood) of three of their
fellow officials who were responsible for his son's death, the *rōnin* seizes
his sword and, in classic *chambara* style, kills a number of the enemy
before he is finally destroyed.

Along with other filmmakers of the postwar period, Kobayashi also directed severe criticism against modern Japanese society. His most ambitious undertaking, for example, was the three-part drama of the horrors of Japan's participation in World War II—the setting is Manchuria—entitled *The Human Condition* (*Ningen no Jōken,* 1958–61). In an interview with the American critic Joan Mellen, Kobayashi said that he regarded *Harakiri* and *The Human Condition* as similar in theme insofar as they both deal with the "tenacious human resilience" of individuals under the authoritarian pressures of society.[24]

Other branches of the performing arts, including the modern theatre *(shingeki)* and *kabuki,* also flourished after the war, though on admittedly much smaller scales and not before overcoming their own particular postwar traumas.

The basis of *shingeki* since its inception has been the theatrical company rather than the independent producer as in American theatre. During the war there was only one active company—the Literary Theatre *(Bungakuza)*—and the number of theatre houses accessible to it was severely reduced by bombing raids. Peace brought a feeling of theatrical revolution within *shingeki* as part of the general hope that accompanied the end of the war.

But the most fundamental difficulties confronting *shingeki* in the postwar period were the same that had always bedeviled it. Foremost was the fact that the very word for theatre—*engeki*—overwhelmingly connoted to the Japanese a presentational rather than representational kind of performing art. Specifically, it meant *kabuki,* and the *shingeki* people had been obliged from the first to try to distinguish theirs as a "new" or "modern" theatre. Even as *shingeki* struggled to establish its own acting and theatrical traditions, it was upstaged by a rapidly rising film industry, which was able to advance just a step behind the cinema in the West to become a truly modern, realistic theatre of representation in its own right. Still another difficulty encountered by *shingeki* in its early stages of development was the deep rift that arose between those who wished to keep it an exclusively literary or theatrical medium and those who aspired to transform it into an ideological *(kannen-teki)* form of theatre. This led, as we have noticed, to the dominance in *shingeki* of proletarian writers in the late 1920s and the 1930s and to its suppression by the military authorities. Once again, in the postwar period, political ideology became a source of contention within *shingeki.*

If *shingeki*'s difficulties remained the same after the war, some of its attempted solutions also evoked a familiar feeling. One of the means by which *shingeki* sought to deal with poor attendance figures, for example, was to stage Western plays in translation, including Shakespeare's *A Midsummer Night's Dream, Romeo and Juliet,* and *Hamlet.* Among contemporary works, Tennessee Williams's *A Streetcar Named Desire* and Arthur

Miller's *Death of a Salesman* (the latter produced by a left-wing theatrical company) enjoyed successful runs. But foreign plays could in the long run contribute little to the advancement of a native theatre, and the relative prosperity *shingeki* has had since the war is attributable also to the original work of Japanese playwrights. Of particular interest has been the writing of plays for *shingeki* by well-known novelists, most notably Mishima Yukio (1925–70) and Abe Kōbō (1924–93).

Mishima, who had strong neoclassical tastes, is perhaps best remembered as a playwright for his use of both the Japanese and Western pasts. Among his writings are modern *nō* plays, several *kabuki* pieces, and works drawn from Western history, such as *Madame de Sade* (1965), which is set at the time of the French Revolution. Abe, on the other hand, devoted himself to avant-garde, experimental theatre, as we can see in such plays as *Friends* (1967) and *The Man Who Turned into a Stick* (1969). But even though Mishima and Abe may differ in the periods— past and present—they chose to explore, they both significantly advanced Japanese theatre by avoiding the pitfalls of earlier, prewar playwrights, who tried to create modern Japanese plays essentially by incorporating into them elements from the realistic tradition of theatre in the west.[25] The plays of Mishima and Abe are original works, free from the constraints of realism, that have served to inspire other playwrights to press forward in the development of a truly modern Japanese theatre.

Kabuki faced a situation and prospects quite different from those of *shingeki* in the postwar period. In its origins, of course, *kabuki* was a bourgeois theatre that the Tokugawa authorities at first had barely tolerated. Yet by modern times *kabuki* had unchallengeably become the main theatre of Japan. Although its low beginning may never have been entirely forgotten, part of its repertory was also viewed as a repository of traditional morality and the feudalistic values of the premodern samurai class. It was for this reason that the military authorities generally favored it during the war[26] and for the very same reason that SCAP cast such a jaundiced eye upon *kabuki* after the war and strictly forebade the performance of "feudalistic" works, such as *Chūshingura* (Treasury of Loyal Retainers), the perennially popular dramatization of the vendetta carried out by forty-seven *rōnin* in the early eighteenth century. But by about 1947 the SCAP-imposed restrictions on *kabuki* were relaxed, and it promptly began to enjoy a brisk revival. Today, *kabuki* enjoys enormous favor and at least one of its actors, Bandō Tamasaburo, is a popular star of the magnitude of a leading rock-and-roll musician.

One of the arts that perforce drew much attention in the postwar period, owing to the destructiveness of the war itself, was architecture. Many of Japan's largest cities, including Tokyo, had been devastated by Allied high-explosive and incendiary bombing raids, and there was a desperate need for new buildings of all kinds. But because of the relatively low priority given by SCAP to the physical reconstruction of Japanese cities and the gap between any drawing up and implementation of large-scale architectural projects, the postwar building boom in Japan did not begin until the early 1950s. To understand the directions then taken in building, it will be helpful to review briefly the general course of architectural development during the preceding century.

Traditional Japanese architecture was based almost entirely on the use of wood in construction. The advent of Western influences about the time of the Meiji Restoration brought a sweeping technological revolution in architecture through the introduction of an array of new building materials, including cement, steel, and bricks. By the beginning of the twentieth century, as modern capitalist industries began to achieve significant growth in Japan, techniques of reinforced-concrete construction were also widely applied in the erection in Tokyo and other great cities of large plant- and office-type buildings.

The earliest Western-style buildings erected during the Meiji period —in a conglomeration of modes, including Gothic, Renaissance, and Baroque—were actually designed by foreign architects, such as the Englishman Josiah Condor, who arrived in Japan in 1877. Among the buildings done by Condor were the National Museum at Ueno Park and the Rokumeikan (Deer Cry Mansion) which, as noted in Chapter 9, became a symbol of what many regarded as the over-Westernization of Japan in the late nineteenth century. Condor taught at the Tokyo Technical College (which later became the Department of Architecture at Tokyo University) and greatly influenced many of the young Japanese architects who rose to prominence in the late Meiji period. But, as one scholar has put it, the Japanese architects of this age used "only the techniques and external forms of the industrial civilization of the West, without understanding its spiritual background. Consequently it was quite natural that they placed more stress on the engineering side in adopting Occidental customs."[27] In addition, the engineering side of architecture was also stressed because of the importance attached by the Japanese government to structural design for the purpose of protection against earthquakes.

It was not until the second decade of the twentieth century—at the same time as the modernist movement in Western architecture commenced—that Japanese architects began to display a more sophisticated and discerning attitude toward the problems and potentialities of modern building construction. Stimulated by the ideas of Walter Gropius, Le Corbusier, and others from the West, they were given new opportunities through increased building demand resulting from the economic boom that, as noted in the preceding chapter, Japan enjoyed when the European powers withdrew from competition for Far Eastern markets during World War I. Among the questions Japanese architects began to grapple with in this period were the relationship between function and decoration (functionalism was then much in vogue in Europe), how materials should be used to accent or enhance their special qualities, and how architecture could best be directed toward humanistic rather than dehumanizing ends. Probably the most important issue approached by Japanese architects during the period of World War I and its aftermath was how Japan's traditional tastes in building could be combined with the modern architectural values of the West. Among the most obvious of these traditional tastes were: the natural use of materials, such as unpainted wood and rough, earthen-type walls; the handling of space—essentially by means of thin, adjustable partitioning—to create a sense of continuity or flow between one part of the interior of a building and another and even between interior and exterior; and an emphasis on geometrically arranged straight lines in design, deriving mainly from retention of the ancient post-and-beam style of construction. All of these qualities are perfectly represented in that most flawless of traditional Japanese architectural masterpieces, the Tokugawa-period Katsura Detached Palace in Kyoto. Yet the modern Japanese themselves remained almost totally oblivious to Katsura's virtues until prodded into reflecting upon them in the 1930s by an expatriate from Nazi Germany, Bruno Taut (1880–1938).

Shortly after Taut's arrival in Japan in 1933, a Japanese architectural authority noted, "Fifty years ago Europeans came and told us, 'Nikkō is the most valuable,' and we thought so too; now Bruno Taut has come and told us, 'It is Ise and Katsura which are the most valuable,' and again we believe."[28] In a speech in 1936 to the Society for International Cultural Relations (Kokusai Bunka Shinkōkai) in Tokyo, Taut had this to say about the Ise Shrine:

> Everything in Ise is artistic, nothing is artificial. There are no peculiarities: the natural wood is faultless and marvellously polished, and the straw roof is equally perfect in its gorgeous curve, without the upcurve of the ridge or of the eaves. Equally flawless is the joining of the wood with the stone of the foundations, and there is no ornament which is not integral to the architectonic character. The golden globules on the cross-beams under the ridge join the harmony of straw and *hinoki* [cypress] wood, and the white papers and green branches of the Shinto sect are unsurpassably in accord with the whole.[29]

Taut went on to observe that, though the "Japanese pretend that the atmosphere of age exerts a particular fascination on them," it is the eternal newness and freshness of the Ise Shrine that impresses him as being most fundamentally Japanese. Of the Katsura Detached Palace, he said:

> . . . only at Katsura does there exist that overwhelming freedom of intellect which does not subordinate any element of the structure or the garden to some rigid system. At Nikkō, as in many architectural attractions of the world,

the effect is gained by quantity—about in the same way that an army of two hundred thousand is larger than one of twenty thousand. At Katsura, on the contrary, each element remains a free individual, much like a member of a good society in which harmony arises from absence of coercion so that everyone may express himself according to his individual nature. Thus the Katsura Palace is a completely isolated miracle in the civilized world. One must speak of its "eternal beauty," which admonishes us to create in the same spirit much more than is the case with the Parthenon, with the Gothic Cathedral or with the Ise Shrine. That which is peculiar to Japan, the local, is insignificant; but the principle is absolutely modern and of complete validity for any contemporary architecture.[30]

For Taut, "Japan's architectural arts could not rise higher than Katsura, nor sink lower than Nikkō."

One of the great events in the history of modern architecture in Japan was the construction of the Imperial Hotel in central Tokyo by Frank Lloyd Wright (1867–1959) between 1919 and 1922. Wright, who had visited Japan as early as 1905, was a keen admirer of East Asian art, acquiring Buddhist statuary and an extensive collection of Japanese woodblock prints from the Edo period. Among the most daring innovators in modern architecture, he forcefully advocated an "organic" approach to design and construction, by which he meant that the architect should not only seek to achieve unity and harmony in the functional features of a building but also allow it—whether home, office building, or hotel—to emerge organically within its particular setting and social context. Facing on Hibiya Park, not far from the emperor's palace, the Imperial Hotel was a low, rambling structure made of reinforced concrete with a brick-encrusted and heavily decorated exterior (fig. 70). In the interior, Wright made dramatic use of space, raising and lowering ceiling height. Determined to achieve total unity of structural planning and decoration, he even went so far as to design personally the contents of the guest rooms, including beds, chairs, tables, and wall hangings. To the undying dismay of its many admirers, Wright's original Imperial Hotel, having survived both the 1923 Tokyo earthquake and the bombing raids of World War II, was demolished in the late 1960s to make way for the present multistory New Imperial Hotel. But the old structure remains vivid in historical memory, not only for its intrinsic qualities as an architectural masterpiece but also as a direct statement to the Japanese by one of the most powerfully individualistic Western artists of the early twentieth century.

One of the most interesting aspects of Wright's impact on Japanese architecture after World War I was that in part it was a kind of feeding back of influences Wright had himself received earlier from the Japanese. Westerners had displayed interest in Japanese architecture, especially the traditional house, since at least the 1870s. The American

Fig. 70   Old Imperial Hotel in Tokyo, designed by Frank Lloyd Wright

Edward Morse (1838–1925), known for his discovery of prehistoric
Jōmon remains at Ōmori in the outskirts of Tokyo, made a detailed study
of Japanese domestic architecture about this time, and in 1885 published
Japanese Homes and Their Surroundings, a text that over the years has
gone through many printings. Styles of Japanese architecture were also
introduced at fairs and exhibitions in the late nineteenth century, most
notably in the display prepared for the World's Columbian Exposition at
Chicago in 1892, which commemorated the four hundredth anniversary
of the discovery of America. Designed and constructed by the Japanese
themselves, the Chicago display was modeled loosely on the Phoenix
Hall of the eleventh-century Byōdōin Temple at Uji. The original Phoenix Hall consists of a central hall with galleries extending like wings to
the right and left (and terminating in open pavilions) and like a bird's
body and tail to the rear. At Chicago the rear gallery was eliminated and
the pavilions were enclosed. This created an arrangement of three linked
structures of extremely graceful design, situated on raised platform floors
and covered with gently sloping and deeply recessed tile roofs. The interior of each structure was designed and decorated to represent a different
period of domestic styling in Japanese history: Fujiwara, Ashikaga, and
Tokugawa.

The Japanese display at the 1892 World's Columbian Exposition,
called the Phoenix Villa, was particularly striking in contrast to the oppressively heavy type of architecture adopted for the general exhibition
halls, which were "cast in the pure classic, or Neo-classic style, employ-

ing the familiar design vocabulary of columns, entablatures, arches, vaults and domes, the group unified by a gigantic architectural order sixty feet in height."[31] Although architects throughout the country visited and were impressed by the Phoenix Villa, it was the Chicago School, including Frank Lloyd Wright, that benefited most from study of this excellent, near-at-hand model of Japanese structure and design, which was presented to the city of Chicago and preserved until 1946. Wright expressed his enthusiasm for traditional Japanese architecture in the following words:

> I saw the native home in Japan as a supreme study in elimination—not only of dirt but the elimination of the insignificant. So the Japanese house naturally fascinated me and I would spend hours taking it all to pieces and putting it together again. I saw nothing meaningless in the Japanese home and could find very little added in the way of ornament [the equivalent of ornament being achieved] by bringing out and polishing the beauty of the simple materials they used in making the building . . . and strangely enough, I found this ancient Japanese dwelling to be a perfect example of the modern standardizing I had myself been working out. The floor mats, removable for cleaning, are all three feet by six feet. The size and shape of all the houses are both determined by these mats. The sliding partitions all occur at the unit lines of the mats [and the] polished wooden posts . . . all stand at the intersection of the mats.[32]

Despite the example of Wright and the promise of more independence and even innovation of approach inherent in the new sentiments of Japanese architects, the 1920s and 1930s witnessed a general continuation of the earlier reliance upon, and imitation of, Western architectural trends.[33] For example, rather than attempt in the best traditional manner—and with the encouragement of Taut—to allow structure to determine design (as in the classical straight-line patterning of buildings, such as Katsura, based on post-and-beam construction), they succumbed to the Western use of massive walls that obliterated all structural features. It is true that, with the approach of the China and Pacific wars, the emergent military leaders of Japan sought to promote the development of a "national style" in modern architecture, but this tended to be an effort more to excise Western elements from Japanese buildings than to encourage the pursuit of new and progressive native lines of development.

Whereas before World War II the Japanese had been influenced chiefly by European architectural styles, after the war the main foreign influence was, probably unavoidably, American. One result of this trend was that, while such countries as England, France, and Germany placed great emphasis on city planning in the rebuilding of their war-torn cities, the Japanese—in the absence of a significant American interest in it—devoted little attention to overall planning once postwar rebuilding had begun in earnest during the early 1950s.[34]

To the general neglect of housing needs, highest priority in the early part of the postwar building boom in Japan was given—especially in the largest cities—to the construction of office space. Also under American influence, the Japanese sought to equip their new office-type and other buildings with the most advanced facilities and amenities, including extensive fluorescent lighting and air conditioning. In addition, both in commercial and industrial construction and in later home building, they tried where possible to use fireproof materials to modify the traditional tinderbox character of cities like Tokyo.

The Japanese had always lived in small wooden homes, usually incapable of accommodating more than one or two families. Hence the construction of multistory concrete apartment buildings in the postwar period constituted a truly revolutionary development in living style for many urban dwellers in Japan. Although even these more modern apartment homes are exceedingly modest by American standards, the Japanese viewed them as first steps toward achievement of what they perceived as a kind of earthly utopia of informal and leisurely living derived from the model provided by the United States.

As part of the postwar building boom, architects experienced a renewal of both self-confidence and pride as Japanese building styles and aesthetic values began truly to attract international attention. One of the leaders in this postwar renewal was Maekawa Kunio, a former student of Le Corbusier and his Cubist-inspired emphasis on geometric forms in architectural design. Among Maekawa's postwar buildings are the main branch of the Japan Mutual Financing Bank (Nihon Sōgo Ginkō, 1952) in Tokyo and the Tokyo International House (Kokusai Bunka Kaikan, 1955), both of which were awarded the annual prize of the Japan Architectural Academy.[35] But the greatest fame in Japan's postwar world of architecture has gone to Tange Kenzō, who began winning prizes in architectural competitions during the war and later was for a time associated with Maekawa. Tange's triumphs include the Hall Dedicated to Peace (Heiwa-ki Kaikan) at Hiroshima and the main Sports Arena for the 1964 Tokyo Olympics (figs. 71–72). In the same way that the 1964 Olympics symbolized for many Japanese the true end of the postwar period and Japan's resumption of international status and dignity, the Sports Arena represents an important milestone in the country's modern architectural history. Far from requiring further tutelage and inspiration from the West, the Japanese now stand among the leaders in international architecture, and architecture has become an aspect of Japanese culture that has exerted great influence on the world outside Japan.

It is often said that postwar Japan evolved into a one-and-a-half-party system. This means that for decades national power was held uninterruptedly by the conservative camp of politicians, who in 1955 merged to form the Liberal-Democratic Party (LDP), and whose opponents in the

Fig. 71   Hiroshima Peace Park *(Japan National Tourist Organization)*

Fig. 72   Swimming Arena for the 1964 Tokyo Olympics, designed by Tange Kenzō *(Consulate General of Japan, New York)*

left-wing, or progressive, camp (led by the Socialist Party) were during the same period consistently held to a minority—and thus a permanently out-of-power—status with no more than one-third of the seats in the Diet.

As the seemingly permanent rulers of the country, the Liberal-Democratic Party pursued policies of economic development and intimate alignment with the United States based on a Mutual Security Pact that made the former conqueror responsible for Japan's national defense. The pact, originally signed in 1950, was a great boon to Japan in enabling it, unlike other major countries, to limit military spending to a small fraction of its national income. At the same time, the pact at times aroused intense hostility among some Japanese and even symbolized the love-hate feelings of Japan for the United States, which derive from the special kind of relationship that evolved between the two countries after the war.

An event that was important in restoring some semblance of equality or at least partnership in relations between the United States and Japan was the rioting in Tokyo in 1960 over renewal of the Mutual Security Pact and the consequent cancellation of President Eisenhower's planned visit to Japan. The leftist-inspired rioting occurred against a confused background of Cold War tensions (including the fear that Japan, with American troops still stationed on its soil, might be the first target of the Soviets in a nuclear war with the United States), resentment against the high-handed tactics of Prime Minister Kishi Nobusuke (1896–1987) in seeking renewal of the pact, and an ambivalent kind of anti-Americanism. For the left wing in Japan, the United States was the principal threat to international peace. A staunch supporter of the conservatives, who were in power, the United States even advocated amendment of the American-imposed 1947 Constitution to eliminate the antiwar article and enable Japan to enter more actively into military association with it. But among the great majority of the Japanese people the United States was probably viewed in 1960 in various, sometimes conflicting ways: as a former enemy, as a humane and beneficent occupier, as an invaluable trading partner, and as a military colossus within the gates of East Asia.

Although Eisenhower was prevented from visiting Japan and Kishi was forced out of office, the Mutual Security Pact was renewed for another ten years and the left-wing opposition was badly fragmented by internal disputes after the rioting. It is therefore debatable who won the victory in 1960. At least one significant result of the incident was a stirring, for the first time in the postwar period, of Japanese nationalism. After a decade and a half of political passivity caused by feelings of guilt and humiliation over the war, action had been taken—whether or not it was fully supported by all of the Japanese people—on a truly national issue, and the United States as Big Brother had been at least partly rebuffed.

This is not to suggest that 1960 marked the charting of a new course for Japan or the definition of a new national purpose. Japan was on the threshold of its decade of greatest material fulfillment, a decade that propelled its gross national product to third highest in the world. What started as a "leisure boom" attained the level of an almost undreamed of prosperity, measured in terms of washing machines, television sets, motor cars, and overseas travel. At the same time, the Japanese were afflicted by those apparent inevitabilities of progress: urban sprawl, pollution, and the psychological tensions and social malaise of the modern condition.

Japan had become a society of mass culture *(taishū bunka)* by at least the late 1920s. Newspapers, books, and magazines had achieved huge circulations; people flocked to department stores and to the movies and theatres; and radio broadcasts were reaching into households throughout the country.[36] Goods of all kinds were being produced, and advertising and marketing were geared to stimulate desire for them and encourage mass consumption. A decade or so later Japan, like other participants in World War II, used the tools of mass culture to promote its aims in what can perhaps be called the first "mass-culture war."

But mass culture as a medium to foster the production of consumer goods declined precipitously during the war. Having chosen to fight a country (the United States) whose economy was some ten times greater than its own,[37] Japan was forced to direct virtually all its wealth and resources into the war effort. By war's end, as we have seen, the Japanese people suffered dire shortages of food, clothing, and the other basic necessities of everyday life. In that sense, mass culture had ground nearly to a halt.

As mass culture gradually revived in the postwar period, it was accompanied by a substantial "Americanization" of life—at least at the popular level—because of the pervasive influence of the United States upon Japan both during and after the Occupation. By about 1955 the Japanese government, having met the basic needs of the people, was able to set new goals in the production of goods for mass consumption, and thereupon embarked upon what became known as Japan's "economic miracle." Year after seemingly endless year Japan scored remarkable increases in gross national product. The stages through which this miracle came to satisfy the desires of Japan's consumers were neatly categorized by the coining of a series of slogans that punned irreverently on the imperial regalia or "three sacred treasures" of emperorship (mirror, sword, and jewel). Thus, during the late 1950s the Japanese people sought to acquire the three S's of *senpūki, sentaku,* and *suihanki* (electric fan, washing machine, and electric rice cooker); during the 1960s it was the three C's of *kaa, kura,* and *kara terebi* (car, air conditioner, and color television); and by the 1970s everyone wanted the three J's of *jueru, jetto,* and *jūtaku* (jewels, overseas vacation, and house).[38] The period of phenomenal economic growth finally came to an end in the 1980s, by which time the Japanese populace had largely obtained all the basic material treasures of a mass-culture society.

The spread of mass culture tends to standardize tastes and reduce class distinctions. The Japanese, with their collectivist ethos, are probably more susceptible than most people to such standardization and to at least the perception that in recent years class distinctions have been substantially reduced. Thus polls indicate that an unusually high number of Japanese—90 percent or more—regard themselves as middle class. If, in fact, contemporary Japanese society has become to a high degree homogenized as "middle class," the homogenization has been due, among other things, to a uniform, nationwide educational curriculum; nearly universal literacy; close to 100 percent ownership of color television sets; and the largest per capita circulation of newspapers in the world.[39] Always one of the world's most ethnically homogeneous people, the Japanese may also have become one of its most homogeneous socially and culturally.

A major phenomenon in postwar Japan has been the spectacular rise in the so-called new religions *(shinkō shūkyō)*. Although loosely categorized as new, many of the most important of these religions were founded before the war, some as early as the mid-nineteenth century. But by far the greatest proliferation of the new religions occurred in the period following World War II. By the end of the Occupation in 1952, for example, their number was estimated at more than seven hundred, a figure that prompted one Western scholar to refer to the immediate postwar years as a time of the "rush hour of the gods."[40]

Despite the diversity of the new religions, they share certain general characteristics. For example, they have tended to spring up during times of intense crisis or social unrest, such as the early Meiji and post-World War II periods; their founders have typically been charismatic figures who have served as vehicles for the revelation of religious truth; they are highly syncretic, often partaking freely of Shinto and Buddhism, as well as Christianity;[41] and they are millenarian in that they characteristically promise the advent of a paradise on earth. Also the new religions have always appealed chiefly to people lower on the social and economic scales: to those who have in some sense been left behind in the march of modern progress.

What makes the new religions most fascinating within the larger context of Japanese cultural history is the degree to which they reflect fundamental religious values and attitudes that have been held since ancient times. This can be seen perhaps most tellingly in the kinds of charismatic figures who have founded new religions, the most interesting of which are the female shamanistic types. Shamanism, as we observed in Chapter 1, derives from northeast Asia and exerted enormous influence on early Japanese religion. It centers on belief in the transmission of a deity's will through a human intermediary, or shaman. This form of divine transmission, known in Japanese as *kami* possession *(kami gakari)*, is vividly described in classical works of literature such as *The Tale of Genji* and entails a process whereby, in the face of personal affliction or natural calamity, the deity believed to be responsible is invited to enter the body of a medium, usually a girl or woman. Once the deity possesses her, the medium enters into an ecstatic, sometimes frenzied state and a voice, clearly not her own, speaks forth to indicate what must be done to placate the aroused deity.

An excellent example of a modern shaman of this sort is Nakayama Miki (1798–1887), founder of Tenrikyō, one of the earliest and most successful of the new religions. A woman of peasant origins (as so many of the founders have been), Nakayama underwent much suffering and experienced personal tragedy in her early life: the famines of the late Tokugawa period, an unhappy marriage, illness and death of her children. Then, in 1838, while serving as the medium for ministration to the leg pains of one of her sons, she was seized by a deity who proclaimed through her mouth that he was "the true and the original god who has descended from Heaven to save all mankind."[42] The deity demanded that Nakayama's body thenceforth be made available to him.

In addition to becoming the instrument for transmission of divine revelations by the "true and original god," Nakayama developed extraordinary powers to heal, and thus entered the tradition of faith healing that has been a powerful and recurrent feature of Japanese folk religion throughout history.

Faith healing, as stressed in Tenrikyō and other new religions, is simply one of a number of concrete promises of personal happiness, material furfillment, and even entry into an earthly paradise that constitute the millenarian aspect of those religions. It is also in this millenarianism that the new religions, otherwise so much within the mainstream of the little tradition of folk religion in Japan, reveal themselves to be products of the modern age. Earlier utopian thinking in Japan about life in this world focused almost invariably on the recapturing or restoration of a golden age, and thus implicitly rejected existing conditions.[43] But the new religions not only do not reject the modern world, they boast that their followers will joyously attain the highest rewards that this world offers. To dramatize this promise, the more affluent of the new religions have constructed lavish national centers—equipped with the most modern luxuries and conveniences—to serve as meccas for visits and pilgrimages of the faithful and to enable them to sample the paradisiacal sweets conjured by their religions. Yet, as Carmen Blacker observes, even in the building of such meccas there is a harking back to the traditional—in this case, an attempt to "impose on the present world a kind of mythical or eschatological geography,"⁴⁴ much like, for example, the representation of the Pure Land Buddhist paradise in the Phoenix Hall and garden of the eleventh-century Byōdōin at Uji.

The most important of the new religions—and one of the most startling religious, social, and political phenomena in postwar Japan—is Sōka Gakkai, the Value Creation Society. Founded in the early 1930s for the purpose of religious education, Sōka Gakkai is a modern outgrowth of a branch of Nichiren Buddhism. In contrast to most of the new religions, which are highly syncretic, it shares the exclusivism and intolerance of other religious sects that have always been the hallmarks of Nichiren Buddhism.

Sōka Gakkai achieved only minor success in prewar days and was even disbanded when its leaders were jailed during the war because of their refusal to show reverence to state Shinto. But after the war, under the dynamic if not fanatical leadership of Toda Josei (1900–1958), the society enjoyed a phenomenal expansion. Employing such strong-arm, browbeating methods of proselytizing as *shakubuku* (breaking and subduing) and seeking to recruit not merely individuals but entire families, Sōka Gakkai claimed a membership by the early 1960s of ten million. In addition, through its political arm, Kōmeitō (Clean Government Party), Sōka Gakkai went to the polls and established itself as the third largest force in the upper house of the Japanese Diet.

Sōka Gakkai is in many ways a model for realization of the expectations that have been aroused by the new religions in postwar Japan. Although intellectuals may shun it and some people may denounce it as neofascist, Sōka Gakkai is one of the greatest mass movements in Japanese history. Along with its vast following, it possesses enormous material opulence, observable in its sumptuous center at the foot of Mount Fuji, which drew more than two million people to its opening in 1958. The attractions of Sōka Gakkai are many. For one thing, it offers people the opportunity to belong to a great and flourishing movement, an opportunity that appealed with particular force to the Japanese in the wake of the widespread social disorientation caused by defeat in war. Sōka Gakkai makes extravagant claims for its power to induce healing through faith, and even boasts that it can prevent illness. Not content with the slogan "Join us and you won't become sick," the society has gone so far as to threaten, "If you don't join us, you will be sure to *get* sick."⁴⁵

If the resurgence of the new religions since the war has directed additional attention to the extraordinary group instincts and group orientation of the Japanese, there has also been much consideration given during the same period to the matter of individualism in a Japan liberated from the anti-individualistic fetters of the *kokutai* ideology. This is probably most conspicuous in the writings of such authors as Mishima Yukio, Abe

Kōbō, and Ōe Kenzaburō (1935–   ), who have subjected the individual to the most intense psychological scrutiny, observing his unlimited potentiality for erratic, perverse, and bizarre behavior and his often desperate struggle against the dictates of social conformity.

Mishima, who committed suicide by disembowelment in 1970 at the age of forty-five, was one of the most fascinating individuals—at least to foreigners—in recent Japanese history.[46] A small and sickly youth of upper middle-class stock (his father was a moderately successful bureaucrat), Mishima had a most unwholesome childhood under the fanatically possessive domination of his grandmother, with whom he lived and in whose bed he slept until age twelve. Quite likely this early experience nourished the homosexuality that became so central not only to his later social behavior but also to his artistic vision.

Mishima attended the lustrous Peers School in Tokyo, where he achieved an outstanding academic record and even received an award from the hand of the emperor for graduating at the head of his class in 1944. He showed considerable precocity in writing, and although, at the urging of his father, he attended Tokyo University Law School and began a career in the Finance Ministry in 1947, he soon abandoned this to become a full-time author. In 1949 he vaulted into fame with the publication of an extraordinary, painfully revealing autobiographical novel entitled *Confessions of a Mask (Kamen no Kokuhaku)*.

One of Mishima's purposes in writing *Confessions of a Mask* was to debunk the I-novelists, many of whom he believed merely chronicled in excruciating detail the dullness of their lives without ever really probing into the dark inner realms of human psychology. Whether or not the I-novelists as a group were, in fact, guilty of not telling the ultimate truth about themselves or getting to the roots of their existences, Mishima himself certainly revealed enough in *Confessions of a Mask* about his own emotional essence to explain the main course of his life and even his manner of death.

The Mishima we see in *Confessions of a Mask* is a narcissistic young man powerfully attracted from an early age to such things as the sight of a night soil man dressed in close-fitting thigh-pullers, the odor of sweat emanating from soldiers, and the "black thickets" in masculine armpits. But far more importantly, these homosexual cravings were associated with an aesthetic of blood and death.[47] This fact is startlingly impressed upon us in the famous passage from *Confessions of a Mask* wherein Mishima reveals that he had his first ejaculation upon viewing a reproduction of Guido Reni's painting of Saint Sebastian in which the martyr is shown tied to a tree, his nearly nude and expiring body pierced with arrows. The effect on Mishima was immediate and fierce:

> That day, the instant I looked upon the picture, my entire being trembled with some pagan joy. My blood soared up; my loins swelled as though in

wrath. The monstrous part of me that was on the point of bursting awaited my use of it with unprecedented ardor, upbraiding me for my ignorance, panting indignantly. My hands, completely unconsciously, began a motion they had never been taught. I felt a secret, radiant something rise swift-footed to the attack from inside me. Suddenly it burst forth, bringing with it a blinding intoxication.[48]

The latter part of *Confessions of a Mask* is devoted to Mishima's determined but futile attempt to prove his normality by courting a young lady named Sonoko. Mishima—or, I should say, the novel's protagonist—derives no pleasure from physical contact with Sonoko, and when she falls in love with him, he balks at marriage. Still, they renew their liaison even after she marries another man and continue until the climactic scene of the book when they visit a rather sleazy dance hall and he sees something that strikes him with the force of a "thunderbolt":

He was a youth of twenty-one or -two, with coarse but regular and swarthy features. He had taken off his shirt and stood there half naked, rewinding a belly-band about his middle. The coarse cotton material was soaked with sweat and had become a light-gray color. He seemed to be intentionally dawdling over his task of winding and was constantly joining in the talk and laughter of his companions. His naked chest showed bulging muscles, fully developed and tensely knit; a deep cleft ran down between the solid muscles of his chest toward his abdomen. The thick, fetter-like sinews of his flesh narrowed down from different directions to the sides of his chest, where they interlocked in tight coils. The hot mass of his smooth torso was being severely and tightly imprisoned by each succeeding turn of the soiled cotton belly-band. His bare, sun-tanned shoulders gleamed as though covered with oil. And black tufts stuck out from the cracks of his armpits, catching the sunlight, curling and glittering with glints of gold.

At this sight, above all at the sight of the peony tattooed on his hard chest, I was beset by sexual desire. My fervent gaze was fixed upon that rough and savage, but incomparably beautiful body. Its owner was laughing there under the sun. When he threw back his head I could see his thick, muscular neck. A strange shudder ran through my innermost heart. I could no longer take my eyes off him.

I had forgotten Sonoko's existence. I was thinking of but one thing: Of his going out into the streets of high summer just as he was, half-naked, and getting into a fight with a rival gang. Of a sharp dagger cutting through that belly-band, piercing that torso. Of that soiled belly-band beautifully dyed with blood. Of his gory corpse being put on an improvised stretcher, made of a window shutter, and brought back here.[49]

Mishima, at about twenty-three, fantasized a death for the young man in the dance hall that was the one he chose for himself some twenty-two years later. It may well be, as Masao Miyoshi hypothesizes,[50] that Mishima's adult life was dominated by a longing for the death he felt he was denied during the war when he failed the physical examination for induction into the army and when all the American bombs missed him.

But it is clear in retrospect that he needed much time to prepare both mentally and physically for what he envisioned as the aesthetically perfect form of self-destruction. In the mid-1950s he took up body-building, and during the radicalism of the 1960s, which accompanied the involvement of the United States in the Vietnam War, he assumed an extreme right-wing political stance based on traditional reverence for the emperor. Mishima transformed himself into a modern-day samurai, a warrior of pure spirit who would think only of one thing: "a sharp dagger . . . piercing [his] torso."

Mishima was a disciplined and prolific writer, producing more than thirty novels and many plays and essays. His output is striking not only for its quantity but also for its thematic diversity. Nevertheless, the Mishima that matters—the Mishima driven by an aesthetic of death as both the ultimate sexual experience and the supreme realization of beauty —is fully adumbrated in *Confessions of a Mask*. In his subsequent writing, Mishima gave probably the most artistic and memorable expression to this aesthetic in *The Temple of the Golden Pavilion (Kinkakuji)*. Published serially in 1956, *The Temple of the Golden Pavilion* was inspired by the burning six years earlier of the fourteenth-century Golden Pavilion (or Temple) by an unbalanced Zen acolyte. The acolyte of Mishima's novel, Mizoguchi, is a young man, rendered inarticulate by a stutter, who enters into the service of the Golden Pavilion during World War II. When he had first been shown the Pavilion by his father on a visit to Kyoto, Mizaguchi had been disappointed to discover that it was "merely a small, dark, old, three-storied building." But after he returned home he found that

> the Golden Temple, which had disappointed me so greatly at first sight, began to revivify its beauty within me day after day, until in the end it became a more beautiful Golden Temple than it had been before I saw it. I could not say wherein this beauty lay. It seemed that what had been nurtured in my dreams had become real and could now, in turn, serve as an impulse for further dreams.
>
> Now I no longer pursued the illusion of a Golden Temple in nature and in the objects that surrounded me. Gradually the Golden Temple came to exist more deeply and more solidly within me.[51]

Mizoguchi fixes on the Golden Pavilion as an ideal of externalized beauty and, at the same time, identifies it with the beauty he feels within himself but cannot bring out because of his speech impediment. All goes reasonably well as long as the war continues, because the danger of the Pavilion's possible destruction by bombing balances Mizoguchi's always threatened interior world of beauty. But, when the war ends, there is an abrupt and terrible change in the relationship between the building and the acolyte:

... from the moment that I set eyes on the temple that day [of surrender], I could feel that "our" relationship had already undergone a change. When it came to such things as the shock of defeat or national grief, the Golden Temple was in its element; at such times it was transcendent, or at least pretended to be transcendent. Until today, the Golden Temple had not been like this. Without doubt the fact that it had in the end escaped being burned down in an air raid and was now out of danger had served to restore its earlier expression, an expression that said: "I have been here since olden times and I shall remain here forever." ...

The most peculiar thing was that of all the various times when the Golden Temple had shown me its beauty, this time was the most beautiful of all. Never had the temple displayed so hard a beauty—a beauty that transcended my own image, yes, that transcended the entire world of reality, a beauty that bore no relation to any form of evanescence! Never before had its beauty shone like this, rejecting every sort of meaning.

It is no exaggeration to say that, as I gazed at the temple, my legs trembled and my forehead was covered with cold beads of perspiration. On a former occasion when I had returned to the country after seeing the temple, its various parts and its whole structure had resounded with a sort of musical harmony. But what I heard this time was complete silence, complete noiselessness. Nothing flowed there, nothing changed. The Golden Temple stood before me, towered before me, like some terrifying pause in a piece of music, like some resonant silence.

"The *bond* between the Golden Temple and myself has been cut," I thought. "Now my vision that the Golden Temple and I were living in the same world has broken down. Now I shall return to my previous condition, but it will be even more hopeless than before. A condition in which I exist on one side and beauty on the other. A condition that will never improve so long as this world endures."[52]

Thus Mizoguchi embarks on the line of thinking that leads to the conclusion that he must destroy the Golden Pavilion in order to live. In this application of Mishima's aesthetic, it is the Golden Pavilion as the embodiment of the highest beauty (in contrast to the beauty that Mizoguchi imagines is within him) that must "die" to realize its finest potential.

Mishima committed suicide with another member of his private army, known as the Shield Society (Tate no Kai), on November 25, 1970, at the headquarters of the Japan Self-Defense Force in Tokyo after exhorting a hastily assembled group of its members to join him in smashing the liberal postwar constitutional structure and restoring, in the name of the emperor, a Japan of "true men and samurai."[53] It is difficult to take seriously the radically right-wing politics Mishima espoused in his last years, especially in view of the fact that for most of his life he had been notably apolitical. It seems far more likely, as suggested earlier, that he conceived these politics as a necessary part of the staging for the glorious and beautiful death he so ardently desired. Also part of the staging was delivery to his publisher on the day he had chosen to die of the final

342
Culture in the Present Age

installment of his last novel, the massive tetralogy entitled *The Sea of Fertility*. Set in the twentieth century and based on the theme of reincarnation through several generations of the soul of a young Japanese aristocrat, *The Sea of Fertility* was obviously intended by Mishima to confirm his stature as one of the world's great writers. But to many critics it confirms, instead, the sad fact that Mishima's best writing had been done years earlier. As Marleigh Ryan observes, "In [the tetralogy's] more than 1,400 pages of plots and subplots, births and rebirths, violence and sickness, we have a repetition of virtually every theme Mishima used in his earlier novels. From peepholes to ritual suicide, we have been through it all before, and we remain curiously unmoved."[54]

Mishima's delvings into the wellsprings of human behavior was characteristically Japanese at least insofar as he limited himself generally to the particularities of his own psyche (however abnormal) as the only source of true experience. Abe Kōbō, on the other hand, transcended this particularism of so many Japanese writers and dealt more universally with the self of modern man. A writer of enormous imaginative power—much influenced by Kafka—who wove his bizarre tales as parables on the plight of contemporary existence, Abe was preoccupied with the themes of personal freedom, the urge to attain it, and the equally powerful urge to prevent or escape from it. In *The Ruined Map* (*Moetsukita Chizu,* 1967), for example, his hero is a private detective investigating a man's disappearance, who eventually confuses his own identity with that of the man he is seeking. The cause of this confusion is suggested in the following dialogue the detective has with a possible witness to the disappearance. The witness speaks first:

> "Why does the world take it for granted that there's a right to pursue people? Someone who hasn't committed any crime. I can't understand how you can assume, as if it were a matter of course, that there is some right that lets you seize a man who has gone off of his own free will."
> "By the same reasoning the one left behind might insist that there was no right to go away."
> "Going off is not a right but a question of will."
> "Maybe pursuit is a matter of will too."
> "Then, I'm neutral. I don't want to be anyone's friend or enemy."[55]

Abe seems to be telling us that some people will always try to escape from the restraints of society and their humdrum existences and that others will just as surely pursue them and attempt to entrap them again. Pursuer and pursued are likely to be motivated by the same force of will and, in their special relationship, may indeed appear to be very similar, if not identical.

Abe's concern was with freedom not as an intellectual ideal but as an emotional craving. The paradox of his message is that freedom, once achieved, may incite the same desire to escape as did one's previous state of real or imagined captivity. Abe's finest statement of this paradox is *The Woman in the Dunes (Suna no Onna,* 1962). Like *The Ruined Map,* it commences with the disappearance of a man, in this case a nondescript schoolteacher who is an amateur entomologist going on a holiday to the seaside in quest of bugs. The man can be seen both as a pursuer of bugs (who possess freedom) and as one who yearns for freedom in his fascination with sand, the natural habitat of the bugs he pursues. No other substance—except water, to which Abe frequently compares it—so clearly represents both freedom and its potential denial. Forever free itself, as it constantly shifts and flows, sand can also relentlessly pursue and totally engulf.

Missing the last bus home, the man accepts shelter for the night in a nearby village, only to discover the following day that he is a prisoner. He has been placed in a house in a deep sand pit to live with a recently widowed but still young woman. Together they constitute one of a score of enslaved families in pits facing the sea that must constantly dig sand to prevent it from inundating the village. Much of *The Woman in the Dunes* is a narrative of the man's schemes and efforts to escape to freedom, but on another level it is the story of how the man, forced into confinement in the microcosmic world of the sand pit, comes to realize the futility for most people of regarding life—whether in his kind of captivity or in society beyond it—as anything other than a pit, a place where freedom is stifled. Some people may think they have round-trip tickets that enable them to come and go as they please, but they need all the strength and will they possess to avoid losing the return halves of their tickets and being forced onto the one-way track that entraps everyone else:

> Got a one-way ticket to the blues, woo, woo. . . .
>
> If you want to sing it, sing it. These days people caught in the clutches of the one-way ticket never sing it like that. The soles of those who have a one-way ticket are so thin that they scream when they step on a pebble. They have had their fill of walking. "The Round-Trip Ticket Blues" is what they want to sing. A one-way ticket is a disjointed life that misses the links between yesterday and today, today and tomorrow. Only the man who obstinately hangs on to a round-trip ticket can hum with real sorrow a song of a one-way ticket. For this very reason he grows desperate lest the return half of his ticket be lost or stolen; he buys stocks, signs up for life insurance, and talks out of different sides of his mouth to his union pals and his superiors. He hums "The One-Way Ticket Blues" with all his might and, choosing a channel at random, turns the television up to full volume in an attempt to drown out the peevish voices of those who have only a one-way ticket and who keep asking for help, voices that come up through the bathtub drain or the toilet hole. It would not be strange at all if "The Round-Trip Ticket Blues" were the song of mankind imprisoned.[56]

After a futile and humiliating attempt to escape from the pit, the man
sets about constructing a ground trap in the hope of ensnaring a crow to
carry his plea for help to the outside world. The trap project has little
chance of succeeding, but it leads the man to an incredible discovery:
beneath the sand there is water that could be invaluable to the villagers.
With this secret knowledge about the water, the man's attitude toward
his situation begins to change, and when shortly thereafter the villagers
forget or neglect to remove the rope ladder leading to the bottom of the
pit, he does not seize the opportunity to make another attempt to
escape. For now he has a "two-way ticket" to life and can afford to weigh
his options more carefully:

> There was no particular need to hurry about escaping. On the two-way ticket
> he held in his hand now, the destination and time of departure were blanks
> for him to fill in as he wished. In addition, he realized that he was bursting
> with a desire to talk to someone about the water trap. And if he wanted to
> talk about it, there wouldn't be better listeners than the villagers. He would
> end by telling someone—if not today, then tomorrow.
> He might as well put off his escape until sometime after that.[57]

The themes of freedom and escape from the fetters of modern society
are important also in the work of Ōe Kenzaburō, although Ōe presents
the issue more clearly as that of alienation and anomie. In Ōe's typical
schema, the individual is caught in a society that makes stifling demands
upon him, demands that he cannot meet and that, therefore, render him
a failure, at least in his own mind. Compounding the personal alienation
and fear that he is going nowhere in life is the more widely shared social
malaise of anomie that sees no direction in the life of society as a whole
(that is, postwar Japan, the home of economic animals who have poured
their souls into the transistor radio).

Such an individual—held in the grip of alienation and anomie—is
Bird, the hero of Ōe's *A Personal Matter* (*Kojinteki na Taiken*, 1964), a
novel startlingly similar in conception and plot to John Updike's *Rabbit,
Run*. As the story begins, we find Bird at age twenty-seven, married and
awaiting the birth of his first child. We learn how he was drunk for four
weeks after his marriage two years earlier, how he had to withdraw from
graduate school, and how he subsequently turned to his father-in-law to
obtain an unpretentious job as teacher in a college-preparatory cram
school. Bird dreams of going to Africa and has just bought a set of
Michelin road maps of the distant continent. Wandering the streets while
waiting for news of his wife from the hospital, Bird is attacked by a gang
of dragon-jacketed hoods and is beaten to the ground:

> It occurred to Bird that the maps must be getting creased between his body
> and the ground. And his own child was being born: the thought danced with
> new poignancy to the frontlines of consciousness. A sudden rage took him,

and rough despair. Until now, out of terror and bewilderment, Bird had been
contriving only to escape. But he had no intention of running now. If I don't
fight now, I'll not only lose the chance to go to Africa forever, my baby will be
born into the world solely to lead the worst possible life—it was like the voice
of inspiration, and Bird believed.[58]

Bird counterattacks and "the joy of battle . . . reawakened in him; it had
been years since he had felt it. Bird and the dragon-jackets watched one
another without moving, appraising the formidable enemy. Time passed,"
and the gang withdrew.

Bird, trapped and bewildered by life, sees in the dragon-jacketed gang
a well-defined enemy he can attack, daringly and against great odds. But
the euphoria he experiences over victory in physical battle is short-lived,
and the oppressiveness of life becomes even more terrifyingly real when
he learns that his baby has been born a monster with a rare brain hernia
protruding from its head. Africa suddenly becomes more unattainable
than ever before, and Bird tries to escape from the dilemma of what to
do about the baby by fleeing in a totally opposite direction. Purchasing a
bottle of whiskey, he seeks sanctuary—in a symbolic kind of return to
the womb—in the dark, cluttered apartment of a former girlfriend. Later,
when the baby fails to die in the hospital as Bird had agonizingly hoped,
he and the girlfriend take custody of it and deliver it to an illicit doctor
for disposal. With the baby gone, they plan to fulfill Bird's dream of
going to Africa.

Ōe had to this point written a splendid and poignantly moving story.
Inexplicably, he chose to conclude it with a brief, less than convincing
epilogue that informs us that Bird came to his senses in time to retrieve
the baby and return it to the hospital, where it was operated on and
fixed—it did not have a brain hernia after all, merely a benign tumor.
Bird's attitude is now mature and stable, and he is planning for the future
of the baby.

In 1994 Ōe became the second Japanese writer, after Kawabata Yasunari, to receive the Nobel Prize in literature. Playing on the title that
Kawabata had used for his 1968 Nobel acceptance speech, "Japan the
Beautiful and Myself," Ōe entitled his speech "Japan the Ambiguous
and Myself." Ōe observed that Kawabata, in the twilight of his career,
had been able to reaffirm his faith in the traditional literary and aesthetic
values of Japan and, in particular, in the spirit of Zen Buddhism. In his
own writing, however, Ōe found himself torn by what he saw as the
"ambiguity" between Japan the traditional and Japan the modern. As he
put it:

After a hundred and twenty years of modernization since the opening up of
the country, contemporary Japan is split between two opposite poles of ambiguity. This ambiguity, which is so powerful and penetrating that it divides

both the state and its people, and affects me as a writer like a deep-felt scar, is evident in various ways. The modernization of Japan was oriented toward learning from and imitating the West, yet the country is situated in Asia and has firmly maintained its traditional culture. The ambiguous orientation of Japan drove the country into the position of an invader in Asia, and resulted in its isolation from other Asian nations not only politically but also socially and culturally. And even in the West, to which its culture was supposedly quite open, it has long remained inscrutable or only partially understood.[59]

One of the most remarkable phenomena of postwar mass (popular) culture has been the boom in comics *(manga)*. In the United States the popularity of printed comics has declined steadily since the 1950s largely because of the competition from television. But in Japan, which, like the United States, has also become one of the world's most television-saturated countries, comics of the "story-line" kind have during the same period exploded in popularity to the point where, in 1980, 27 percent— or 1.8 billion—of the books and magazines published in Japan were comics.[60] But what is perhaps even more astounding than the sheer volume of comics publications is that comics are voraciously read by adults as well as youngsters. Thus, for example, to the great surprise of many foreign visitors, it is not at all uncommon to see well-dressed businessmen riding the subway thoroughly and unself-consciously engrossed in reading comic books.

Japan has a comics tradition, especially in caricature, dating back to ancient times. As noted in Chapter 4, caricature-like sketches can be found on the walls of Hōryūji Temple and in the collection of documents in the Shōsōin storehouse of the Nara period. These sketches appear to have provided at least some of the inspiration for the drawing of probably the most famous caricatures of premodern Japanese history, the Animal Scrolls attributed to the priest Toba (see figs. 28–29). In the Tokugawa period, Hokusai is especially remembered for his caricatures and comical sketches and stylistically can probably be regarded as the father of modern Japanese comics. Hokusai is also credited with coining the word *manga*, which is still used today for comics.

One of the most popular subjects of postwar comics has been science fiction. Another has been the samurai, Japan's equivalent, in terms of manly ethos, of the American cowboy. But the Japanese have never developed the kind of "war comics" that have been so popular in the United States. Even during World War II, neither comics nor movies portrayed the Japanese soldier, for example, as a tough he-man out to slaughter the enemy. Rather, the focus was more on relations among soldiers bonded by battle and on the simple and pure way they fought for their country and sometimes died for it.[61] Since the war, for fairly obvious reasons, Japanese artists of comics and other media have made no attempt to glorify war. On the contrary, some have drawn antiwar comics while others have given their attention to the sad plight of the civilian in a war-devastated Japan. Keiji Nakazawa's *Hadashi no Gen (Barefoot Gen)*, for example, tells the story of a boy named Gen in Hiroshima on the day the first atomic bomb was dropped.[62] "Unaware of the hell that was approaching in the sky, Hiroshima began the day as usual." Gen, setting out for school, is stopped by a lady who asks him where a certain class is to be held. As he starts to answer, Gen notices a single B-29 in the sky and wonders why the sirens have not sounded. Within seconds the bomb plummets and "like a wind from hell, the atomic cloud roared up six miles into the sky over Hiroshima . . . and in the city, time stopped."

Gen, dazed, pulls himself out of the rubble. The body of the lady is nearby, her face melted almost beyond recognition. As Gen runs through the flattened city calling for his father, mother (who is pregnant), sister, and brother, the people he sees "look like monsters." At last he finds what used to be his house. His mother kneels beside it, but his father, sister, and brother are trapped beneath the collapsed roof. Gen and his mother try desperately to pry the roof up with pieces of timber, but before they can succeed the house is engulfed by a fire sweeping through the city. The mother screams that she wants to die with her husband and other children, but Gen drags her away and "as they escape the flames, Gen's mother goes into labor, and with no one to help them, they bring a new life into the dying city." In the last frames the mother, holding the baby aloft, implores her, "When you grow up you must *never* let this happen again!"

For a country that has one of the lowest rates of violence and crime in the world, Japan produces many comics that depict acts of extreme violence, including scenes of almost unmatchable blood and gore. Frederik Schodt describes one comic, for example, that depicts suffering peasants in the medieval age and that features "heads rolling, eyes gouged out, and showers of blood (created by soaking a brush in ink and then blowing on it)."[63] And for a country that is puritanical in regard to sex and pornography, Japan tolerates a remarkable amount of sex of all kinds in its comics. Artists are not allowed to draw explicit sexual acts but, limited only by their imaginations and their skill with the brush, they are able to craft scenes of both "normal" and deviant sexual activities that leave very little to readers' imaginations.

Erotic art has a long tradition in Japan. Woodblock artists in the Tokugawa period, for example, produced great quantities of erotic prints, called "spring pictures" *(shunga)*, that are fully explicit and show men and women in every conceivable—and some inconceivable—position of intimacy. Some prints depict people with oversized sexual organs; others show them engaged in sex with animals. In Japan today, public display of spring pictures is generally suppressed. But the spirit of spring pictures lives on in the work of the many *manga* artists who have been influenced by them.

Science fiction, violent action, samurai stories, sports—these are among the standard fare of boys' comics. Although recently some of this fare has also been served up to girls, the style and subject matter of girls' comics have always differed greatly from those of boys. At one time, girls' comics (whose artists now are almost all women) were concerned exclusively with romance and love, and these subjects remain the basis for nearly all comics for girls. In girls' comics the main characters are always depicted as young, with pretty, innocent faces, and huge, dreamy eyes. Many look more Caucasian than Japanese (the West being viewed in this regard as a place of romance), and they live in a total fantasy world to which Japanese girls appear to be especially attracted because the customs and mores of their country have kept them largely segregated from boys through at least the teen years.

In girls' comics, in particular, homosexuality, bisexuality, and cross-dressing are common, and boys and girls are often, if not usually, androgynously portrayed. A taste for the androgynous has deep roots in Japanese culture. This stems at least in part from the fact that the traditional clothing of men and women—the kimono in its various forms—has often been similar if not identical. In many Tokugawa-period woodblock prints, for example, men and women are dressed exactly alike. Frequently their faces are also drawn in identically conventionalized form, and sometimes even their hairdos are the same. Although usually the top of a man's head is shaved, and thus distinct from a woman's, there are pictures of young men (without shaved pates) and women who cannot be distinguished one from another. In some spring pictures, for example, we find young men and women making love whose sex can be identified only by their genitalia.

Cross-dressing and at least the suggestion of homosexuality or bisexuality have been common in Japanese theatre from at least the time of *kabuki* in the Tokugawa period. In the all-male *kabuki,* the actor playing the part of *onnagata* or female impersonator represents idealized womanhood. Some *onnagata* in earlier times remained cross-dressing impersonators even in their private lives; and it has often been contended, as noted in Chapter 7, that the *onnagata*'s specialized style of femininity cannot be matched even by real women. In the all-female Takarazuka Revue of the twentieth century, as we saw in the last chapter, women cross-dress to play men's roles, and often are the acknowledged stars of Takarazuka. The Takarazuka audiences are composed mostly of teenage girls, and it is not uncommon for them to form "crushes" on the male impersonators. Parents do not necessarily object to their daughters having these crushes or regard them as lesbianism. As Antonia Levi puts it, "[M]any parents consider it nicer, 'purer' if the first object of a young girl's affection is female rather than male."[64]

Boys portrayed in girls' comics are almost always feminine in appearance or at least androgynously like girls. Sometimes the boys are homosexually drawn to each other and make love. But in the same way that the attraction of teenage girls to the male impersonators of the Takarazuka Revue is not necessarily regarded as lesbianism, this kind of lovemaking of boys in comics is not thought to be real homosexuality. The boys are engaged in a "pure," highly aestheticized form of love that transcends the distinction between homosexuality and heterosexuality.

In the late 1980s a young writer with the curious pen name of Yoshimoto Banana (1964–) appeared on the literary scene like a meteor. Her novels and novellas were immediately and enormously popular. Some have been awarded high literary prizes, and several, including *Kitchen*, *N.P.*, and *Lizard*, have already been translated into English. Yoshimoto Banana is unquestionably a cultural phenomenon. But what makes her particularly unusual is that she emerged from the world of pop culture. Indeed, she herself says that she was inspired to become a writer by the comics.

Although many critics have lavishly praised Yoshimoto, some have not known what to make of her. Should she be regarded as a writer of "serious literature," or should she be considered the producer of works that, like the other artifacts of pop culture, are meant to be "consumed"? Yoshimoto herself has confused the issue by saying that whenever she publishes a new novel, she wants copies of her other works to be removed from the booksellers' shelves.[65]

Yoshimoto writes of a world quite at variance with what has long been perceived as "traditional Japan": that is, a place of tight social organization (beginning with the nuclear family), a powerful work ethic, and firmly established institutions. In Yoshimoto's books, virtually nothing is said about social organization, work ethic, or institutions. Most of the main characters have no meaningful family ties or are members of artificially constructed or dysfunctional families, and often they have little or no occupational motivation. They seem to float rudderless through life, frequently yearning for love but fearful they will not find it and that their lives will, instead, be a series of despairing, lonely days. Death is a persistent theme. People are left alone by the deaths—sometimes violent deaths—of family members, lovers, and friends. Mikage, the principal character in *Kitchen*, for example, reflects on how death and fate have treated her as she tries to absorb the shock of the news that the person she had come to regard as a surrogate mother has been brutally murdered:

When my parents died I was still a child. When my grandfather died, I had a boyfriend. When my grandmother died I was left all alone. But never had I felt so alone as I did now.

From the bottom of my heart, I wanted to give up; I wanted to give up on living. There was no denying that tomorrow would come, and the day after tomorrow, and so next week, too. I never thought it would be this hard, but I would go on living in the midst of a gloomy depression, and that made me feel sick to the depths of my soul. In spite of the tempest raging within me, I walked the night path calmly.[66]

Mikage's surrogate "mother," Erico, is in fact a cross-dressing, transsexual man. She is the real father and ersatz mother of Yuichi, who befriends Mikage when her grandmother and sole remaining relative dies and has her move in with him and Erico. The three—Erico, Yuichi, and Mikage—form a congenial but rather strange family. The relationship between Mikage and Yuichi, which is the central story of *Kitchen*, is ambiguous. For most of the book they appear to behave like brother and sister, and there is no suggestion of romantic attraction. They seem, indeed, to be like some of the androgynously similar but essentially sexless characters who appear in girls' comics.

Erico, who works in a gay bar, is stabbed to death by a crazed patron who at first thought she was a real woman. Proving her physical prowess, Erico manages to club her attacker to death even as she is dying. But Erico's death destroys the "family" and ruptures the already fragile emotional structure supporting the lives of Mikage and Yuichi. Yuichi will probably muddle on. But we fear that Mikage, devastated by the loss of Erico and burdened with a morbid, despairing outlook on life, will fare worse. There is within Mikage, however, a powerful survivalist instinct that emerges even when her thoughts are the darkest: "Always defeated —defeated we make dinner, we eat, we sleep. Everyone we love is dying. Still, to cease living is unacceptable."[67]

It is at this point that Mikage finds strength and the purpose to go on in her long-professed love of kitchens. In the opening lines of *Kitchen*, Mikage informs us, "The place I like best in this world is the kitchen." Her grandmother has just died and "now only the kitchen and I are left. It's just a little nicer than being all alone." A moment later she states, more emphatically, "I often think that when it comes time to die, I want to breathe my last in a kitchen."[68] Acting upon this kitchen fixation, Mikage takes up cooking and becomes an assistant to a cooking teacher. With a job and newly found purpose, she realizes—suddenly and intuitively—that she also wants to continue to be with Yuichi, and at *Kitchen*'s end it appears that the two will remain together. Yet even at this stage there is scarcely a hint of real sexual attraction or romanticism. In a world where there is constant death and loss and where loneliness always threatens, Mikage and Yuichi seem more than content to settle for companionship.

Even as Yoshimoto Banana skyrocketed to fame as a writer and "Banana-mania" swept the country in the late 1980s and the early 1990s,

Japan was undergoing major changes. The postwar "economic miracle" that had propelled Japan's economy to number three and then to number two in the world came to an end before the 1980s were over, and Japan slipped into a recession that lasted throughout the 1990s. Politically, the era of the one-and-a-half-party system, which kept the Liberal-Democratic Party in power for nearly four decades, also ended when the LDP, rocked by a steady stream of scandals, was forced to relinquish the office of prime minister in 1993 to an opposition leader at the head of a coalition government. But this transference of power proved no solution to either Japan's economic or political problems. Prime ministers came and went frequently during the 1990s, and the Japanese government failed to convince many in Japan or elsewhere that it had either the political will or the policies to lift the country out of a chronic recession caused in large part by bad loans overseas and a banking system that partly collapsed under the weight of them. In the euphoric days of the economic miracle it was even suggested that the twenty-first century would be a "Japanese century." That seems like a distant dream now, as Japan enters the new century with more problems than prospects.

If there is a central theme to this book, it is that the Japanese, within the context of a history of abundant cultural borrowing from China in premodern times and the West in the modern age, have nevertheless retained a hard core of native social, ethical, and cultural values by means of which they have almost invariably molded and adapted foreign borrowing to suit their own tastes and purposes.

But the Japanese have also exported their own culture in modern times, and in the process have exerted a great influence on world art and fashion. Exhibitions of arts and crafts, ranging from ancient Buddhist statuary and paintings to the utensils of the tea ceremony and signs used by merchants in the Tokugawa and Meiji periods, have drawn large crowds in the United States and other countries. Touring theatrical groups performing plays from the puppet and *kabuki* theatres are perennially popular abroad. Japanese tastes in architecture, interior decoration, and garden design are known and imitated throughout the world; and Japanese designers such as Ise Miyake and Hanae Mori have ascended to high levels in the field of women's fashion. Clearly, major aspects of Japanese culture have become an important and vital part of the lives of people everywhere.

Notes

Chapter 1 The Emergence of Japanese Civilization

1. Keiji Imamura, *Prehistoric Japan*, p. 26.

2. Scholars continue to debate how rice got to Japan: From south China? From central China? Via the Korean peninsula? See ibid., pp. 130–31.

3. Even more recently, some scholars have hypothesized that this "cultural transformation" was accompanied by a great influx of people from the continent over a long period of time. One scholar, for example, estimates that several million people entered Japan during the thousand years following commencement of the Yayoi period. Ibid., p. 155.

4. Quoted in Ryūsaku Tsunoda, William T. deBary, and Donald Keene, eds., *Sources of Japanese Tradition*, p. 8.

5. Quoted in Agency for Cultural Affairs, ed., *Japanese Religion*, pp. 37–38.

6. W. G. Aston, tr., *Nihongi*, p. 77.

7. They calculated in Chinese-style units of sixty-year periods.

8. See Gari Ledyard, "Galloping Along with the Horseriders: Looking for the Founders of Japan."

9. Walter Edwards, "Event and Process in the Founding of Japan: The Horse-rider Theory in Archaeological Perspective."

10. Many scholars, especially Korean historians, insist that Mimana, which was supposedly in the territory the Koreans called Kaya, never existed: in other words, Japan did not establish a territorial enclave in Korea during this early age.

11. Tsunoda, deBary, and Keene, *Sources of Japanese Tradition*, pp. 9–11.

Chapter 2 The Introduction of Buddhism

1. This date appears in *Nihon Shoki*. Other sources give 538 as the year of the "official" introduction of Buddhism to Japan.

2. Another term for Hinayana is Theravada, "Doctrine of the Elders."

3. A translation of the Constitution can be found in Tsunoda, deBary, and Keane, *Sources of Japanese Tradition*, pp. 50–53. The quotations here are from this translation.

4. Another term for this form of poetry is *tanka* or "short poem."

5. Donald Keene, ed., *Anthology of Japanese Literature*, pp. 37–38.

6. Ibid., pp. 46–47.

7. Ibid., pp. 51–52.

8. Donald Keene, tr., *Essays in Idleness: The Tsurezuregusa of Kenkō*, p. 7.

9. Keene, *Anthology of Japanese Literature*, p. 80.

Chapter 3 The Court at Its Zenith

1. Tsunoda, deBary, and Keene, *Sources of Japanese Tradition*, p. 122.

2. G. B. Sansom, *Japan, A Short Cultural History*, p. 228.

3. There are two forms of *kana: katakana* and *hiragana. Hiragana* is the principal form used, along with Chinese characters, in writing Japanese. Use of *katakana* is restricted primarily to the phonetic reproduction of foreign words and names, and to printing on public signs and the like.

4. There were two titles for regent: *sesshō* for a minor emperor and *kampaku* for an emperor who had reached his majority.

5. A mission was planned for 894 but was never dispatched.

6. Keene, *Anthology of Japanese Literature*, p. 80.

7. Quoted in Earl Miner, ed., *Japanese Poetic Diaries*, p. 26.

8. Keene, *Anthology of Japanese Literature*, p. 76.

9. Tsunoda, deBary, and Keene, *Sources of Japanese Tradition*, p. 180.

10. Keene, *Anthology of Japanese Literature*, pp. 90–91.

11. Ibid., p. 82.

12. Edward Seidensticker, tr., *The Gossamer Years*, p. 167.

13. Keene, *Anthology of Japanese Literature*, pp. 67–68.

14. Lady Murasaki, *The Tale of Genji*, translated by Arthur Waley, pp. 22–23.

15. Ivan Morris, tr., *The Pillow Book*, 1:7–8.

16. Murasaki Shikibu, *The Tale of Genji*, translated by Edward Seidensticker, 1:437.

17. William and Helen McCullough, trs., *A Tale of Flowering Fortunes*, 2:515–16.

18. The chronological and annals and biographies forms of organizing history derived from China. An annals and biographies history was basically a topically, rather than a chronologically, arranged work. The two principal topics were the annals of emperors and the biographies of court ministers and other prominent people.

19. Helen McCullough, tr., *Ōkagami*, p. 208.

20. *Namu Amida Butsu* or "Hail Amida Buddha!"

21. Tsunoda, deBary, and Keene, *Sources of Japanese Tradition*, pp. 202–3.

Chapter 4 The Advent of a New Age

1. The term "samurai," although generally used today when speaking of Japan's premodern warriors, was in early times only one designation among many for these fighting men. Probably the most common term was *tsuwamono;* another was *bushi,* which means something like "military gentry."

2. Taira (also known as Heike) and Minamoto (also known as Genji) were two surnames given to princes who were excluded from the imperial family in a process of "dynastic shedding" that was used periodically to reduce the family's considerable size. The imperial family itself has no surname.

3. The wars are known as the Former Nine Years War, 1056–62, and the Later Three Years War, 1083–87. Both wars have misleading designations, since the first lasted six years and the second, four.

4. This struggle is also known as the Gempei War, a designation derived from the *gen* of Genji (Minamoto) and the *hei* (changed phonetically to *pei*) of Heike (Taira).

5. This war tale is called *Shōmonki* or *Masakado-ki.*

6. Cited in Paul Varley, *Warriors of Japan, As Portrayed in the War Tales*, p. 85.

7. Cited in Paul Varley, "Warriors as Courtiers: The Taira in *Heike Monogatari*," in Amy Heinrich, ed., *Currents in Japanese Culture*, p. 62.

8. The Kakuichi version, compiled in 1371.

Chapter 5 The Canons of Medieval Taste

1. Keene, *Anthology of Japanese Literature*, p. 197.

2. William R. LaFleur, *The Karma of Words: Buddhism and the Literary Arts in Medieval Japan*, pp. 60–79.

3. Keene, *Anthology of Japanese Literature*, pp. 206–7.

4. Ibid., pp. 195–96.

5. Robert Brower and Earl Miner, *Japanese Court Poetry*, p. 245.
6. Quoted in Earl Miner, *An Introduction to Japanese Court Poetry*, p. 102.
7. From the *Shinkokinshū* in Keene, *Anthology of Japanese Literature*, p. 194.
8. Tsunoda, deBary, and Keene, *Sources of Japanese Tradition*, p. 193.
9. Hōjō Masako (1157–1225) was Yoritomo's wife.
10. Later in the century imperial princes were substituted for the Fujiwara.
11. The former emperor was Gotoba (1180–1239), and the brief conflict became known as the Jōkyū War.
12. Sansom, *Japan, A Short Cultural History*, p. 334.
13. Ibid.
14. Tsunoda, deBary, and Keene, *Sources of Japanese Tradition*, p. 219.
15. Ibid., p. 234.
16. Heinrich Dumoulin, *A History of Zen Buddhism*, p. 126.
17. Some scholars contend that the storm of 1274 was not a typhoon inasmuch as it occurred in November, after the typhoon season.
18. Quoted in William Wayne Farris, *Heavenly Warriors*, p. 331.
19. Quoted in Varley, *Warriors of Japan*, p. 183.
20. *Kamikaze* pilots often wore headbands *(hachimaki)* emblazoned with the words "Seven Lives!"
21. Keene, *Essays in Idleness*, p. 23.
22. Ibid., p. 70.
23. Following a Chinese practice, the medieval Japanese designated five Zen temples in Kyoto and five in Kamakura as the leading Zen institutions of their respective cities.
24. Donald Keene, *Nō: The Classical Theatre of Japan*, p. 25.
25. Tsunoda, deBary, and Keene, *Sources of Japanese Tradition*, p. 289.
26. During the *shite*'s absence from the stage, there is a *kyōgen* (discussed below) in which the priest speaks to a man of the locality and learns more about the history of the Shrine in the Fields.
27. Matsukaze is the *shite* and Murasame is a companion *(tsure)*.
28. Donald Keene, ed., *Twenty Plays of the Nō Theatre*, pp. 31–32.
29. Arthur Waley, *The Nō Plays of Japan*, p. 73.
30. Shinkei, *Sasamegoto*, in Kidō Saizō and Imoto Nōichi, eds., *Renga Ronshū, Haironshū*, p. 175.
31. Keene, *Anthology of Japanese Literature*, pp. 315–16.
32. Tsunoda, deBary, and Keene, *Sources of Japanese Tradition*, p. 244.
33. Ibid., p. 245.
34. Later, the tea of Uji, south of Kyoto, became esteemed as Japan's best. Uji tea remains the best today.
35. Competitions in the arrangement of flowers and the identification of different kinds of incense were also popular.
36. "Ami" was taken from the first two syllables of Amida.
37. Murai Yasuhiko, "Shukō Kokoro no Fumi," in Hayashiya Tatsusaburō, ed., *Kodai-Chūsei Geijutsu Ron*, p. 448.

Chapter 6 The Country Unified

1. European records say that the Portuguese first reached Japan in 1542.
2. Michael Cooper, ed., *They Came to Japan*, p. 60.
3. Ibid., p. 40.
4. Ibid., p. 42.
5. During the Tokugawa period, the Dutch were known not as *namban* but as *kōmō*, "redheads."
6. Geoffrey Parker, *The Military Revolution*, p. 140.

7. Cooper, *They Came to Japan*, p. 134.

8. C. R. Boxer, *The Christian Century in Japan, 1549–1650*, pp. 195–96.

9. Ibid., pp. 207–8.

10. See the description of Azuchi Castle's paintings in Carolyn Wheelright, "A Visualization of Eitoku's Lost Paintings at Azuchi Castle," in George Elison and Bardwell L. Smith, eds., *Warlords, Artists, and Commoners*, pp. 87–111.

11. Haga Kōshirō, "The *Wabi* Aesthetic Through the Ages," in Paul Varley and Kumakura Isao, eds., *Tea in Japan*, p. 200.

12. Ibid.

Chapter 7 The Flourishing of a Bourgeois Culture

1. For example, Ronald Toby in *State and Diplomacy in Early Modern Japan*.

2. From 1633 until 1764 the Dutch went annually to Edo. Later they went every other year, then every fourth year. See Marius Jansen, "Japan in the Early Nineteenth Century," in Jansen, ed., *Cambridge History of Japan*, 5:89.

3. Endō Shūsaku, *Silence*, pp. 96–97.

4. Ibid., p. 236.

5. Nishiyama Matsunosuke, *Edo Culture*, pp. 35–36.

6. Sansom, *Japan, A Short Cultural History*, p. 465.

7. Maruyama Masao, *Studies in the Intellectual History of Tokugawa Japan*, p. 24.

8. Scholars estimate that male literacy in Japan by the end of the Tokugawa period was more than 40 percent, a figure that compares favorably with, and in many cases is higher than, European literacy rates for the same period.

9. For example, Herman Ooms in *Tokugawa Ideology*.

10. Sōtatsu, Kōrin, and the group of painters they influenced are known as the Rimpa school.

11. Nishi Kazuo and Hozumi Kazuo, *What Is Japanese Architecture?*, tr. by H. Mack Horton, p. 133.

12. Ihara Saikaku, *Nihon Eitai Gura*, pp. 112–13.

13. E. S. Crawcour, "Some Observations of Mitsui Takafusa's *Chōmin Kōken Roku*," *Transactions of the Asiatic Society of Japan*, 3rd series, vol. 8 (Tokyo, 1961), p. 70.

14. Ibid., p. 88.

15. *Uki* can be written with two characters, one meaning "wretched" and the other "floating"; *yo* means "world."

16. I have used Ivan Morris' translations for the titles of all the Saikaku works mentioned here.

17. Ihara Saikaku, *The Life of an Amorous Woman and Other Writings*, pp. 124–25.

18. Ibid., pp. 202–3.

19. The term *bunraku* is taken from a famous puppet theatre, the Bunrakuza, established in Osaka in the nineteenth century. Another term for the puppet theatre is *jōruri*, adopted from the name of Princess Jōruri, a character who appears in some early puppet plays.

20. Donald Keene, *Bunraku: The Art of the Japanese Puppet Theatre*, p. 31.

21. Donald Keene, tr., *Four Major Plays of Chikamatsu*, pp. 51–52.

22. Keene, *Anthology of Japanese Literature*, pp. 369 and 371.

23. Quoted in Ivan Morris, *The World of the Shining Prince*, p. 202.

24. Liza Crihfield, "Geisha," in *Kōdansha Encyclopedia of Japan*, 3:15.

Chapter 8 Heterodox Trends

1. For example, Harold Bolitho in *Treasures Among Men: The Fudai Daimyō in Tokugawa Japan*.

2. Quoted in Conrad Totman, *Early Modern Japan*, p. 171.

3. Tsunoda, deBary, and Keene, *Sources of Japanese Tradition*, p. 399.

4. Sokō, in fact, did not use the word *bushidō*, but, rather, *shidō*.

5. The scholar was Tsurumi Shunsuke. See Henry D. Smith II, "Rethinking the Story of the 47 Rōnin: Chūshingura in the 1980s" (paper prepared for the Modern Japan Seminar, Columbia University, April 30, 1990).

6. My discussion of this division of opinion is based on Eiko Ikegami, *The Taming of the Samurai: Honorific Individualism and the Making of Modern Japan*, pp. 228–33.

7. Only forty-six *rōnin* committed suicide. The forty-seventh had returned to Akō after the murder of Kira to inform the domain about what had happened and was not arrested by the shogunate.

8. Donald Keene, tr., *Chūshingura: The Treasury of Loyal Retainers*.

9. The shogunate forbade the staging of current events. Hence theatrical producers presented the *rōnin* story as an occurrence of the Muromachi period. The "Kira character" was given the name of one of Ashikaga Takauji's lieutenants, Kō no Moronao.

10. Yamamoto Tsunetomo, *Hagakure*, translated by William Scott Wilson, p. 29.

11. Ibid., p. 30.

12. Mishima Yukio, *The Way of the Samurai: Yukio Mishima on Hagakure in Modern Life*, translated by Kathryn Sparling.

13. The word "mirror" in traditional Chinese and Japanese thought means the use of history as a "reflector" of proper and moral ways of governance.

14. Tsunoda, deBary, and Keene, *Sources of Japanese Tradition*, p. 533.

15. Ibid., pp. 534–35.

16. Honda Toshiaki is the principal subject of Donald Keene's *The Japanese Discovery of Europe*.

17. Harold G. Henderson, *An Introduction to Haiku*, p. 86.

18. Ibid., pp. 89 and 101.

19. A translation of *The Classic of Tea* can be found in Lu Yü, *The Classic of Tea,* translated by Frances Ross Carpenter.

20. The term appears to have been coined by a Nagasaki interpreter during the course of translating Englebert Kaempfer's *History of Japan* into Japanese. See Toby, *State and Diplomacy in Early Modern Japan*, pp. 12–14.

21. Tsunoda, deBary, and Keene, *Sources of Japanese Tradition*, pp. 595–96.

22. Bob Wakabayashi, *Anti-Foreignism and Western Learning in Early-Modern Japan*, p. 13.

Chapter 9 Encounter with the West

1. The imperial seat was at this time moved to Edo and the city renamed Tokyo or Eastern Capital.

2. Tsunoda, deBary, and Keene, *Sources of Japanese Tradition*, p. 644.

3. Hirakawa Sukehiro, "Japan's Turn to the West," in Jansen, ed., *Cambridge History of Japan*, 5:460.

4. Eugene Soviak, "On the Nature of Western Progress: The Journal of the Iwakura Mission," in Donald H. Shively, ed., *Tradition and Modernization in Japanese Culture*, p. 12.

5. Yomiuri Shinbun Sha, ed., *Meiji Ishin* in *Nihon no Rekishi*, 10:230.

6. Ibid., p. 234.

7. Donald Keene, ed., *Modern Japanese Literature*, p. 31.

8. Hirakawa, "Japan's Turn to the West," pp. 470–72.

9. Yomiuri Shinbun Sha, *Meiji Ishin*, p. 230.

10. Fukuzawa Yukichi, *An Encouragement of Learning*, p. 1.

11. Quoted in A. M. Craig, "Fukuzawa Yukichi: The Philosophical Foundations of Meiji Nationalism," in Robert E. Ward, ed., *Political Development in Modern Japan*, pp. 120–21.

12. See the discussion of this memorial in Peter Duus, *Modern Japan,* pp. 108–9.

13. The rescript is translated in full in John K. Fairbank, Edwin O. Reischauer, and Albert M. Craig, *East Asia: The Modern Transformation,* p. 276.

14. Quoted in Kenneth Pyle, "Meiji Conservatism," in Jansen, *Cambridge History of Japan,* 5:691.

15. In this discussion of Tokutomi and the "new generation," I have used Kenneth B. Pyle, *The New Generation of Meiji Japan.*

16. The following comments on Christianity in the Meiji period have benefited from my reading of Irwin Scheiner, *Christian Converts and Social Protest in Meiji Japan.*

17. Another incident that occurred about this time involved a professor from Tokyo Imperial University, Kume Kunitake, who was dismissed from his position for writing an article in which he called Shinto a primitive form of heaven-worship.

18. Tsunoda, deBary, and Keene, *Sources of Japanese Tradition,* p. 856.

19. Ibid., p. 857.

20. From a passage given in G. B. Sansom, *The Western World and Japan,* p. 414.

21. The novelist was Yamada Bimyō. Quoted in Masao Miyoshi, *Accomplices of Silence,* pp. 3–5.

22. An excellent monograph dealing with Tsubouchi and Futabatei Shimei and containing a translation of the latter's novel *The Drifting Cloud* is Marleigh G. Ryan, *Japan's First Modern Novel: Ukigumo of Futabatei Shimei.*

23. Keene, *Modern Japanese Literature,* p. 57.

24. Robert H. Brower, "Masaoka Shiki and *Tanka* Reform," in Shively, *Tradition and Modernization,* p. 418.

25. Ibid., p. 396.

26. Sansom, *The Western World and Japan,* p. 404.

27. For a discussion of Kawakami, see John M. Rosenfield, "Western-style Painting in the Early Meiji Period and Its Critics," in Shively, *Tradition and Modernization.*

28. For the following remarks on music in the Meiji period, I have relied in particular on William P. Malm, "The Modern Music of Meiji Japan," in Shively, *Tradition and Modernization.*

29. Ibid., p. 260.

30. The present Kabukiza in Tokyo, however, is still another building, erected by others in 1889.

Chapter 10 The Fruits of Modernity

1. Kenneth B. Pyle, "Meiji Conservatism," in Jansen, *Cambridge History of Japan,* 5:696.

2. Japan regained this territory after defeating Russia in 1905.

3. The Taishō emperor, Meiji's son, acceded to the throne in 1912. The reign period to which he has given his name was 1912–26.

4. Edward Seidensticker, *Kafū the Scribbler,* p. 49.

5. Nagai Kafū, *The River Sumida,* in Keene, *Modern Japanese Literature,* pp. 196–97.

6. Tanizaki's title for this book was *Sasame Yuki (Thin Snow),* but it has been translated into English by Edward Seidensticker as *The Makioka Sisters.* It deals with the decline of an Osaka merchant family in the period before World War II. See the next chapter for a discussion of this work.

7. Tanizaki Junichirō, *Some Prefer Nettles,* translated by Edward Seidensticker.

8. Ibid., p. 26.

9. Ibid., pp. 152–53.

10. Natsume Sōseki, *Kokoro,* pp. 240–41.

11. Ibid., p. 245.

12. Carol Gluck, *Japan's Modern Myths,* p. 221.

13. Kano Masanao, *Taishō Demokurashii*, p. 71.

14. Quoted in Gluck, *Japan's Modern Myths*, p. 222.

15. E. H. Gombrich, *The Story of Art*, p. 422.

16. Shiga Naoya, *A Dark Night's Passing*, translated by Edwin McClellan.

17. Kobayashi Hideo. Quoted in William F. Sibley, *The Shiga Hero*, p. 1.

18. Shiga, *A Dark Night's Passing*, pp. 350–51.

19. Ibid., p. 352.

20. Kodama Kōta et al., *Nihon Bunka-shi Taikei* (Outline of the Cultural History of Japan), 12:202–3.

21. G. H. Healey, Introduction to Akutagawa Ryūnosuke, *Kappa*, translated by Geoffrey Bownas, p. 23. The remark is attributed to Kikuchi Kan.

22. Ibid., pp. 29–30.

23. This tale was also made into an extremely popular film, *The Gate of Hell (Jigokumon)*, but the screenplay was based on a version by Kikuchi Kan, not Akutagawa.

24. Keene, *Modern Japanese Literature*, pp. 302–6.

25. The Shōwa reign was 1926–89.

26. Keene, *Modern Japanese Literature*, pp. 336–37.

27. Jeffrey Dym, "Benshi, Poets of the Dark: Japanese Silent Film Narrators and Their Forgotten Narrative Art" (Ph.D. diss., University of Hawai'i, 1998).

28. Based on thoughts expressed by Donald Richie in *Japanese Cinema*, pp. 70–71.

29. Benito Ortolani, "Fukuda Tsuneari: Modernization and Shingeki," in Shively, *Tradition and Modernization*, p. 486.

30. Quoted in A. Horie-Webber, "Modernization of the Japanese Theatre: The Shingeki Movement," in W. G. Beasley, ed., *Modern Japan*, p. 160.

31. Ibid., p. 161.

32. Ibid.

33. This discussion of opera and the Takarazuka Revue is based largely on Roland Domenig, "Takarazuka and Kobayashi Ichizō's Idea of *Kokumingeki*," in Sepp Linhart and Sabine Frühstück, eds., *The Culture of Japan as Seen Through Its Leisure*, pp. 267–84.

34. J. L. Anderson, "Takarazuka Kagekidan (Takarazuka Opera Company)," in *Kōdansha Encyclopedia of Japan*, 7:318.

35. Maruyama Masao, *Thought and Behavior in Modern Japanese Politics*, p. 69.

36. Robert K. Hall, ed., *Kokutai no Hongi: Cardinal Principles of the National Entity of Japan*, p. 54.

37. Miyoshi, *Accomplices of Silence*, p. 98.

38. Ibid., p. 104.

39. Kawabata Yasunari, *Snow Country*, pp. 6–9.

40. Ibid., p. 24.

41. Dan van der Vat, *The Pacific Campaign*, p. 373.

42. Donald Keene, *Landscapes and Portraits*, pp. 303–5.

43. van der Vat, *The Pacific Campaign*, p. 373.

Chapter 11 Culture in the Present Age

1. Theodore McNelly, ed., *Sources in Modern East Asian History and Politics*, pp. 169–70.

2. Asahi Shimbun, ed., *Pacific Rivals*, pp. 134–35.

3. Hugh Borton, *Japan's Modern Century*, p. 572.

4. Comments on the postwar "end of the I-novel tradition" can be found in Yoshida Seiichi and Inagaki Tatsurō, eds., *Nihon Bungaku no Rekishi* (History of Japanese Literature), 12:410–11.

5. Dazai Osamu, *No Longer Human*, pp. 124–25.

6. Dazai Osamu, *The Setting Sun*, p. 166.

7. Ibid., pp. 132–33.

8. Yoshida and Inagaki, *Nihon Bungaku no Rekishi,* 12:410.

9. Masao Miyoshi in *Accomplices of Silence.*

10. Tanizaki, *The Makioka Sisters,* p. 99.

11. Tanizaki Junichirō, *In Praise of Shadows,* pp. 20–21

12. Quoted in John Nathan, *Mishima: A Biography,* p. 83.

13. Kawabata Yasunari, *Japan the Beautiful and Myself,* pp. 46–47, 52.

14. Kawabata Yasunari, *The Sound of the Mountain,* p. 12.

15. Ōoka Shōhei, *Fires on the Plain,* p. 216.

16. In a translator's introduction to the Penguin edition of *Fires on the Plain,* Ivan Morris points out that the hero did not commit the "ultimate abomination": he did not kill another person in order to eat his flesh.

17. Noma Hiroshi, *Zone of Emptiness,* p. 286.

18. Ibuse Masuji, *Black Rain,* pp. 296–97.

19. Richie, *Japanese Cinema,* p. 58.

20. Joseph L. Anderson and Donald Richie, *The Japanese Film,* p. 162.

21. Ibid., p. 176.

22. Richie, *Japanese Cinema,* p. 64.

23. Based on Ueda Akinari's *Ugetsu Monogatari,* written in the late eighteenth century. See Ueda Akinari, *Ugetsu Monogatari: Tales of Moonlight and Rain.*

24. Joan Mellen, *Voices from the Japanese Cinema,* p. 147.

25. Ted T. Takaya, ed. and tr., *Modern Japanese Drama: An Anthology,* p. xxx.

26. Although it too was banned in the later stages of the war as an unnecessary extravagance.

27. Kawazoe Noboru, *Contemporary Japanese Architecture,* p. 19.

28. Quoted in Bruno Taut, *Fundamentals of Japanese Architecture,* p. 6.

29. Ibid., pp. 15–16.

30. Ibid., pp. 19–20.

31. Clay Lancaster, *The Japanese Influence in America,* pp. 76–77.

32. Quoted from Wright's *Autobiography,* ibid., p. 88.

33. Yamamoto Gakuji, *Nihon Kenchiku no Genkyō* (The Present State of Japanese Architecture), pp. 23–24.

34. Kodama Kōta et al., *Nihon Bunka-shi Taikei,* 13:287.

35. Maekawa's 1955 International House has been torn down and replaced by another, larger structure.

36. For this discussion of mass culture I have learned much from Marilyn Ivy, "Formations of Mass Culture," in Andrew Gordon, ed., *Postwar Japan as History,* pp. 239–58.

37. Irie Akira, *Shin-Nihon no Gaikō* (New Japanese Diplomacy), p. 24.

38. William W. Kelly, "Finding a Place in Metropolitan Japan: Ideologies, Institutions, and Everyday Life," in Gordon, *Postwar Japan as History,* p. 195.

39. Ivy, "Formations of Mass Culture," in Gordon, *Postwar Japan as History,* p. 239.

40. H. Neill McFarland, *The Rush Hour of the Gods.*

41. Harry Thomsen, *The New Religions of Japan,* p. 16.

42. Carmen Blacker, "Millenarian Aspects of the New Religions in Japan," in Shively, *Tradition and Modernization,* p. 575.

43. This was true, for example, of the spirit of the Meiji Restoration.

44. Blacker, "Millenarian Aspects," p. 587.

45. Thomsen, *The New Religions of Japan,* p. 90.

46. Nathan Glazer, citing a poll by the Japanese newspaper *Asahi,* notes that Mishima is one of the very few Japanese whom even a small percentage of Americans can identify by name. See Akira Irie, *Mutual Images,* p. 142.

47. This theme is developed in John Nathan's biography of Mishima, *Mishima: A Biography.*

48. Mishima Yukio, *Confessions of a Mask,* p. 40.

49. Ibid., pp. 251–52.

50. Miyoshi, *Accomplices of Silence,* p. 157.

51. Mishima Yukio, *The Temple of the Golden Pavilion,* p. 29.

52. Ibid., pp. 63–64.

53. Nathan, *Mishima: A Biography,* p. 275.

54. Marleigh Ryan, "The Mishima Tetralogy," p. 165.

55. Abe Kōbō, *The Ruined Map,* p. 162.

56. Abe Kōbō, *The Woman in the Dunes,* pp. 161–62.

57. Ibid., p. 239.

58. Ōe Kenzaburō, *A Personal Matter,* pp. 15–16.

59. Ōe Kenzaburō, *Japan the Ambiguous and Myself,* p. 117.

60. Frederik L. Schodt, *Manga! Manga!,* p. 12.

61. Ibid., p. 75.

62. An English translation of *Hadashi no Gen* can be found in Nakazawa Keiji, *Barefoot Gen, A Cartoon Story of Hiroshima.*

63. Schodt, *Manga! Manga!,* p. 124.

64. Antonia Levi, *Samurai from Outer Space: Understanding Japanese Animation,* pp. 10–11.

65. John Whittier Treat, "Yoshimoto Banana Writes Home," in Treat, ed., *Contemporary Japan and Popular Culture,* p. 280.

66. Yoshimoto Banana, *Kitchen,* p. 48.

67. Ibid., p. 82.

68. Ibid., pp. 3–4.

Glossary

apure *après-guerre*
aragoto "rough business" style of *kabuki* acting
benshi silent-film narrator
biwa Japanese lute
bugaku ancient court dance
bummei kaika civilization and enlightenment
bunjin "literati" artists
bunraku the puppet theatre
burai-ha "dissolutes," a designation bestowed upon a group of writers in the period
    following World War II
bushidō "the way of the warrior"
chanoyu the tea ceremony
chashitsu tea room
chōka "long poem"
chōnin townsman of the Tokugawa period
chū loyalty
daibutsu great buddha
daisu lacquered stand (for *chanoyu*)
dengaku "field music"
dōbōshū "companions" or art connoisseurs of the Muromachi shogunate
dogū earthen figurine of the Jōmon period
dōtaku bronze "bell" of the tomb period
emaki horizontal, narrative picture scroll
fudai daimyō vassal or hereditary daimyo of the Tokugawa period
fukko return to antiquity
fukoku-kyōhei "Enrich the country and strengthen its arms"
fusuma sliding door
gagaku "elegant music" of the Japanese court
garan plan of a Buddhist temple compound
geisha "person of accomplishment"
gembun-itchi movement to "unify the spoken and written languages"
genrō body of governmental "elders"
gijin man of high moral purpose
giri duty
hachi wide-mouthed pottery
haikai "light verse" of the Tokugawa period
haiku seventeen-syllable poetic form
hakama a divided skirt worn by men
han daimyo domain
haniwa terra cotta figurine of the tomb period

harai   internal purification or exorcism in Shinto
heimei   quality of "openness and candor" seen in the *haniwa* figurines
himorogi   area marked off by rocks and ropes
inja   a person who has withdrawn from society
iwasaka   area marked off by rocks
jidaimono   historical play
junshi   following lord in death
kabuki   plebeian theatre
kagura   Shinto music
kaizuka   shell mound
kakekotoba   "pivot word" of poetry
kakemono   vertical, hanging scroll
kami   Shinto deity
kamigakari   possession by a deity or spirit
kamikaze   wind of the gods
kana   Japanese syllabary
kanga   Chinese picture
kannen-teki   ideological
kanzen chōaku   "virtue is rewarded and vice is punished"
karamono   Chinese article
kare-sansui   type of garden called a "withered landscape"
katakiuchi   vendetta
katsureki   "living history" play of modern *kabuki*
kessai   external purification in Shinto
ki   ether, substance
kō   filial piety
kōan   Zen problem
kofun   tomb
kogaku-ha   Ancient Studies school of Tokagawa-period Confucianism
kōgo   vernacular Japanese
kokkeibon   "witty book"
kokugaku-ha   National Learning (Neo-Shinto) school of the Tokugawa period
kokusui hozon   "preservation of the national essence"
kokutai   national polity
kōshoku   erotic
koto   Japanese zither
kugutsu   puppeteer of the late Heian and Kamakura periods
kyōgen   light or comic theatre of the Muromachi period
magatama   curved jewel of the Japanese imperial regalia
makoto   sincerity
manga   comics
mappō   latter days of the Buddhist law
matsuri   festival
michi   way
michiyuki   theatrical "lovers' journey"
minken   people's rights
miyabi   courtly refinement
moga   "modern girl"
monogatari   tale
monomane   acting technique—the "imitation of things"
mono no aware   a "sensitivity to things"
mugen   "ghostly dream" (*nō* play)
mujō   Buddhist idea of impermanence

mukyōkai   "non-church" movement
namban   literally, "southern barbarians"—form of culture
nembutsu   invocation in praise of Amida buddha
nijiriguchi   "crawling in" entrance to tea room
nikki   diary
ninjō   human feelings
nishiki-e   "brocade," multicolored woodblock print
nō   classical theatre of the Muromachi period
okashi   lightness or wit
onnagata   female impersonator of the *kabuki* theatre
raigō   pictorial representation of the coming of Amida at the time of death
rangaku   Dutch Studies
rekishi monogatari   historical tale
renga   linked verse
ri   reason or principle
rōnin   masterless samurai
sabi   loneliness
sakoku   "closed country"
samisen   Japanese banjo-like musical instrument
sangiri   "cropped hair" play of modern *kabuki*
sankin kōtai   alternate attendance
sansui   landscape (literally, "mountains and water")
sarugaku   "monkey music"
satori   Buddhist enlightenment
sencha   infused tea
seppuku   disembowelment
sewamono   contemporary or domestic play of the puppet and *kabuki* theatres
sharebon   "amorous book"
shasei   realistic depiction
shimai   climactic dance in a *nō* play
shimpa   "new school" of theatre of the Meiji period
shin   mind
shinden   domestic architectural style of the Heian period
shingeki   modern theatre
shingon   true words
shinigurui   "death frenzy"
shinkō shūkyō   "new religions" of modern Japan
shishi   men of high purpose
shishōsetsu   I-novel
shite   protagonist of *nō* play
shoin   domestic architectural style of the medieval age
shōji   sliding door covered with translucent rice paper
shomin-geki   popular, or home, drama
sonnō-jōi   "Revere the Emperor! Oust the Barbarians!"
sui   chic
sukiya   "room or building of taste"
sumi-e   monochrome ink painting
taikyoku   supreme ultimate
taishū bunka   mass (popular) culture
tanka   short (thirty-one-syllable) poem
tatami   rush matting
tatarigami   malevolent spirit
tateana   pit-dwelling

tennō   emperor
tenshu   castle donjon
tōcha   tea-judging contests
tokonoma   alcove
torii   entranceway to a Shinto shrine
tozama daimyō   "outside" daimyo of the Tokugawa period
tsū   savoir faire
tsure   "companion" of a *nō* play
tsuwamono   warrior
uji   clan
ukiyo-e   "pictures of the floating world"
uta-monogatari   poem-tale
wabi   aesthetic of the tea ceremony
wabicha   tea ceremony based on th aesthetic of *wabi*
wagoto   "soft business" style of *kabuki* acting
waka   thirty-one-syllable poem
waki   subordinate actor of a *nō* play
yamazato   mountain village
yojō   resonances
yomihon   historical novel
yūgei   elegant pastime
yūgen   mystery and depth
zuihitsu   miscellany or "running brush"

Selected Bibliography

Abe Kōbō. *The Box Man.* Translated by E. Dale Saunders. New York: Knopf, 1974.
———. *The Ruined Map.* Translated by E. Dale Saunders. New York: Knopf, 1969.
———. *The Woman in the Dunes.* Translated by E. Dale Saunders. New York: Knopf, 1964.
Agency for Cultural Affairs, ed. *Japanese Religion.* Tokyo: Kōdansha, 1972.
Akutagawa Ryūnosuke. *Kappa.* Translated by Geoffrey Bownas. London: Peter Owen, 1970.
Anderson, Joseph L., and Donald Richie. *The Japanese Film.* New York: Grove Press, 1959.
Asahi Shimbun, ed. *Pacific Rivals.* New York: Weatherhill, 1972.
Aston, W. G., tr. *Nihongi.* London: George Allen and Unwin, 1896.
Beasley, W. G., ed. *Modern Japan.* Berkeley: University of California Press, 1975.
Bolitho, Harold. *Treasures Among Men: The Fudai Daimyō in Tokugawa Japan.* New Haven, Conn.: Yale University Press, 1974.
Borton, Hugh. *Japan's Modern Century.* New York: Ronald Press, 1970.
Boxer, C. R. *The Christian Century in Japan, 1549–1650.* Berkeley: University of California Press, 1951.
Brower, Robert H., and Earl Miner. *Japanese Court Poetry.* Stanford, Calif.: Stanford University Press, 1961.
Cooper, Michael, ed. *They Came to Japan: An Anthology of European Reports on Japan, 1543–1640.* Berkeley: University of California Press, 1965.
Covell, Jon Carter. *Under the Seal of Sesshū.* New York: De Pamphilus, 1941.
Crawcour, E. S. "Some Observations on Mitsui Tadafusa's *Chōmin Kōken Roku.*" *Transactions of the Asiatic Society of Japan,* 3rd series, vol. 8 (Tokyo 1961).
Dazai Osamu. *No Longer Human.* Translated by Donald Keene. New York: New Directions, 1958.
———. *The Setting Sun.* Translated by Donald Keene. New York: New Directions, 1956.
Domoulin, Heinrich. *A History of Zen Buddhism.* New York: McGraw-Hill, 1963.
Duus, Peter. *Modern Japan.* Second edition. Boston: Houghton Mifflin, 1998.
Dym, Jeffrey. "Benshi, Poets of the Dark: Japanese Silent Film Narrators and Their Forgotten Narrative Art." Ph. D. dissertation. University of Hawai'i, 1998.
Edwards, Walter. "Event and Process in the Founding of Japan: The Horserider Theory in Archeological Perspective." *The Journal of Japanese Studies,* vol. 9, no. 2 (Winter 1983).
Elison, George, and Bardwell L. Smith, eds. *Warlords, Artists, and Commoners.* Honolulu: University of Hawai'i Press, 1981.
Endō Shūsaku. *Silence.* Translated by William Johnston. Tokyo: Tuttle, 1969.
Fairbank, John K., Edwin O. Reischauer, and Albert M. Craig. *East Asia: The Modern Transformation.* Boston: Houghton Mifflin, 1965.

Farris, William Wayne. *Heavenly Warriors*. Cambridge, Mass.: Harvard University Press, 1992.

Fukuzawa Yukichi. *An Encouragement of Learning*. Translated by David Dilworth and Umeyo Hirano. Tokyo: Sophia University, 1969.

Gluck, Carol. *Japan's Modern Myths*. Princeton, N.J.: Princeton University Press, 1985.

Gombrich, E. H. *The Study of Art*. London: Phaedon, 1950.

Gordon, Andrew, ed. *Postwar Japan as History*. Berkeley: University of California Press, 1993.

Hall, Robert K., ed. *Kokutai no Hongi: Cardinal Principles of the National Entity of Japan*. Translated by John O. Gauntlett. Cambridge, Mass.: Harvard University Press, 1949.

Hayashiya Tatsusaburō, ed. *Kodai-Chūsei Geijutsu Ron*. Tokyo: Iwanami Shoten, 1973.

Heinrich, Amy, ed. *Currents in Japanese Culture: Translations and Transformations*. New York: Columbia University Press, 1997.

Henderson, Harold G. *An Introduction to Haiku*. New York: Doubleday, 1958.

Ibuse Masuji. *Black Rain*. Translated by John Bestor. Tokyo: Kōdansha, 1969.

Ihara Saikaku. *The Life of an Amorous Woman and Other Writings*. Edited and translated by Ivan Morris. New York: New Directions, 1963.

————. *Nihon Eitai Gura*. Tokyo: Meiji Shoin, 1975.

Ikegami, Eiko. *The Taming of the Samurai: Honorific Individualism and the Making of Modern Japan*. Cambridge, Mass.: Harvard University Press, 1995.

Imamura, Keiji. *Prehistoric Japan: New Perspectives on Insular East Asia*. Honolulu: University of Hawai'i Press, 1996.

Irie, Akira. *Mutual Images*. Cambridge, Mass.: Harvard University Press, 1975.

————. *Shin-Nihon no Gaikō*. Tokyo: Chūō Kōron Sha, 1991.

Jansen, Marius, ed. *The Cambridge History of Japan*. Vol. 5. Cambridge: Cambridge University Press, 1989.

Kano Masanao. *Taishō Demokurashii*. Tokyo: Shōgakkan, 1976.

Kawabata Yasunari. *Japan the Beautiful and Myself*. Translated by Edward G. Seidensticker. Tokyo: Kodansha, 1969.

————. *Snow Country*. Translated by Edward G. Seidensticker. New York: Knopf, 1956.

————. *The Sound of the Mountain*. Translated by Edward G. Seidensticker. New York: Knopf, 1970.

————. *Thousand Cranes*. Translated by Edward G. Seidensticker. New York: Knopf, 1959.

Kawazoe, Noboru. *Contemporary Japanese Architecture*. Tokyo: Kokusai Kōryū Kikin, 1973.

Keene, Donald. *Bunraku: The Art of the Japanese Puppet Theatre*. Tokyo: Kōdansha, 1965.

————. *The Japanese Discovery of Europe, 1720–1830*. Revised edition. Stanford, Calif.: Stanford University Press, 1969.

————. *Japanese Literature: An Introduction for Western Readers*. New York: Grove Press, 1955.

————. *Landscapes and Portraits: Appreciations of Japanese Culture*. Tokyo: Kōdansha, 1971.

————. *Nō: The Classical Theatre of Japan*. Tokyo: Kōdansha, 1966.

————, comp. and ed. *Anthology of Japanese Literature*. New York: Grove Press, 1955.

————, ed. *Modern Japanese Literature: An Anthology*. New York: Grove Press, 1956.

————, ed. and tr. *Twenty Plays of the Nō Theatre*. New York: Columbia University Press, 1970.

————, tr. *Chūshingura: The Treasury of Loyal Retainers*. New York: Columbia University Press, 1971.

————, tr. *Essays in Idleness: The Tsurezuregusa of Kenkō.* New York: Columbia University Press, 1967.

————, tr. *Four Major Plays of Chikamatsu.* New York: Columbia University Press, 1961.

Kidō Saizō and Imoto Nōichi, eds. *Renga Ronshū, Haironshū.* Tokyo: Iwanami Shoten, 1961.

Kondō Ichitarō. *Japanese Genre Painting: The Lively Art of Renaissance Japan.* Translated by Roy Andrew Miller. Tokyo: Tuttle, 1961.

Kuck, Loraine. *The World of the Japanese Garden.* New York: Walker-Weatherhill, 1968.

La Fleur, William R. *The Karma of Words: Buddhism and the Literary Arts in Medieval Japan.* Berkeley: University of California Press, 1983.

Lancaster, Clay. *The Japanese Influence in America.* New York: Walton Rawls, 1963.

Lane, Richard. *Masters of the Japanese Print.* New York: Doubleday, 1962.

Ledyard, Gari. "Galloping Along with the Horseriders: Looking for the Founders of Japan." *The Journal of Japanese Studies,* vol. 1, no. 2 (Spring 1975).

Levi, Antonia. *Samurai from Outer Space: Understanding Japanese Animation.* Chicago: Open Court, 1996.

Linhart, Sepp, and Sabine Frühstück, eds. *The Culture of Japan as Seen Through Its Leisure.* Albany: State University of New York Press, 1998.

McCullough, Helen, tr. *Ōkagami, the Great Mirror.* Princeton, N.J.: Princeton University Press, 1980.

McCullough, William, and Helen McCullough, trs. *A Tale of Flowering Fortunes.* Stanford, Calif.: Stanford University Press, 1980.

McFarland, H. Neill. *The Rush Hour of the Gods.* New York: Harper & Row, 1967.

McNelly, Theodore, ed. *Sources in Modern East Asian History and Politics.* New York: Appleton-Century-Crofts, 1967.

Malm, William P. *Japanese Music and Musical Instruments.* Tokyo: Tuttle, 1959.

Maruyama Masao. *Studies in the Intellectual History of Tokugawa Japan.* Translated by Mikiso Hane. Princeton, N.J.: Princeton University Press, 1974.

————. *Thought and Behavior in Modern Japanese Politics.* Edited by Ivan Morris. London: Oxford University Press, 1963.

Mellen, Joan. *Voices from the Japanese Cinema.* New York: Liveright, 1975.

Michener, James A. *The Floating World.* New York: Random House, 1954.

Miner, Earl. *An Introduction to Japanese Court Poetry.* Stanford, Calif.: Stanford University Press, 1968.

————, ed. *Japanese Poetic Diaries.* Berkeley: University of California Press, 1969.

Minichiello, Sharon A., ed. *Japan's Competing Modernities: Issues in Culture and Democracy, 1900–1930.* Honolulu: University of Hawai'i Press, 1998.

Mishima Yukio. *After the Banquet.* Translated by Donald Keene. New York: Knopf, 1963.

————. *Confessions of a Mask.* Translated by Meredith Weatherby. New York: New Directions, 1958.

————. *The Sailor Who Fell From Grace with the Sea.* Translated by John Nathan. New York: Knopf, 1965.

————. *The Temple of the Golden Pavilion.* Translated by Ivan Morris. New York: Knopf, 1958.

————. *The Way of the Samurai: Yukio Mishima on Hagakure in Modern Life.* Translated by Kathryn Sparling. New York: Basic Books, 1977.

Miyoshi, Masao. *Accomplices of Silence: The Modern Japanese Novel.* Berkeley: University of California Press, 1974.

Morris, Ivan. *The World of the Shining Prince.* New York: Knopf, 1964.

————, ed. *Modern Japanese Stories.* Tokyo: Tuttle, 1962.

————, tr. *The Pillow Book of Sei Shōnagon*. New York: Columbia University Press, 1967.

Murasaki, Lady. *The Tale of Genji*. Translated by Arthur Waley. New York: Modern Library, 1960.

Murasaki Shikibu. *The Tale of Genji*. Translated by Edward G. Seidensticker. New York: Knopf, 1976.

Nagai Kafū. *The River Sumida*. In *Modern Japanese Literature*, edited by Donald Keene. New York: Grove Press, 1956.

Nakazawa Keiji. *Barefoot Gen, A Cartoon Story of Hiroshima*. Philadelphia: New Society Publishers, 1987.

Nathan, John. *Mishima: A Biography*. Boston: Little, Brown, 1974.

Natsume Sōseki. *Kokoro*. Translated by Edwin McClellan. Chicago: Henry Regnery, 1957.

Nishi Kazuo and Hozumi Kazuo. *What Is Japanese Architecture?* Translated by H. Mack Horton. Tokyo: Kōdansha, 1983.

Nishiyama Matsunosuke. *Edo Culture: Daily Life and Diversions in Urban Japan, 1600–1868*. Translated by Gerald Groemer. Honolulu: University of Hawai'i Press, 1997.

Noma, Hiroshi. *Zone of Emptiness*. New York: World, 1956.

Ōe Kenzaburō. *Japan the Ambiguous and Myself*. Tokyo: Kōdansha, 1995.

————. *A Personal Matter*. Translated by John Nathan. New York: Grove Press, 1969.

Ōoka Shohei. *Fires on the Plain*. Translated by Ivan Morris. New York: Knopf, 1957.

Ooms, Herman. *Tokugawa Ideology: Early Constructs, 1570–1680*. Princeton, N.J.: Princeton University Press, 1985.

Paine, Robert T., and Alexander Soper. *The Art and Architecture of Japan*. Baltimore, Md.: Penguin Books, 1955.

Parker, Geoffrey. *The Military Revolution*. Cambridge: Cambridge University Press, 1988.

Pyle, Kenneth B. *The New Generation of Meiji Japan*. Stanford, Calif.: Stanford University Press, 1969.

Richie, Donald. *Japanese Cinema*. New York: Doubleday, 1971.

Ryan, Marleigh G. *The Development of Realism in the Fiction of Tsubouchi Shōyō*. Seattle: University of Washington Press, 1975.

————. *Japan's First Novel: Ukigumo of Futabatei Shimei*. New York: Columbia University Press, 1967.

————. "The Mishima Tetralogy." *The Journal of Japanese Studies*, vol. 1, no. 1 (Autumn 1974).

Sansom, G. B. *Japan, A Short Cultural History*. New York: Appleton-Century-Crofts, 1931.

————. *The Western World and Japan*. New York: Knopf, 1958.

Scheiner, Irwin. *Christian Converts and Social Protest in Meiji Japan*. Berkeley: University of California Press, 1970.

Schodt, Frederik L. *Manga! Manga!* New York: Kōdansha, 1983.

Seidensticker, Edward. *Kafū the Scribbler*. Stanford, Calif.: Stanford University Press, 1965.

————, tr. *The Gossamer Years*. Tokyo: Tuttle, 1964.

Shiga Naoya. *A Dark Night's Passing*. Translated by Edwin McClellan. Tokyo: Kodansha, 1976.

Shively, Donald H. *Tradition and Modernization in Japanese Culture*. Princeton, N.J.: Princeton University Press, 1971.

Sibley, William F. *The Shiga Hero*. Chicago: University of Chicago Press, 1979.

Takaya, Ted T., ed. and tr. *Modern Japanese Drama: An Anthology*. New York: Columbia University Press, 1979.

Tanizaki Junichirō. *Diary of a Mad Old Man.* Translated by Howard Hibbett. New York: Knopf, 1965.
————. *In Praise of Shadows.* Translated by Thomas J. Harper and Edward G. Seidensticker. New Haven: Leete's Island Books, 1977.
————. *The Makioka Sisters.* Translated by Edward G. Seidensticker. New York: Knopf, 1957.
————. *Some Prefer Nettles.* Translated by Edward G. Seidensticker. New York: Knopf, 1955.
Taut, Bruno. *Fundamentals of Japanese Architecture.* Tokyo: Society for International Cultural Relations, 1936.
Terry, Charles S., ed. *Masterworks of Japanese Art.* Tokyo: Tuttle, 1956.
Thomsen, Harry. *The New Religions of Japan.* Tokyo: Tuttle, 1963.
Toby, Ronald. *State and Diplomacy in Early Modern Japan: Asia in the Development of the Tokugawa Bakufu.* Princeton, N.J.: Princeton University Press, 1984.
Totman, Conrad. *Early Modern Japan.* Berkeley: University of California Press, 1993.
Treat, John Whittier, ed. *Contemporary Japan and Popular Culture.* Honolulu: University of Hawai'i Press, 1996.
Tsunoda, Ryūsaku, William T. deBary, and Donald Keene, eds. *Sources of Japanese Tradition.* New York: Columbia University Press, 1958.
Ueda Akinari. *Ugetsu Monogatari: Tales of Moonlight and Rain.* Translated by Leon Zolbrod. Vancouver: University of British Columbia Press, 1974.
van der Vat, Dan. *The Pacific Campaign: The U.S.-Japanese Naval War, 1941–1945.* New York: Touchstone, 1992.
Varley, Paul. *Warriors of Japan, As Portrayed in the War Tales.* Honolulu: University of Hawai'i Press, 1994.
Varley, Paul, and Kumakura Isao, eds. *Tea in Japan: Essays on the History of Chanoyu.* Honolulu: University of Hawai'i Press, 1989.
Wakabayashi, Bob Tadashi. *Anti-Foreignism and Western Learning in Early-Modern Japan: The New Thesis of 1825.* Cambridge, Mass.: Harvard University Press, 1986.
Waley, Arthur. *The Nō Plays of Japan.* New York: Grove Press, 1957.
Ward, Robert Edward, ed. *Political Development in Modern Japan.* Princeton, N.J.: Princeton University Press, 1968.
Yamamoto Tsunetomo. *Hagakure.* Translated by William Scott Wilson. Tokyo: Kōdansha, 1979.
Yomiuri Shimbun Sha, eds. *Meiji Ishin.* Vol. 10 of *Nihon no Rekishi.* Tokyo: Yomiuri, 1964.
Yoshimoto Banana. *Kitchen.* Translated by Megan Backus. New York: Washington Square Press, 1993.

Index

About the Author

PAUL VARLEY received his M.A. and Ph.D. degrees from Columbia University, where he taught for many years in the Department of East Asian Languages and Cultures. Among his publications are *The Ōnin War, Imperial Restoration in Medieval Japan, The Samurai, A Chronicle of Gods and Sovereigns, Tea in Japan* (edited with Kumakura Isao), and *Warriors of Japan, As Portrayed in the War Tales.* He is professor emeritus at Columbia University and Sen Sōshitsu XV Professor of Japanese Cultural History at the University of Hawai'i.